Kein deutschsprachiger Lit

Who Were the First Christians?

Who Were the First Christians?

Dismantling the Urban Thesis

THOMAS A. ROBINSON

OXFORD
UNIVERSITY PRESS

OXFORD
UNIVERSITY PRESS

Oxford University Press is a department of the University of Oxford. It furthers
the University's objective of excellence in research, scholarship, and education
by publishing worldwide. Oxford is a registered trade mark of Oxford University
Press in the UK and certain other countries.

Published in the United States of America by Oxford University Press
198 Madison Avenue, New York, NY 10016, United States of America.

Library of Congress Cataloging-in-Publication Data
Names: Robinson, Thomas A. (Thomas Arthur), 1951– author.
Title: Who were the first Christians? : dismantling the urban thesis /
Thomas A. Robinson.
Description: New York City : Oxford University Press, 2016. |
Includes bibliographical references and index.
Identifiers: LCCN 2016010012 (print) | LCCN 2016034113 (ebook) |
ISBN 9780190620547 (cloth : alk. paper) | ISBN 9780190620554 (updf) |
ISBN 9780190620561 (epub)
Subjects: LCSH: Church history—Primitive and early church, ca. 30-600. |
Christians. | Cities and towns—Religious aspects—Christianity.
Classification: LCC BR166 .R635 2016 (print) | LCC BR166 (ebook) |
DDC 270.1—dc23
LC record available at https://lccn.loc.gov/2016010012

In memory of my father
and for my brother

Contents

Preface

IN THE RICH world of scholarship on the early Christian movement, debates get settled and settled debates get shaken back to life. Three matters have nagged me over years of teaching in the field. One is the near-consensus opinion that early Christianity was almost exclusively an urban movement. The second is the routinely touted figure that the Christian movement numbered about 6 million (or about 10% of the Roman Empire) around 300 C.E. The third is the portrait of the complexion of the Christian movement, where opinions have shifted from a largely lower-class movement of the masses to an upwardly mobile movement of middle-class respectability.

All three matters may be significantly affected by a largely neglected subject—that is, the pre-Constantinian presence of Christianity in the countryside, where at least 80% of the empire's population lived. This book is an exploration into these matters. I examine various ways by which scholars have attempted to count the number of Christians in the Roman Empire, from the mathematically impossible scenarios of a massive Christian growth to scenarios of such low growth rates that the supposed success of the Christian movement is portrayed more as an illusion than a triumph. My most direct challenge is against the urban thesis. It is my sense that the Christian movement was, in terms of its territory, more present in the countryside and, in terms of its complexion, more rustic in its character than the urban thesis has generally recognized.

Although hundreds of scholars are regularly engaged with these issues, three names stand out prominently in current scholarship: Wayne Meeks, Ramsay MacMullen, and Rodney Stark. Their provocative and influential works will be the focus of much of my work here.

Who Were the First Christians?

I
_____

Introduction

MUST HISTORIANS COUNT?

The Need for Numbers

How many Christians were there in the Roman Empire? There were none at the beginning of the first century. That we can say with certainty. But any number after that is difficult—indeed, impossible—to determine, though that has not prevented numerous scholars from stating, with what appears to be a considerable sense of certainty, what the numbers were. In particular, it is widely asserted that there were 6 million Christians in the Roman Empire in the year 300 c.e., or about 10% of the total population of the empire. But this number rests neither on a reliable ancient number nor on any reliable modern method to calculate such a number. It is a guess, and we have no way to determine whether it is a good guess or a bad guess.[1] And the same is true for any attempt to count the number of Christians for any other period of the empire.

The situation is much the same for the size of the Jewish population in the Roman Empire.[2] Again, numbers are confidently offered, though the various proposals put forward (from 2 million to 10 million or more) hardly inspire confidence. These numbers are no more than guesses, and

_____

1. Rodney Stark believes that he can establish the 10% number as reasonable, and many have followed him. I find Stark's work flawed (see Appendix B). For a detailed discussion, see chapter 3: "Counting Romans and Christians." For a short review of such matters, see Robert M. Grant's "The Christian Population of the Roman Empire," chapter 1 in his book *Early Christianity and Society* (San Francisco: Harper & Row, 1977), 1–12.

2. See chapter 4: "Counting the Jewish Population."

no number has reliable ancient evidence on its side. As with the Christian population, so with the Jewish population—numbers fail us.

Even the total population of the Roman Empire cannot be determined with certainty, though it is more likely that the population of the empire can be determined than its Christian or Jewish component. At least with the total population, some techniques for measuring have been developed, though all such methods have their limitations. For example, one might try calculating city size from the area enclosed by city walls. Or one might try determining population size based on the food necessary to sustain one person, and then measuring the agricultural land in use and the yield of crops in that area. But even here the results are troubling. Numbers from 40 million to 120 million can be found in recent scholarship.[3] Whether one scholar's proposal for calculating the size of the population of the Roman Empire will win the day against the others is yet unclear—and perhaps unlikely.

But do we need exact numbers, or even rough numbers? With regard to Christians and Jews in the Empire or in the urban areas, is not the illuminating measure the *proportion* of the population that was Jewish or Christian, whatever the actual numbers might have been? While this is true, the reality is that unless we have raw numbers for these populations to start with, our attempt to provide percentages becomes guesswork, based perhaps on impressions, but impressions not substantial enough to treat the percentages we offer as anything more than guesses. Even Ramsay MacMullen, who had offered estimates earlier in his career and still tries to wrestle something concrete for the numbers game, in his most recent work has called any estimate "perfectly arbitrary"—well, anything, that is, more precise than a range of 1% to 40%![4] And he notes that although Harnack's 7% to 10% calculation of Christians in the empire around the year 300 C.E. is widely accepted, "no one attempts to justify his guess."[5]

How badly disadvantaged are we, then, if we can determine neither the size nor the proportion of ancient populations? Can we proceed with much confidence in any area of study of the ancient world without some sense of roughly credible numbers? Michael E. Jones put our dilemma

---

3. See chapter 3: "Counting Romans and Christians."

4. Ramsay MacMullen, *The Second Church: Popular Christianity* A.D. 200–400 (Atlanta: Society of Biblical Literature, 2009), 102.

5. MacMullen, *The Second Church*, 173n20.

this way. Although admitting that estimates of population "must rest on dubious bases" and that such numbers are "extremely conjectural," Jones concludes:

> For studies of social, economic and military questions, however, some estimate of population is indispensable. We are forced either to argue our historical interpretations without the vital consideration of population or make the best estimate possible and risk the retribution of critics who justifiably denounce dubious methods and evidence. The second choice seems better to me.[6]

Two of the best-known recent scholars who have dealt with the growth of early Christianity concur: numbers are important—even crucial. Ramsay MacMullen, noted for his many works on the religious complexion of the Roman Empire and of the Christian growth within that world, argues that we need something more concrete to describe the Christian population than that provided by the general terms we find in the ancient literature—words such as "crowds" or "numerous," for example. According to MacMullen:

> anyone interested in how the church grew, the rate of increase, its effect and its historical consequences, *must* have specific numbers to be compared with each other across time. For such a purpose, words without numerical meaning have no meaning at all.[7]

The other scholar who has gained considerable recognition for his efforts to explain the rise of Christianity and to tag numbers to that rise is Rodney Stark. The concluding chapter of his book *Cities of God* is titled: "Why Historians *Ought* to Count."[8]

But MacMullen's "must" and Stark's "ought" do not mean that historians "can" count, though both MacMullen and Stark believe we can and offer to show us how. They are even prepared to provide concrete numbers. Unfortunately, that does not fix our problem. Indeed, the problem of

---

6. Michael E. Jones, *The End of Roman Britain* (Ithaca, NY: Cornell University Press, 1996), 263.

7. MacMullen, *The Second Church*, 102 (emphasis mine).

8. Rodney Stark, *Cities of God: The Real Story of How Christianity Became an Urban Movement and Conquered Rome* (New York: HarperCollins, 2006), 209–222 (emphasis mine).

numbers is amplified rather than resolved by the very specific efforts made by MacMullen and Stark, for the numbers they offer differ radically. In fact, one cannot find any two scholars in the field whose reconstructions provide conclusions that are such polar opposites. Stark has Christians saturating the cities of the Roman Empire by the time of Constantine. MacMullen has Christians representing but a small minority for the same period. Maybe, then, our question should not be "Can historians count?" but "Can historians count accurately?"[9]

Counting Romans, Jews, and Christians

If it is recognized that historians must count and if it is assumed that under somewhat ideal circumstances that they can count accurately, a crucial question remains. What, exactly, are historians counting? If it is the population of the empire, then they are counting people—people of all types, with the only condition being their residence in a defined geographical and political area called the Roman Empire.[10] Simply put, anyone taking up space within the boundaries of the empire counts in the calculation of the empire's population, for the various techniques to determine the size of the population, from the dimensions of a city's walls to the crop yields of surrounding fields, or some other measure, at best simply provide a count of all bodies present. It is more an aerial view, where head counts are possible but nothing more specific.

It is one thing to count the number of people in the empire; it is quite another matter to count subgroups within that population, particularly groups that are spread widely but unevenly across the empire, and whose identity is rooted in matters of religious belief or ancestral heritage, or some other such marker. Consider the difference between calculating the population of Egypt and calculating the number of people in the empire who have Egyptian ancestry, where factors such as migration or expulsion or forced resettlement can scatter the geographical boundaries of "Egyptian" and where matters such as intermarriage or, in Judaism, conversion, can shatter neat boundaries of ethnic identity. The moment some

---

9. See Appendixes A and B.

10. Of course, this broad definition puts aside the question of the status of residency—whether citizen, resident alien, recent immigrants, slaves brought from outside the boundaries of the empire, or a host of other inhabitants whose residency was temporary in some way or other.

other condition is placed on a population count than mere physical presence in a particular area under examination, things become profoundly complicated, for the techniques we have for determining population do not have the power to offer anything more discriminating than a roughly calculated head count, whether of a city or of an empire. But such numbers are not helpful to our primary concern. We are interested in the number of Jews and Christians within that raw count of the empire's population. No method—crude or refined—exists for that kind of discrimination within a population. A head count of the population determined by crop yields, for example, cannot tell us how many of those consuming the harvests of an area were Jewish and how many were of some other identity.

And that is only the beginning of the problems confronting any attempt to calculate the number of Christians and Jews in the ancient world. Consider the Jewish population. It is difficult enough to establish the Jewish population of Judaea, where some of the districts might be assumed to be largely Jewish, but even there, proposed numbers range widely. When a calculation of the number of Jews within the mixed populations of the diaspora is attempted, the effort collapses completely.[11] Complicating the matter even further is the issue of the definition of a Jewish person. The most obvious would seem to be ancestral heritage. One might also count the proselyte along with native-born Jews. God-fearers, no matter how sympathetic to Judaism, would probably not be counted. Further, there is the more recent controversy regarding what the term "Jew" was intended to specify. Did it have the religious connotations now commonly associated with it, or was it intended to identify simply a Judean, with cultural and ancestral overtones, but religious aspects neither necessarily dominant nor even necessary?[12]

Even were we able to put boots on the ground so that we could observe the population of the Roman Empire face-to-face, we would find it difficult to distinguish between a Jewish or a Christian person and others in the larger society, a point that both Jews and Christians made.[13] Imagine, then, trying to do a head count of a subgroup within these populations from a position

---

11. See chapter 4.

12. For a review of the debate, see Seth Schwartz, "How Many Judaisms Were There? A Critique of Neusner and Smith on Definition and Mason and Boyarin on Categorization," *JAJ* 2 (2011): 208–238.

13. Justin, *Dial.* 16; *Letter to Diognetus* 5.1–4.

two thousand years later, largely dependent on literary remains. Historians who have examined the ancient literature for comments relative to the question of proselytes, for example, disagree whether a scattered few non-Jews converted or whether the Jewish population ballooned through large-scale Gentile conversion. And what of significant Jewish conversion to Christianity, as some propose? Do such individuals count as Jews or Christians, or both?

Supposing that an ethnic or ancestral marker of some kind might be found to identify the Jewish element within the larger population, such features fail completely to identify Christians. What kind of marker would we use to identify Christians within the larger population (other than for the few who wrote Christian literature, or became a Christian martyr, or had some Christian token on their gravestone, or advanced sufficiently within the hierarchy of the church to make some bishops' list preserved by one of the ancient Christian historians)? At best, such markers would identify a few hundred. A further problem is that Christian identity could be sketched in different ways, from narrow to broad. One might count only the baptized, or the baptized and the catechumen, or those formally associated with the movement (baptized and catechumen) along with anyone who had some interest in the movement.

But whatever factor of identity we might make primary, none helps us with the task of counting, for how can we use such markers to distinguish one resident from another in the rough head count of the Roman population? Yet, in spite of the bleak possibility of reliably calculating the number of Jews or Christians in the empire, scholars still offer numbers, as though who is to be counted is obvious and the task of counting possible. Perhaps that is because of the general conviction that numbers are necessary. But it is not numbers that are necessary. It is reasonably reliable numbers that are. These we don't have, and it is highly unlikely that we ever will.

Religion as an Aspect of Identity

No one has set out to count the number of *pagans* in the empire. For those who wish to have those numbers, the assumption is that once Jews and Christians have been counted, anyone left over would fit neatly under the category of "pagan." But in recent years, some protest has arisen over the appropriateness of marking off all the multiform complexities making up Greco-Roman religious sensibilities in the Roman Empire into one generic category. Coupled with this protest has been a suspicion of the adequacy of the category of religion as an identity marker.

One thing is certain though. For Christians, religion was the primary marker. Indeed, religion was not simply the primary marker of identity; it was their only marker. No common ancestry, no common geography, no common language, no common cultural features could be appealed to in order to distinguish the Christian from others in the empire. In fact, except in religion, Christians would have been indistinguishable from those around them who had been born and raised in the same area.

Some have argued that the very notion of religion as a distinctive and meaningful concept did not exist in the ancient world until Christianity came along and forcefully put that concept into play.[14] If this is so, then perhaps this taints the now commonly used division of the ancient world, where religion marks off Jew, Christian, and pagan. If religion is a category of Christian coining, are we not subjecting the whole of the ancient world to the perceptions and partitions that suited the Christian agenda and vision? Can we work with a view of the ancient world created by Christians to mark off their own identity and at the same time do justice to the diverse complexity of religious sensibilities in the ancient Mediterranean that were not Christian? Can we lump together all the polytheisms in the ancient Mediterranean as though they were largely the same thing? Or is such a term as paganism or polytheism, as Garth Fowden has asserted, merely a name given "by the lazy cunning of Christian apologists, who could then use their most salacious material to discredit all their opponents at one go"?[15] Is Maijastina Kahlos perhaps on the mark by calling the Christian lumping together of all their polytheistic opponents the

---

14. For a careful discussion of the matter, see John North, "The Development of Religious Pluralism," in *The Jews among Pagans and Christians in the Roman Empire*, ed. Judith Lieu, John North, and Tessa Rajak (London: Routledge, 1992), 174–193. See, too, E. A. Judge, "The Beginning of Religious History," *JRH* 15 (1989): 394–412; E. A. Judge, "Was Christianity a Religion," in *The First Christians in the Roman World: Augustan and New Testament Essays*, ed. E. A. Judge and James R. Harrison (Tübingen: Mohr Siebeck, 2008), 404–409; Jonathan Z. Smith, "Religion, Religions, Religious," in *Critical Terms for Religious Studies*, ed. Mark Taylor (Chicago: University of Chicago Press, 1998), 269–284.

15. Garth Fowden, review of Lane Fox, *JRS* 78 (1988): 176. Probably Fowden was exaggerating for effect when he spoke of the lazy cunning of Christian apologists, for it is hardly accurate to describe the early Christian apologetic effort as lazy. It is ripe and rich with the rhetoric of the day—an entirely appropriate forum and format for the matter to which the apologists directed their energies. Fowden may be more correct about the cunning of the apologists—just read a few pages of Tertullian—but the "lazy" apologists of the time, whoever they were, would have disappeared from history, with neither their writings read nor their manuscripts copied. As for salacious material, Christian apologists might well have used that when they found it, but that is hardly descriptive of most of their apologetic writing. The salacious material is

creation of a "straw man," making it "easier to shoot at one target than to go through all the rival groups one at a time"?[16] Can something as multi-form as the religious expression found from Britain to Mesopotamia and from cat-worshipping Egypt to the classically beautiful human forms of the Greek pantheon, in some way, be the same thing? Can a collective or general term really play fair with the diverse world it is supposed to represent?[17] Should we not speak at least of paganisms or polytheisms, particularly when the trend now is to shy away from general terms, so much so that even the use of well-established terms such as Judaism and Christianity are now more likely to be rejected and replaced by the plural forms *Judaisms* and *Christianities*, on the assumption that each was, within itself, diverse.

All scholars of the period recognize that each of these religions cap-tured by a general term, such as Judaism, Christianity, or paganism, en-compassed a range of diversity. But whether we need to be constantly reminded of this diversity every time we talk about these traditions is another matter. Sometimes, the general term is exactly the term we need for what we are attempting to identify. Of course, general terms will not catch every nuance of diversity in the concrete manifestations designated by a general term, and there will be times, of course, when general terms obscure and another term might be more appropriate. But there will be times when a general term will not only be the most appropriate term but will be crucial to an understanding of a group's perceptions of their world.

Whether or not Christians invented the category of religion should not be the central issue, though it has become one of the hot topics in the field. Rather, the question is whether the larger world would have understood

---

generally part of the apologists' argument to refute charges against Christians by turning the tables and using the mythological traditions of the Greco-Roman world to show that these gods are immoral and not deserving of the respect paid to them. For the most part, such material is a very small part of apologetic writing. Consider Theophilus of Antioch, *Autol.* 1.9; 3.8, for example.

16. Maijastina Kahlos, *Debate and Dialogue: Christian and Pagan Cultures c. 360–430* (Aldershot: Ashgate Publishing, 2007), 68.

17. Frank R. Trombley, *Hellenic Religion and Christianization, c. 370–529* (Leiden: E. J. Brill, 1993), ix–x, provides some sane advice on the use of terms. Edward J. Watts, *The Final Pagan Generation* (Oakland: University of California Press, 2015), 221n2, comments: " 'pagans,' however imprecise the term, is preferable to a long phrase along the lines of 'non-Jewish devotees of traditional Mediterranean gods.' " I have discussed the use of plural terms for Judaism and Christianity at some length in my *Ignatius of Antioch and the Parting of the Ways: Early Jewish-Christian Relations* (Grand Rapids, MI: Baker Academic, 2009), 214–219.

the new category when they were confronted by it. In other words, would the concept of religion have been incomprehensible when encountered? Even if it were the case that the larger Greco-Roman world had to be confronted by stark, uncompromising monotheistic claims for the issue to become much a matter for reflection, when so confronted, did the concept of religion fit that world and make sense? I think that it did. Indeed, in so far as the Greco-Roman world identified either Jews or Christians as those who did not worship the gods, there is at least a hint of some identity marker within Greco-Roman sensibilities that distinguished between those who worshipped the gods and those who did not, whether by denying all gods (the atheists) or clinging to one god in such a way that other gods were conspicuously disregarded or dismissed (Jews and Christians).[18] In the trial of Cyprian (257 C.E.), for example, the charge was that he had not observed Roman religion (*Romana religio*). Cyprian's reply was that he was a Christian and knew of no other gods.[19] Whatever *Romana religio* meant (and perhaps it meant different things to different people), Cyprian's reply indicates what the term meant to him or at least how he wished to use the term in the particular context of the trial. For Cyprian, the gods were the central feature and their worship the central flaw. At this point, the two sides seem to be talking the same language, or they are at least appropriating similar boundary markers, however baffling or blundering they may have each found the other.

It is clear that early Christians viewed the world of polytheism as a common, collective web of thinking and acting, which differed from Christianity as the night differed from the day. For example, Origen spoke twice of atheist or godless polytheism (τῆς ἀθέου πολυθεότητος; τὴν ἄθεον πολυθεότητα) to describe Greco-Roman religious beliefs.[20] In the third-century *Hortatory Address to the Greeks*, the author spoke of "the doctrines of polytheism" (τῶν τῆς πολυθεότητος δογμάτων) and the "adherents of

---

18. Whether it is enough to think of Greco-Roman "religion" largely in terms of one imprecise aspect of civil life and responsibilities is a matter for debate. North, "The Development of Religious Pluralism," 180–187, who is sympathetic to the idea, nonetheless recognizes that there were some Greco-Roman groups in that world that had a more precise sense of their religious character apart from the general civic character of religion.

19. *Acta proconsularia, CSEL* III.3, 110. Cited in Stephen Mitchell, *A History of the Later Roman Empire A.D. 284–641* (Oxford: Blackwell, 2007), 240. According to Mitchell, this is the oldest preserved use of the phrase *Romana religio*. I would add that even were it the first use of the phrase, the concept could have been considerably older.

20. Origen, *Cels.* 1.1; 3.73.

polytheism" (τοὺς τὴν πολυθεότητα ἀσπαζομένους).[21] Eusebius spoke of Christian converts having "rejected all the polytheism (πολυθεῖας) of the demons, and confessed that there is only one God, the Creator of the universe."[22] He had just used an even more odious expression to describe the world of Greco-Roman paganism—"the ancient disease of the superstition of idols" (παλαιᾷ νόσῳ δεισιδαιμονίας εἰδώλων).[23] This is how at least some early Christians, if not most, saw and described the religious world in which they lived—in general and sweeping terms.

And Christians were not the first to group the diverse Greco-Roman polytheism into one religious mass, and by both general and specific attack, to offer a blanket dismissal of all of it. Jews had already divided their world between those who worshipped one god and those who worshipped many, using the very general term ἔθνη (translated as the Gentiles or the nations), for those of the world beyond Judaism.[24] However general this term may appear, clearly it was specific enough to be used as an identity marker. Philo perhaps deserves the credit for coining the more obvious religiously loaded word "polytheism,"[25] though the ἔθνη term was sufficient as a religious marker too. Whether polytheists saw themselves so united, Christians and Jews certainly held this non-nuanced view of the larger world of Greco-Roman religion.[26]

The problem in forbidding the use of these terms is that such sweeping terms reflect a natural way by which groups define themselves and

---

21. *Hortatory Address to the Greeks* 23. This third-century work was attributed to Justin Martyr.

22. Eusebius, *Hist. eccl.* 2.3.2. The word is used elsewhere by Eusebius who speaks of the "madness of polytheism" (τῆς πολυθέου μανίας) *Life of Constantine* 2.45, and the "error of polytheism" (πολυθέον πλάνην) *Life of Constantine* 4.75.

23. Eusebius, *Hist. eccl.* 2.3.2.

24. For example, Psalm 115:2; 135:4, 15; 1 Chronicles 17:21.

25. Philo is credited with the coining of the word polytheism (polytheistic): *Virtues* 39.214; *Rewards* 28.162; *Eternity* 1; *Migration* 12.40; *Heir* 36.169; *Names* 37.205; *Decalogue* 14.65; *Spec. Laws* 4.34.178; *Creation* 61.171; *Confusion* 11.42. It was not the main word used for the non-Jewish world. Jews generally referred to the non-Jewish world as simply the nations (ἔθνη) or (ἐθνικοι). Christians in the earliest period used ἔθνη (over 160 uses in the New Testament, by almost all writers). Most of Paul's uses of the word are in Romans and Galatians. The author of Luke-Acts uses the term frequently in both Luke and Acts, but the use in Acts is three times more frequent. The word "polytheism" does not occur in the New Testament.

26. See Ishay Rosen-Zvi and Adi Ophir, "Paul and the Invention of the Gentiles," *JQR* 105 (2015): 1–41, for a review of the debate and a twist to the common view. The authors contend that Judaism had a more nuanced perspective on the matter, and that it was Paul who sharpened the categories into the way that they have come to be used, a use then adopted by the

dismiss others, drawing boundaries that mark off the "them" and the "us," with little if any attention to or interest in the diversity of the other. There is nothing particularly inappropriate or surprising about such perception. Indeed, to dismiss the early Christian perception of the world divided between Christians and pagans[27]—or by some other tag for the world of polytheism—is to miss a key element for understanding the new Christian movement. The lumping of this diversity together was intentional. It was not due to an oversight or misconception on the part of Christians. To expect or to demand nuance on this matter is unreasonable. Nuance is probably the first thing to go out the window when a movement draws boundaries to differentiate itself within and from the larger world. The use of a general term for the diverse polytheism of the day certainly did not mean that Christians and Jews had no awareness of the diversity within Mediterranean religion. Quite the opposite. They delighted in pointing out the diversity of polytheism.[28] But they thought they observed something else—a common and flawed core of that religious world—and that was critically important.

Of course, that kind of division of the ancient world is a theological construct, but we should not expect something different or something more "accurate." This is a matter of group self-identification and boundary marking—a reflection of how they saw the world or how they made sense of the world they saw. All boundary markers have that quality. Take the "Greek/Barbarian" division, for example. It was equally a construct, and it "failed" to treat individually each group within the orbit of the broad term that marked off everything that was not Greek. But that lack of nuance of diversity was not a reflection of either oversight or

---

later rabbinic tradition. See, too, Isabella Sandwell, *Religious Identity in Late Antiquity: Greeks, Jews and Christians in Antioch* (Cambridge: Cambridge University Press, 2007).

27. Christians had to factor in Judaism as well. They did this in a variety of ways, though always retaining their vision of the larger world as one of polytheism. By viewing Judaism not so much as false but as obsolete, abandoned, replaced, superseded, disobedient, or some other image of dismissal, Judaism need not complicate the debate over one god or many for Christian apologists.

28. Dionysius, bishop of Alexandria in the mid-200s, in response to the prefect Aemilianus' accusation that Christians did not worship the gods, pointed out that "Not all men worship all gods, but each one certain whom he regards as such" (Eusebius, *Hist. eccl.* 7.11.8). And Theophilus of Antioch points out the varying beliefs about the gods (*Autol.* 3.7). Tertullian, *Nat.* 2.12, mockingly comments on the multitude of gods: the greater and the lesser ones, the old and the novel, the male and the female, the unmarried and the married, the clever and the unskilled, the rustic ones and the town ones, the national and the foreign ones.

ignorance. Rather, it was intentional and fundamental to the boundaries being set.

Alan Cameron's observation is worth attention here. Speaking in defense of the usefulness and appropriateness of "the lumping together of all non-Christian cults (Judaism excepted) under one label" and arguing largely against Garth Fowden and John North, who object to such generalization, Cameron comments that from the early Christian perspective "those who refused to acknowledge the one true god, whatever the differences between them, were for all practical purposes indistinguishable." To those who may object that the term pagan "flattens out the diversity of religious experience" of non-Christians, Cameron comments: "Of course it does."[29] And that is the point. The flattened portrait of polytheism is a key to understanding early Christianity's sense of its position and purpose in the larger world and against the world of religious options in the marketplace.[30]

The Rural Factor

A curious matter comes to light when we examine the ways scholars have counted the number of Jews and Christians (or pagans, for that matter) in the empire. The rural areas, comprising perhaps as much as 85% of the empire's population, are overlooked. Most do not see this as a problem, for the dominant assumption has been that Jews outside of Palestine and Christians everywhere were residents of cities. But this "urban thesis" that has dominated discussions of Jews and Christians in the Roman Empire cannot be maintained. As it is routinely presented, it fails the test of the mathematical possible and of the cultural probable, as I will show in the chapters that follow, where I focus on two things. One is the weaknesses and inadequacies of the urban thesis. The other is how important the rural element is for an adequate reconstruction of the growth of Christianity in the Roman Empire. In challenging the universally accepted thesis of the urban character of early Christianity, I am attacking about the only thing on which MacMullen and Stark agree—that Christianity was an urban

---

29. Alan Cameron, *The Last Pagans of Rome* (Oxford: Oxford University Press, 2011), 27.

30. Harold Remus, "The End of 'Paganism'?" *Studies in Religion* 33 (2004): 191–208, argues for the term "polytheism" in place of "paganism," following a trend in recent scholarship. For my purposes here, the matter does not need resolution.

religion in the first three centuries and that the countryside did not become part of Christian interest or success until at least the Constantinian period or even later.

I am not arguing that by considering the rural dimension of Christianity we can establish firm numbers. I am doubtful that even remotely reliable numbers can be offered. But by looking at the rural as well as the urban landscape, we may be able to suggest ways in which theories of the expansion of early Christianity might need to be modified or, in some cases, completely abandoned, and perhaps new ones adopted. And we might gain a deeper appreciation for the complex and diverse makeup of the early Christian movement, as well as its growth throughout the empire, even if we cannot take a precise measure of its membership by counting heads still wet with the waters of baptism.

2

The "Urban" Thesis

The Current Consensus

Efforts to determine the number of Christians in the Roman Empire run head-on into a basic assumption about the character of early Christianity: it was, supposedly, an *urban* religion. This is the view of almost every recent scholar of the early church. Some will make exceptions for isolated areas, but the general picture is confidently asserted—the Christian church in the Roman world was centered in cities, and its structure and concerns reflected an urban context.

But the empire was not largely urban. A large part of the population lived outside the cities and even more would have been farmers, with some living in the city but working plots of land in the countryside. These people, if not always rural, were at least rustic. If such a dominant element in the population of the empire is excluded from the body of potential converts for early Christianity, then we are confronted either with scandalously low numbers of Christians at the time of Constantine or with cities saturated with Christians, neither scenario which seems to reflect the impression left by the overall evidence.

In spite of the seriousness of the problem, the matter of rural Christians is almost never discussed, except to say that there were none—or so few that they can be largely disregarded in reconstructions of pre-Constantinian Christianity.[1] To illustrate the wide acceptance of the urban thesis, I quote

---

1. Wayne A. Meeks, *The First Urban Christians: The Social World of the Apostle Paul* (New Haven and London: Yale University Press, 1983), 73, states that "there may well have been members of the Pauline communities who lived at the subsistence level, but we hear nothing of them." Granted, certainly we hear nothing of them in the modern literature, but perhaps we should not be surprised to hear nothing about them in the Pauline material either, written as it was in the early months of gathering a few people into small, newly

here numerous leading scholars of early Christianity. Ramsay MacMullen perhaps best captures the situation when he states: "in estimating the place of Christianity in the whole empire, the weight of representation must fall on the cities, not the countryside. Almost everyone agrees that the new faith only very slowly reached out into the farming population."[2] In another place, speaking of the pre-Constantinian period, MacMullen simply comments that Christians "are not heard of in the countryside."[3]

W. H. C. Frend, the scholar who has given the most attention to this matter over the years,[4] claims that between Paul and the beginnings of monasticism, Christianity was an urban religion.[5] He further says: "The church's progress during the second century committed it even further to an urban environment," asserting that "With few exceptions, the Christian groups in the second century were found in cities." and that "The third century continued developments already discernible in the late-second. . . . Its urban character, however, was emphasized to an even greater degree than before."[6] In another article, Frend reaffirms

---

established Christian assemblies. The serious question is whether people from the countryside or people of rustic sensibilities in urban areas came to constitute a significant part of the Christian movement from the earliest days. I argue in this book that they do.

2. Ramsay MacMullen, *The Second Church: Popular Christianity* A.D. 200–400 (Atlanta: Society of Biblical Literature, 2009), 101–102. He expresses the same sentiment in his earlier *Christianizing the Roman Empire (A.D. 100–400)* (New Haven: Yale University Press, 1984), 83.

3. MacMullen, *Christianizing the Roman Empire*, 103.

4. R. A. Markus, in the Presidential Address of a meeting of the Ecclesiastical History Society, spoke of the dichotomy of town and countryside, and he pointed, in particular, to Frend's use of the concept: "in the hands of William Frend—the Rostovtzeff of ecclesiastical history—it showed its power to illuminate, even to transform, the study of ancient heresy and schism" [Markus, "Country Bishops in Byzantine Africa," in *The Church in Town and Countryside*, Studies in Church History XVI, ed. Derek Baker (Oxford: Basil Blackwell, 1979): 1].

5. Such comments about the urban character of early Christianity appear across Frend's many writings, so much so that one of the Variorum Reprints of Frend's writings was released in 1980 under the title *Town and Country in the Early Christian Centuries* (London: Variorum Reprints, 1980). For our purposes, the following articles of Frend are particularly important: "Town and Countryside in Early Christianity," in *The Church in Town and Countryside*, Studies in Church History XVI, ed. Derek Baker (Oxford: Basil Blackwell, 1979), 25–42; "The Winning of the Countryside," *JEH* 18 (1967): 1–14; "The Failure of Persecutions in the Roman Empire," in *Studies in Ancient History*, Past and Present Series, ed. M. I. Finley (London and Boston: Routledge and Kegan Paul, 1974), 263–287; "Early Christianity and Society: A Jewish Legacy in the Pre-Constantinian Era," *HTR* 76.1 (1983): 53–71. Frend does make an exception for Phrygia, where he finds an early rural Christianity [W. H. C. Frend, *The Rise of Christianity* (Philadelphia: Fortress Press, 1984), 38–39].

6. Frend, "Town and Countryside in Early Christianity," 34, 35, 37.

this view: "The main weakness of the Church in the first half of the third century was that, except perhaps in parts of Asia Minor, it was almost entirely an urban organization."[7] And in his classic work on the Donatists, Frend repeatedly makes his case that Christianity was largely urban until the latter half of the third century, at which time it began to gain rural adherents.[8]

Other scholars hold the same opinion. Robert Browning says that Christianity in the first three centuries was "essentially an urban religion, spreading from city to city and leaping over the intervening country-side."[9] Derek Baker, the editor of a collection of papers titled *The Church in Town and Countryside*, introduced the volume with the comment that "Christianity was in origin predominantly an urban phenomenon—a fact overshadowing its early development."[10] Wayne Meeks and Robert Wilken concur, stating emphatically that early Christianity was a "mostly urban" movement, "streetwise and cosmopolitan."[11] Indeed, it is Meeks, through his widely read and praised book *The First Urban Christians*, who is primarily responsible for the now near-universal assumption of the urban character of early Christianity.[12] Rodney Stark, in his two popular books on the subject, *The Rise of Christianity* and *Cities of God*,[13] follows Meeks, as he had in an earlier article, where he said: "For sociologists, the most important single fact about early Christianity is that it was, at least subsequent to the crucifixion, an urban movement."[14] Indeed, the

---

7. Frend, "The Failure of the Persecutions in the Roman Empire," 268.

8. Frend, *The Donatist Church: A Movement of Protest in Roman North Africa* (Oxford: Clarendon Press, 1952).

9. Robert Browning, *The Emperor Julian* (Berkeley: University of California Press, 1976), 160.

10. Baker, *The Church in Town and Countryside*, xv.

11. Wayne A. Meeks and Robert L. Wilken, *Jews and Christians in Antioch in the First Four Centuries of the Common Era* (Missoula, MT: Scholars Press, 1978), 1.

12. Meeks, *The First Urban Christians*, 32–34. That books deals with the setting of churches within Paul's orbit. Meeks develops the urban theme for the period beyond Paul more explicitly in his *The Origins of Christian Morality* (New Haven and London: Yale University Press, 1993), 37–51.

13. Rodney Stark, *The Rise of Christianity* (Princeton: Princeton University Press, 1996), 57; *Cities of God: The Real Story of How Christianity Became an Urban Movement and Conquered Rome* (New York: HarperCollins, 2006).

14. Rodney Stark, "Antioch as the Social Situation for Matthew's Gospel," in *Social History of the Matthean Community*, ed. David L Balch (Minneapolis: Fortress Press, 1991), 189.

subtitle of Stark's second book on the topic, *Cities of God*, is *The Real Story of How Christianity Became an Urban Movement and Conquered Rome*. Henry Chadwick comments that "almost all the evidence concerning the shape of second-century Christianity shows the churches to be organized around the town."[15] Peter Brown describes "the average adherents" of Christianity as "industrious townfolk."[16] Henri Marrou speaks of missionaries who were "at work in the last decades of the fourth century, when the movement of evangelisation, for long confined to the towns, finally spread to the countryside."[17] Robin Lane Fox says that it was not until the mid-fourth century that Christianity turned to the countryside.[18] A. H. M. Jones, earlier than any of the authors quoted above, concluded that Christianity became "very rapidly an essentially urban religion."[19] Perhaps the most sweeping statement comes from Paula Fredriksen, who states that "for its first three centuries, Christianity *in all its varieties* remained an urban phenomenon."[20] These quotes come from many of the leading scholars of early Christian history, and numerous more quotes of similar kind could be gleaned from almost any current book on early Christianity.[21] In some cases, comments of like kind were being made a

---

15. Henry Chadwick, "The Role of the Christian Bishop in Ancient Society, in *Protocol of the Colloquy of the Center for Hermeneutical Studies in Hellenistic and Modern Culture* (Berkeley, CA: The Center for Hermeneutical Studies in Hellenistic and Modern Culture, 1980), 1.

16. Peter Brown, *The Rise of Western Christendom: Triumph and Diversity*, A.D. 200–1000, 2nd ed. (Oxford: Blackwell, 2003), 69.

17. Jean Daniélou and Henri Marrou, *The Christian Centuries*, vol. 1, *The First Six Hundred Years*, trans. Vincent Cronin (London: Darton, Longman and Todd, 1964), 296.

18. Robin Lane Fox, *Pagans and Christians* (New York: Alfred A. Knopf, 1987), 46.

19. A. H. M. Jones, *The Greek City: From Alexander to Justinian* (Oxford: Clarendon Press, 1940), 298. Jones does admit there were "local variations," with rural churches in such areas as in Bithynia, Cyprus, and Cyrenaica.

20. Paula Fredriksen, "Christians in the Roman Empire in the First Three Centuries," in *A Companion to the Roman Empire*, ed. David S. Potter (Oxford: Blackwell, 2006), 587 (emphasis mine). Most scholars would allow for a rural presence, and perhaps a rural origin, for at least some forms of Christianity, such as Montanism and segments of Donatism.

21. Abraham J. Malherbe, *Social Aspects of Early Christianity*, 2nd ed. (Philadelphia: Fortress Press, 1983), 63 (though with qualification); David E. Aune, *Prophecy in Early Christianity and the Ancient Mediterranean World* (Grand Rapids, MI: Eerdmans, 1983), 243; Ben Witherington III, *Conflict and Community in Corinth: A Socio-rhetorical Commentary on 1 and 2 Corinthians* (Grand Rapids, MI: Eerdmans, 1995), 23n63; M. Eugene Boring, *Revelation, Interpretation: A Bible Commentary for Preaching and Teaching* (Louisville, KY: John Knox, 1989), 87; James S. Jeffers, *Conflict at Rome: Social Order and Hierarchy in Early Christianity* (Minneapolis: Fortress Press, 1991), 1.

hundred years ago,[22] well before Meeks made it the consensus opinion. The thesis of a largely urban Christianity sweeps on with hardly a voice of dissent.

The Problem with the Urban Thesis

Not only do early church scholars routinely declare that Christianity was largely urban, many are prepared to offer fairly precise numbers for the size of the Christian movement in the Roman Empire around the year 300 C.E., just before Constantine, the first Christian emperor, came on the scene. The common number offered is 6 million Christians in an empire of 60 million, or 10% of the population.

But there are problems with the numbers and the methods used in attempting to determine the various matters of the demography of early Christianity. The one fundamental and insurmountable problem in the estimates of Christian adherents in the early period relates directly to the supposed urban character of early Christianity. The problem is this: most of the population of the empire was rural. If Christians were largely urban and if the empire was largely rural, even with remarkable success in the urban areas, Christianity could have represented at best only a small proportion of the overall population of the empire by the time of Constantine—much smaller than the 10% that is often maintained. Indeed, if the empire was 10% urban (as many of those quoted above would have maintained) and Christians, at 10% of the empire, were themselves largely urban, Christians would have made up the entire population of all urban areas by the year 300 C.E. Even with a higher rate of urbanization (20%), Christians (at 10% of the population of the empire) would have made up half the population of all cities of the empire. Given that Christians would have been far more numerous in the eastern part of the empire, Eastern cities would have been swamped with Christians even in a fairly urbanized empire. If, on the other hand, Christians constituted only 10% of the urban population (or even double that) and if the adherents of Christianity throughout the empire were primarily urban, then Christians would have made up only 1% to 4% of the population of

---

22. For earlier views similar to Meeks, see, for example, S. Angus, *The Environment of Early Christianity* (New York: Charles Scribner's Sons, 1915). Angus says that the church "apparently attempted no peasant mission" and that it was "practically confined to Greek-speaking people" (212).

the empire in the year 300,[23] a scenario equally problematic and one that would require a radical rethinking of the Christian presence (and success or lack thereof) in the empire. Strangely, the mathematical impossibilities facing most of the reconstructions offered seem to have escaped notice even by those who are generally meticulous in their scholarship.[24] The problem with using numbers in this way is that no one would propose them if the blunt reality of the situation were spelled out. Yet some such highly unlikely scenario is required by the assumptions that are commonly accepted in the urban thesis.

It is my contention that the rural element may be part of the solution, for if Christianity had even a most minimal success in the countryside, gaining but a small percentage of the rural inhabitants, the number of rural Christians easily could have equaled—or indeed surpassed—that of urban Christians in the early period, simply by reason of the fact that the overall rural population was so much more numerous than the urban. Only under a rural scenario of some sort can the total population of Christians in the empire number several million without swamping the cities with Christians. The other scenario would be simply to reduce the total number of Christians in the empire at the time of Constantine. We could then make all Christians urban without swamping cities with Christians. But even under that scenario, a rural component in the Christian membership is likely, given that the rural and the rustic populated cities almost as much as they did the countryside, as we shall see.

In the examination that follows, I consider in some detail various aspects of the "urban thesis." It is my contention that (1) the widely accepted numbers of Christians in the empire at the time of Constantine simply do not work without a substantial rural element in the church; (2) the

---

23. The 1% calculation is based on urbanism at 10% and Christians at 10% of the urban population of cities. The 4% is based on a more generous calculation of urbanism at 20% and Christians at 20% of the population of cities.

24. Consider, for example, MacMullen, who is far more cautious than most regarding Christianity's expansion. In some earlier works, he had asserted that the church "started out as an urban phenomenon and continued in that tendency" until about 400 c.e. He further asserted that "the countryside lagged far behind the cities in degree of Christianization." And he recognized that "a great majority of the empire's total population lived outside of cities" (*Christianizing the Roman Empire*, 83). Few would disagree with MacMullen on these points, nor with his claim that the Christian population of the empire in 312 c.e. was about 5 million (85). Yet on that scenario, all urban areas of the empire would have been quite crowded with Christians by the time of Constantine's conversion, a position that MacMullen did not hold. Or consider Rodney Stark, who states that the

urban thesis rests on no convincing evidence for the pre-Constantinian period and most of the assumptions that exclude the possibility of a rural Christianity fail on close examination;[25] (3) the urban–Christian/rural–pagan dialectic is useful as a description only of the post-Constantinian era, and even then it captures not the reality, but at best an impression (based on the proportion of the respective populations that had converted rather than actual numbers of urban and rural Christians); (4) proponents of the "urban thesis" have a tendency to tip the scales unfairly in favor of their theory, routinely dismissing as insignificant or unrepresentative any evidence that points to an early rural Christianity; and (5) the stark lines drawn between the urban and the rural do not reflect the realities of the relationship between city and countryside in the ancient world where early Christianity developed.

Dissenting Voices

There have been a few warnings about aspects of the urban thesis. Robert Markus, in his address to a conference on the theme of the church in town and countryside, offered a rare caution about the use of the notion of town and countryside as an interpretative tool. He spoke of "its limitations, its liability to obscure and to distort."[26] Few have heeded his warning.

More recent still is the volume from the third "Shifting Frontiers in Late Antiquity" conference, where much of the discussion has challenged the sharp dichotomy between city and country that is often assumed by those who promote the "urban thesis." Presenters there used terms such as "paper thin" (xxi), "chosen illusion" (xxi), "more mental than actual"

---

urban population of the empire was only 5% (3 million). Yet, if Christians comprise 10% of the population of the empire (as Stark holds), there would have been 6 million Christians, making as many rural Christians as urban. And that scenario has every resident of every city a Christian. Stark does not seem to be aware of the problem this makes for his urban thesis. See Appendix B.

25. The typical arguments that dismiss the possibility of rural Christianity are as follows: (1) the conservative nature of the countryside; (2) the near-unbridgeable boundaries between the city and the countryside, often with an emphasis on the linguistic barriers; (3) the need for the dislocation that the city environment creates in order for new religious movements to take root; and (4) the example of Paul's city-centered mission. These matters are dealt with later in chapter 6.

26. Markus, "Country Bishops in Byzantine Africa," 1.

(139) to describe the "frontier" between country and city.[27] Numerous other scholars express similar cautions.[28]

Stephen Mitchell, in his comprehensive work on Anatolia, offers a number of comments on the rural situation. Speaking of the centuries before the 300s, he states: "An important thread that runs through the history of Anatolian Christianity ... is the paramount importance of the rural churches."[29] Of the area around Eumenia, Mitchell comments: "It is worth emphasizing that the stereotype of the early Christians as an urban sect has little validity here."[30] Richard A. Fletcher notes "a few tiny fragments of evidence which suggest an early rural dimension to the spread of Christianity in, for example, Syria, Egypt or Asia Minor." In the same context, he comments that "very many farmers" would have lived in urban space. And he notes that Christianity viewed as an "urban religion" is a truism, and "like all truisms ... need[s] some qualification."[31]

What should at least open the door for a conversation about early rural Christianity are comments made by the authors of two recent and detailed works that update and extend Adolf Harnack's classic work on the expansion of Christianity in the pre-Constantinian period. Both authors conclude that some attention must be given to the presence of Christianity in rural areas. Roderic Mullen cautions that in light of the evidence from the upper Tembris Valley, "it may be unwise to conclude that the countryside was largely devoid of Christians." Further, he challenges Rodney Stark's conclusion about the lack of rural Christians, noting that "the religiously

---

27. The papers from this third conference were published in Thomas S. Burns and John W. Eadie, eds., *Urban Centers and Rural Contexts in Late Antiquity* (East Lansing: Michigan State University Press, 2001). Even in this collection, the "urban thesis" is affirmed in the introductory comments (xxi), though other articles, such as David Riggs' ("Paganism between the Cities and Countryside of Late Roman Africa," 285–300) challenge the supposed sharp dichotomy between the country and the city (287). Also of special importance is J. F. Drinkwater, "Women and Horses and Power and War," 135–146. Diverse as the results are from this conference, it is likely that more thorough and cautious conclusions about the nature of the rural and urban environments of early Christianity are now in order, and the stark line between city and countryside often drawn in scholarship may need to be set aside or much more heavily qualified.

28. See chapter 5.

29. Stephen Mitchell, *Anatolia: Land, Men, and Gods in Asia Minor* (Oxford: Clarendon Press: 1993), II.68.

30. Mitchell, *Anatolia*, II.58.

31. Richard A. Fletcher, *The Barbarian Conversion: From Paganism to Christianity* (New York: H. Holt and Co., 1998), 15.

discontented, the relatively deprived, and religious seekers from privileged backgrounds" (individuals that Stark sees as the natural audience for the Christian message) could be found in rural areas too. Mullen concludes by stating: "one suspects that the surviving evidence is skewed toward urban areas simply by virtue of the greater density of population to be found there."[32] Ten years after Mullen's work, William Tabbernee edited a volume by leading researchers in a range of geographical areas important to early Christianity, all with a careful eye to archaeological evidence in particular.[33] Tabbernee comments about this volume: "From the data presented, there are some surprises in store for those who think that early Christianity was primarily an urban phenomenon."[34] In regard to Italy, for instance:

> this examination of the spread of Christianity in Italy before Constantine qualifies the commonly accepted theory that Christian growth was initially and primarily an urban phenomenon. Among the Italian episcopates identified, no less than half were from small towns, some quite a distance from the coast. Modern studies about the Christianization in northern Italy show a similar balance between urban and rural.[35]

But perhaps the most unlikely voice on this issue comes from the scholar most associated with the urban thesis—Wayne Meeks. In one of Meeks' latest writings, there is recognition of the existence of an early rural Christianity. Meeks comments: "as the [Christian] movement spread, beginning in the second century, back into the countryside, the urban bishops presided, in principle, also over the Christians in the towns and

---

32. Roderic L. Mullen, *The Expansion of Christianity: A Gazetteer of Its First Three Centuries* (Leiden and Boston: Brill, 2004), 9. Mullen was able to make use of archaeological findings unavailable to Harnack, as well as better editions of some of the texts. Nonetheless, Harnack still must be the starting point. See chapter 7.

33. William Tabbernee, ed., *Early Christianity in Contexts: An Exploration across Cultures and Contexts* (Grand Rapids, MI: Baker Academic, 2014).

34. Tabbernee, *Early Christianity in Contexts*, 8. That is not to say that Tabbernee's work proposes a sweeping early conversion of the countryside. In many areas of the empire and its periphery, the contributors argue for an urban Christianity with little early evidence for a rural Christian presence.

35. Robin M. Jensen, et al., "Italy and Environs," in *Early Christianity in Contexts: An Exploration across Cultures and* Contexts, ed. William Tabbernee (Grand Rapids, MI: Baker Academic, 2014), 207.

villages dependent upon their city—the region known as the chōra."[36] But Meeks leaves the matter of this rural Christianity otherwise unexplored. That is unfortunate. A new series entitled *The First Urban Churches*, though clearly inspired by Meeks' most influential work, *The First Urban Christians*, suggests some focus on the countryside—the "hinter of city life" and the "nearby small villages," warning that "a totally 'urban' lens . . . might oversimplify the social, parochial, and geographical complexities of ancient life."[37]

There seem to be adequate informed reservations about the urban thesis to probe the rural earth more thoroughly for evidence of the presence of Christianity in the countryside in the first three centuries, and it is this neglected *chora*—the countryside of the second and third centuries—that guides much of the present volume.

36. Wayne A. Meeks, "Social and Ecclesial Life of the Earliest Christians," in *The Cambridge History of Christianity*, vol. 1, *Origins to Constantine*, ed. Margaret Mary Mitchell and Frances Margaret Young (Cambridge: Cambridge University Press, 2006), 153. Meeks is primarily interested here in the development of church office from a body of elders as the principal authority to a single bishop, who is superior to the body of elders.

37. James R. Harrison, "The First Urban Churches: Introduction," in *The First Urban Churches*, vol. 1, *Methodological Foundations*, ed. James R. Harrison and L. L. Welborn (Atlanta: SBL Press, 2015), 7.

3

Counting Romans and Christians

The Accepted Numbers

A detailed article by Keith Hopkins offers a useful summary of the near-consensus opinions on most of our questions, and for the most part, these are the numbers that I will use in this book, though I will factor in shifts in scholarly opinion since Hopkins wrote.[1] Hopkins laid out the general consensus clearly. Although all the numbers are subject to ongoing revision, no radically new consensus seems to be developing. It needs to be pointed out, in fairness to Hopkins, that he presented his work as "an experiment in both method and substance,"[2] though many who have adopted his numbers have done so with considerably more certainty than Hopkins would have endorsed. With these qualifications in mind, my intention is neither to defend Hopkins' numbers nor to dismiss them. I merely wish to show how the commonly accepted numbers fail, and how even more recent revisions to the popular numbers fail too.

Hopkins gave the following population figures for the beginning of the 300s c.e. The total population of the empire was around 60 million;[3] the east was slightly more populous and urbanized.[4] Hopkins puts the

---

1. Keith Hopkins, "Christian Number and Its Implications," *JECS* 6 (1998): 185–226.

2. Keith Hopkins, "Christian Number and Its Implications," 185.

3. Hopkins, "Christian Number and Its Implications," 195.

4. Hopkins, "Christian Number and Its Implications," 195, n19. But opinions differ on this matter. While most would agree with Hopkins, Walter Scheidel, "Demography," in *The Cambridge Economic History of the Greco-Roman World*, ed. Ian Morris and Richard P. Saller (Cambridge: Cambridge University Press, 2007), 47, places only 35%–40% of the population of the empire in the Greek eastern half.

population of the east at 35 million, and the urban population at 15% (9 million empire wide; 5.25 million in the east),[5] though the degree of urbanization is a matter of considerable dispute.[6] About 80% of the total population was engaged in farming (48 million).[7] Jews made up 7% to 8% of the total population (4.2–4.8 million),[8] and most of these lived outside of Palestine (about 80%, or 3.36–3.84 million).[9] Further, most of those Jews were urban.[10] Christians numbered 10% (about 6 million) of the total population of the empire around 300 C.E.[11] And Christians, like Jews, were mainly urban.[12]

---

5. Hopkins, "Christian Number and Its Implications," 195n20.

6. The size of ancient cities and the proportion of urban dwellers in the empire are debated matters. Richard L. Rohrbaugh pointed out that recent trends in scholarship (as of 1991) spoke of smaller-size cities, and of a smaller proportion of urban population ["The Pre-Industrial City in Luke-Acts: Urban Social Relations," in *The Social World of Luke-Acts: Models for Interpretation*, ed. Jerome H. Neyrey (Peabody, MA: Hendrickson, 1991), 125–149]. Twenty-five years after Rohrbaugh's article, many scholars are still proclaiming smaller-sized cities, based on newer or more refined methodologies. For example, see J. W. Hanson, "The Urban System of Roman Asia Minor and Wider Urban Connectivity," in *Settlement, Urbanization and Population*, ed. A. Bowman and A. Wilson (Oxford: Oxford University Press, 2011), 229–275. But there has been a significant change in spite of that similarity. That is in regard to the degree of urbanization. Whereas Rohrbaugh said that in most cases only 5%–7% of the people lived in cities (133), some newer scholarship proposes much higher rates of urbanization, up to 35% in Egypt. Bagnall and Frier, for example, place the urban segment at about a third of the population [Roger S. Bagnall and Bruce W. Frier, *The Demography of Roman Egypt* (Cambridge: Cambridge University Press, 1994), 56]. But much depends on what size of settlement is considered urban. See chapter 5 for a detailed discussion.

7. Hopkins, "Christian Number and Its Implications," 207. The matter is complicated because of the fluid boundaries between city and countryside, with farmers often living in towns and traveling to their plots outside the city each day.

8. Hopkins, "Christian Number and Its Implications," 213–214, works with 7% to 8%, which gives him 4.2–4.8 million Jews in the empire, though he would be happier with a much lower number of 3 million.

9. Hopkins, "Christian Number and Its Implications," 213. This is a more disputed matter, though numbers as high as 80% for the percentage of the Jewish population living in the diaspora are sometimes given (see chapter 4).

10. Hopkins, "Christian Number and Its Implications," 214. See chapter 4 for further discussion.

11. Hopkins, "Christian Number and Its Implications," 194. This figure is in line with Robert M. Grant's suggestion that the Christian population was less than 7.5 million, and perhaps much less [*Early Christianity and Society: Seven Studies* (San Francisco: Harper & Row, 1977), 8]. Grant's first chapter, "The Christian Population of the Roman Empire," has much useful information on demography.

12. Hopkins, "Christian Number and Its Implications," 195n20.

Let us examine the number most important to our concerns: the number of Christians in the empire in the year 300 C.E., just before the rise to power of Constantine, whose reign would bring substantial change to the religious dynamics of the empire. Most writers on early Christianity routinely assert that about 10% of the population of the empire was Christian, without any hint to their readers how arbitrary such a number is or how cautious experts are becoming about such a matter. From professional to popular writers and from scholarly to popular presses, the 10% number is touted. Take the case of a recent book by one of the best-known authors in the field of early Christianity. Bart Ehrman, in his 2009 book *Jesus, Interrupted: Revealing the Hidden Contradictions in the Bible (and Why We Don't Know about Them)*, simply states as fact that Christians were about 10% of the Roman Empire at the beginning of the 300s. No word of caution is offered about how much of a wild guess the number really is.[13] A host of other authors follow suit.[14]

In part, a certain level of satisfaction with this 10% number is a consequence of the work of Rodney Stark, who has shown that a mere 40% per decade increase (3.42% annual increase) in the Christian movement would have produced 6 million Christians by the year 300 C.E. Four matters have made Stark's projections of early Christian growth seem compelling. One, Stark presents Mormonism as a new religion that had precisely that kind of growth, thus he has a concrete example of such growth.[15] Two,

---

13. Bart D. Ehrman, *Jesus, Interrupted: Revealing the Hidden Contradictions in the Bible (and Why We Don't Know about Them)* (New York: HarperCollins, 2009), 244, though in an earlier book, Ehrman states that Christians "comprised far less than 10% [*The New Testament: A Historical Introduction to Early Christian Writings*, 3rd ed. (New York, Oxford University Press, 2004), 423]. Which it is does not seem to matter.

14. The following is but a small sampling: E. Glenn Hinson, *The Evangelization of the Roman Empire: Identity and Adaptability* (Macon, GA: Mercer University Press, 1981), 25; Laurie Guy, *Introducing Early Christianity: A Topical Survey of Its Life, Beliefs and Practices* (Downers Grove, IL: InterVarsity Press, 2004), 10, 112; Peter J. Leithart, *Defending Constantine: The Twilight of an Empire and the Dawn of Christendom* (Downers Grove, IL: InterVarsity Press, 2010), 39; William Farina, *Perpetua of Carthage: Portrait of a Third-Century Martyr* (Jefferson, NC: McFarland, 2009), 78; Megan Hale Williams, "Lessons from Jerome's Jewish Teachers: Exegesis and Cultural Interaction in Late Antique Palestine," in *Jewish Biblical Interpretation and Cultural Exchange: Comparative Exegesis*, ed. Natalie B. Dohrmann and David Stern (Philadelphia: University of Pennsylvania Press, 2008), 71–72; James Carroll, *Constantine's Sword: The Church and the Jews: A History* (Boston: Houghton Mifflin Company, 2001), 176; Bruce Chilton, "Tolerance and Controversy in Classical Christianity," in *Religious Tolerance in World Religions*, ed. Jacob Neusner and Bruce Chilton (West Conshohocken, PA: Templeton Foundation Press, 2008), 134.

15. Stark, *The Rise of Christianity*, 7. The Mormon rate of growth was 43%.

Stark points out that his projections fall almost exactly where various early church scholars have thought the size of the Christian movement was in 300 C.E.[16] Three, the exponential factor in Stark's 40% growth equation seems to explain how Christianity's numbers could increase so rapidly in the latter half of the third century, thus making sense of a situation where there appear to be so few Christians before 250 C.E. and yet so many by the year 300. And, four, taking a 30% growth rate per decade or a 50% growth rate would seem to give impossibly low or high numbers, respectively, thus making 40% look right. It seems, then, that Stark has both statistics and scholarship on his side. What could be more convincing? Unfortunately, Stark's numbers fail for a variety of reasons and at a number of points, a matter I lay out in Appendix B.

The Population of the Roman Empire

What is troubling about any of the numbers offered is that, at the very best, these are guesses and must continue to be guesses. To demonstrate how problematic a quest for reliable numbers for any of these matters is, let us examine current scholarship on the simple and most fundamental question: the size of the population of the Roman Empire in the year 300 C.E.[17]

The most widely repeated numbers given in recent scholarship range between 50 and 60 million. This reflects little change in the size of the population of the Roman Empire proposed in the first systematic study

---

16. Stark, *The Rise of Christianity*, 4–13.

17. For a review of some of the numbers offered over the past couple of centuries, see Michael E. Jones, *The End of Roman Britain* (Ithaca, NY: Cornell University Press, 1996), 261–263. Jones thinks the population of the empire may have doubled from Augustus to Alexander Severus. He proposes a population of 50–60 million at the time of Alexander Severus (208–235), which he calls a "conservative estimate." Frank McLynn, *Marcus Aurelius: A Life* (Cambridge, MA: Da Capo Press, 2009), 3–4, lists a number of different estimates, one as high as 130 million. Bruce W. Frier, "Demography," in *The High Empire A.D. 70–192, CAH*, vol. 11, ed. A. K. Bowman, P. Garnsey, and D. Rathbone (Cambridge: Cambridge University Press, 2000), 812–816, works with the data supplied by Colin McEvedy and Richard Jones, *Atlas of World Population History* (New York: Facts On File, 1978). Frier reduces the population by 10% in the latter part of the second century to account for the impact of a series of plagues. Angus Maddison, *Contours of the World Economy, 1–2030 AD: Essays in Macro Economic History* (New York: Oxford University Press, 2007), 11–68, offers more details, but basically follows McEvedy and Jones. The most common number of 60 million at the time of Constantine is used by Hopkins, "Christian Number and Its Implications," 191–192. It is important to remember that Hopkins is more skeptical in regard to numbers and more nuanced in his use of them than many. He calls the initial use of these "estimates" as "only a heuristic device" (192).

of the issue by Julius Beloch in 1886, a defining work on the issue.[18] Elio
Lo Cascio, in spite of criticism of Beloch, recognizes that Beloch's work
is "the key-stone of all modern investigation on size, structure, and, to a
certain extent, dynamics of ancient populations ... still unparalleled in its
scope," and "at the root of all modern debates and controversies" regarding the population of the ancient world.[19] Beloch estimated the population to have been about 54 million at the time of Augustus (beginning of
the Common Era), with populations roughly equal between the western
and eastern parts of the empire. Adolf Harnack accepted the 54 million
number.[20] Even though Beloch revised his numbers upward (to 100 million) later in his life,[21] and even though there has been sharp criticism
of Beloch's methods almost from the beginning,[22] most modern scholars
accept numbers in the 50 to 60 million range. Tim Parkin, for example,
who cautions against almost all of the methods by which ancient numbers have been determined, including those by Beloch, nonetheless uses
Beloch's numbers for the size of the Roman Empire.[23]

But there is a vast range of estimates regarding the population of the
Roman Empire beyond the 50 to 60 million figure that the majority of
scholars use.[24] Figures earlier than Beloch were often considerably higher—
as much as 130 million. Gibbon reckoned that slaves alone numbered

---

18. Karl Julius Beloch, *Die Bevölkerung der griechisch-römischen Welt* (Leipzig: Verlag von
Duncker & Humblot, 1886), 507.

19. Elio Lo Cascio, "The Size of the Roman Population: Beloch and the Meaning of the
Augustus Census Figures," *JRS* 84 (1994): 23.

20. Adolf Harnack, *The Mission and Expansion of Christianity in the First Three Centuries*,
trans. and ed. James Moffatt (New York: G. P. Putman's Sons/London: Williams & Norgate,
1908), 8.

21. Lo Cascio, "The Size of the Roman Population," 28n29. Frier, "Demography," 81n95,
dismisses Beloch's revised figures as "considerably less credible."

22. Lo Cascio, "The Size of the Roman Population," 23–40, presents his own criticisms and
notes the criticism of many others. For a sympathetic review of Beloch's work and an assessment and dismissal of much of the criticism of Beloch, see Glen W. Bowerstock, "Beloch and
the Birth of Demography," *TAPA* 127 (1997): 373–379.

23. Tim G. Parkin, *Demography and Roman Society* (Baltimore: Johns Hopkins University Press,
1992), 4–66. Some difficulties in determining the population of specific areas are examined
in Robert Witcher, "Missing Persons? Models of Mediterranean Regional Survey and Ancient
Populations," in *Settlement, Urbanization and Population*, ed. A. Bowman and A. Wilson, Oxford
Studies in the Roman Economy 2 (Oxford: Oxford University Press, 2011), 36–75.

24. This high number has made its way on popular internet sites, as in the Khan Academy Big
History Project, 7.3: Agriculture and Civilization: Greco-Roman (https://www.khanacademy.

60 million.[25] And many modern scholars lean toward higher numbers, too, as Michael Jones points out. Jones speaks of Beloch's numbers as "underestimates or minimums."[26] Walter Scheidel offers a possible high of 72 to 76 million in the mid-second century C.E.[27] Peter Fibiger Bang is prepared to speak of a high of 80 million, though he warns that this would be only under the most optimistic conditions.[28] On the other side, lower numbers than those commonly used are offered, somewhere around 40 to 45 million,[29] which is 20% to 25% lower than Beloch's number, and 25% to 33% lower than the widely accepted number of 60 million.

Further, even if our numbers were more properly estimates rather than guesses, the population of the Roman Empire was hardly a stable one, for the size would have fluctuated, with droughts, famine, epidemics, war, and other economic disruptions on the one hand reducing the population, and periods of peace and prosperity on the other perhaps providing the right conditions for growth. In regard to the empire's total population, some have estimated a 10% decline in a two-decade period of crises starting in 165 C.E.,[30] with some scholars speculating that in some areas there may have been a decline of as much as 30%,[31] since the decline would

org/partner-content/big-history-project/agriculture-civilization/first-cities-appear/a/greco-roman). For the 120,000,000 number, see note in Philip Schaff, *History of the Christian Church*, vol. 1 (New York: Charles Scribner's Sons, 1882), 79n1; William Stevenson, *Historical Sketch of the Progress of Discovery, Navigation and Commerce, from the Earliest Records to the Beginning of the Nineteenth Century* (Edinburgh: William Blackwood, 1824), 198.

25. Edward Gibbon, *The Decline and Fall of the Roman Empire*, intro. by Antony Lentin and Brian Norman (Ware, Kertfordshire: Wordsworth Editions, 1998), 36. For a discussion of Gibbon's contribution, see Jan N. Bremmer, *The Rise of Christianity through the Eyes of Gibbon, Harnack and Rodney Stark*, 2nd ed. (Groningen: Barkhuis, 2010), 2–24.

26. Jones, *The End of Roman Britain*, 2. Jones follows Pierre Salmon, *Population et dépopulation dans l'Empire romain* (Brussels: Latomus, 1974). Jones offers a brief survey of population figures in an appendix (261–263).

27. Scheidel, "Demography," 47–48.

28. Peter Fibiger Bang, *The Roman Bazaar: A Comparative Study of Trade and Markets in a Tributary Empire* (Cambridge: Cambridge University Press, 2008), 115.

29. Maddison, *Contours of the World Economy, 1–2030 AD*, 32–43, discusses the debate regarding the population of the Roman Empire, as well as questions about urbanization. Maddison looks, in particular, at the works of McEvedy and Jones, *Atlas of World Population History* (Hammondsworth: Penguin Books, 1978); and Frier, "Demography," 787–816.

30. David Stone Potter, *The Roman Empire at Bay, AD 180–395* (London: Routledge, 2004), 17.

31. The impact of the Antonine plague on the Roman Empire is much debated. See comments in Dionysios Ch. Stathakopoulos, *Famine and Pestilence in the Late Roman and Early*

not have occurred evenly across the empire. Calculating the population of the Roman Empire becomes, then, somewhat a shot in the dark at a moving target.[32] And trying to determine the Christian population would be a particularly blind shot. Further complicating our quest for numbers, many scholars offer a number for the population of the Roman Empire, without even specifying for what period that number applies. That makes the number largely useless.

It is important at this point to note that Hopkins had misgivings about some of the evidence and figures that he used in his influential article.[33] Others, too, have expressed a need for caution. Bruce Frier, another recent investigator on the subject, calls himself an agnostic on questions of population because the surviving evidence seems "exceedingly fragile both in its quantity and quality." He expresses little confidence that we can arrive at "more than vague (if arguably 'educated') guesses as to gross population levels and change."[34] Fergus Millar captures the uncertainty of our numbers when he speaks of the "modern estimates (or rather guesses)" regarding the population of the Roman Empire.[35] Frank McLynn speaks of demography as "an esoteric science, where inexact or incomplete data have to be 'guesstimated.'"[36] Jan Bremmer says that the numbers are based

---

Byzantine Empire: A Systematic Survey of Subsistence Crises and Epidemics, Birmingham Byzantine and Ottoman Monographs (Aldershot: Ashgate Publishing, 2004), 94–95. See, too, R. P. Duncan-Jones, "The Impact of the Antonine Plague," *JRomArch* 9 (1996): 108–136; R. J. Littman and M. L. Littman, "Galen and the Antonine Plague," *AJP* 94 (1973): 243–244; and Walter Scheidel, "A Model of Demographic and Economic Change in Roman Egypt," *JRomArch* 15 (2002): 97–114. Scheidel uses Littman's figures of 7 to 10 million deaths over the twenty-five years of the plague (pp. 254–255), a 14% to 20% loss of the population (p. 99).

32. That is not to say that the effort to count should be abandoned. For a review of the effort from times past to the present, see Walter Scheidel, "Progress and Problems in Roman Demography," in *Debating Roman Demography*, ed. Walter Scheidel (Leiden: Brill, 2000), 1–82. See, too, Scheidel, "Roman Population Size: The Logic of the Debate," Princeton/Stanford Working Papers in Classics (Stanford University, 2007).

33. Hopkins, "Christian Number and Its Implications," 191–193.

34. Bruce W. Frier, "More Is Worse: Some Observations on the Population of the Roman Empire," in *Debating Roman Demography*, ed. Walter Scheidel (Leiden: Brill, 2000), 139. See, too, Scheidel, "Progress and Problems in Roman Demography," 143.

35. Fergus Millar, *Rome, the Greek World and the East*, vol. 1. *The Roman Republic and the Augustan Revolution*, ed. Hannah M. Cotton and Guy M. Rogers (Chapel Hill: University of North Carolina Press, 2002), 31.

36. Frank McLynn, *Marcus Aurelius: A Life* (Cambridge, MA: Da Capo Press, 2009), 3.

on "quicksand."[37] Michael Jones concludes that "estimates must necessarily be extremely conjectural. Some would say impossible." Such estimates rest on "dubious bases" and "scattered and fragmentary" evidence, according to Jones.[38] Lo Cascio noted that those studying ancient populations were shifting from macrodemographic to mircodemographic problems, because "estimating the size of an ancient population is thought of as an almost impossible exercise, given the uncertainties in the source material."[39]

These are not new warnings. Seventy-five years ago, Gaetano Salvemini warned that "given the scarcity of the sources, it is not possible to arrive at a safe conclusion" on estimates of the population of the Roman Empire.[40] Little suggests that we are any better off today. Whether "a rough estimate is better than no estimate at all" will be argued differently by scholars of different temperaments.[41]

The Problem of the Christian Numbers

About thirty-five years ago, Robert M. Grant offered a similar judgment, not on the size of the empire's population but on the size of the Christian population. It "cannot be regarded as close to a solution," he said.[42] Peter Brown, who has made significant contributions to the study of early Christianity, spoke with similar warning about the numbers offered in regard to the percentage of Christians in the Roman Empire. He noted that the figure usually given (between 5% and 10%) is "of course, a

---

37. Bremmer, *The Rise of Christianity through the Eyes of Gibbon, Harnack and Rodney Stark*, 50.

38. Jones, *The End of Roman Britain*, 263.

39. Lo Cascio, "The Size of the Roman Population," 40.

40. Gaetano Salvemini, *Historian and Scientist: An Essay on the Nature of History and the Social Sciences* (Cambridge, MA: Harvard University Press, 1939), 44.

41. Lo Cascio, "The Size of the Roman Population," 40, quoting P. A. Brunt quoting D. L. Glass. Some might argue that demography offers better results when focused on questions of "population structure and dynamics" rather than on an attempt to determine the size of a population (see Neville Morley, "Demography and Development in Classical Antiquity," in *Demography and the Graeco-Roman World: New Insights and Approaches*, ed. Claire Holleran and April Pudsey (Cambridge: Cambridge University Press, 2011), 14–36.

42. Robert M. Grant, *Early Christianity and Society* (San Francisco: Harper & Row, 1977), 5, though his chapter "The Christian Population of the Roman Empire" attempts to work out possible numbers for some situations.

guess."[43] Unfortunately, few who tout such numbers seem to have any of Brown's sense that it is simply a guess.

Our difficulties lie not simply because two thousand years separate us from the people we want to count. Even had a count been attempted at the time, the task would not have been easy and the result would not have been reliable, for much would have depended on the self-identification of individuals as Christians. As the author of the *Letter to Diognetus* pointed out:

> For Christians are not distinguishable from other people either by country, language, or customs. For nowhere do they live in their own cities, speak some unusual dialect, or practice an uncommon lifestyle . . .. while living in both Greek and barbarian cities according to each one's lot and following local customs with respect to clothing and food and the rest of life. . .[44]

Simply put, we cannot establish either the size or the proportion of the Christian movement in the empire as a whole or in its urban areas. But all is not lost. We can at least test the common numbers offered to see whether a reconstruction of the early Christian movement based on such numbers can fit the Roman world as we know it from other evidence or approaches. In other words, we can at least identify and rule out impossible scenarios, and this, in itself, would be of considerable value to the field. Specifically, the most common scenario put forward fails at this point. The implications of a 10% Christian population and a largely urban Christian membership have, quite simply, not been thought through, and this has allowed an impossible reconstruction of the Christian situation in the Roman Empire at the beginning of Constantine's reign to become a near-consensus view in scholarly and popular literature alike.[45]

Few show any awareness of the nuances of the problem. Paul McKechnie, in a popular-level book, at least recognizes the difficulty of

---

43. Peter Brown, *Poverty and Leadership in the Later Roman Empire*, The Menahem Stern Jerusalem Lectures (Hanover, NH: University of New England Press, 2002), 17.

44. *Letter to Diognetus* 5.1–4.

45. See, for example, Michael Novak, *The Universal Hunger for Liberty: Why the Clash of Civilizations Is Not Inevitable* (New York: Basic Books, 2004), 4, who lists the Christian population at 10%, but nonetheless states that mostly Christianity "thrived in urban pockets"— an impossible reconstruction. One might excuse that kind of oversight by someone not an expert in the field. The problem is that scholars of early Christianity have routinely asserted the same thing.

these numbers, though he fails to see just how serious the problem is. He argues that Christians made up a "good-sized minority," and he recognizes that if Christians were to make up much more of the empire, a large number of Christians would need to be rural. But he rejects that option, saying that "to believe that (say) 20% or 25% were Christian before Constantine, one would have to posit a very substantial rural expansion of Christianity before legalization, and this seems improbable; certainly, tangible evidence of it is lacking."[46] What McKechnie fails to note, however, is that if the Christian population of the empire was even as low as 10% (far lower than his low) and if Christians made up one-third of the urban population (if that is what McKechnie's "good-sized minority" might be taken to be), then there would have been as many rural Christians as urban ones—some 3 million in each area. But at least McKechnie is aware there could be a problem, though he misses how low the numbers of Christians must be for the rural problem not to come into play.

The commonly used number of Christians in the empire is problematic enough, but, as we will see, it becomes even more problematic when we set it beside some of the Jewish numbers that have been offered, along with the supposedly urban character of the Jewish diaspora.[47] Such numbers would require that, by the year 300, everyone residing in cities was either a Jew or a Christian! Indeed, we could double the urban population of the east, and still stock all the cities largely with Jews and Christians. Even if a substantial number of converts to Christianity came from Judaism during this period, the numbers would remain still large enough to present profound difficulties. Such overwhelming Christian and Jewish presence in the cities would revolutionize our understanding of almost every aspect of Christianity (and, indeed, of the Roman world and of Judaism). No one holds such a view. It doesn't pass the sniff test of the plausible. Some adjustments become necessary.

We have very few ancient comments about the size of the Christian population in any area for any period. The clearest hint is a comment by Chrysostom, speaking about the situation in Antioch near the end of the 300s. He stated that the Christian population of the city was

---

46. Paul McKechnie, *The First Christian Centuries: Perspectives on the Early Church* (Downers Grove, IL: InterVarsity Press, 2001), 55.

47. See chapter 4.

about 100,000, and that Christians made up more than half of the population.[48] Various conclusions have been drawn from these statements. When one considers that Chrysostom's comment comes after more than a half-century of imperial favoritism to Christianity and relates to a city that had a long and significant Christian presence, we are probably not far off the mark in estimating that somewhat under 20% of the population of Antioch would have been Christian by the time of Constantine's conversion.[49] But if there was little Christian presence in the countryside, then, based on Antioch as a template, we are left with under (and perhaps well under) 4% of the empire in the Christian fold by the time of Constantine. And that is giving the benefit of a doubt at every point: 20% Christians in cities and 20% urbanization of the empire.[50] If we opted for a lower degree of urbanization (say, 10%) and a lower proportion of Christians among the urban population (10%), then the number of Christians in the empire would not have exceeded 600,000 by the time of Constantine—one-tenth of what is commonly thought. And were we to take a 10% Christian population in cities and Stark's numbers (5% urbanization, and an urban-centered Christianity), there would have been only 300,000 Christians by the year 300—not the 6 million that Stark contends. Stark takes no note of this situation. Even the most generous use of these numbers would require a rethinking of scores of major

---

48. Chrysostom, *Homily 85 on the Gospel of Matthew, Homily 11 on the Acts of the Apostles,* uses the number 100,000 for Christians. For a discussion of the merits of these passages for determining the population of Antioch, see Glanville Downey, "The Size of the Population of Antioch," *TAPA* 89 (1958): 86–89, and MacMullen, *The Second Church,* 147n36.

49. There is likely to have been a swelling of Christian numbers as pagans followed Constantine into the church. Of course, Chrysostom could have been wrong, but he is as likely to have had as reliable information as anyone.

50. Recently, some scholars are proposing that the urbanization of the empire was higher than has generally been accepted. Some claim, at least in the provinces of Italy and Egypt, urbanization as high as 30% and in other areas as high as 20% to 25%. See, for example, the chapters in A. Bowman and A. Wilson, eds., *Settlement, Urbanization and Population,* Oxford Studies in the Roman Economy 2 (Oxford: Oxford University Press, 2011). Note Wilson's article in particular ("City Sizes and Urbanization in the Roman Empire," 161–195). Also, much lower numbers are being proposed for the population of what had been considered some of the major cities of the empire. For example, see J. W. Hanson, "The Urban System of Roman Asia Minor and Wider Urban Connectivity," in *Settlement, Urbanization and Population,* ed. A. Bowman and A. Wilson, Oxford Studies in the Roman Economy 2 (Oxford: Oxford University Press, 2011), 229–275. Ephesus, traditionally viewed as one of the great cities of the empire, with perhaps a population of almost a quarter of a million, is calculated to have a population of between 22,400 and 89,600, depending on population density (p. 254).

questions about the nature of early Christianity and of the Christian conversion of the empire. And adopting Stark's even more problematic numbers would bring almost everything commonly said about early Christian growth crashing down, though Stark believes what he has offered confirms what has generally been said about early Christian numbers.

Clearly, either the frequently repeated number of 6 million Christians in the empire or the frequently assumed urban character of the Christian population is untenable. Where the problem lies is difficult to specify, though one thing is certain: given how few Christians there were anywhere in the empire, especially during the first two hundred years, even a small rural Christian element will require at least some qualification of the "urban thesis." Indeed, with only the most minimal success in the countryside, the number of rural Christians easily could have equaled the number of urban Christians, simply based on the overwhelmingly rural population of the empire in Constantine's time. This is rarely recognized in modern scholarship. For example, although Frank Trombley, in *The Cambridge History of Christianity*, estimates that Christians in the countryside to have been 5% to 10% of the total rural population around 300 c.e., he does not address its implications.[51] Such percentages as he suggested would add up to 2.5 to 5 million rural Christians in the empire, which—even taking his lower number—would make rural Christians a near-majority of the overall Christian population (2.5 million of 6 million), and taking the higher number would make most of the Christians of the empire residents of the countryside (5 million of 6 million). Trombley's otherwise extremely useful article illustrates how easy it is to overlook basic implications of the numbers routinely offered.

The Rural Christianity Factor

It is my contention that the urban–Christian/rural–pagan dichotomy that is so frequently proposed is appropriate only in a post-Constantinian

---

51. Frank Trombley, "Overview: The Geographical Spread of Christianity," in *The Cambridge History of Christianity*, vol. 1, *Origins to Constantine*, ed. Margaret Mary Mitchell and Frances Margaret Young (Cambridge: Cambridge University Press, 2006), 310. It is unclear whether Trombley is speaking only of Phrygia or for the empire generally, though he quotes Origen in this context, and Origen's comment seems to be broad rather than a narrow specifying of a particular territory.

environment. It is only then that the proportion of Christians in cities becomes sufficiently high to allow us to speak of cities as "Christian." The countryside would continue to appear pagan, however, even if the number of rural Christians had kept pace with the number of urban Christians. Thus, even in this post-Constantinian context when one might talk of the "urban" character of Christianity and the contrasting pagan character of the countryside, that portrait may be more a matter of perception than of reality, at least in terms of actual numbers.[52]

To complicate the matter further, what counts as urban is a matter of considerable variation. Some scholars count any settlement over one thousand as urban; others require a population considerably larger.[53] Then there is the question regarding what portion of the urban population was either rural (or rustic) in its habits and work or rural in its origin, having moved from the countryside to the city for some reason or other. These crucial matters are taken up later at various points in this book. For now, we simply look at the basic problem of numbers, quite apart from how those numbers have been determined.

The following tables help to clarify the numbers under a variety of situations, even the most supportive of which is not persuasive for the urban thesis. Table 3.1 reflects the situation in which early Christianity is largely urban. As has been mentioned earlier and is evident from the table, it is difficult to speak of even a 10% Christian population in the empire by the time of Constantine (as is routinely done) without putting the urban Christian population at an unrealistically high percent.

What becomes clear from Table 3.1 is that the thesis of a largely urban Christianity runs into considerable problems, even when that thesis is given every advantage. Take the widespread view that Christians numbered 6 million in an empire of 60 million, or 10% of the population in the year 300. Even setting the urbanization rate of 25% (which is generously high), every urban area of the empire would have had 40% of its population claiming Christian identity prior to Constantine. Further, given that

---

52. At times, an author will mention that it is the *proportion* of the urban population as compared to the *proportion* of the rural population that is the point. But one should not stop there, for equally important is what that indicates about the *actual* number of rural Christians compared to urban Christians. See, for example, the comment by Rodney Stark, *The Rise of Christianity*, 10.

53. See chapter 5.

Table 3.1 Proportion of Christians in Empire (based on 60 million population in empire with no rural Christians)

	Roman Population				
10% Urbanization (6 Million)			15% Urbanization (9 Million)		
		Christian Population			
% Urban	Total %	Total*	% Urban	Total %	Total*
10	1.0	0.6	10	1.5	0.9
20	2.0	1.2	20	3.0	1.8
30	3.0	1.8	30	4.5	2.7
40	4.0	2.4	40	6.0	3.6
50	5.0	3.0	50	7.5	4.5
67	6.7	4.5	67	10.0	6.0
100	10.0	6.0	100	15.0	9.0

*In millions

	Roman Population				
20% (12 Million) Urban in Empire			25% (15 Million) Urban in Empire		
		Christian Population			
% Urban	Total %	Total*	% Urban	Total %	Total*
10	2.0	1.2	10	2.5	1.5
20	4.0	2.4	20	5.0	3.0
30	6.0	3.6	30	7.5	4.5
40	8.0	4.8	40	10.0	6.0
50	10.0	6.0	50	12.5	7.5
67	13.5	8.1	67	16.8	10.1
100	20.0	15.0	100	25.0	15.0

Christians were mainly in the eastern part of the empire, all eastern cities would have had a significant majority of its population Christianized. And if we work with the more likely lower rates of urbanization, all cities would be saturated with Christians, a scenario no one espouses.

Were we to concede that even a small portion of the rural area had converted to Christianity (as illustrated in Table 3.2), the dynamics would

Table 3.2 Equal Number of Rural and Urban Christians
(based on 60 million population in empire)

Roman Population							
10% Urbanization (6 Million)				15% Urbanization (9 Million)			
Christian Population as Percent of Empire							
Urban	Rural	Total	Million	Urban	Rural	Total	Million
10	1.1	2.0	1.2	10	1.6	3.0	1.8
20	2.2	4.0	2.5	20	3.5	6.0	3.6
30	3.3	6.0	3.6	30	5.3	9.0	5.4
33	3.7	6.7	4.0	33	5.8	10.0	6.0
40	4.4	8.0	4.8	40	7.1	12.0	7.2
50	5.6	10.0	6.0	50	8.8	15.0	9.0

Roman Population							
20% Urbanization (6 Million)				25% Urbanization (9 Million)			
Christian Population as Percent of Empire							
Urban	Rural	Total	Million	Urban	Rural	Total	Million
10	2.1	4.0	2.4	10	2.6	5.0	3.0
20	4.3	8.0	4.8	20	5.6	10.0	6.0
25	5.6	10.0	6.0	25	6.6	11.7	7.0
30	6.8	12.0	7.2	30	8.8	15.0	9.0
33	7.7	13.3	8.0	33	10.0	16.7	10.0
40	9.5	15.0	9.6	40	12.5	20.0	12.0
50	12.5	20.0	12.0	50	16.7	25.0	15.0

change considerably, and in such a way as to challenge the urban thesis head-on. For example, with the urban population at 15% of the empire, when Christians make up 10% of the empire, 33% of the urban population would need to be Christian but only 5.8% of the rural population would need to be for there to have been *an equal number of urban and rural Christians*. Yet the impression would be quite different. The cities would be starting to look quite Christian at 33%; the countryside would still look solidly pagan with only 5.8% Christians in it.

Table 3.3 shows various situations for urban and rural percentages, with Christians making up 10% of the empire. It is plain to see how difficult it is to speak of the commonly used figure of a Christian population of 10% at the time of Constantine without including in that number rural Christians into the millions. For example, even with an unrealistically high 40% of the population of cities Christianized (3.6 million), there still would need to be 2.4 million rural Christians (or 4.7% of the countryside) to bring the total number of Christians to 10% of the empire.

From these tables, two points need to be kept in mind. (1) Only a small *percentage* of the rural population would need to have converted for there to have been equal numbers of rural and urban Christians. (2) Given the high proportion of rural residents in the empire, the countryside would have appeared to be quite unchristianized compared to the urban areas, even when the actual numbers of urban and rural Christians were the same, or when rural Christians outnumbered urban Christians.

Table 3.3 Urban and Rural Christian Population (based on 60 million population in empire with Christians at 10% (6 million))

Urban Population of the Empire							
10%		15%		20%		25%	
6 million		9 million		12 million		15 million	
Christian Population (%)							
Urban	Rural	Urban	Rural	Urban	Rural	Urban	Rural
10	10.0	10	10.0	10	10.0	10	10
20	8.9	20	8.2	20	7.9	20	6.7
30	7.8	30	6.5	30	5.0	30	3.3
40	6.7	40	4.7	40	2.5	40	0.0
50	3.6	50	2.9	50	0.0		
100	0.0	67	0.0				

Why does this matter? The urban thesis that has dominated most of the reconstructions of early Christian growth cannot support the structure built upon it. Unless a rural dimension for early Christianity is brought into play, it would appear that either the number of Christians in the empire at the time of Constantine was considerably lower than the 6 million commonly touted or all urban areas were saturated with Christians. Either scenario would force a massive rethinking of nearly every aspect of early Christianity and the Roman Empire.

4

Counting the Jewish Population

Jews in the Roman Empire

Calculating the number of Jews in the Roman Empire is considerably more difficult than calculating the total population of the empire, which is difficult enough. Indeed, the task of counting the Jewish population is impossible—to put the matter bluntly.

It is not just distance in time that complicates the matter. Even if field surveys and crop yields might provide a basis for a rough calculation of high and low population possibilities for the Jewish inhabitants of specific areas in Palestine, outside of Palestine (and even within large areas of Palestine), the Jewish population was mixed with the non-Jewish population. And that mixture cannot be sifted by any mechanism at hand to leave only Jews in the count. Indeed, it may have been difficult even at the time to count the number of Jews. Shaye Cohen points out that what identified an individual as Jewish in the ancient world was not their "looks, clothing, speech, names or occupations"—not even circumcision. For all practical purposes, what identified an individual as a Jew was the individual's self-identification. One was recognized as a Jew only because one self-identified as a Jew.[1]

Granted, the larger society knew that circumcision was a distinctive marker,[2] but such a marker was functional only if, as Cohen put it, the

---

1. Shaye J. D. Cohen, "'Those Who Say They Are Jews and Are Not': How Do You Know a Jew in Antiquity When You See One?" in *Diasporas in Antiquity*, Brown Judaic Studies 288, ed. Shaye J. D. Cohen and Ernest S. Frerichs (Atlanta: Scholars Press, 1993), 3.

2. Circumcision was a marker for Jews even though other groups in the ancient world practiced circumcision too (Herodotus, *Hist.* I.104.3). Paul used the label "the circumcised" for Jews, even when he was writing to a Gentile audience (Gal 2:7, 6:11).

pants were down! Justin, writing in the second century and speaking of Jewish identity, does not mention the pants, but he seems to agree that Jews were indistinguishable from other men except for their circumcision. That, of course, meant, that under normal circumstances an individual could not be identified as Jewish.[3] When the Roman authorities made some effort to identify the Jewish population for the purpose of taxation after the Jewish War, it was circumcision that was considered the marker of the Jew by the authorities. At least, that seems to have been the deciding mark when a more rigorous enforcement of the *Fiscus Judaicus* was put into play under Emperor Domitian.[4] But while it may have been possible to distinguish the Jewish element (or the male Jewish element) within Roman society, no such records, if collected, survive. We are thus left in a position where even our best efforts to calculate the Jewish component of the empire hit a brick wall.

One wonders, then, what modern historians are counting when they offer a calculation of the size of the Jewish population in the Roman Empire. Certainly, the widely varying results do not encourage confidence. Keith Hopkins is perhaps the most cautious. He has Jews making up 7% to 8% of the empire's population (4.2 to 4.8 million), taking the number that was the most widely accepted at the time. But Hopkins recognized that this number might be high and suggested that 5% (3 million) was perhaps correct, though he expressed caution about any of the numbers, speaking of the "hopelessly inadequate data" on which the number rests.[5]

Others have offered numbers, both lower and higher than those used by Hopkins, and usually without the cautions Hopkins pointed to. On the higher side are numbers proposed by scholars such as F. J. Foakes Jackson and Kirsopp Lake, who spoke of 6 to 7 million Jews in an empire of 60 to 70 million, or 10% of the empire.[6] Salo Baron, whose work is

---

3. Justin, *Dial.* 16, "For you are not recognised among the rest of men by any other mark than your fleshly circumcision." Justin did note that the Sabbath and various festivals as well as observance of the law were expected behaviors too.

4. M. D. Goodman, "Nerva, the Fiscus Judaicus and Jewish Identity," *JRS* 79 (1989): 40.

5. Keith Hopkins, "Christian Number and Its Implications," *JECS* 6 (1998): 213–214.

6. F. J. Foakes Jackson and Kirsopp Lake, *The Beginnings of Christianity* (London: Macmillan and Co., 1920), I.159, following Jean Juster, *Les juifs dans l'Empire romain. Leur condition juridique, économique et sociale* (Paris: Librairie Paul Geuthner, 1914), I.212. Juster specifies that number for the situation before the war of 70 C.E.

followed by many, claimed that Jews made up one-eighth of the population of the empire, and that 20% of the eastern empire, where more Jews lived, was Jewish.[7] Louis Feldman agrees.[8] James Jeffers places the Jewish population of the empire at 6.5 to 8.5 million;[9] Rodney Stark claimed that Jews made up 10% to 15% of the empire: 6 to 9 million Jews in an empire of 60 million people.[10] Peter Richardson says Jews made up one-seventh of the empire "by some estimates." He offers no other options.[11]

On the other hand, significantly lower numbers have been offered, though often without any indication where the numbers come from. David Wenham and Steve Walton, for example, state that there were 3.5 million Jews in the empire.[12] Leonard Glick works with a similar number— 3 to 4 million.[13] Darrell Bock simply noted that estimates for Jews in the empire run from 1 million to 8 million, without indicating who holds these positions.[14] Peter Davids speaks of a "safely conservative" estimate of 2 million Jews "spread unevenly over the Roman and Parthian worlds,"[15] which must reduce the Jewish population of the Roman Empire to not

---

7. S. W. Baron, *A Social and Religious History of the Jews*, 2nd ed. (New York: Columbia University Press, 1952), I:170, 370–372.

8. Louis H. Feldman, *Jew and Gentile in the Ancient World: Attitudes and Interactions from Alexander to Justinian* (Princeton: Princeton University Press, 1993), 92; Louis H. Feldman and Meyer Reinhold, *Jewish Life and Thought among Greeks and Romans* (Minneapolis: Fortress Press, 1996), 124. In another work, Feldman, *Jewish Life and Thought among Greeks and Romans: Primary Readings* (London: Continuum, 1996), 266, sets the number at "at least a tenth of the population of the Roman Empire" (emphasis mine).

9. James S. Jeffers, *The Greco-Roman World of the New Testament Era: Exploring the Background of Early Christianity* (Downers Grove, IL: InterVarsity Press, 1999), 213.

10. Rodney Stark, *Cities of God: The Real Story of How Christianity Became an Urban Movement and Conquered Rome* (New York: HarperCollins, 2006), 6.

11. Peter Richardson, *Building Jewish in the Roman East* (Waco, TX: Baylor University Press, 2004), 336.

12. David Wenham and Steve Walton, *Exploring the New Testament: A Guide to the Gospels & Acts* (Downers Grove, IL: IVP Academic, 2005), 43.

13. Leonard B. Glick, *Marked in Your Flesh: Circumcision from Ancient Judea to Modern America* (New York: Oxford University Press, 2005), 29.

14. Darrell L. Bock, *Studying the Historical Jesus: A Guide to Sources and Methods* (Grand Rapids, MI: Baker Academic, 2002), 109. Bock does not indicate who proposes these numbers.

15. Peter H. Davids, *The First Epistle of Peter*, NICNT (Grand Rapids, MI: Eerdmans, 1990), 46n3. He does recognize a higher number of 4 million too (p. 46).

more than a million and a half, and perhaps substantially fewer.[16] The various lower numbers mentioned above for the Jewish population of the empire clash with numbers often put forward for the Jewish population for Palestine on its own, where numbers between 2 and 5 million are offered by some, numbers greater than that proposed by others for the entire Jewish population of the empire.[17] And most numbers are offered without specifying the period, even though the Jewish population, with a series of devastating wars, cannot have had a stable population.

The numbers look like a guessing game, where a player is merely to pick a number from 1 to 10—any number. There is no consensus, or anything that looks like it could develop into a consensus. Everett Ferguson simply points out the range of numbers that have been proposed, while noting that estimates of the number of Jews in the empire are "little more than guesses."[18] Irina Levinskaya warns that "one must be cautious rather than confident" on demographic matters until we have more archaeological information and a more secure methodology.[19] And even earlier, Dora Askowith spoke of the possibility of calculating the Jewish population of the empire from numbers offered by Beloch and Harnack, but cautioned that the result (4.5 million), though interesting, would probably be an "excessive estimate."[20]

There does, however, appear to be the beginning, at least, of a trend to be more suspicious of the higher numbers regarding the total Jewish population of the empire. The editors of *The Jews among Pagans and Christians*, for

---

16. A still useful article, both for its review and defense of low numbers and for its cautions, is C. C. McGown's 1947 article, which compares the population of Palestine near the end of the British mandate to the situation of the first century [C. C. McGown, "The Density of Population in Ancient Palestine," *JBL* 66 (1947): 425–436].

17. Jack Pastor, *Land and Economy in Ancient Palestine* (London: Routledge, 1997), 6–8, reviews some of the debate about the population of Palestine. See, too, M. Broshi, "The Population of Western Palestine in the Roman-Byzantine Period," *BASOR* 26 (1979): 1–10.

18. Everett Ferguson, *Backgrounds of Early Christianity*, 3rd ed. (Grand Rapids, MI: Eerdmans, 2003), 427.

19. Irina Levinskaya, *The Book of Acts in Its Diaspora Setting*, vol. 5, *The Book of Acts in Its First Century Setting* (Grand Rapids. MI: Eerdmans, 1996), 23.

20. Dora Askowith, *The Toleration and Persecution of the Jews In the Roman Empire*, vol. 1, *The Toleration of the Jews under Julius Caesar and Augustus* (New York: Columbia University, 1915), 52. Askowith's assessment of her number as probably an "excessive estimate" is misinterpreted as a "reasonable estimate" when referred to by Lewis S. Feuer, "The Sociobiological Theory of Jewish Intellectual Achievement: A Sociological Critique," in *Ethnicity, Identity, and History. Essays in Memory of Werner J. Cahnman*, ed. Joseph B. Maier and Chaim I. Waxman (New Brunswick, NJ: Transaction, 1983), 102.

example, speak of the "high (if not inflated) estimates of the Jewish population of the Diaspora."[21] Much earlier, Victor Tcherikover questioned the
bases upon which the high numbers rested.[22] Recently, Seth Schwartz set
the population of Palestine in the middle of the first century at 1 million,
of which half probably were Jews, critiquing the way crop yields have been
used to argue for a much larger population.[23]

What is most problematic about the high numbers often offered for Jews
in the empire is that the estimate of 6 to 7 million seems to be based entirely
on a misreading of a medieval text, a passage that should never have been
considered in attempts to determine the Jewish population of the empire.
The number comes from a comment made by the thirteenth-century author
known as Bar Hebraeus.[24] Tcherikover suspected that Bar Hebraeus was
confused, but he was unable to prove it, though he had already provided
a number of reasons for caution about the high numbers. Further examination showed that Tcherikover was on the right track. Shortly after the
publication of the Hebrew edition of Tcherikover's book, Judah Rosenthal
pointed out that Bar Hebraeus' number is identical to the number found in
Eusebius' *Chronica*, but in the Eusebian passage the number specifies the
total number of Roman citizens (not Jews), as determined by a census in the
reign of Claudius.[25] Although the error was pointed out in 1951, and others

---

21. Judith Lieu, John North, and Tessa Rajak, eds., *The Jews among Pagans and Christians in the Roman Empire* (London and New York: Routledge, 1992), 5.

22. Victor Tcherikover, *Hellenistic Civilization and the Jews*, trans. S. Applebaum (Philadelphia: Jewish Publication Society of America, 1959), 292–295.

23. Seth Schwartz, "Political, Social, and Economic Life in the Land of Israel, 66–c. 235," in *The Cambridge History of Judaism*, vol. 4, *The Late Roman-Rabbinic Period*, ed. Steven T. Katz (Cambridge: Cambridge University Press, 2006), 23, 38–41.

24. Bar Hebraeus, a Syriac bishop of a Monophysite church, was one of the most learned men of his age. He wrote extensively on a wide range of topics. E. A. W. Budge, trans., *The Chronography of Gregory Abu'l Faraj, The Son of Aaron, The Hebrew Physician Commonly Known as Bar Hebraeus Being the First Part of His Political History of the World* (London: Oxford University Press, 1932).

25. Eusebius' number is 1 million greater than that provided by Tacitus (*Ann.* 11.25) for this census. For the various places Eusebius's number (or a variant of it) has been used, see Abraham Wasserstein, "The Number and Provenance of Jews in Graeco-Roman Antiquity: A Note on Population Statistics," in *Classical Studies in Honor of David Sohlberg*, ed. Ranon Katzoff, with Yaakov Petroff and David Schaps (Ramat Gan, Israel: Bar Ilan University Press, 1996), 310nn. See, too, Judah Rosenthal, "Bar Hebraeus and a Jewish Census under Claudius," *Jewish Social Studies* XVI (1951): 267–268, and Brian McGing's review of the debate about this data in "Population and Proselytism: How Many Jews Were There in the Ancient World?" in *Jews in the Hellenistic and Roman Cities*, ed. John R. Bartlett (London: Routledge, 2002), 93–94.

since then have called attention to the problem of Bar Hebraeus' number,[26] that number is still presented by many as reliable.

Abraham Wasserstein mentions other numbers that might be offered, dismissing all such numbers as no more secure, even as approximations. Nor can the proportion of Jews in the empire be established, he warns, pointing out that 11%, for example, is no safer than 5%.[27] Wasserstein's conclusion provides a sound caution for the field:

> The minima established are no more solidly grounded than the maxima. Our evidence does not enable us to offer well-founded estimates of that kind; it is not representative and it is not comprehensive. We cannot hope to establish any reliable estimates of absolute numbers or relative proportions. We cannot even be sure of the orders of magnitude involved. All that our evidence allows us to say is that at certain periods of ancient history, e.g., in the first Christian century, before the catastrophes of 70, 117 and 135 CE, the number of Jews in some places (and their prominence in the life of those places) was such as to create the impression that the Jewish population was very numerous, and that this impression may well represent a truth that is important but not precisely quantifiable.[28]

Yet Wasserstein cautions that the locations where Jews were both numerous and visible may have provided a "misleading impression that their numbers, both absolutely and proportionately, were larger than they really were."[29] Brian McGing is of similar mind. Of numbers in such ancient sources as Josephus and Philo, McGing concludes that they are "so tendentious and unreliable as to be virtually without value."[30]

---

26. Leonard Victor Rutger, *The Hidden Heritage of Diaspora Judaism*, 2nd ed. (Leuven: Peeters, 1998), 202–203; Louis H. Feldman, *Judaism and Hellenism Reconsidered* (Leiden: Brill, 2006), 185n15.

27. Wasserstein, "The Number and Provenance of Jews in Graeco-Roman Antiquity: A Note on Population Statistics," 312–313. Wasserstein also points out that the 7 million number taken from Bar Hebraeus' account is "based on what even the most charitable of critics must judge to be very shaky evidence" (309), and McGing, "Population and Proselytism," 88, states that "it is high time that the evidence of Bar Hebraeus was given a decent burial."

28. Wasserstein, "The Number and Provenance of Jews in Graeco-Roman Antiquity," 313.

29. Wasserstein, "The Number and Provenance of Jews in Graeco-Roman Antiquity," 313.

30. McGing, "Population and Proselytism," 105.

The simple reality is that, as John Barclay states, "it is impossible to give even approximate figures" for the number of Jews in the Roman Empire.[31] That was twenty years ago, and things have not changed. Most recently, Shlomo Simonsohn notes "the fallacy of basing demography on insufficient data, questionable sources and the like" and warns that "figures even approaching a limited degree of precision must fail due to the . . . paucity of reliable data."[32] More bluntly still, he dismisses all the numbers that had been offered for the Jewish population of the empire, pointing out that they were "so discrepant, so unproven and so unreliable, that they met with the incredulity of many scholars, time and time again."[33] Any numbers, then, are speculative, at best, and there is no way to confirm or refute any of the various numbers offered. McGing put the matter sharply:

> I do not believe we have the first notion of how many Jews there were in the ancient world, even roughly speaking, nor do we have the means to discover it. This may sound like a counsel of despair, but pretending otherwise and basing important theories on wishful thinking, will get us nowhere.[34]

I see nothing that would lead me to a conclusion different from McGing's. We would be better served by heavily qualifying what we say about numbers, at least until more adequate evidence to support one guess over another is found.

But whatever numbers we work with—or with none at all—some conclusions and cautions can be drawn. For one thing, if we make Jews in the diaspora largely urban (as most do), even low numbers for Jews in the empire would make Jews the dominant minority in the cities of the empire (particularly the eastern cities) and the higher numbers sometimes proposed would require that the cities of the Roman Empire be largely saturated with Jews.[35] The urban thesis commonly touted for diaspora Jews clearly faces problems.

---

31. John M. G. Barclay, *Jews in the Mediterranean Diaspora: from Alexander to Trajan (323 BCE–117 CE)* (Edinburgh: T & T Clark, 1996), 4n1.

32. Shlomo Simonsohn, *The Jews of Italy: Antiquity* (Leiden: Brill, 2014), 107–108.

33. Simonsohn, *The Jews of Italy: Antiquity*, 113n70.

34. McGing, "Population and Proselytism," 106.

35. Even a diaspora population of 1.5 million Jews with most of them situated in urban areas of the eastern empire would have a quarter of all eastern cities consisting of Jewish residents (calculated on an eastern population of 35 million and an urbanization of 15%). See Tables 4.1 and 4.2.

On the other hand, if we set the Jewish population of the empire very low, some contend it would then be difficult to account for the strength of the Jews to organize and carry off one revolt after another in the period from 66 to 135 C.E.[36] Others have pointed out, however, that such resistance may only indicate strengths in fairly limited areas of the empire and under special conditions, so that the rebellions cannot speak to the strength of the Jewish presence throughout the empire.[37] And the contrast between Palestine and the diaspora must be factored in also, with Jews clearly a more dominant part of the population in Palestine. Yet the diaspora revolts of 115–117 C.E. do show a Jewish population of some strength, even though the Jewish rebels were defeated in the end— indeed, in some areas, perhaps even annihilated. It seems, however, that the Jewish community at the beginning of the revolt apparently thought itself powerful enough to attack and win against local populations (both in cities and in the countryside) and even against the Roman garrisons. At least, there is no evidence that Jews who revolted in the diaspora were subject to the kind of unbearable repression that might have compelled them to engage in hopeless revolt. Further, when the Jews attacked, they appear to have read the immediate situation correctly, for they were able to wreak havoc upon the residents of the land and even against armed Roman garrisons.[38]

After these rebellions, the situation would have changed somewhat. A substantial number of Jews would have been slaughtered in the revolts, a substantial number reduced to slavery, and survivors left destitute. But we cannot be very specific about the impact of these revolts, other than to say that the status, strength, and size of the Jewish population of the Roman Empire would have been diminished. To what measure the strength and number of Jews in the empire declined is largely guesswork, even though

---

36. William Horbury, "Jewish-Christian Relations in Barnabas and Justin Martyr," in *Jews and Christians: The Parting of the Ways A.D. 70 to 135*, ed. J. D. G. Dunn (Tübingen: J. C. B. Mohr, 1992). Reprint, with new English translations: (Grand Rapids, MI: Eerdmans, 1999), 318, contends these various revolts of Jews are "no small proof of Jewish strength and numbers." Horbury makes the same point in "The Jewish Dimension," in *Early Christianity: Origins and Evolution to AD 600*, ed. Ian Hazlett (London: SPCK, 1991), 40, where he calculates that Jews made up 8% to 9% of the Roman Empire.

37. Wasserstein, "The Number and Provenance of Jews in Graeco-Roman Antiquity," 313.

38. E. Mary Smallwood, *The Jews under Roman Rule: From Pompey to Diocletian* (Leiden: Brill, 1976), 389. Much besides the motives of this war is unclear. Even the chronology is uncertain, as is the involvement of Parthian Jews and Palestinian Jews.

some ancient numbers are provided,[39] and some scholars have tried to calculate the percentage of the Jewish population destroyed. For example, Naomi Pasachoff and Robert Littman claim that as a result of the Jewish War of 66–73 c.e., one-tenth of the entire Jewish population of the Roman Empire was destroyed.[40] They do not indicate how they arrived at this number, but if the Jewish population of the empire was around 5 million, the loss of half a million Jews in the first revolt may be possible, but the actual situation cannot be determined with any certainty. It will not help much to turn to Josephus, who set the number killed in the siege of Jerusalem alone at over 1 million, a number which according to many modern scholars is roughly the size of the entire Jewish population of Palestine in the first century—or even double that size![41] But all of this is guesswork. Numbers fail us.

In the discussion below, I will use commonly accepted low numbers for Jews in the empire. I do so not because I have confidence in these numbers but only to show how even the most cautious numbers fail many of the theories about the urban character of diaspora Judaism and of early Christianity. I will assume 4.2–4.8 million Jews in the empire.[42] Were we

---

39. Allen Kerkeslager, "The Diaspora from 66 to c. 235 CE," in *The Cambridge History of Judaism*, vol. 4, *The Late Roman-Rabbinic Period*, ed. Steven T. Katz (Cambridge: Cambridge University Press, 2006), 53–68, points to the disappearance of Jewish communities in Egypt, Cyrenaica, and Cyprus as a result of the revolt of 115–117, speaking of the "unmitigated savagery" that Jewish populations faced and stating that "the campaign of ethnic cleansing appears to have been a devastating success" (62). It is not possible to establish the degree to which the Jewish population was reduced, but a significant loss must be factored in. Cassius Dio, *Roman History*, 68.32 reports that the Jews killed 220,000 in Cyrenaica and in Egypt and Cyprus 240,000, though it is unclear whether the author means that 240,000 were killed in Egypt and Cyprus together or just in Cyprus. Although we cannot trust ancient numbers, certainly the sense of the scope of the slaughter is conveyed.

40. Naomi E. Pasachoff and Robert J. Littman, *A Concise History of the Jewish People* (Lanham, MD: Rowman and Littlefield, 2005), 91.

41. Ancient numbers generally are viewed by modern scholars as notoriously unreliable. Nevertheless, we can gain an impression from the following ancient comments that the loss of life was considerable. Josephus claims that 1,100,000 died in the siege of Jerusalem alone (70 c.e.). Another 97,000 were sold into slavery (*Jewish War*, 6.9.3). Seth Schwartz, *The Ancient Jews from Alexander to Muhammad* (Cambridge: Cambridge University Press, 2014), 83, dismisses Josephus' numbers for the dead but thinks the number of captives may be possible. Substantial Jewish communities in the eastern Mediterranean were wiped out or expelled in the revolts of 115–117 c.e. A Roman historian indicated that 580,000 Jews were killed in the Bar Kochba revolt (Dio Cassius, *Roman History*, 69.14.1).

42. This is based on the Jewish population of the empire at 7%. Hopkins uses this number, though he thinks the number may be "inflated."

to subtract a million for Jews in Palestine (which may be too high[43]), that would leave 3.2–3.8 million diaspora Jews in the empire. Were I to take some of the higher numbers offered, the chance of finding any way to reconcile the size of the Jewish population of the diaspora with the supposed urban character of diaspora Jews would become even more remote.

Jews in the Eastern Empire

As we have seen, it is regularly assumed in conjunction with the discussion of the Jewish population of the Roman Empire that (1) the majority of these Jews lived in the eastern part of the empire, and (2) the overwhelming majority of the diaspora Jews was urban. The first assumption is sound; the second is far less certain.

There is no question that the Jewish diaspora in the eastern part of the empire was considerably more extensive than in the western part.[44] One might reasonably draw that conclusion based simply on matters of geography and politics, without any appeal to ancient literature or archaeology. Most diaspora Jews would have settled into eastern areas of the empire simply for reasons of proximity, for Palestine was part of the east, and this area would have been the most familiar. Further, the strongest foreign influence encountered by the Jews of Palestine for some three hundred years before the Roman presence was from the Greek Ptolemaic and Seleucid empires, both eastern. These realms, which became part of the eastern Roman Empire, had long accommodated large numbers of Jewish immigrants, from slaves, to mercenaries, to free. Large cities such as Alexandria and Antioch and various cities of Asia Minor and Syria contained large Jewish populations.[45] In addition, it is thought by some that the east contained about 60% to 65% of the total population of the Roman Empire.[46] Thus, even if the proportion of Jews in the population was roughly the

---

43. Hopkins, "Christian Number and Its Implications," 213.

44. See the information in M. Stern, "The Jewish Diaspora," in *The Jewish People in the First Century*, ed. S. Safrai and M. Stern (Assen/Maastricht: Van Gorcum/Philadelphia: Fortress, 1987), I.117–122.

45. The evidence mainly comes from Josephus and Philo for Alexandria and from Josephus alone for Antioch (Philo, *Flaccus* 43, 55; Josephus, *J.W.* 2.488; Josephus, *Ag. Ap.* 2.4. See Diana Delia, "The Population of Roman Alexandria," *TAPA* 118 (1988): 175–292; Glanville Downey, "The Population of Antioch," *TAPA* 89 (1958): 84–91.

46. The matter is debated. Baron, *A Social and Religious History of the Jews*, I:170.

same in the western and the eastern sections of the empire (which no one claims), more Jews would have been in the east simply by reason of the fact that this was where the majority of the population of the empire resided.[47]

The ancient literature also points in that direction. Numerous comments locate Jews in particular towns or provinces, and generally such locations are eastern. Although Jews could be found in all areas of the Roman Empire, ancient evidence suggests that writers informed about the situation located Jews primarily in the eastern empire, even when they were trying to make a case that Jews lived throughout the vast reaches of the Roman Empire. The author of Acts presents a list of areas from which Jews of "every nation under heaven" were gathered in Jerusalem on the Feast of Pentecost. Of the fifteen specific areas listed, only Rome is west of the eastern shore of the Aegean Sea. Even the areas of Greece (the Roman provinces of Achaia and Macedonia) are omitted, although, oddly, the author knows that Jews live there.[48] In the second relevant text, a letter from King Agrippa I (preserved in Philo's *Embassy to Gaius*) records the presence of Jews throughout the eastern Mediterranean and Mesopotamia, but when Philo wanted to make the case that Jews were spread throughout Europe (the west) as well, basically he adds only the areas of Greece.[49] The story is much the same when we appeal to Josephus on these matters.[50] In some ways, the statement that most of the Jews of the diaspora lived in the eastern half of the empire is so obviously correct that a defense of the position need not be offered, and we might accept with some confidence Baron's conclusion that the "overwhelming

---

47. Hopkins, "Christian Number and Its Implications," 195, n20.

48. Acts 2:1, 5–11. Later in his work, the author of Acts speaks of various cities on the western coast of the Aegean Sea and in areas of Greece, though nothing from Greece makes his list here. This apparent discrepancy between the list of all nations under heaven from which Jews had come and the omission of areas from the list where the author knows Jews lived has puzzled scholars. Some think that the author was simply appropriating similar lists found in some ancient works on history or geography [Gary Gilbert, "The List of Nations in Acts 2: Roman Propaganda and the Lukan Response," *JBL* 121 (2002): 497–529].

49. Philo, *Embassy* 36.281–284. Of the twenty areas Philo listed, nine of them are clustered in a small area roughly covering modern Greece. Everything else is east. Thus, though the list appears much longer than that of the author of Acts, it really covers basically the same territory—the eastern Mediterranean, and more vaguely, areas of Mesopotamia. Acts covers areas beyond the Roman Empire (Parthia, Media, Elam, Mesopotamia, and Arabia). Philo is more interested in the Roman world.

50. Josephus, *Ant.* 1.6.1–4.

majority" of Jews were in the eastern part of the empire.[51] We might somewhat cautiously reckon that three-quarters of diaspora Jews were eastern,[52] since the eastern empire was both more populous and the more likely habitat of diaspora Jews, whose homeland and pre-Roman diasporas were largely eastern. Even though that number involves a measure of guessing, the number is somewhat more defensible than assertions that posit one in five people in the Mediterranean as Jewish, as is sometimes done.[53] But whether one kind of number is all that better than another is the question, for as Hans Conzelmann cautioned, speculations about the eastern diaspora are "absolutely guesswork."[54]

The Urban Character of Diaspora Judaism

Now to the question of the urban character of diaspora Jews. As we have seen, almost hand in hand with the assumption of the urban character of early Christianity is an even more questionable assumption of the urban character of diaspora Judaism.[55] Most scholars who argue for a largely urban Christianity argue, as well, for a largely urban Jewish diaspora, if they address the matter at all.[56] Some scholars, such as Colin Hemer, take the urban character of diaspora Jews a step further. Hemer contends that not only were Jews usually found in cities, but that they normally resided

---

51. Baron, *A Social and Religious History of the Jews*, I:170.

52. That would give us between 2.4 and 2.9 million Jews in the eastern part of the empire if we wanted to put some number to it. The number is based on a Jewish diaspora of 3.2–3.8 million, calculated by taking Hopkins' number of Jews in the empire ("Christian Number and Its Implications," 213), and subtracting 1 million for Jews who live in Palestine, (which is probably high), and then taking 75% of that for Jews in the eastern part of the empire.

53. Jack N. Lightstone, "Urbanization in the Roman East and the Inter-Religious Struggle for Success," in *Religious Rivalries and the Struggle for Success in Sardis and Smyrna*, ed. Richard S. Ascough (Waterloo, ON: Wilfrid Laurier University Press, 2005), 237.

54. Hans Conzelmann, *Gentiles, Jews, Christians: Polemics and Apologetics in the Greco-Roman Era* (Minneapolis: Fortress, 1992), 16.

55. The nature of diaspora Judaism has some importance to what we can say about the character of early Christianity, which is the key matter of interest in this book. My discussion of diaspora Judaism here is a peripheral discussion, largely addressed to illustrate the difficulty of maintaining the widely accepted urban description of early Christianity.

56. W. H. C. Frend, *The Rise of Christianity* (Philadelphia: Fortress, 1984), 30–43. Wayne A. Meeks, *The First Urban Christians: The Social World of the Apostle Paul* (New Haven: Yale University Press, 1983), 34; Wayne A. Meeks and Robert L. Wilken, *Jews and Christians in Antioch in the First Four Centuries of the Common Era* (Missoula, MT: Scholars Press, 1978),

in cities that were economically strong.[57] Baron's view is similar. He comments: "Jewry's numerical weight was accentuated by its preponderantly urban character. Although thousands were swept by the storms of national or individual life into the remotest hamlets and villages, the large majority doubtless inhabited the big commercial and cultural centers."[58] Uriah Engelman, in his influential but controversial work, asserted that the Jewish population of the Roman Empire was "an urban one consisting mainly of artisans."[59] Jack Lightstone puts numbers to this: when Rome conquered Palestine, Jews would have made up 10% of the population of the empire. Further, Lightstone asserts, since Jews were mainly eastern, Jews made up 20% of the eastern part of the empire. Adding the urban locale of diaspora Judaism, Lightstone contends that Jews made up "a significant proportion of the population of cities and towns."[60]

Such a reconstruction of the Jewish situation in the empire is suspect at a number of levels. For one thing, as noted above, the most recent trend in scholarship is to lower the count of Jews in the empire. Further, a supposedly prosperous Jewish population overlooks the mass of Jews who existed on the same level as most of the population of the empire, close to poverty. E. Mary Smallwood put the matter bluntly: "The prosperous Jew, envied for his wealth, was a figure of the mediaeval world, not of the Roman."[61] Claudia Setzer describes the Jews of North Africa as "a few of

---

1; Rodney Stark, *The Rise of Christianity* (Princeton: Princeton University Press, 1996), 57; Thomas Sowell, *Migrations and Cultures: A World View* (New York: Basic Books, 1996), 236; A. H. M. Jones, *The Later Roman Empire, 284–602: A Social Economic and Administrative Survey*, vol. 2 (Oxford: Basil Blackwell, 1964), 941.

57. Colin J. Hemer, *The Letters to the Seven Churches of Asia in Their Local Setting*, JSNTS 11 (Sheffield: JSNT Press, 1986), 160. Jeffers, *The Greco-Roman World of the New Testament Era*, 213, comments that "most Jews in the dispersion lived in cities, where they could pursue a variety of trades."

58. Baron, *A Social and Religious History of the Jews*, I:170.

59. Uriah Zevi Engelman, *The Rise of the Jew in the Western World: A Social and Economic History of the Jewish People of Europe* (New York: Behrman's Jewish Book House, 1944), 16.

60. Lightstone, "Urbanization in the Roman East and the Inter-Religious Struggle for Success," 237.

61. E. Mary Smallwood, "The Diaspora in the Roman Period before CE 70," in *The Cambridge History of Judaism*, vol. 3., ed. William Horbury, W. D. Davies, and John Sturdy (Cambridge: Cambridge University Press, 1999), 173. She also pointed to the law in Rome that if the corn-doles fell on the Sabbath, Jews could collect their portion on the next day, using that concession as indication of the poverty of a segment of Jewish society (171) and commenting that "the average social and economic level of Roman Jews seems to have remained consistently low" (173).

prominence, a majority of needy."[62] Nothing suggests a different story for Jews in other areas of the diaspora.

But even were we to dismiss these points, there remains a profound problem in the numbers routinely offered. If Jews made up 20% of the east and if they were largely urban, Jews would have made up almost the entire population of all eastern cities and towns, since the urban population of the eastern empire generally is estimated at 15% to 20%. But, as we have already seen, based on the urban thesis and the common numbers asserted for the Christian movement, Christians would have populated all that urban space. There would have been no room for an equally numerous urban Jewish population.

In the examination following, I attempt to show how difficult it is to work with even the most restrained numbers that have been offered. Take, for example, Hopkins' numbers of about 5.25 million residents of urban areas of the eastern part of the empire, excluding Palestine.[63] If we have 2.4–2.9 million Jews in the eastern part of the empire, between 41% and 50% of the inhabitants of cities and towns in the eastern Mediterranean would have been Jewish, if, as it often is assumed, diaspora Jews were largely urban, and if the urban population is at 15% of the total.[64] This is, quite simply, an impossible reconstruction, even for Alexandria, the city that is thought to have had the largest Jewish population of any city in the empire. Suppose we increase the urban population of the east to 20%, the numbers we confront are still impossible, for we would have between 31% and 37% of all urban areas Jewish. This is in addition to crowds of Christians that must have inhabited these cities too, if Christianity was, as Judaism supposedly was, itself largely urban and eastern. If we were to take the numbers of Baron, an even more inconceivable scenario would arise. Baron, who holds that Jews were largely urban, states that "every fifth 'Hellenistic' inhabitant of the eastern Mediterranean world was a Jew."[65] Using Baron's numbers, if diaspora Jews were mainly urban, *every resident of eastern cities must have been Jewish*, assuming the eastern empire

---

62. Claudia Setzer, "The Jews in Carthage and Western North Africa, 66–235 CE," in *The Cambridge History of Judaism*, vol. 4, *The Late Roman-Rabbinic Period*, ed. Steven T. Katz (Cambridge: Cambridge University Press, 2006), 71.

63. Hopkins, "Christian Number and Its Implications," 195, n20.

64. Table 4.2.

65. Baron, *A Social and Religious History of the Jews*, I:171.

to be about 20% urban. Such numbers cannot work. No one would assert that eastern cities were so predominately Jewish, yet many scholars work with numbers that demand that.

Consider Wayne Meeks' influential approach. Meeks spends several pages early in *The First Urban Christians* dealing with the Jewish population of cities, and he concludes that "there was a substantial Jewish population in virtually every town of any size in the lands bordering the Mediterranean." He uses a number of 10% to 15% for the total Jewish population of cities, and he contends that it was perhaps even higher for Alexandria.[66] But Meeks paints himself into a corner with such numbers. If cities in the empire contain a Jewish population of 10% to 15%, then urban Jews would have numbered only between 600,000 and 900,000, if, as is commonly thought, the total urban population of the empire was around 6 million.[67] Yet Meeks thinks there were 5 to 6 million Jews in the diaspora, and he seems to think that Jews in the Roman Empire were generally urban, even contrasting the rural Jews of Galilee and Mesopotamia to the urban diaspora in Roman provincial cities.[68] But taking Meeks' numbers, a considerable majority of diaspora Jews must have been rural.[69] Yet in neither of Meeks' main books is this significant population of rural Jews in the Roman Empire recognized. Meeks simply treats diaspora Jews as largely urban, missing entirely the impossibility of the numbers making any sense in a largely urban context.[70] Rodney Stark has a similar problem but with even more impossible numbers.[71]

---

66. Meeks, *The First Urban Christians*, 34.

67. Or between 900,000 and 1,350,000 Jews if the urban population is 9 million.

68. Meeks, *The First Urban Christians*, 34. In another work, Meeks points again to the rural and small-town context of Palestinian Judaism ["Breaking Away: Three New Testament Pictures of Christianity's Separation from the Jewish Communities," in *"To See Ourselves as Others See Us": Christians, Jews, "Others" in Late Antiquity*, ed. Jacob Neusner and Ernest S. Frerichs (Chico, CA: Scholars Press, 1985), 115]. Most scholars would grant that Jews in Palestine were more rural, and often a contrast is made between Jews in Palestine and Jews in the diaspora [Joshua J. Schwartz, "The Material Realities of Jewish Life in the Land of Israel, 235-638," in *The Cambridge History of Judaism*, vol. 4, *The Late Roman-Rabbinic Period*, ed. Steven T. Katz (Cambridge: Cambridge University Press, 2006), 433–434].

69. Counting diaspora Jews at 5 to 6 million and urban diaspora Jews at 600,000 to 1,350,000, 75% to 90% of diaspora Jews must have been rural.

70. Meeks, *The First Urban Christians*, 34; *The Origins of Christian Morality*, 43–45.

71. See Appendix B.

Given the significant rural Jewish population required (but not admitted) in Meeks' reconstruction, much more attention needs to be given to the phenomenon of rural diaspora Judaism, a study that likely would have implications for a discussion of the rural environment in which Christianity could have taken root. Meeks leaves a number of tantalizing questions unaddressed. What kind of Judaism was practiced in the cities if rabbinic Judaism was largely small town or rural in its early centuries, as Meeks claims? What kind of engagement did rural Jews have with their rural pagan neighbors and with their urban kinsmen? And what of Meeks' assertion that "the massive confrontation between 'apostolic Christianity' and 'normative Judaism' which even now haunts the imagination of students of Christian origins, never happened"?[72] These are all largely unexplored areas, yet they are some of the most crucial and tantalizing issues for the debate regarding Jewish-Christian relations and identity, and these kinds of issues are probably more substantial and revolutionary than the more famous claim Meeks made about the urban character of early Christianity.

A Rural Jewish Diaspora?

As the following tables show, under almost any scenario, the number of rural Jews in the empire must have been greater (and probably considerably greater) than the number of urban Jews. Even under the unlikely scenario where Jews constitute 15% of the urban population and 7% and 8% of the total population of the empire (Tables 4.1 and 4.2), rural Jews would still have constituted a clear majority of the Jewish population. Such a clear rural majority is widely accepted for the situation of Jews in Palestine,[73] yet when that question is framed for the diaspora, a starkly

---

72. Meeks, "Breaking Away: Three New Testament Pictures of Christianity's Separation from the Jewish Communities," 115.

73. Jacob Neusner, "The Experience of the City in Late Antique Judaism," in *Approaches to Ancient Judaism*, vol. 5, ed. William Scott Green (Atlanta: Scholars Press, 1985), 37–52, contends that rabbinic literature rose in the town and village, not the city, and Jews were largely rural in Palestine and Mesopotamia, at least. Neusner does not comment on how much this rural setting holds for Jews in the Roman diaspora as well. He dismisses the city/country dialectic as not of much significance (44, 46). What the role and reach of the rabbinic movement were in either Palestine or the diaspora are matters of considerable debate, with the period of initial influence being moved later and later, and with the rural/urban issue mixed into the discussion. About the same time as Neusner's writing, Shaye J. D. Cohen concluded that the second-century rabbis were "prosperous, rural and landowning—not poor, urban or

Table 4.1 Jewish population of Roman Empire (excluding Palestine) (based on 60 million population in empire and a Jewish population of 7% (rows 1–3) and at 8% (rows 4–6))

1	2	3	4	5	6
% Urban in Empire	Total Urban Population (millions)	Total Jewish Population (millions)	Jewish % of Urban Areas	Jewish Rural Population (millions)	% Rural Jews
10	6	3.2	53	2.3	72
15	9	3.2	36	1.9	59
20	12	3.2	27	1.4	44
10	6	3.8	63	2.9	76
15	9	3.8	42	2.5	66
20	12	3.8	32	2.0	53

Column 3: excluding 1 million for Palestine.
Column 4: if Jewish population largely urban.
Columns 5 and 6: rural numbers if Jews constitute 15% of urban population.

Table 4.2 Jewish Population of Eastern Roman Empire (excluding Palestine) (based on 39 million population in eastern empire and a Jewish population of 7% (rows 1–3) and at 8% (rows 4–6))

1	2	3	4	5	6
% Urban in Empire	Total Urban Population (millions)	Total Jewish Population (millions)	Jewish % of Population	Jewish Rural Population (millions)	% Rural Jews
10	3.9	2.4	25	1.8	75
15	5.8	2.4	36	1.5	64
20	7.8	2.4	49	1.2	51
10	3.9	2.9	20	2.3	80
15	5.8	2.9	30	2.0	70
20	7.8	2.9	40	1.7	60

Column 3: excluding 1 million for Palestine.
Column 4: if Jewish population largely urban.
Columns 5 and 6: rural numbers if Jews constitute 15% of urban population.

opposite reconstruction is routinely proposed: diaspora Jews were supposedly urban dwellers.

But a number of scholars have acknowledged—cautiously in some cases—
the likelihood of a rural dimension of diaspora Judaism. Frend admits that
"there may have been something that could be termed a rural Dispersion."[74]
E. Mary Smallwood comments that most of the Jews of Palestine were agricultural rather than commercial in the first century, though she does not
carry that observation over to the diaspora.[75] Tessa Rajak recognizes that,
though we "cannot say much about rural settlements," it is clear that there
were rural Jews, though all numbers are "highly speculative."[76]

Martin Hengel is much more specific: in the early Hellenistic period
in Egypt, Jews were "pre-dominantly a peasant people,"[77] and he provides
a brief discussion of the character of diaspora Judaism in his chapter titled
"Jews in a Greek-Speaking Environment: Mercenaries, Slaves, Peasants,
Craftsmen and Merchants." His is a far more nuanced and adequate
treatment of the Jewish diaspora than what is reflected in the sweeping statements often confidently made about the urban character of the
Jewish diaspora. Hengel further points to Josephus' comment that Jews
were not merchants but peasants.[78] Similarly, Tcherikover thinks that Jews

---

mercantile" ["The Place of the Rabbi in Jewish Society in the Second Century," in *The Galilee
in Late Antiquity*, ed. Lee Levine (Cambridge, MA: Harvard University Press, 1989), 157–173].
In later works, Cohen admits that he may have "overdrawn the rural-urban contrast" ["The
Rabbi in Second-Century Jewish Society," in *The Cambridge History of Judaism*, vol 3, ed.
W. D. Davies, Louis Finkelstein, William Horbury, and John Sturdy (Cambridge: Cambridge
University Press, 1999), 1201]. Hayim Lapin, *Rabbis as Romans: The Rabbinic Movement in
Palestine, 100–400 C.E.* (Oxford: Oxford University Press, 2012), 6, argues for a more urban-
centered rabbinic movement. John Robert Mandsger, "To Stake a Claim: The Making of
Rabbinic Agricultural Spaces in the Roman Countryside," Ph.D. diss., Stanford University,
2014, examines the rural dimension. For a summary of the debate, see Schwartz, *The Ancient
Jews from Alexander to Muhammad*, 98–123. Whatever the solution to these questions, it does
not remove the problem of numbers that I have identified confronting the thesis of a largely
urban Jewish diaspora.

74. Frend, "Town and Countryside in Early Christianity," 35.

75. E. Mary Smallwood, *The Jews under Roman Rule: From Pompey to Diocletian* (Leiden: Brill,
1976), 122.

76. Tessa Rajak, "The Jewish Community and Its Boundaries," in *The Jews among
Pagans and Christians in the Roman Empire*, ed. Judith Lieu, John North, and Tessa Rajak
(London: Routledge, 1992), 10.

77. Martin Hengel, *Jews, Greeks and Barbarians: Aspects of the Hellenization of Judaism in the
Pre-Christian Period*, John Bowden, trans. (Philadelphia: Fortress, 1980), 87.

78. Hengel, *Jews, Greeks and Barbarians*, 91, referring to Josephus, *Ag. Ap.* I.60.

were spread throughout Egypt and offers evidence for Jews in villages there.[79] Wasserstein speaks of an early rural Jewish presence in Ptolemaic Egypt (or even earlier, in the Persian period).[80] Applebaum thinks that for Pamphylia the evidence suggests "a considerable part of the Jewish population of the region was rural, and unattached to city communities."[81] For almost every other area of the empire, Applebaum's conclusion is the same: diaspora Jews had a considerable rural contingent.[82] More recently, Stephen Mitchell, in his detailed study of Anatolia, questions the supposed urban character of diaspora Judaism. He comments: "The conventional picture of diaspora Jews as a distinct urban minority group, which earned a living from crafts and trade, has never carried much conviction."[83] He reminds us that the Jewish settlers under Antiochus III were "first and foremost farmers," and offers a range of evidence for rural Jewish presence in Asia Minor.[84]

The Jewish population of the diaspora, then, was not strictly urban; indeed, it may have been substantially rural. We might reach that conclusion even without the supporting evidence from specific areas simply by looking at the population of Palestine itself. A largely rural population of a million or less at home is unlikely to have produced a non-agricultural thriving urban population of several million for the diaspora. Indeed, how a small, largely rural Jewish population in Palestine could have produced a Jewish diaspora population into the many millions—urban or rural—is baffling.[85] With the revolts of the late first and early second centuries, the lot

---

79. Tcherikover, *Hellenistic Civilization and the Jews*, 285–286.

80. Wasserstein, "The Number and Provenance of Jews in Graeco-Roman Antiquity," 314–315.

81. S. Applebaum, "The Organization of the Jewish Communities in the Diaspora," in *The Jewish People in the First Century*, ed. S. Safrai and M. Stern (Assen/Maastricht: Van Gorcum/ Philadelphia: Fortress, 1987), 701–727.

82. Applebaum, "The Social and Economic Status of Jews in the Diaspora," 486.

83. Stephen Mitchell, *Anatolia: Land, Men, and Gods in Asia Minor* (Oxford: Clarendon Press: 1993), II.35.

84. Mitchell, *Anatolia: Land, Men, and Gods in Asia Minor*, 35–37.

85. A heated debate has arisen regarding whether a large Jewish diaspora population requires a considerably successful proselyting mission. For the classic positions of this matter, see Louis H. Feldman, *Jew and Gentile in the Ancient World: Attitudes and Interactions from Alexander to Justinian* (Princeton: Princeton University Press, 1993), and Martin Goodman, *Mission and Conversion: Proselytizing in the Religious History of the Roman Empire* (Oxford: Clarendon Press, 1995).

of many of these Palestinian Jewish farmers was to be forcefully deported
to other lands in the empire.[86] In such cases, the transplanted Jewish population would most likely have been settled as farmers since that was the
skill most of them had, and that is what most people in the empire worked
at. Such deportees would not have had the skills or resources to succeed in
the cities, and if transported there would have become merely part of the
mass of the urban poor. Further, the number of prosperous urban Jews in
Palestine would never have been large, and certainly not large enough to
fill the urban areas of the empire with many millions of Jewish artisans
and merchants, even if every Jewish resident of Palestine—rich or poor,
urban or rural—left their homeland for the diaspora.

A Proposed Solution

It is much easier to get a sense of the size and strength of the Jewish
population of the Roman Empire than the strength of the Christian
population—and, as we have seen, it is none too easy to get anything but
a most vague sense of the Jewish presence in the empire. Whatever Jews
and Christians may have claimed about the size of their respective communities, Jews, at least, had some evidence much more concrete in their
favor. The various revolts that Jews raised against the Romans and the size
of the Roman army necessary to suppress the revolts reveal a somewhat
substantial Jewish presence in at least some areas of the empire—at least
in certain periods.

But, as we have seen, if Jews were numerous, then they cannot have
been largely urban, for under such a scenario they would have saturated all
the urban areas of the empire. Herein may lie a clue to one of the elements
in early Christian growth in the Roman countryside. Once we grant a rural
Jewish diaspora, whatever its size, we have potential Christian links to the
countryside, which is our concern in this work. At least, the countryside
would no longer necessarily present itself as a completely alien world in
which Christianity could offer nothing intelligible and with whom there
would have been no shared sensibilities. Stark, who spends much of his
time arguing for the importance of Jewish networks in explaining the
growth of urban Christianity, fails to address how such networks might

---

86. Kerkeslager, "The Diaspora from 66 to c. 235 CE," speaks of the Jewish farmers in
Cyrenaica (57).

have worked in rural areas. That is because he adopted wholesale the urban thesis of diaspora Judaism.

That is not to say that Christians were able to exploit these kinds of contacts with rural Jewish communities. The matter of Jewish/Christian relations in the first three centuries is one of the most disputed issues in scholarship on early Christianity. All I am saying here is that a rural Jewish presence does present the possibility of an early Christian presence in the countryside. I will not press that point, because it seems to me that the evidence points away from a Jewish audience to a pagan one for the success of Christianity. The question of Christian engagement with paganism, both rural and urban, has been sometimes shortchanged, particularly as theories of the massive Jewish component in early Christian membership have been advanced. Such theories may well need to be challenged. Christianity in the first three centuries may have grown not by winning Jews but by winning pagans—even pagans in the countryside.[87] Yet for those who argue, as Stark does, for substantial Christian success among the Jewish population, a rural dimension must be brought into play.

The following assumptions underlie the current discussion of the Christian and the Jewish population of the Roman Empire in the first three centuries of the Common Era. (1) Jews and Christians in the empire were largely urban. (2) Christians made up about 10% of the empire around 300 c.e. (3) Jews made up slightly under 10%. (4) The urban population of the empire was roughly 10% to 20%. These numbers are the most frequently

---

87. The question of Jewish conversion to Christianity and the Jewish complexion of the Christian church in the first few centuries is part of the debate often labeled "The Parting of the Ways." Unlike Stark and many others, I consider the Christian movement to have become rapidly and widely a Gentile movement, as I have argued in *Ignatius of Antioch and the Parting of the Ways: Early Jewish-Christian Relations* (Grand Rapids, MI: Baker Academic, 2009). One point that is often not given its due in the discussion is the perception of the civil authorities and informed critics of Christianity on the matter. The Christian movement is treated as something different from Judaism early and routinely in the trial of Christians. Note, too, a curious matter that arises in Origen's response to Celsus. Origen, *Cels.* 2.1, is baffled that Celsus had his Jewish polemicist address Jewish converts to Christianity rather than converts from paganism. If Celsus really had wanted to address the Christian movement, Origen contends, it would have made better sense to have addressed pagan converts, since that was the background of Christian converts. Origen seems to know only the Ebionites who are Jewish converts to Christianity. According to Origen, most Jews had not converted to Christianity (3.1). This became a problem for the Christian attempt to appropriate (or expropriate) Jewish tradition, and Christian apologetic efforts deal regularly with the matter of Jewish unbelief. The apologists tend to handle that problem not by pointing to vast numbers of Jews in the Christian movement but rather to what they contended was a history of Jewish unbelief going back almost to the beginning of Jewish history.

proposed, though there are those who call for higher numbers and those who call for lower numbers. But whether lower or higher, the proposals offered to date are not sufficiently radical or novel enough to resolve the problems confronted when a largely urban identity for Jews and Christians is asserted.

Based on such assumptions, an impossible situation emerges. There simply are too many Jews and Christians filling the urban spaces of the empire for there to be any room left for anyone else. We could increase the urban proportion of the empire to 20% and reduce the Jewish and Christian numbers by half and still have cities half full of Jews and Christians throughout the empire—a situation so bordering on the impossible that few would consciously propose any such reconstruction, and none could adequately defend it.[88] And the situation gets much worse. Since most Jews and Christians are found in the eastern part of the empire in this period, the proportion of Jews and Christians in the cities would squeeze out almost everyone else, even with a 20% urbanization of the area.

Small adjustments to these basic numbers will not solve the problem. For example, making the eastern part of the empire somewhat more urbanized than the western (while sound) will still leave cities largely saturated with Jews and Christians. And more radical proposals, though perhaps alleviating somewhat the problem of numbers, appear no more convincing. For example, we could say that large numbers of Jews became Christians, thus counting such people only once in the calculation of populations. But we would need to have such a massive flood of Jews into Christianity (perhaps nearly 50%) for that proposal to resolve the basic problem of numbers. And if there was such a mass movement, that changes almost everything we know about Jews and Christians in this period, though some will argue toward that end.[89]

Clearly, many of the statements routinely offered about the proportion of Jews in the empire, the size of the Jewish diaspora, and the urban

---

88. Stark's extreme position (5% urbanization in the empire, 9 million Christians when Constantine become emperor, and Christians largely urban) would require not just a saturation of cities with Christians but a *triple* saturation—a scenario that Stark does not seem to realize is demanded by his numbers. Granted, there is no such thing as a triple saturation, but that is my point—the scenario required by the numbers is impossible. See Appendix B for a detailed discussion of Stark's work.

89. Stark proposes a significant contingent of Jews moving into Christianity. For some observations of the problems of Stark's proposal, see Appendix B.

character of diaspora communities need to be reexamined or more cautiously stated. Where our numbers have failed is not clear. Were there
fewer Jews in the empire? Were far more Jews crowded into Palestine
and far fewer in the diaspora? Was the Roman Empire much more highly
urbanized? Were Jews of the diaspora less urbanized?[90] And, of course,
there is always that overarching problem of specifying what exactly defines
"urban" in antiquity?

We probably need to admit the possibility, if not likelihood, that a far
greater proportion of Jews in the Roman Empire was rural. As well, we
may also need to posit a lower number for the total Jewish population
in the empire than has been commonly accepted, which many scholars
believe to be inflated. And we probably need to recognize that almost all
of the numbers proposed are arbitrary (and, in most cases, useless, and
even misleading). Perhaps the best position to take regarding the matter
of Jewish population in the ancient world is that of Stern. He admits that
we cannot determine any figures about the Jewish population in Palestine
or the Diaspora,[91] though we can say "the total Jewish population of the
Roman Empire outside Palestine, and of the Parthian Empire, including the huge Jewish community of Babylonia, considerably exceeded the
number of Jews living in their homeland."[92] We have no reliable numbers
for the Jewish population in Palestine or the diaspora that would allow us
to say anything more specific, and certainly nothing that would require a
largely urban diaspora.[93]

---

90. Hopkins treats the Jewish diaspora as largely Roman ("Christian Number and Its
Implications," 213). Many who have examined the Jewish diaspora have not specified clearly
whether their numbers are for the Roman Empire only or for all Jews outside Palestine,
including those in Mesopotamia. Emperor Trajan invaded Mesopotamia in 114, and Rome
experienced various losses and gains in this troubled territory over the next few hundred
years. M. Stern, "The Jewish Diaspora," II:117, thinks that most diaspora Jews were under
Roman influence from the time of Augustus. Even were we to reduce the number of Jews
in the Roman diaspora by guessing that 20% of the diaspora may have lived outside the
Roman Empire, there would still be 2.4 to 2.9 million Jews in the eastern Empire (excluding
1 million in Palestine), and, if diaspora Jews are mainly urban, these Jews would constitute
about a third of the population of cities, numbers significantly high to suggest an error
somewhere.

91. Stern, "The Jewish Diaspora," 119.

92. Stern, "The Jewish Diaspora," 122.

93. Tcherikover, *Hellenistic Civilization and the Jews*, 286–295, dismisses the number of
1 million that Philo offered for the Jewish population of Egypt (*Flaccus* 43), and he offers
various grounds for suspicion in regard to ancient numbers.

Indeed, we must consider a rural element of the diaspora, first of all by being more careful about the divide we make between the urban and the rural. The kind of divide often proposed by those who argue for the urban thesis simply fails to reflect the realities of life as lived in the ancient world, as we will see in the next chapter. If our new reconstruction places Christians and Jews in the countryside as well as in urban areas, the pressures the urban thesis has put on the population of cities, saturating the cities of the empire with Jews and Christians, is largely addressed.

For the remainder of this book, I attempt to show that the hypothesis of a pre-Constantinian rural Christianity deserves consideration. If I fail at that, I will be satisfied to have shown how the common numbers routinely offered regarding Jews and Christians in the Roman Empire and the urban complexion of both groups fail—and fail badly.

5

Urban and Rural Relationships

General Views

The oft-repeated notion of a stark dichotomy in the Greco-Roman world between rural and urban areas—whether cultural, religious, or linguistic—may be misleading. The line between rural and urban was ambiguous at best. City and country were interwoven in ways that prevent neat definition, and the urban and rural worlds were never mutually isolated enclaves where members of one rarely entered the other. Modern portraits of the divide between city and countryside that Christians supposedly faced when they attempted to take their message to rural areas are overblown. The interchange between city and countryside was frequent and matter-of-course.[1]

Over the past twenty years, numerous historians with considerable credentials have challenged the view of a sharp divide between the urban and rural worlds of the ancient Mediterranean. In spite of that, stark boundaries between city and countryside are still routinely assumed in reconstructions of the early church. I quote here a number of recent scholars on the subject to demonstrate just how explicit scholars have been about the inadequacy of the traditional view of a rural/urban dichotomy.

---

1. For a still useful survey of the overly ambitious efforts of sociologists to draw a sharp line between the urban and the rural, see the 1963 article by Francisco Benet, "Sociology Uncertain: The Ideology of the Rural-Urban Continuum," *Comparative Studies in Society and History* 6 (1963), 1–23. Benet offers a number of useful illustrations from both modern and ancient societies. For an influential work emphasizing the divide, see the last three chapters of A. H. M. Jones, *The Greek City from Alexander to Justinian* (Oxford: Clarendon Press, 1940), 259–304. For an analysis of Jones' work on the city, see Luke Lavan, "A.H.M. Jones and 'The Cities' 1964–2004," in *A.H.M. Jones and the Later Roman Empire*, ed. David M. Gwynn (Leiden: Brill, 2008), 167–192.

Andrew Wallace-Hadrill noted over twenty-five years ago that scholarship now tended to be more skeptical about portraits of sharp divisions between town and country.[2] He noted that the new tendency in scholarship was "to undo the separation of town and country and reunite the town with its non-urban environment."[3] In 1996, shortly after Wallace-Hadrill's comment, Richard Rohrbaugh reviewed the recent social-science literature on the relation between the rural and the urban, noting that the general conclusion was that "in both modern and ancient worlds the city [had] never been an isolated construct."[4] Peter Garnsey cautioned against drawing the lines too sharply between city and country,[5] and Robert Markus expressed similar reservations.[6] Stephen Mitchell described the city as "symbiotically inseparable from the rural territories."[7] Walter Scheidel described the urban/rural divide of the Greek *poleis* of the eastern Mediterranean as "exceedingly permeable."[8] Robin Lane Fox detailed the substantial links between city and the countryside.[9] John North had strong words for many of the claims of a sharp divide between the urban and rural worlds, dismissing such conclusions as being founded on a "bogus set of assumptions."[10] North argued that many rural residents moved to cities and many farm

2. John Rich and Andrew Wallace-Hadrill, eds., *City and Country in the Ancient World*, Leicester-Nottingham Studies in Ancient Society 2 (London: Routledge, 1991), ix.

3. Andrew Wallace-Hadrill, "Introduction," in *City and Country in the Ancient World*, ed. John Rich and Andrew Wallace-Hadrill (London: Routledge, 1991), 1. He notes, too, the particular difficulty for the ancient historian caused by what the word πόλις could mean.

4. Richard L. Rohrbaugh, "The Preindustrial City," in *The Social Sciences and New Testament Interpretation*, ed. Richard L. Rohrbaugh (Peabody, MA: Hendrickson, 1996), 115–119.

5. Peter Garnsey, *Famine and Food Supply in the Graeco-Roman World* (Cambridge: Cambridge University Press, 1988), 62.

6. Robert Markus, "Country Bishops in Byzantine Africa," in *The Church in Town and Countryside*, Studies in Church History XVI, ed. Derek Baker (Oxford: Basil Blackwell, 1979), 1–2.

7. Stephen Mitchell, *A History of the Later Roman Empire A.D. 284–641* (Oxford: Blackwell, 2007), 302.

8. Walter Scheidel, "Demography," in *The Cambridge Economic History of the Greco-Roman World*, ed. Walter Scheidel, Ian Morris, and Richard P. Saller (Cambridge: Cambridge University Press, 2007), 77.

9. Robin Lane Fox, *Pagans and Christians* (New York: Alfred A. Knopf, 1987), 40–46.

10. John A. North, "Religion and Rusticity," in *Urban Society in Roman Italy*, ed. T. J. Cornell and Kathryn Lomas (London: UCL Press, 1995), 144.

workers lived in cities, and some even tilled plots of land within the city or in the suburbs—all of which weakens the stark urban/rural dialectic often assumed.[11] Donald Engels challenged the gulf between the urban and the rural and argued that the city attracted and served the rural population as much as the rural population served the city, providing not just manufactured goods but religion as well.[12] Roger Bagnall, when discussing rural Egypt, stated: "above all the village was not a closed community . . . . The villages were inextricably tied to the metropolitan economy and population. The view of the village in isolation, then, is only a partial one, which must be completed by its external relationships."[13] Francisco Benet states simply: "The isolation of rural communities is of course a myth."[14] Kenneth Harl, speaking more generally of the situation, stated: "The image of the ancient city as a parasite on the countryside, ultimately a Marxist construct, is not very illuminating," noting that shrines, public buildings, markets, and games "wove residents of cities, villages, and rural demes or townships into a community."[15] Even a leading historian such as Liebeschuetz, who argued for a sharp divide between city and country dwellers in the area around Antioch, admitted that there were perhaps other ways of reading the evidence.[16] And Wayne Meeks, though speaking of the traditionalism of the countryside, recognized that "there was a steady seepage of values from polis to village," on the one hand and, on the other, "some flow of values in the opposite direction," though he did not consider what this might mean to the development of a rural Christian presence.[17] And in terms of Christianity, Richard Fletcher spoke of the urban thesis as a

---

11. North, "Religion and Rusticity," 144–145.

12. Donald Engels, *Roman Corinth: An Alternative Model for the Classical City* (Chicago: University of Chicago Press, 1990),

13. Roger S. Bagnall, *Egypt in Late Antiquity* (Princeton: Princeton University Press, 1993), 121.

14. Benet, "Sociology Uncertain: The Ideology of the Rural-Urban Continuum," 10.

15. Kenneth W. Harl, "From Pagan to Christian in Cities of Roman Anatolia during the Fourth and Fifth Centuries," in *Urban Centers and Rural Contexts in Late Antiquity*, ed. Thomas S. Burns and John W. Eadie (East Lansing: Michigan State University Press, 2001), 307.

16. J. H. W. G. Liebeschuetz, *Antioch: City and Imperial Administration in the Later Roman Empire* (Oxford: Clarendon Press, 1972), 61–62.

17. Wayne A. Meeks, *The Moral World of the First Christians: The Social World of the Apostle Paul* (Philadelphia: Westminster Press, 1986), 39.

"truism" that needs qualification, particularly for the eastern empire, where there were signs of some early rural penetration by Christianity.[18]

Yet in spite of such warnings, the great gulf between city and countryside is routinely asserted by those who maintain the urban thesis. A much more nuanced view is necessary, one that does not split the Roman world between a vast countryside and densely populated cities, with each clearly distinguishable from the other. Rather, the ancient world is better viewed more as a continuum, running the gamut from a few huge metropolises to a number of smaller cities and towns of considerably varied sizes, to villages and settlements, some perhaps no more than a few hovels—all of them accommodating to some degree rural residents, who worked the fields beyond during the day but made their homes at night in an assortment of settlements, from bustling cities to small villages.[19] And even that kind of general description may need to be substantially qualified. Scheidel contends that cities were either very large or quite small; few cities of intermediate size existed.[20] The editors of *Urban Centers and Rural Contexts in Late Antiquity* lament the wide use of the term "city," suggesting that only a few centers deserved that term in the Roman Empire. They list only eight that should qualify; all others would be counted simply as "towns," or for the smaller still, simply as villas, villages, and hamlets.[21]

In some cases, it is possible that the urban/rural ratio *within* cities was 1:1 or even 1:2, where large numbers of the farmers lived within the city and walked to their plots each morning. Mogens Hansen calculates that one-half to two-thirds of the population of most areas would have lived within the walls of the towns and cities, challenging the older views of Moses Finley and his followers regarding the "consumer city."[22] Even

---

18. Richard Fletcher, *The Barbarian Conversion: From Paganism to Christianity* (Berkeley: University of California Press, 1997), 15.

19. See S. W. Baron, *A Social and Religious History of the Jews*, 2nd ed. (New York: Columbia University Press, 1952), I:71–72.

20. Walter Scheidel, "Demography," in *The Cambridge Economic History of the Greco-Roman World*, ed. Walter Scheidel, Ian Morris, and Richard P. Saller (Cambridge: Cambridge University Press, 2007), 79.

21. Thomas S. Burns and John W. Eadie, eds., *Urban Centers and Rural Contexts in Late Antiquity* (East Lansing: Michigan State University Press, 2001), xii, list Rome, Carthage, Trier, Constantinople, Alexandria, Antioch, Serdica (Sofia), and Thessalonica.

22. Mogens Herman Hansen, *The Shotgun Method: The Demography of the Ancient Greek City-State Culture* (Columbia: University of Missouri Press, 2006), 64–76, examines Greece and Greek colonies. Although we cannot simply assume a similar distribution in the Roman

where some provincial towns did not accommodate farmers as residents within their walls—as Duncan-Jones concludes from the significant proportion of urban space given over to public buildings, leaving little room for residential space—he sees this as proof that urban space was intended for a population much larger than what might fit within the city walls. He states: "when we speak of city population in the sense true in our period, it is unhistorical to exclude the citizens who lived on the soil, and to count only those who lived *intra muros*."[23] In either of these scenarios—farmers living within city walls or beyond them—the dividing line between city and countryside becomes at least blurred, if not nonsensical and unworkable. And the flipside of farmers residing within cities must be considered too, for urbanites of adequate resources spent much of their time outside the city, in their sometime luxurious and sometimes modest rural estates, blurring further the urban and the rural domains.[24]

If we still felt it necessary to have some kind of urban/rural divide, it might be more insightful to draw a line between remote villages and those villages located closer to towns and cities where exchange with the urban environment would have been commonplace. Villages close to towns and cities—as most villages probably were—were interwoven with at least some of the aspects of urban life. Further, not only were villages often close to more urbanized areas, towns and cities themselves were often very close to each other, and in some areas only a few miles apart.[25] Thus, it may be considerably more helpful to dismiss the dialectic of an urban/rural divide, and replace it with a more graduated scale representing a village's proximity and accessibility to a more urbanized area. We, then,

---

Empire, such a study as Hansen's should caution against assuming the countryside was filled with farmers isolated from and unfamiliar with urban environments.

23. R. P. Duncan-Jones, "City Population in Roman Africa," *JRS* 53 (1963): 86.

24. Paul Erdkamp, "Urbanism," in *The Cambridge Companion to the Roman Economy*, ed. Walter Scheidel (Cambridge: Cambridge University Press, 2012), 241–265; Dennis P. Kehoe, *Law and the Rural Economy in the Roman Empire* (Ann Arbor: University of Michigan Press, 2007).

25. See Norman J. G. Pounds, "The Urbanization of the Classical World," *Annals of the Association of American Geographers* 59 (1969): 135–157; in particular the maps on pp. 136, 155. See also Joseph Bingham, *Origines Ecclesiasticæ: The Antiquities of the Christian Church*, vol. 1 (London: Henry G. Bohn, 1846), 352–389, who provides a detailed list of areas with bishops. Or simply consider Ignatius' letters. Three were written to churches close together: Ephesus, a port; Magnesia, about 12 miles away; and Tralles, about the same distance further along the Meander Valley. All were fairly large centers. Anyone living in the surrounding countryside had relatively easy access to an urban area.

would find that a significant part of the rural landscape was tied closely to towns and cities. In fact, much of the urban and rural life of the empire would have flowed together.

At the same time, not every area was the same, as A. H. M. Jones reminds us. Some areas were considerably more tribal than others, and in some cases, towns, not cities, were the main locales of rural engagement with trade and the marketplace.[26] But on the whole it appears difficult to make an urban/rural divide very meaningful in most areas of the Mediterranean.[27]

The Problem of Definition

When we speak of city, or town, or village, what exactly are we talking about, and how do we distinguish one from the others? The matter is not a simple one, though it might appear that there is no problem at all when we hear scholars speaking of over 500 cities in Spain, 500 in Asia, 500 in Italy, 200 in Africa Proconsularis, and various other determinations.[28] Surely, then, there must be something that marks a settlement as a city, distinguishing it from other settlements that are considered towns or villages. And surely there must be some way to distinguish the urban from the rural so that when we talk about the degree of urbanization in the Roman Empire, it identifies and counts something. But no. The terms "city" and "urban" are tossed around in modern scholarship largely without definition, and the three things that most seem likely to serve as discriminating markers (status, size, and structure) do not help—or at least do not help in ways that are of much use to the questions of urbanization or urban/rural relations. And that is quite apart from the question of whether we should even be trying to find the boundaries of a strict dichotomy between country and city.[29]

---

26. A. H. M. Jones, *Cities of the Eastern Roman Provinces* (Oxford: Clarendon Press, 1937), 295. Jones was speaking about Syria in this context.

27. For a review of the debate about urbanization and some of the difficulties in estimating ancient urbanization, see Scheidel, "Demography," 74–85.

28. Mary T. Boatwright, *Hadrian and the Cities of the Roman Empire* (Princeton: Princeton University Press, 2000), 3n3, lists some of the figures offered, noting that most do not specify the period for which the number is proposed.

29. John Dominic Crossan, *The Birth of Christianity* (New York: HarperCollins, 1998), 215–218, provides a clear and brief summary and critique of some scholarly positions on rural and urban.

Status

In some ways, the distinction between what was a city and what was not is, from one perspective, primarily a legal one of a *granted* status, specifying the city from which the surrounding lands would be organized and taxed.[30] Thus, the status of "city" was not necessarily indicative of size or degree of urbanization.[31] Take, for example, the lands of Pamphylia, Pisidia, and Lycaonia. Jones points out that "some small communities were granted the rank of cities," and that many small cities were "little larger than villages."[32] Speaking of the province of Asia, Jones notes a similar condition, where the government granted city status to villages.[33] And Libanius of Antioch noted that some large villages were as populous as many cities.[34]

Scheidel puts the matter simply: urban status was a legal construct, and some small settlements may have been more urban in name than in nature."[35] Given that labels and realities could be quite different, it is unlikely that a suitable rule can be put in place by which one can determine whether a settlement of a particular size qualified as a village, town, or city, or what settlements should be included in a calculation of the urbanization of the empire.

---

30. The Greek half of the Roman Empire had a considerable web of cities dotting the landscape when Rome took over. The west was less organized or urbanized, which required a more intentional approach to the foundation of cities. See Ray Laurence, Simon Esmonde Cleary, and Gareth Sears, *The City in the Roman West c. 250 BC–c. AD 250* (Cambridge: Cambridge University Press, 2011), and Mireille Corbier, "City, Territory and Taxation," in *City and Country in the Ancient World*, ed. John Rich and Andrew Wallace-Hadrill (London and New York: Routledge, 1991), 211–239.

31. Erdkamp, "Urbanism," 241–265, discusses the problem of definition in terms of economic matters, showing how mixed together the urban and the rural could be. See, too, Kehoe, *Law and the Rural Economy in the Roman Empire*, 165. Kevin Butcher, *Roman Syria and the Near East* (London: The British Museum Press; Los Angeles: Getty Publications, 2003), 135, points out that there was little difference between small cities and the larger villages in economic terms.

32. Jones, *Cities of the Eastern Roman Provinces*, 146.

33. Jones, *Cities of the Eastern Roman Provinces*, 94.

34. Libanius, *Or.* 11.230, cited in Ramsay MacMullen, "Market-Days in the Roman Empire," *Phoenix* 24 (1970): 335.

35. Scheidel, "Demography," 78–79.

Size

Keith Hopkins, in an effort to bring some specification to the debate, calculates the urban population of the empire by including the residents of all towns of two thousand or more people. This allowed him to set the urban population of the empire at 15%, which he adjusts to 20% in the east and 10% in the west.[36] Hopkins recognized that the size of two thousand was arbitrary, but at least one knows what Hopkins is counting. Raymond Goldsmith went even lower than Hopkins, who had already set the bar fairly low. He counted as urbanites anyone in towns of a population of a thousand or more, which gave him an urbanization of 9% to 13% in the empire.[37] Others have opted for a much higher bar for the urban label. Angus Maddison opts for a 10,000 level.[38] J. C Russell sets his low at 10,000 also, which gives him an urban population of 4.1% of an empire of 44 million.[39] Under Russell's scenario, the urban population of the empire would be fewer than 2 million, hardly a situation where we could count crowds of 6 million urban Christians, as many suppose there to have been. Andrew Wilson opts for 5,000 residents for city status and argues for an urbanization at 13.4%.[40] Roger Bagnall speaks of villages

---

36. Keith Hopkins, "Christian Number and Its Implications." *JECS* (1998): 203n36.

37. Raymond W. Goldsmith, "An Estimate of the Size and Structure of the National Product of the Early Roman Empire," *Review of Income and Wealth* 30 (1984): 272.

38. Angus Maddison, *Contours of the World Economy, 1–2030 AD: Essays in Macro-economic History* (Oxford: Oxford University Press, 2007), 40–43. Maddison provides a useful review of the varied estimates.

39. J. C. Russell, *Late Ancient and Medieval Population*, Transactions of the American Philosophical Society, n.s. 48.3 (Philadelphia: American Philosophical Society, 1958), 80.

40. Andrew Wilson, "City Sizes and Urbanization in the Roman Empire," in *Settlement, Urbanization and Population*, ed. A. Bowman and A. Wilson, Oxford Studies in the Roman Economy 2 (Oxford: Oxford University Press, 2011), 191. This requires a population of 55 million in the empire. Wilson also offers numbers for other scenarios. Counting urbanism as towns of 1,000, urbanism would rise to 18.9%, but the urban percentage would decline if the size requirement for a town was larger (to 9.8% based on towns of 5,000 or more and the population at 75 million). Wilson prefers the 5,000 benchmark "to ensure that one is counting a predominantly non-agricultural population" (p. 180), though how the 5,000 benchmark, rather than some other number, ensures that is not clearly established, since even large cities could have a substantial element of their population engaged in agriculture. See Hansen, *The Shotgun Method: The Demography of the Ancient Greek City-State Culture*, 73–76, who calls the 5,000 minimum a "stiff requirement," opting for a 1,000 figure (73). For a brief summary of the matter specifically in regard to Italy, see Alessandro Launaro, *Peasants and Slaves: The Rural Population of Roman Italy (200 BC to AD 100)* (Cambridge: Cambridge University Press, 2011), 28–30.

with a population from a few hundred to 5,000 or more, and he judges there to have been between 2,000 and 2,500 such villages in Egypt.[41] In a later book, Bagnall adjusts the maximum size of a village population down to 4,000,[42] which supposedly marks the minimum size of a settlement to be counted as a city by Bagnall. A. H. M. Jones counted 650 cities in Africa but later pointed out that the term *civitas* (or Greek πόλις) could refer even to a group of scattered villages, a matter that Maddison uses to show "how easy it is to exaggerate the degree of urbanization in the Roman world."[43]

But more often than not, scholars have offered comment about the percentage of urban dwellers in the empire without indicating how that number was determined, almost as though it was an unstated and obvious given—which it definitely is not. Anyone wishing to comment on the extent of urbanization must at least indicate what size of settlements falls within the definition of urban, or if something other than size is offered for the identifying mark of the urban, such investigators must explain how we are to use that to calculate concrete numbers regarding urbanization. Otherwise, the comments mean little.

Structure

Under the influence of idealistic or obsolete views of the Greek *polis*, some have thought that particular urban amenities and infrastructure define a city. A list of such desirable features is provided by Pausanius for the Greek city: theater, agora, gymnasium, government buildings, and fountains.[44] Maddison adds to the lists of desirable amenities of a Roman city: aqueducts, baths, public toilets, sewers, drains, warehouses, granaries, cemeteries, jails, law courts, circuses, hippodromes, libraries, and of

---

41. Bagnall, *Egypt in Late Antiquity*, 110. Also, see D. W. Rathbone, "Villages, Land and Population in Graeco-Roman Egypt," *PCPS* 216, n.s. 36 (1990): 103–142.

42. Roger S. Bagnall and Bruce W. Frier, *The Demography of Roman Egypt* (Cambridge: Cambridge University Press, 1994), 56.

43. Maddison, *Contours of the World Economy*, 60n1. Maddison refers to A. H. M. Jones, *The Decline of the Ancient World* (Holt, Rinehart and Winston, 1966), 237–239 and A. H. M. Jones, *The Roman Economy: Studies in Ancient Economic and Administrative History* (Oxford: Blackwell, 1974), 4.

44. Pausanius, *Descr.* 10.4.1. Clement, *Recognitions* 2.62, lists what is expected of a great city: gates, walls, baths, streets, markets, and the like. John D. Grainger, *The Cities of Seleukid Syria* (Oxford: Clarendon Press, 1990), 63–65, notes the varied uses of the term *polis*.

course temples, among other things.[45] But, as Robin Osborne points out, the model city is "something of a fictional construct,"[46] and Scheidel dismisses those who attempt to define ancient cities either in terms of ideal types or of shared characteristics.[47]

Arbitrary Boundaries

MacMullen sums up the difficulties of trying to specify the degree of urbanization, pointing out that it

> depends on one's definition of a "city" as opposed to a "village." I think that kind of division is not even possible. At best, it is a definition that would vary from place to place and would perhaps even be defined on different aspects. We cannot go by what some official designation might tell us, since the recognition of such a status sometimes reflected simply imperial favour, and nothing more discerning.[48]

Similarly, Scheidel comments that the percent of the urban population of the empire "cannot be reliably determined for any particular region or period of the Greco-Roman world."[49] And Maddison says much the same thing: "it is difficult to distinguish between urban and smaller aggregations."[50]

If the matter of what constitutes an urban area is so wide-ranging and arbitrary, we might be wise to be cautious about proposing any stark urban/rural distinction since we would not know where to draw the line. Indeed, we could not even assume that the line should be drawn for all clusters of populations in the same way and at the same level—or if a line should be drawn at all.[51] Neville Morley has taken issue with the very

---

45. Angus Maddison, *Contours of the World Economy*, 41.

46. Robin Osborne, "Pride and Prejudice, Sense and Subsistence: Exchange and Society in the Greek City," in *City and Country in the Ancient World*, ed. John Rich and Andrew Wallace-Hadrill (London and New York: Routledge, 1991), 121.

47. Scheidel, "Demography," 81–82.

48. MacMullen, *The Second Church*, 31.

49. Scheidel, "Demography," 75.

50. Maddison, *Contours of the World Economy*, 41.

51. The distinction between urban and rural often fails to recognize the diversity in the kinds of settlements that served the needs of the inhabitants of the empire. For North

foundation of the rural/urban distinction that has driven much of scholarship, stating that "there was no clear political or social divide between town and countryside."[52] That leaves unresolved key issues regarding the composition of the early Christian movement.

Rural/Urban Contacts

Contacts between the urban and the rural environs would have been fostered by a variety of situations. The most obvious contacts were created by the regular visits from farmers and craftsmen when they brought their goods to market, and, in a reverse movement, by wealthy city residents who spent considerable time at their country estates.

But the contact may have been more significant than that. According to some of the latest studies, the vast majority of the rural population may actually have lived in small urban centers or even in large cities, leaving each day to work their fields, sometimes remaining overnight in a small shelter on their plots, or perhaps for several nights at key points in the planting and harvest season, but maintaining their permanent home in a village, town, or even a city. Scheidel thinks that most of the "urban" residents actually farmed land, and he speaks of the "sociopolitical fusion between town and country that was a defining characteristic of Greek and Roman civilization."[53] He further contends that only the largest cities would have consisted of a majority of non-farmers.[54] Paul Erdkamp speaks of 80% to 90% as the "common estimate" for the proportion of the population engaged in agriculture, noting, too, that a sizeable part of the farming population would have lived in cities.[55] For Erdkamp, the smaller the town,

---

Africa, David J. Mattingly and R. Bruce Hitchner, "Roman Africa: An Archaeological Review," *JRS* 85 (1995): 186, speak of provincial capitals, ports of trade, new foundations, indigenous towns, cult centers, military towns, industrial towns, other small towns (including subcategories for agricultural towns/agglomerations, roadside settlements).

52. Neville Morley, *Metropolis and Hinterland: The City of Rome and the Italian Economy 200 B.C.–A.D. 200* (Cambridge: Cambridge University Press, 1996), 22, deals with the concept of the consumer city, and he dismisses views that make the city into the economic engine while neglecting the countryside (21–24).

53. Scheidel, "Demography," 79–80. Osborne, "Pride and Prejudice," 120, notes the phenomenon of farmers choosing to live in the city rather than on their land.

54. Scheidel, "Demography," 77.

55. Erdkamp, "Urbanism," 246.

the more of its population that would have been engaged in agriculture, and he cautions against underestimating the number of "city-dwelling agricultural workers."[56] But not everyone would agree, leaving the matter of where the majority of farmers lived unsettled,[57] as well as the question of the minimum size of a settlement for it to be counted as urban.

In some ways, cities and towns were merely areas of the countryside where people had clustered in greater numbers, and it was in such clusters that most people lived. A few of these clusters grew to be quite large, but most were relatively small. Whether large or small, many of the inhabitants of such clusters worked the lands surrounding these towns. Reflecting this reality, Scheidel suggests that it would be more accurate to speak of agrarian and non-agrarian sectors than of countryside and city.[58]

Even large cities could have had a good portion of their population who daily left for the fields, for it would have been a relatively short walk from towns or cities to plots in the countryside.[59] For anyone who has visited the ruins of an ancient Greco-Roman city (such as Ephesus, for example), this arrangement becomes strikingly obvious. Ephesus, one of the prominent cities of the Roman Empire, was hardly a mile square, and tourists can easily walk from one length of the ruins to the other in less than a half hour. A farmer living just inside the city walls could easily walk a considerable distance into the countryside within an hour, passing by a landscape of fields and orchards as he walked to his own field. And where farmers lived outside the city, they would have clustered in nearby towns and villages, and they would have come into the more densely populated areas to bring their produce to market.

Even the idea of walls providing a clear boundary for defining urban and rural space fails, for not every city had walls and not every small town lacked them. Rome itself went for about three hundred years without walls,

---

56. Erdkamp, "Urbanism," 246–247.

57. In agreement with Scheidel, see Cam Grey, *Constructing Communities in the Late Roman Countryside* (Cambridge: Cambridge University Press, 2011), 46–48. Grey, noting the mobility of the rural population, speaks of the boundaries between the rural and the urban as "permeable" and of the terms as being of a "somewhat elastic category" (29). For a different view of where farmers resided, see Peter Garnsey, *Cities, Peasants and Food in Classical Antiquity: Essays in Social and Economic History* (Cambridge: Cambridge University Press, 1998), 107–133, a chapter titled "Where Did Italian Peasants Live?"

58. Scheidel, "Demography," 75.

59. Morley, *Metropolis and Hinterland*, 38, speaks of 5 kilometers as the comfortable distance one might walk from the city to its less densely populated outskirts.

for in the imperial period the city had outgrown the old Servian walls of Republican times, and there was no pressing need for invincible Rome at its height to build walls. Dionysius of Halicarnassus, who lived in Rome in the time of Augustus, said that there was not a clue where the city ended and the countryside began, giving the "impression of a city stretching out indefinitely."[60] The Aurelian walls which one now sees were not built until 271–275 C.E., and this building project corresponded with a spate of wall building in various parts of the empire at the time, due in part at least to the threat from barbarian invaders.[61] For many locales in which the Christian movement made its way in the Roman world, the city and the countryside literally would have flowed into each other, without wall or other significant marker—except in so far as cemeteries might provide some indication.[62]

With or without walls, MacMullen's colorful description of the urban/rural situation is apt: "It was as if the city each morning drew in and exhaled a deep breath of country air."[63] David Riggs, addressing the same matter, points out that regardless of whether the farmer lived within the city or simply nearby, "most people breathed in a steady dose of both town and country air."[64] Duncan-Jones challenges the view of a sharp line between countryside and city, which he considers more applicable to modern cities than ancient ones where the rural was much more included in the life of the city.[65] Even for those who lived outside the city, many lived close

60. Dionysius of Halicarnassus, *Roman Antiquities* 4.13.4–5. The republican walls were in a state of ruin in Dionysius's day.

61. Hendrik W. Dey, *The Aurelian Wall and the Refashioning of Imperial Rome, AD 271–855* (Cambridge: Cambridge University Press, 2011), 110–111, and he notes wall building *"en masse* in previously secure interior regions of the empire" (102). Ray Laurence, Simon Esmonde Cleary, and Gareth Sears, *The City in the Roman West, c.250 BC–C.AD 250* (Cambridge: Cambridge University Press, 2011), 141, recognize that a number of cities did not have walls, though they argue that walls, along with streets and temples, were generally important aspects in new city building.

62. J. M. C. Toynbee, *Death and Burial in the Roman World* (Baltimore: Johns Hopkins University Press, 1971), 73–75.

63. Ramsay MacMullen, "Market-Days in the Roman Empire," *Phoenix* 24.4 (1970): 337. See, too, Brent D. Shaw, "Rural Markets in North Africa and the Political Economy of the Roman Empire." *Antiquités africaines* 17 (1981): 37–84.

64. David Riggs, "The Continuity of Paganism between the Cities and Countryside of Late Roman Africa," in *Urban Centers and Rural Contexts in Late Antiquity*, ed. Thomas S. Burns and John W. Eadie (East Lansing: Michigan State University Press, 2001), 288.

65. Richard Duncan-Jones, *The Economy of the Roman Empire: Quantitative Studies*, 2nd ed. (Cambridge: Cambridge University Press, 1982), 259–260.

enough to the city to visit it often. It was not miles but minutes that separated many "rural" dwellers from the city streets.[66]

Given the considerable contact between the urban and the rural, opportunities for Christian links into the countryside and contact with rustics
and rurals certainly existed. Whether Christians took advantage of these
contacts to share the Christian message is the question. We are in no position simply to assume that they did not, and perhaps we should assume
that they did unless there is evidence to the contrary.

We do have a clear example of a mission to the countryside by a
group strikingly similar to the Christian movement—and, indeed,
a movement born from the Christian environment. This movement,
Manichaeism, may be suggestive of the kind of perspective regarding
a rural mission that one might anticipate among Christians themselves. In a story involving Mani's first church, established in the village
of Diodorus, there was a catholic presbyter in an already established
Christian church there.[67] The Christian church was clearly the older one
in this village, and indeed may have been the initial source of converts
to Mani's movement. Further, Mani (216–276/7) is said to have sent
his close disciples "through various cities and villages, with the view of
securing followers."[68] That Mani targeted villages as well as cities does
not require that Christians did the same, but it is suggestive of the kind
of scope one might expect in the Christian mission. If we have no reservation about speaking of Mani's rural successes and interests, what
gives us pause when speaking about Christian success or interest in the
countryside, especially when, in the story of the first encounter between
Mani and the church, the contact is rural and the Christian assembly is
the older?

---

66. One study of the distribution of bars in Pompeii suggests that such establishments
were placed to service people coming from areas outside the city [Steven J. R. Ellis, "The
Distribution of Bars at Pompeii: Archaeological, Spatial and Viewshed Analyses," *JRomArch*
17 (2004): 371–384]. See, too, Peter Oakes, "Contours of the Urban Environment," in *After
the First Urban Christians: The Socio-Scientific Study of Pauline Christianity Twenty-Five Years
Later*, ed. Todd D. Still and David G. Horrell (London/New York: T & T Clark, 2009), 28.

67. Archelaus, *Acts of the Disputation with Manes*, 39.

68. Archelaus, *Acts of the Disputation with Manes*, 53. It might be argued that this means only
that Manichaean missions were widespread, though it is clear that Manichaeism had rural
success in the 300s. Jason BeDuhn, *Augustine's Manichaean Dilemma*, vol. 1, *Conversion and
Apostasy, 373–388 C.E.* (Philadelphia: University of Pennsylvania Press, 2010), 335n9, speaks
of the "unusual inclusion of rural settlements" in orders to expel or exile Manichaeans.

Supplying the Cities with Food

The countryside has always been essential to cities. In the modern world, with better modes of transportation and means of preserving produce (particularly with refrigeration), the consumer is often far removed from the producer in distance and in thought. Not so in the ancient world. Most of the produce had to be grown on the land near the urban settlements. Land transport of foodstuffs was prohibitively expensive for any shipment over even a moderate distance, since the animals that were necessary to haul the produce overland would have consumed much of the value of the cargo along the way.[69] Thus, most of a city's food supply would have come from nearby villages or plots of lands farmed by residents of the cities. Port cities would have had an additional advantage of being able to import grain by ships, which was the least expensive mode of shipment of foodstuffs, but even port cities would have depended on the local farmers for much of their produce.[70] That does not mean that everyone who lived in the countryside and were involved with crops or cattle would have made their way regularly into the city. Many must have barely scraped by, having little surplus to bring to market. But many would have routinely come to the city market, at least in sufficient enough numbers to meet the needs of the urban population dependent on others for food.[71] Such markets would have linked rurals not just to the city but to rurals from other settlements, who came to a common market.

In addition to agricultural produce, the countryside would have been a supplier of animals for sacrificial meat and meat for the marketplace. The shepherds and sheep on the hillsides around Bethlehem in the Christmas nativity story capture a slice of life where livestock in the fields often would have been being raised to supply sacrificial victims for temples, which in the case of Judea would have been limited to the one in Jerusalem, but in most areas could have included a multitude of temples. The degree

---

69. Stephen Mitchell, *History of the Later Roman Empire*, 303. Donald Engels, *Roman Corinth*, 75, spoke of a maximum distance of 60 miles for the land transport of food.

70. Mitchell, *A History of the Later Roman Empire*, 304, points out that coastal cities could become much larger than inland cities due to the access to cheaper food supply transported by boats.

71. L. de Ligt, *Fairs and Markets in the Roman Empire: Economic and Social Aspects of Periodic Trade in a Pre-industrial Society* (Leiden: Brill, 1993). Morley, *Metropolis and Hinterland*, 166–169, deals with peasant marketing, noting the regular weekly (eighth-day) markets frequented by small rural farmers.

to which the city elite or the temple organization may have owned rural land for raising animals for sale for sacrificial purposes is another matter, though whatever the arrangement, some engagement between urban and rural players would have been necessary.

Supplying the Cities with Clothing and Manufactured Goods

Not every agricultural activity was for food or sacrifice. Animal skins, tanned into leather, provided a common material in the ancient world used in the manufacture of numerous items, from tents to footwear. Whether the manufacturing was done in the cities or in the countryside, some contacts with the countryside would have been necessary in order to obtain the raw materials or the finished products. Fabric for clothing also had to be woven, and though the ideal wife might take on that duty herself, one could buy linen or other fabrics that had been woven by others. An illustration of this kind of market economy is reflected in the story of the execution of Peter, the bishop of Alexandria, in the last year of the Great Persecution. An aged man and woman were coming into the city from some "smaller towns" (*oppidis*). One had four hides to sell; the other had two sheets of linen.[72] As Paul Erdkamp has noted, the rural areas supplied a range of specialized labor in producing goods for the urban market, and he found no useful economic boundary separating rural and urban areas.[73]

Supplying the Cities with People

Food and clothing were not the only crucial commodities that the country-side supplied to cities. Almost as important, the country supplied the city with people, a fact usually overlooked in the discussion of the supposed urban character of early Christianity. According to some who have studied the urban

---

72. *The Genuine Acts of Peter*. Both were Christians, the woman being an aged virgin. They appear in the story because they are Christian and witness to Peter's death and provide aid to him. The hides and fabrics that they had brought to the city to sell became the blankets upon which Peter knelt at his beheading. They also witness to the economic links that bound city and countryside together.

73. Erdkamp, "Urbanism," 242, concentrates on economic matters, skirting the heated debate of the city as consumer vs. producer, and he looks for the "shades of grey" that some-times gets overlooked by the emphasis on ideal types.

areas of the Roman Empire, cities generally had neither a high enough birth rate nor an adequate life expectancy among residents to keep their populations stable.[74] Walter Scheidel speaks of the "negative growth rates" of large cities, which had to be "counterbalanced by immigration,"[75] and he describes urban centers as "consumers of men" because of the high death rates in towns.[76] Thus, city populations would have been in deficit if cities were unable to attract newcomers, although we do not know what numbers may have been involved in the movement of rural residents to address this deficit. John North contends that a "high percent" of the urban poor would have consisted of immigrants from the countryside.[77] Meeks recognizes this kind of rural movement to the cities, but he does not address how such movement might affect his thesis of the urban character of early Christianity.[78]

Rural dwellers would have moved to the city for a variety of reasons— obviously none of which was a sense of obligation to keep the city population stable. Mohammed Abd-el-Ghani describes the numerous attractions of a city like Alexandria, and speaks of the "Egyptian country-folk who would be lured from their home villages in the 'chora' to the magnificent capital and prolong their stay there as much as they could,"[79] providing Alexandria with

---

74. Walter Scheidel, "Progress and Problems in Ancient Demography," in *Debating Roman Demography*, ed. Walter Scheidel (Leiden: Brill, 2001), 118–180. The matter is debated, especially in the most recent literature. See Saskia Hin, *The Demography of Roman Italy: Population Dynamics in an Ancient Conquest Society 201 BCE–14 CE* (Cambridge: Cambridge University Press, 2013), 210–257; Saskia Hin, "Revisiting Urban Graveyard Theory: Migrant Flows in Hellenistic and Roman Athens, in *Migration and Mobility in the Early Roman Empire*, ed. Luuk de Ligt and Laurens E. Tacoma (Leiden: Brill, 2016), 234–263; Elio Lo Cascio, "The Impact of Migration on the Demographic Profile of the City of Rome: A Reassessment," in *Migration and Mobility in the Early Roman Empire*, ed. Luuk de Ligt and Laurens E. Tacoma (Leiden: Brill, 2016), 23–32. All sides, however, agree that some level of migration needs to be factored into the analysis of urban populations.

75. Scheidel, "Demography," 41–42, 84.

76. Scheidel, "Demography," 83. Morley, *Metropolis and Hinterland*, 39–40, thinks that this deficit phenomenon applied to urban areas as small as a few thousand. Morley also notes that migrants from the countryside would have faced new diseases, and as a group may have had a higher death rate (39–46).

77. John A. North, "Religion and Rusticity," in *Urban Society in Roman Italy*, ed. T. J. Cornell and Kathryn Lomas (London: UCL Press, 1995), 139.

78. Wayne A. Meeks, *The Moral World of the First Christians* (Philadelphia: Westminster Press, 1986), 39.

79. Mohammed Abd-el-Ghani, "Alexandria and Middle Egypt: Some Aspects of Social and Economic Contacts," in *Ancient Alexandria between Egypt and Greece*, ed. W. V. Harris and Giovanni Ruffini (Leiden: Brill, 2004), 161.

a "dense rural population from the villages of Middle Egypt,"[80] According to El-Abbadi, the rural element in the Alexandrian population may have doubled after the Romans took over.[81] Although these comments relate specifically to Alexandria, there is little reason to dismiss the attraction of rural dwellers to other cities too. Benet, summarizing the conclusion of Janet Abu Lughod, points out that the ties between modern Cairo and the villages "are enhanced, not destroyed, because new migrants seek out well known 'successes' from their village to give them employment, so that residential and work clusters of people from the same villages result."[82] It is less clear how immigrants in the ancient world made their homes in their new cities. While evidence for Jews suggest some kind of clustering in enclaves, it is less clear for others, and even for Jews there were no rigid boundaries.[83]

Some scholars have made the newly arrived rural residents the main source of converts for Christian churches (and Jewish synagogues) in the cities. Magnus Zetterholm, for example, uses the influx of rural newcomers into the city as a cornerstone in his thesis regarding the development of Christianity in Antioch. Using theories of Rodney Stark,[84] Zetterholm

---

80. Abd-el-Ghani, "Alexandria and Middle Egypt," 163.

81. Cited in Abd-el-Ghani, "Alexandria and Middle Egypt," 163.

82. Benet, "Sociology Uncertain," 9, referring to Janet Abu-Lughod, "Migrant Adjustment to City Life: The Egyptian Case," *American Journal of Sociology*, 67.1 (1961): 30–31.

83. Laurens E. Tacoma, "Migrant Quarters in Rome?" in *Integration in Rome and in the Roman World: Proceedings of the Tenth Workshop of the International Network Impact of Empire*, Impact of Empire 17, ed. Gerda de Kleijn and Stéphane Benoist (Leiden: Brill, 2014), 127–146. Shlomo Simonsohn, *The Jews of Italy: Antiquity* (Leiden: Brill, 2014), 78–80, notes that Philo (*Embassy*, 23) placed most Jews in the Trastevere neighborhood, though, as Simonsohn points out, Jews resided in other neighborhoods and that Trastevere was the area where most newly arrived immigrants initially settled, no matter where they had come from. Hin, *The Demography of Roman Italy*, 216, finds evidence of perhaps some clustering of migrants from the same geographical origin in the fact that particular distinctive religious symbols sometimes are discovered in clusters. Christopher Haas, *Alexandria in Late Antiquity: Topography and Social Conflict* (Baltimore: Johns Hopkins University Press, 1997), 49, calls attention to not only Jewish enclaves in Alexandria, but to others (Lycians and Phrygians), and to one section that seemed to house people from the Egyptian countryside.

84. Stark, *The Rise of Christianity*, 147–162, made much of the theory of networks to explain the spread of Christianity. The idea of networks has become in recent years an interpretive key for the spread of various kinds of ideas and movements, as in Anna Collar, *Religious Networks in the Roman Empire: The Spread of New Ideas* (Cambridge: Cambridge University Press, 2013). Philip A. Harland, "Connections with Elites in the World of the Early Christians," in *Handbook of Early Christianity: Social Science Approaches*, ed. Anthony J. Blasi, Jean Duhaime, and Paul-André Turcotte (Walnut Creek, CA: AltaMira Press, 2002), 389–392, emphasizes the importance of family networks in the composition of Greco-Roman

thinks the rural newcomers lacked or lost social networks when they made their homes in the cities, and that the synagogue and church were able to supply a replacement network and attract at least some of these newcomers.[85]

What Zetterholm and Stark do not deal with is the flip side of this equation. If Christianity was drawing substantial numbers of new members from newcomers to the city, these members would have been primarily rural in their sensibilities and recently rural in their residence. Granted, they had become dwellers in cities, but they can hardly be described as urban rather than rural. They are dwellers in cities but not necessarily "city-dwellers." As North points out, such individuals,

> so far from being thoroughly urban, would have been born and brought up in the country. For them, at least, there can hardly have been any gap of sophistication between their own ideas and those of the villages in which they had been born and grown up.[86]

Furthermore, unless all contact to their past was cut by their move to the city, at least some of these newcomers (and perhaps most) would have retained contact of some kind with relatives in the countryside. Further, it is not clear that all newcomers to the city remained in the city permanently. Surely some departed for the countryside again after a period of city life—a prodigal son story repeated thousands of times across the

---

associations and in the Christian communities. I find the concept of networks useful in explaining how Christianity may have crossed the boundaries between the urban and rural domains. But networks have a flip side. Not only do networks provide links along which new ideas might more easily flow, they also provide powerful, ready-made barriers. Early Christian authors highlighted such barriers, noting in particular the opposition from and severing of networks with one's own relatives (sometimes forced and sometimes voluntary) (Matt 10:21–22, 34–37; 19:29). Indeed, the Christian church is often presented as a new and more important family unit (Mark 3:31–35).

85. Magnus Zetterholm, *The Formation of Christianity in Antioch: A Social-Scientific Approach to the Separation between Judaism and Christianity* (London: Routledge, 2003), follows Stark's basic thesis, though Zetterholm emphasizes the attraction of the synagogue for the newly arrived rural migrants to the city in a way that Stark does not. From this group of newly converted "Jews," Zetterholm thinks Christianity drew heavily for its initial base of members when political changes made association with the synagogue less advantageous (42). Stark does not speak of Judaism as a midpoint for rural residents moving from paganism to Christianity, though he should not be adverse to this since he sees Judaism generally in such a role in urban areas, which is where he has located most of the Jewish diaspora.

86. North, "Religion and Rusticity," 139.

empire. Indeed, the story of the prodigal suggests that some movement from the countryside to the city, and back again, was part of the world of experience of early Christians, or at least an occurrence familiar to them.[87] Such movement of rural people into the cities and the departure of some back to life in the country would have established a strong and exploitable network for Christian expansion into the rural empire, even where the church might not otherwise have a dedicated mission to the villages.[88]

There is yet another link that connected the city with the countryside. A story in Matthew's gospel speaks of a landowner who, in need of workers for his vineyard, goes to the market where he finds people who are hanging around hoping to be hired. This shows a further aspect of interchange between the city and the countryside,[89] and it may enable us to suggest a bit of detail to the complexion of early Christian churches, adding a rural or rustic dimension to urban Christian assemblies. I offer the following as a provisional and speculative effort to understand one possible element in the rural/urban world of Christianity.

Some have argued that young single men formed a significant component of rurals who moved to urban centers, either for work or for better marriage opportunities in a tight marriage market.[90] According to Jonathan Reed, possibly one in every ten young rural males (between the ages of 15 and 24) moved to the city.[91] If that was the case, such a group would have constituted about a tenth of the urban population (816,000 in a population of 9 million). Add to this the number of native residents of the city in that

---

87. Luke 15:11–32.

88. Jonathan L. Reed, "Instability in Jesus' Galilee: A Demographic Perspective," *SBL* 129 (2010): 363, contends that large numbers of single young males migrated to the cities, and he notes a variety of ways that links back to the countryside could have been maintained. Although his work is focused on Galilee, he notes parallels with what other investigators have noted for Egypt.

89. Matt 20:1–15.

90. Several things would have made the search for a wife difficult for a young man. Women often married young and many died in childbirth. The widowed husband, often older, tended to remarry. Women rarely married after the age of thirty or thirty-five. Each of these factors increased the number of men looking for wives while decreasing the number of women who would be available for marriage. See Roger S. Bagnall and Bruce W. Frier, *The Demography of Roman Egypt* (Cambridge: Cambridge University Press, 1994), 123–127, 165. Also, Reed, "Instability in Jesus' Galilee," 345, 362–363.

91. Reed, "Instability in Jesus' Galilee," 362. Morley, *Metropolis and Hinterland*, 49, simply says that migrants tended to be adults between 15 and 30 years.

age group (another 1.41 million), and the young male population of cities would stand at about 25% of the population.[92] Whether that is a reasonable reconstruction is another matter, though it is likely that such a group formed a considerable element in a city's population.

Is there evidence that young males became part of the Christian movement in sufficient number to evoke comment or attention? Various passages in early Christian literature refer to young men, often treating them in one way or another as a recognizable group, or suggesting possibly some awareness of a distinctive group.[93] More important, perhaps, is that some texts deal quite explicitly and in detail with the matter. Take Celsus' criticism of Christianity's effort in the marketplace to attract hearers, which, Celsus says, avoids assemblies of wise men, turning rather to young men, or a mob of slaves or to some gathering of the unintelligent.[94] Although Origen dismisses Celsus' comment as merely an effort to abuse Christians, Origen goes on at length to defend the Christian practice of attracting and instructing young men, who in the context of Celsus' attack must be seen largely as part of the urban rabble.

In another passage, roughly dated between Celsus' criticism of the Christian movement attracting young rabble and Origen's defense of Christians for having that interest (and apparently success), Tertullian addresses the matter of young males in the church. In this case, it is not that the group is noticeable but rather that it is not. These are celibate males who, as a group, are not recognized by some distinctive mark, in contrast to celibate women, who are distinctly identified by the veil. For our purposes, the passage points to an element of celibate young men in the church,

---

92. The calculation of the number of young men relies on Table 3 in Bruce W. Frier, "Demography," in *The High Empire* AD *70–192, CAH*, vol. 11, ed. A. K. Bowman, P. Garnsey, and D. Rathbone (Cambridge: Cambridge University Press, 2000), 795. The 1.41 million native males in that category was determined by taking the 9 million urban figure and reducing it by 816,000 (the number of rural residents in that age group who had moved to the city). This left a native urban population of 8,840,000, and 16% of that came to 1.41. Of course, many more residents of cities would have been themselves migrant (older men, women of various ages, etc.), along with the younger migrant males who have grown older since their arrival in the city, but these remain indeterminables. Even the number of young single rural men who moved to cities is a guess and serves only to sketch one particular scenario.

93. I am not suggesting a technical term is in place, but only that some recognition of young men in the Christian assembly is being made: Acts 2:17; 5:6, 10; Titus 2:6; 1 John 2:13, 14. If the church did attract a considerable number of young men, might we have some of the roots of monasticism there?

94. Origen, *Cels.* 50.

in this case distinguishable, or at least potentially distinguishable, from other young men in the assembly.[95]

Such observations may allow us to add a bit of color to the portrait—in this case, not of the rural church but of the urban. Young men, perhaps many single and with rural roots, may have been a fixture of most urban churches. This would have brought a rural dimension into the church, and perhaps in time even into the leadership. And some links between the countryside and the city must have been fostered by such members.

For our purposes, it is enough to note that if cities consisted of a large number of recently arrived and somewhat displaced country residents, and if these newcomers constituted a significant source of religious converts, then the popular view of the urban character of early Christianity must be modified to take into account this constituent of the church's membership, for this would have added a distinctly rural element into the Christian mix. Thus, whatever the reality of the rural presence in a city's population—whether newly arrived or settled for generations and working the fields beyond the walls—Christian contact with rurals and rustics would not have been unusual.

Supplying the Cities with Religion

Temples both dotted the countryside and clustered in and around cities.[96] Even those temples that we might consider urban often were outside the city, since the right of sanctuary granted to temples often necessitated that the temple not be within the city, where such a right might be considerably more disruptive.[97] In some cases, the greatest and most famous temples

---

95. Tertullian, *Virg.* 10. Tertullian is fighting for a more rigorous adoption of the veil as the mark of the female who has taken a vow of celibacy. In context, it appears that the male group in question is distinguishable from other young males in the assembly by having taken some kind of vow of celibacy. For one thing, these young men are presented as a counterpart to vowed celibate young women, and not all young unmarried women are in that group. Further, they want their celibate commitment recognized. Given the strict sexual code of early Christian assemblies, the unmarried (male or female) would have been expected to be celibate. What seems to be at issue here is something different—a vow of a permanent celibate life.

96. Béatrice Caseau, "The Fate of Rural Temples in Late Antiquity and the Christianization of the Countryside," in *Recent Research on the Late Antique Countryside*, Late Antique Archaeology 2, ed. William Bowden, Luke Lavan, and Carlos Machado (Leiden: Brill, 2004), 105–144.

97. See S. R. F. Price, *Rituals and Power: The Roman Imperial Cult in Asia Minor* (Cambridge: Cambridge University Press, 1984), 191–196; Angelos Chaniotis, "The

lay not only outside the cities but sometimes at a considerable distance from any urban area.[98] Such temples would have brought urban and rural together, for inhabitants of both worlds would have journeyed to the temples for similar reasons. One might find devout pagan pilgrims, going from temple to temple, awed at the sight of a grand temple or hushed in the shade of a sacred grove, perhaps even sharing the road on occasion with a Christian who might have sought to engage them in a debate about the gods. And there would have been the simply curious also—both pagan and Christian—interested in seeing any worthwhile site along the way that his or her travels necessitated.[99]

Robin Lane Fox, looking at temples that dotted the rural landscape and the numerous festivals held in cities, concluded that "just as the countryside ran into the town, so the ebb and flow of people joined the two landscapes in honour of the gods."[100] He emphasizes the travel involved in Greco-Roman religion, as city residents visited rural sites, often at a considerable distance, and as rural dwellers, providing a "reverse traffic," came to town for the festivals. It was clearly not Christians who invented the idea of pilgrimage.[101] After presenting the case for the substantial links between rural and urban Greco-Roman religion—"the pagan gods ... brought the towns and countryside into persistent contact," as he says—Lane Fox then asserts that not until after Constantine were Christians "turned likewise to the countryside beyond"[102]—this in spite of his showing in the very

---

Dynamics of Rituals in the Roman Empire," in *Ritual Dynamics and Religious Change in the Roman Empire*, ed. Olivier Hekster, Sebastian Schmidt-Hofner, and Christian Witschel (Leiden: Brill, 2009), 8–10.

98. Take the case for the Temple of Artemis of Ephesus. It was about 4 kilometers from the gates of Ephesus. Another temple, to Apollo (Artemis's twin) was in Didyma, 17 kilometers along the sacred way from Miletus. Didyma was the second most renowned oracle after Delphi. Delphi was itself 15 kilometers from the port of Kirrha. Pilgrims visiting such sites or processions parading to such sites would have brought city and countryside into close proximity.

99. It would be wrong to think that every Christian ran from pagan temples in fear. Some may have found religious sites the ideal place for speaking about Jesus. The Acts portrayal of Paul visiting the Areopagus, even if fictional, suggests a world in which such encounters were not inconceivable.

100. Lane Fox, *Pagans and Christians*, 44.

101. Lane Fox, *Pagans and Christians*, 41–46; Jaś Elsner and Ian Rutherford, eds., *Pilgrimage in Graeco-Roman and Early Christian Antiquity: Seeing the Gods* (Oxford: Oxford University Press, 2005).

102. Lane Fox, *Pagans and Christians*, 46.

same context the considerable links between pagan urban religion and pagan rural religion. But that is precisely the question. The rural/urban connection of Greco-Roman religion, perhaps, should have caused Lane Fox to ask whether Christianity, too, might not have developed urban and rural links. Lane Fox does not seem to notice that Christianity's failure to penetrate the countryside would have made Christianity somewhat an anomaly in that period if it failed to reach out to or establish links with the countryside. Was Christian attention to or presence within the country-side really so delayed, making it an anomaly within the general pattern of how ancient religion functioned across its urban and rural areas? Perhaps Christianity was odd in that way, but such a judgment would need detailed defense, which Lane Fox does not provide.

Soldiers, Slaves, Convicts, and Exiles

Christianity had a body of potential missionaries produced, quite unin-tentionally, by Roman authorities who took action against Christian un-desirables. Those convicted of being Christian were oftentimes exiled to remote areas or sent to the mines. Although all modern commentators on early Christianity recognize such treatment of Christians, few (if any) have investigated how such action may have contributed to the spread of Christianity. Such neglect is understandable in some ways, for we have almost no reports for the period during which Christians suffered exile or worked as convict labor, while we do have literature about what hap-pened when they returned to their churches after release or what they did while in prison awaiting their trial, where occasional stories of conver-sion of guards can be found.[103] Of course, it might be that contacts and even conversions of fellow convicts had little impact on the makeup of the Christian community, for life was harsh and brief for those sentenced to the mines. A convert to Christianity there might have found some solace for himself, but his sphere of influence would have been minimal. Yet there perhaps would have been cases where contact led to conversion, and cases where a slave gained freedom or an exile was allowed back, and re-turned a different person. The story of what occurred during the periods of exile and forced labor is largely untold, though the world in which exiles,

---

103. Candida R. Moss, *The Other Christs: Imitating Jesus in Ancient Christian Ideologies of Martyrdom* (New York: Oxford University Press, 2010), 104.

slaves, and convicts were a considerable segment of the population may have further blurred urban and rural boundaries and may have been a setting of Christian witness.

Although we do not have reports about the actions of Christians in exile or in ancient Roman gulags, we can make some reasonable guesses from what we do know. Some of these convicts would have been church leaders. Others would have been average Christian lay people caught in the net. And some would have been intense zealots, a few of whom bordered on the insane, seeking out an opportunity to be tried and convicted as Christians.[104] All would have had one thing in common: they would have already been tested publicly for their faith and had stood firm. Of course, what we do not know is how they acted in exile or the labor camps. Some may have simply become mute, having lost everything, overwhelmed by the recognition of their plight, and pained, knowing that their family had been reduced to a condition of absolute poverty because of their action, with no way for them now to aid their loved ones or themselves. But others must have considered their new situation as another opportunity to live and die for Christ, with their firm conviction and zeal undiluted by their added hardship. That these individuals spoke to none, that they impressed none, that they won none to the Christian cause, is unlikely.

The matter of the spread of Christianity among the Roman army must also be considered. Some soldiers may have been Christians who were conscripted into the army; some may have converted to Christianity during their army career. But there is no doubt that there was a Christian presence in the army.[105] Most of the soldiers would have been stationed near the borders of the empire (thus in more rural areas), and many soldiers would have settled as farmers on nearby lands upon retirement. To what degree that would have helped established a Christian presence in

---

104. That is not to place martyrs generally into a category of the mentally unstable or abnormal, though martyrs have baffled both the ancient civil authorities and a good number of modern scholars. See Candida R. Moss, *Ancient Christian Martyrdom: Diverse Practices, Theologies, and Traditions* (New Haven: Yale University Press, 2012), 6–8, for a brief review of and challenge to the treatment of early Christian martyrdom as some kind of mental dysfunction in the scholarship of the last two centuries. Yet it must be admitted that some martyrs likely were unstable, whether from the specific anxieties related to a persecution or from a general instability that may have marked much of their lives even under more normal conditions.

105. Eusebius, *Hist. eccl.*, records instances of Christian soldiers being targets in some of the persecutions of Christians: under Decius (7.11.17–20) and in the Great Persecution (8.4.1–3).

rural areas is impossible to establish, but it is one more aspect of life in the Roman Empire that points to the likelihood of some Christian presence in the countryside.

Conclusion

Sharp lines between city and countryside and between urban and rural worlds fail to do justice to the reality of two entities linked by a multitude of contacts and associations. Only at the extremes might one speak of two worlds. For most, the urban and the rural flowed together or ebbed to and fro, making sharp boundaries arbitrary and misleading.

But does that mean the urban thesis regarding the composition of members in the early Christian movement fails? Was not Paul, missionary extraordinaire, focused on cities? And was not the Christian message wrapped in Greek language and sensibilities? And even if Christians had decided to leave the cities and port their message into the language of the surrounding countryside, would they have had any success there given how conservative the countryside tends to be, particularly in matters of religion?

These matters are the subject of the next chapter.

6

Supposed Barriers to Christian Success in the Countryside

The Urban Character of Paul's Mission

The most influential work that propelled the urban thesis to dominance is Wayne Meeks' groundbreaking book, *The First Urban Christians*, largely based on Meeks' study of Paul.[1] Under the influence of Meeks' work, many not only assert an urban mission of Paul but an almost exclusively urban complexion of early Christian churches until the time of Constantine or later. Further, many treat Paul's practice, as portrayed by Meeks, as a template for early Christian mission generally.[2] Two questions must be considered. One, does Meeks' depiction of the urban focus of Paul's mission exclude a rural mission or a rustic element in the early Pauline communities? Two, whatever is determined to be the practice of Paul, does Paul's practice have much relevance to the debate regarding Christian presence in the countryside or Christian interest in the rural population?

First to Meeks' description of Paul's mission. Meek refers to Paul's list of dangers and abuses he suffered on his missions as recorded in 2 Corinthians 11:26: "on frequent journeys, in danger from rivers, danger from bandits, danger from my own people, danger from Gentiles,

---

1. Indeed, such is the subtitle of Meeks' influential work, *The First Urban Christians: The Social World of the Apostle Paul* (New Haven and London: Yale University Press, 1983).

2. E. Glenn Hinson, *The Evangelization of the Roman Empire: Identity and Adaptability* (Macon, GA: Mercer University Press, 1981), 33–43, thinks that Paul's method was normal up to the conversion of Constantine. So, too, Rodney Stark, *Cities of God: The Real Story of How Christianity Became an Urban Movement and Conquered Rome* (New York: HarperCollins, 2006), 25–26.

danger in the city, danger in the wilderness, danger at sea, danger from false brothers and sisters." From this passage, Meeks asserts that Paul "divides the world into city, wilderness and sea .... His world does not include the *chora*, the productive countryside; outside the city there is nothing—*eremia*."[3] But surely Meeks is forcing this passage to carry a weight it was never intended to carry—and that it cannot carry. More troubling than the flawed and strained interpretation Meeks gives to this passage is that this is the key passage that Meeks appeals to for Paul's supposed dismissal of the countryside and his supposed focus on urban areas.

All Paul is asserting in this passage is that he, as a representative of Christ, has been in danger everywhere and from everyone. He is not asserting anything about the *chora*. Paul simply lists off all his sufferings—much greater than any of his competitors, he wants his audience to know—and he lists these over a much longer passage than Meeks quotes (11:26–28).[4] Further, it is not as though Paul did not speak of the countryside—in spite of what Meeks asserts. Paul does speak in this passage of dangers from bandits, which has a more rural tone to it, and dangers from rivers, which most likely has a rural setting, where some crossings might be risky when, for example, the river's flow was stronger than normal. Although rivers might flow through cities, it is more likely that bridges would have been part of the infrastructure there, unless Paul, like soldiers in the army of Maxentius fleeing from Constantine's forces, chose to wade the flowing Tiber rather than use the Milvian Bridge.

I will not press the point further, for I think it is ill-advised to make Paul's words anywhere in this passage exclude or include the countryside—or anything else.[5] The omission of the word *chora* in this passage simply has no relevance to the assertion of an urban-focused mission, and it is certainly not a key to it.

This is not the only passage that Meeks calls in to support his narrow reading of Paul's urban-focused mission. "The author of Acts hardly errs," Meeks tells us, "when he has Paul boast to the tribune, astonished that Paul knows

---

3. Meeks, *The First Urban Christians*, 9.

4. Meeks, *The First Urban Christians*, 9.

5. I was discussing Meeks' treatment of this passage in 2 Corinthians with some colleagues, when one of them (Jim Linville) commented that, contrary to Meeks, it would seem that Paul was rather fond of the countryside if it is the one thing he left out in his list of all the dangerous and horrible places he had experienced.

Greek, that he is 'a citizen of no mean city.' "[6] But, really, does this in any way suggest that Paul has no interest in the countryside or that his focus must be exclusively urban, as Meeks suggests? If we allow this passage in Acts to be used in the way that Meeks has used it—which it should not be—then surely note should be taken of comments by the same author that do speak of Paul and the countryside. In one passage, the author portrays Paul's message as spreading throughout the countryside (χώρας).[7] In another passage, the author writes that Paul and his companions fled to Lystra and Derbe, cities of Lycaonia, and to the surrounding country (περίχωρον).[8] Again, I will not press that point, for I am certain we would be far better served if we distanced ourselves from such inventive readings of any of these ancient texts, though such comments about Paul and the countryside do raise some questions about the supposedly urban-centered Pauline mission.[9]

It seems that Paul's mission is viewed as urban-focused because extant writings from Paul are addressed primarily to churches in cities. From the undisputed letters, four cities are addressed: Rome, Corinth, Thessalonica, and Philippi. Of the other undisputed letters, one is to a region (Galatia) and one to an individual (Philemon), both of which could have had an urban address. Other cities, too, can be associated with Paul's missions from the undisputed letters, where Damascus, Antioch, Ephesus, Cenchreae, and Troas are all mentioned by Paul. From the disputed letters, further cities could be added: Colossae, Laodicea, and Hierapolis. But making a list of cities (whether long or short) misses two crucial points. One, Paul may see the countryside included in the orbit of the *polis*, since *polis* and countryside together were a fundamental unit of the economic and political structure of Greco-Roman society. Two, when Paul spoke of his mission, he did not speak particularly of cities. Rather, he spoke of regions or provinces, and his reference generally is to churches of provinces rather than to churches

---

6. Acts 21:39. Meeks, *The First Urban Christians*, 9.

7. Acts 13:49 (my translation). Many English translations read region rather than countryside. The Greek is χώρας. In another passage in Acts, Paul chooses to travel overland, though others in the party opt to go by boat (20:13–15).

8. Acts 14:6.

9. Although I am critical of Meeks' reading of these passages and his exclusion of the countryside, there is little doubt that Meeks has provided numerous insights of enduring worth. For an evaluation of Meeks' work twenty-five years after its publication, see Todd D. Still and David G. Horrell, eds., *After the First Urban Christians: The Socio-Scientific Study of Pauline Christianity Twenty-Five Years Later* (London: T & T Clark, 2009).

in individual cities. The following provinces are explicitly listed, and often proceeded by the phrase "churches of": Judaea, Syria, Cilicia, Galatia, Asia, Macedonia, Achaia, Illyricum, and Spain.[10] With the disputed letters considered too, Dalmatia and Crete could be added.[11] Paul's vision is regional and larger. The question whether this included the countryside is more likely to be settled by looking at the general relationship between urban and rural areas in the empire than by some curious reading of a passage from Paul.

But even if Meeks' curious reading of Paul's comment about his mission is allowed to stand, that mission really has almost no relevance to the debate about the urban and rural spheres of Christian activity. Three points are important here. One, Paul's was not the only mission.[12] Two, Paul's mission was not entirely urban. And, three, it would not have been at all obvious—even to those who might have sought to emulate Paul—that Paul had a particular pattern of mission.

Regarding the first point, we need to note that even in Paul's letters themselves, we learn of a number of Christian missionaries who were not part of Paul's enterprise, and there were others, though associated with Paul in some way, who might be more accurately described as freelance missionaries than as delegates of Paul.[13] Various Christian missionaries may have centered their missions in cities—we simply do not know, and though we might think this a likely conclusion, we must be careful not to simply assert what we hope to establish. In the next chapter, I present evidence of at least some Christian presence in the countryside in the second century. Although we cannot say how churches came to be established there, some kind of rural mission is perhaps the most natural explanation.

Even were all early Christian missions focused on urban centers, we could not disassociate these missionaries entirely from rural encounters,

---

10. Judaea (Gal 1:22, 1 Thess 2:14); Syria (Gal 1:21); Cilicia (Gal 1:21); Galatia (1 Cor 16:1, Gal 1:2); Asia (Rom 16:5, 1 Cor 16:19); Macedonia (Rom 15:26, 2 Cor 1:16; 8:1; 1 Thess 1:7; 4:10); Achaia (Rom 15:26; 1 Thess 1:7); Illyricum (Rom 15:19); Spain (Rom 15:24, 28).

11. Dalmatia (2 Tim 4:10); Crete (Titus 1:5). The passage in Titus gives instructions to appoint elders in each city (πόλις), which Meeks might have used to argue that this author saw cities as crucial centers in the Christian mission, Meeks, however, does not appeal to this passage.

12. Even in the Acts account, which makes Paul look like the missionary par excellence, other missionaries beyond Paul's orbit are active (8:5; 21:8), as they are in Paul's own writings (1 Cor 3:5; 9:5; 2 Cor 11:4, 13, 23).

13. 1 Cor 1:12; 3:4–6, 21; 4:6; 16:12; 2 Cor 10:15–16; 11:1–12, 13; Gal 2:7–9.

for missionaries would have been itinerant. They journeyed from city to city, and that meant that they had opportunities for rural contact, for between each city was the rural world, and as we have seen, even cities themselves had a substantial component of those of rustic and rural complexion. Christian missionaries stayed in village inns and they bought food at small local markets. Although early Christians emphasized the importance of offering hospitality to traveling preachers,[14] there would have been many occasions where itinerant preachers had to take accommodations in rural inns or some such establishment. Although the one story we have about a Christian traveler taking up such accommodations is ripe with the fantastic (obedient bedbugs that leave the bed on command), the other elements of the story are quite appropriate to the scene: a Christian traveler takes accommodations in a rural inn and finds that he is sharing his bed with bedbugs.[15]

Such missionaries traveled along roads that led past local sites, including rural temples, which were the main points of interest in the countryside—and they likely visited some of these sites, perhaps with the curiosity of a tourist.[16] That the numerous rural religious sites never drew a Christian preacher's interest is doubtful. That such encounters never led to discussions about the gods is improbable. That these conversations never led to interest in the Christian option and the occasional conversion is unlikely. Whatever we make of the story of Paul publically addressing people about religious matters among the altars of the Areopagus, there is nothing far-fetched about a Christian taking the opportunity afforded by a local religious feature to talk about the Christian message. And there is nothing far-fetched about having such a scene played out in the environment of a rural temple, of which there were thousands. And we can assume that no insurmountable linguistic barrier routinely presented itself at rural temples, for rural temples often served urban dwellers too or were visited by urban travelers.[17]

---

14. See Andrew Arterbury, *Entertaining Angels: Early Christian Hospitality in Its Mediterranean Setting* (Sheffield: Sheffield Phoenix, 2005).

15. *Acts John* 60–61.

16. We know of traveling Christian preachers in the early period not so much by their own record but by advice given to churches regarding hospitality and the limits to hospitality. See Arterbury, *Entertaining Angels*, 122–131.

17. See Ramsay MacMullen, *Paganism in the Roman Empire* (New Haven: Yale University Press, 1981), 18–34; Robin Lane Fox, *Pagans and Christians* (New York: Alfred A. Knopf, 1987), 41–46.

The focus on Paul's urban mission (or on any itinerant Christian mission) must not overlook the inescapable rural aspect—cities were dots on a rural landscape. The image of Christian missionaries jumping from city to city fits the situation of modern travel, where airports provide portals from city to city, blotting out the rural reality between. This was not the reality of the early Christian missionaries. Indeed, the busy network that Christians developed linking congregations far and wide would have presented regular contact with the countryside and inescapable contact with some of its residents, quite apart from the flow of the countryside into the city that was a matter of course in the ancient world. I am not arguing that a massive Christian mission developed from these contacts; I am merely pointing out that the focus on the urban character of early Christian missionary activity has led to a stark neglect of the rural aspect of travel as people moved from city to city through the rural landscape.

The presentation of Paul's mission in the New Testament is, at best, a sketch, and perhaps idealized. Many of the features of Paul's mission come from the presentation in Acts, which seems to jump from city to city as Paul spreads the Christian message into Asia Minor and Greece, and then moves on to Rome itself. This urban focus reflected in Acts is taken as accurate by most scholars,[18] even by those who judge most of the portrait of Paul in Acts as unreliable. Yet, even taking the Acts' portrait of Paul's mission as reliable, we learn, at most, how Paul's mission was initiated. We find nothing in this account that would preclude a mission extending into the surrounding towns and rural settlements, and certainly nothing that suggests that it would have taken over two hundred years for the church to begin to expand from its urban base into the countryside.

Finally, I doubt that Paul had as clear a pattern for mission in his mind that many Pauline scholars would lead us to believe, or, if he had, when that pattern became clear to him, whether from the start or later, toward the end as he reflected on his work. Even if Paul had an intentional urban focus, I doubt that the urban focus that supposedly marked Paul's missionary agenda would have been obvious to even the most committed

---

18. For example, Christine Trevett, *Montanism: Gender, Authority and the New Prophecy* (Cambridge: Cambridge University Press, 1996), 16, comments: "Paul tended to concentrate upon the educated urban synagogue goers, as Acts 13–19 illustrates." But as I have argued elsewhere, what Acts indicates, at best, is a failed mission to the synagogue and a rapid turn to a Gentile audience [*Ignatius of Antioch and the Parting of the Ways: Early Jewish-Christian Relations* (Grand Rapids, MI: Baker Academic, 2009), 54n42].

devotee of Paul or the Pauline tradition.[19] In some cities, Paul stayed for a year or more; in others, he remained only briefly, sometimes because he was under threat, but not always.[20] It cannot be assumed that Paul did not reflect on the countryside in those cities where he resided for longer periods. Indeed, perhaps the opposite should be assumed: the longer Paul remained in a city, the greater the likelihood of rural contacts. At best, Paul's letters and Acts give us only a glimpse of Paul's work. It is unlikely any ancient church leader sat down to analyze Paul's writings to determine Paul's mission strategy or, if on doing so, would have discovered an urban agenda. If anything, the ancient reader looking to Paul's work as a template (though the very idea may be quite silly and unlikely) is more likely to have noted that Paul's mission was to everyone anywhere—even if Paul is more idealistic than descriptive in his comments to that effect.[21]

A more probable view of the matter of Paul's "urban mission" is provided in a few short sentences by Jürgen Becker. The passage deserves to be quoted in full since it is an alternative reading that is at least as credible as Meeks' view—and perhaps considerably more probable. It is an attractive view, also, since it offers areas for further reflection and is not dogmatic in the way that many of the sweeping statements in support of the urban thesis tend to be. Becker comments:

> Paul was thus selective in choosing the targets of his mission. It is his social background that plays a dominant role here and elsewhere.

---

19. My sense is that no one in the ancient world would have detected a missionary strategy of Paul from reading Paul's letters or Acts. Indeed it has been pointed out that the now common view of Paul's "missionary journeys" does not seem to have been suggested by any commentator on Acts before J. A. Bengel's 1742 *Gnomon Novi Testamenti* [John T. Townsend, "Missionary Journeys in Acts and European Missionary Societies," in *SBL 1985 Seminar Papers*, ed. Kent Harold Richards, SBLSP 24 (Atlanta: Scholars Press, 1985), 433–438], cited by Leif E. Vaage, "Ancient Religious Rivalries and the Struggle for Success Christians, Jews, and Others in the Early Roman Empire," in *Religious Rivalries in the Early Roman Empire and the Rise of Christianity*, ed. Leif E. Vaage (Waterloo, ON: Wilfrid Laurier University Press, 2006), 16. Also in that volume, see Terence L. Donaldson, "'The Field God Has Assigned': Geography and Mission in Paul," 109–137, for a review of the discussion regarding Paul's perception of his work.

20. It is difficult to reconstruct Paul's movement solely on the basis of his undisputed letters, where a case might be made for an extended stay only for Ephesus (1 Cor 16:8). If Acts is used, a case can be made for Corinth (Acts 18:1, 11). Acts also places Paul in Antioch for a year before the start of his mission (11:26) and in Rome for two years at the end of the story (28:14, 30).

21. Romans 10:12–13; 1 Corinthians 9:20–23. See Ksenija Magda, *Paul's Territorial and Mission Strategy* (Tübingen: Mohr Siebeck, 2009), for a recent attempt to address this question.

Did his origins not perhaps force him to go into the cities because he did not speak the respective provincial dialects? Did he have to trust that the urban Christianity of a particular city would spread into the provinces through some degree of multilingualism? If this was the design of his mission, it was evidently successful, as Pliny the Younger (*Letters* 10.96), an impartial witness, confirms a little more than two generations after Paul: "The plague of superstition [i.e., Christianity] has not only spread over the cities, but also over the villages and rural areas." Later still, Tertullian (*Apologeticum* 1.7) will confront the emperor with the statement: "There are loud complaints that we have taken over the entire city, and [that there are already] Christians in the countryside, the villages, and the islands."[22]

Nothing about Paul's mission is of such weight that we are forced to assume either a disinterest by Christians in the countryside or a disability of the Christian message to attract some of the rural population in some way. Meeks' curious reading of key passages leaves one with a sense of unease.

The most significant question to address is not whether Paul had a particular method or, if he had, whether it would have been detectable to the reader of Acts and Paul's letters. The question is why Paul's practice is used as a guide when we have a much more explicit portrait of early Christian practice in the account about Jesus. Repeatedly the gospels record that Jesus had an interest in or was active in villages—in fact, in all the towns and villages.[23] Three elements of note arise from such presentation in the gospels. First, the authors of the gospels are writing after Paul's mission and a decade or more after Paul's death. Their presentation of a more inclusive urban *and* rural mission should serve as a balance to the emphasis often put on Paul's *urban* mission. Second, given the prominence of the gospels in the life of the early Christian churches, Christians would have regularly heard of Jesus' interest in and mission to villages.

---

22. Jürgen Becker, chapter 4, "Paul and His Churches," in *Christian Beginnings: Word and Community from Jesus to Post-Apostolic Times*, ed. Jürgen Becker, Reinhard Krauss, trans. (Louisville, KY: Westminster/John Knox Press, 1993), 134–135. It is unclear why Becker has inserted the words "that there are already" into the text. The Latin reads simply: "*Obsessam vociferantur civitatem; in agris, in castellis, in insulis Christianos; omnem sexum, aetatem, condicionem, etiam dignitatem transgredi ad hoc nomen quasi detriment maerent.*"

23. Matt 9:35; Mark 1:45; 5:14; 6:6, 56; 8:27; Luke 5:17; 8:1; 13:22; John 3:22.

It hardly matters whether the stories reflect Jesus' actual practice (as is likely) or whether they simply reflect what Christian writers in the latter part of the first century thought would have been Jesus' practice. Indeed, if the latter case, then that might serve as evidence for Christian practice in the late-first-century communities in which the gospels had their origin, placing villages within the orbit of Christian interest. Third, and perhaps most important, these stories are not presented merely as interesting features of Jesus' activities, which some might find attractive and want to imitate. Rather, on occasion, the gospels present a mission to villages as a command.[24]

Of course, the question of Paul's methods or the custom of Jesus becomes largely passé if, as many now contend, the church had no significant mission outreach after Paul until the time of Constantine.[25] Ramsay MacMullen puts the position bluntly: "after Saint Paul, the church had no mission, it made no organized or official approach to unbelievers; rather, it left everything to the individual."[26] He points to the "very scanty evidence about preachers in the second and third centuries."[27] In part, this caution regarding public preaching stems from the danger that Christians could face if they became a visible cause of concern to the authorities, according to MacMullen.[28] But surely MacMullen overstates his case when he claims that Origen could only find itinerant preachers servicing the already converted.[29]

---

24. Matt 10:11; Luke 9:6.

25. For a review of the debate, see Robert L. Plummer, *Paul's Understanding of the Church's Mission: Did the Apostle Paul Expect the Early Christian Communities to Evangelize?* (Milton Keyes, UK: Paternoster, 2006), 1–42. For a review along with extensive bibliographic material, see J. Patrick Ware, *The Mission of the Church: In Paul's Letter to the Philippians in the Context of Ancient Judaism*, NovTSup 120 (Leiden: Brill, 2005), 1–19. See, also, John P. Dickson, *Mission-Commitment in Ancient Judaism and in the Pauline Communities: The Shape, Extent and Background of Early Christian Mission* (Tübingen: Mohr Siebeck, 2003); and Ian H. Henderson, "Mission and Ritual: Revisiting Harnack's 'Mission and Expansion of Christianity,'" in *The Changing Face of Judaism, Christianity and Other Greco-Roman Religions in Antiquity*, ed. Ian H. Henderson and Gerbern S. Oegema (Gütersloh: Gütersloher Verlagshaus, 2006), 34–56.

26. MacMullen, *Christianizing the Roman Empire*, 34.

27. MacMullen, *Christianizing the Roman Empire*, 34.

28. MacMullen, *Christianizing the Roman Empire*, 35.

29. MacMullen, *Christianizing the Roman Empire*, 35. Origen, *Cels.* 3.9, speaking of the effort to spread Christianity widely, mentioned that some preachers go to the villages and cottages, not just to the cities. Origen, *Cels.* 3.9.

While there may have been a limited or largely nonexistent mission throughout the second and third centuries (though we certainly do not have sufficient information about Christian expansion during this time to determine that), we do know that Christianity grew in this period, whether by organized efforts from bishops or by occasional accidental encounters of individuals. For the question of rural Christian success, it matters not how the church grew. Indeed, if Christian growth was largely dependent on individual contacts and social relationships, then the countryside may well have been as much a field for Christian growth as the urban settlements, as I argue at various points in this work.

The Conservative Nature of the Countryside

Another supposed obstacle to successful Christian expansion into the countryside arises from the general assumption that the countryside was (and is) more conservative than the city. For example, Ramsay MacMullen points to

> the central characteristic of villages—their conservatism. They and their population hovered so barely above subsistence level that no one dared risk a change. Conservatism in its root sense, simply to hang on to what one had, was imposed by force of circumstances. People were too poor, they feared to pay too heavy a price, for experiment of any kind. So the tortoise never moved, it never changed its ways.[30]

Along similar lines, Frank Trombley states: "agriculturists were conservative on matters of religious belief and practice, fearing violations of the 'peace of the gods' .... Christianity first took root in the nearer territories of the towns where urban attitudes prevailed."[31] Everett Ferguson offers a

---

30. Ramsay MacMullen, *Roman Social Relations*, rev. ed. (New Haven: Yale University Press, 1974), 27. MacMullen offers too exaggerated a contrast between urban and rural environments, where risk to life, liberty, and livelihood were always near at hand for large segments of either population.

31. Frank Trombley, "Overview: The Geographical Spread of Christianity," in *The Cambridge History of Christianity*, vol. 1, *Origins to Constantine*, ed. Margaret M. Mitchell and Frances M. Young (Cambridge: Cambridge University Press, 2006), 311. See, too, Neil Christie, *From Constantine to Charlemagne: An Archaeology of Italy, AD 300–800* (Aldershot: Ashgate Publishing, 2006), 112. But Dominic Crossan, *The Birth of Christianity: Discovering What Happened in the Years Immediately after the Execution of Jesus* (New York: HarperCollins,

similar but expanded portrait: "The most conservative elements in pagan society—the aristocracy and the rural peoples—proved most resistant to Christianity. Its initial success came among city-dwellers, those always most open to new ideas and to change."[32]

Even Greco-Roman culture supposedly failed to penetrate the country-side, it is asserted.[33] The assumption seems to be that if the dominant culture could not penetrate the countryside, there was little if any chance for an insignificant peripheral movement, without resources or reputation, to succeed there. The problem for Christian success in the countryside is amplified, according to some scholars, by Christianity's early identification with and use of Greco-Roman culture and language in the church's interests and mission. That would hardly have endeared the Christian effort in the countryside, where Greco-Roman culture supposedly had failed to penetrate and had been roundly rebuffed by the native population.

Two cautions must be raised against this kind of presentation. For one thing, it appears that Greco-Roman culture had been adopted to a lesser or greater degree in many, if not perhaps most, areas of the empire—urban and rural. A. H. M. Jones uses the ability to speak Greek as his primary marker to determine whether Greek culture had spread to the country-side. The results are varied. In some places, Jones finds that the native languages had largely died out. In other areas, a widespread bilingualism seems in evidence. And in some places, the native languages appear to have survived as the dominant language of town and countryside.[34] Thus, the argument of a linguistic barrier that prevented Christian expansion into the countryside would have relevance only in specific areas. But even

---

1998), 415, turns the structure on its head, making urban Christianity conservative and rural Christianity "more subversive and with social reformist tendencies." Although Crossan admits the rural nature of earliest Christianity, he sees Christianity becoming largely urban (p. 416). Crossan builds upon Dimiritus J. Kyratatas, *The Social Structure of the Early Christian Communities* (Brooklyn, NY: Verso, 1987), 92, 95.

32. Everett Ferguson, *Backgrounds of Early Christianity*, 3rd ed. (Grand Rapids, MI: Eerdmans, 2003), 608.

33. Meeks, *The First Urban Christians*, 14–15. The leading American historian of the Roman Empire in his day, Chester G. Starr, helped spread this view in his widely used introduction [*The Roman Empire: 27 B.C.–A.D. 476* (New York: Oxford University Press, 1982), 91–108].

34. A. H. M. Jones, *The Greek City from Alexander to Justinian* (Oxford: Clarendon Press, 1940), 288–295. Greek seems to have been widely used in the Phrygian countryside, and Latin similarly widely used in the African countryside. And Greek was used along with Coptic in rural areas of Egypt. Even restless and resistive Palestine bore many marks of accommodation to and adoption of the dominant culture.

in these areas, the linguistic barrier is not evidence that Christianity was unable to penetrate the countryside, for the church had ways to overcome language barriers, as we will see.

Further, any presentation of the countryside as a uniformly conservative monolith is problematic. We are warned in one of the recent investigations of the urban and rural empire that "the countryside was much more complex than the urban accounts suggest, with conditions from region to region so remarkably different that it would be more accurate to speak of countrysides in late antiquity."[35] Further, even were we to suppose that the countryside was more conservative than the city, it is quite another matter to assume that such conservatism successfully turned back attempts by Christians to win converts there. Indeed, as we will later see, there is evidence for a considerable rural Christian population in various areas of the empire by the latter half of the third century, and a century before that Montanism had experienced considerable rural success, and even earlier Christians were found in both urban and rural areas of Pontus.[36] Such successes demonstrate that, whatever the conservative nature of the countryside, Christianity had the means to overcome that barrier, at least in some areas, long before Constantine's conversion and without imperial patronage.

Further, we must recognize that the assumption that rural attitudes in the Roman Empire were more conservative than urban attitudes is largely untested. Yet that cliché is touted out as though it is a law of human experience, able to be applied wholesale to every situation without needing to look at the actual realities on the ground. Surely areas of Phrygia and North Africa stand as warnings against depending much on that assumption for the world of early Christianity.

The Case of Alexander, the "Oracle Monger"

Consider the reception of Alexander of Abonoteichus, a second-century soothsayer and healer, whom Lucian of Samosata, a Cynic rhetorician, labels the "Oracle Monger" or "False Prophet." Lucian, a rationalist of the first order, was intent to expose Alexander as a charlatan. According to

---

35. Thomas S. Burns and John W. Eadie, eds., *Urban Centers and Rural Contexts in Late Antiquity* (East Lansing: Michigan State University Press, 2001), xxiv.

36. See chapter 7.

Lucian, masses of people over a large area were taken in by Alexander's wondrous human-headed snake and Alexander's supposed skill at prophecy, healing, and exorcism.[37] Alexander's career ran from about 150 to 170 C.E., a period important in making some sense of Christianity's expansion.

As for Christianity's rural success, we learn several things from Lucian's story of Alexander. First, the kinds of things highlighted in Christianity (healings, exorcisms, prophecy) were closely parallel to Alexander's own claims and skills. Both brought the divine close, often in quite dramatic ways. Further, nothing in Lucian's account suggests that there was a difference in urban and rural sensibilities related to Alexander's success.[38] Indeed, according to Lucian, when Alexander first showed his mysterious snake, his town became "over-full of people"[39] from the area of Paphlagonia, an old territory on the south coast of the Black Sea between Pontus and Bithynia. However accurate Lucian may have been, writing some thirty years after an event he had not personally observed,[40] his sense is that urban and rural residents alike would have been drawn to (or, in Lucian's opinion, duped by) the promises and the pizzazz of Alexander's presentation. That Christians could have had some comparable success even in the countryside and with "thick-witted, uneducated" people[41] is suggested by Alexander's own success, where people of all levels of society sought Alexander's help and found hope in his miraculous gifts. The needs and hopes of the rural resident (if we can ever draw a clear line between rural and urban resident) did not differ much from that of others. A conservative countryside is not without its religious quests for protection from malevolent forces and benefit from powers beyond, nor are rural dwellers necessarily scared off by the unconventional and the novel. If Alexander could sell his wares successfully in that religious and psychic marketplace, Christianity might have some success in the same environment.

---

37. Lucian, *Alexander the False Prophet*, in *Lucian*, vol. 4, A. M. Harmon, trans., LCL (Cambridge, MA: Harvard University Press, 1925), 173–253.

38. Although Lucian locates Alexander in cities, he does so to emphasize Alexander's greater danger than some brigand who operates in the forests and mountains (*Alex.* 2).

39. Lucian, *Alex.* 15.

40. Lucian was a vigorous critic of Alexander, and he met him once, on which occasion he bit Alexander's hand rather than kiss it (*Alex.* 55, 57).

41. Lucian, *Alex.* 17, παχέσι καὶ ἀπαιδεύτοις, as Lucian labels Alexander's audience. Later (30), Lucian speaks of those easily duped as ἰδιῶται.

And there is some evidence that Christianity had that kind of success. According to Lucian, Alexander numbered two groups as his worst enemies: the Cynics and the Christians.[42] How much Cynics and Christians had in common is debated.[43] In regard to the story at hand, both saw Alexander as a deceitful trickster. But Cynics came to that conclusion because they were rationalists. Christians came to the same conclusion, but for an entirely different reason—they were Alexander's close competitors.

In order to take some suspicion off himself, Alexander called attention to the Christians, charging that they had come to fill (ἐμπεπλῆσθαι) Pontus.[44] It hardly makes sense for Alexander to have called attention to the Christians in the way that he did unless Christians were already under suspicion. The point that Alexander wanted to make was not about shameful or repulsive Christian conduct. That Christians are known and despised is assumed. It is the size of the movement that Alexander sought to use to turn the spotlight from himself. Obviously there is rhetorical excess in Alexander's comment: Christians did not "fill" the cities and countryside. But it is clear that they were numerous enough to be noticed and to have become a matter of some concern. It is also clear that Christians had penetrated the countryside with some success—or at least the perception of the populace was that they had. This evidence is in line with Pliny's investigation a half-century earlier that found a Christian presence in both city and countryside in roughly the same area.

Urban and Rural Conservatism

It might be argued that those who had the most to lose from a change in the religious structure were those who gained most from the control of the religious structure, which would make the conservatism of the urban elite a more important element in the resistance to Christianity than the

---

42. Lucian, *Alex.* 25, 38.

43. The case has been argued for Cynic influence on some Christian preachers, who by lifestyle or maxims, behaved or sounded like Cynics. Jesus and Paul both have been claimed. See, for example, the survey by F. Gerald Dowing, *Cynics, Paul and the Pauline Churches* (London: Routledge, 1998). And, of course, there is the work of John Dominic Crossan, *The Birth of Christianity* (San Francisco: HarperCollins, 1998). Crossan's work provoked a detailed critique by N. T. Wright. "A New Birth?" *SJT* 53 (2000): 72–91.

44. Lucian, *Alex.* 25.

supposed conservatism of the countryside. When confronted with a new and more powerful god, what is the risk to the average person, whose benefits from religion primarily lie in the area of physical and mental well-being and security, which Christianity promised as much as any of the gods in the marketplace?[45] But for the priests and the powerful, the established religion offered more than personal well-being. It offered a stable economic and political structure. Until the Constantinian revolution, Christianity could have offered little of that.

Further, the sword of "conservatism" cuts both ways. Even if the countryside was more conservative (which has yet to be established or really even defined for this context), should we conclude that the Christian message would have faced a stiffer resistance there than elsewhere? Or if a stiffer initial resistance, may that resistance not have been more easily overcome by the kind of emphases that marked early Christian contact? Some recent work on conversion has pointed to the importance of miracles and exorcisms in gaining conversions.[46] Such displays would have been at least as effective in the countryside as in the city, and perhaps more so. Indeed, it might be argued that the countryside would have been the easiest field for preaching success, where cult and priest often would have had fewer resources for such a battle. What happened when a Christian leader displayed some special power, either in a healing or exorcism, or in some other kind of challenge to a local priest or temple or to a local magician? If the local religion was seen to be discredited or if the local priest was converted or a local magician bested, what effect might this have on

---

45. There will always be some risk in conversion from the stigma of nonconformity and the potential jeopardy to social status. It is possible that the anonymity one might find in a city could help hide one's Christian affiliation, though we have no evidence to indicate that such anonymity caused Christian success in urban areas and denied it success in the countryside. Further, even for those in larger urban areas, individuals primarily lived their lives and found their identity in small neighborhoods. One did not live in a city; one lived in a neighborhood within a city that was probably not much larger than a village—not so different from urban life for most city-dwellers today.

46. Note here Ramsay MacMullen's work on the importance of miracles, healings, exorcisms, and supernatural kinds of encounters to the majority of individuals who sought aid from the Christian god and joined the Christian church [MacMullen, *Christianizing the Roman Empire (A.D. 100–400)* (New Haven: Yale University Press, 1984)]. See, too, MacMullen, "Conversion: A Historian's View," *SecCent* 5 (1985–1986): 67–81; and "Two Types of Conversion to Early Christianity," *VC* 37 (1983): 174–192. Not everyone agrees with MacMullen. For a discussion of MacMullen's work and opposition to it, see James A. Kelhoffer, *Miracle and Mission: the Authentication of Missionaries and Their Message in the Longer Ending of Mark* (Tübingen: Mohr Siebeck, 2000), 281–283.

the whole village? We know that pagan priests did convert to Christianity.[47] The conversion of one priest in a large urban temple may have had little impact on the overall religious state of affairs in the city, but the conversion of the lone priest of a local rural shrine must have made more than a slight religious ripple in the immediate area; indeed, it may have become a pivotal event for the community.

When we investigate Christian expansion in the countryside during the period for which evidence is plentiful, we find miracles and exorcisms and other kinds of encounters with the divine are treated as effective tools for conversion.[48] Indeed, even the most basic story Christians told about Jesus featured him as a healer and exorcist of considerable skill. Thus, both in message and method, Christians presented themselves as a source of relief for both mental and physical ailments, and they gained a reputation for a certain expertise in this regard, whatever the suspicions were about the source of that power. In the Greco-Roman mind, healings were possible, exorcisms were possible, divine encounters were possible, but one had to be careful to get the real thing, or at least to get it from a safe source.[49] Christian use of sorcery was one of the common charges brought against Christians to discredit their powers, as we learn from Celsus' fairly informed critique of the Christian movement.[50]

But how would this have worked at the level of the world as lived? Whatever the rumors and charges that may have circulated regarding Christian practice of harmful magic, once an individual, perhaps in great

---

47. Montanus was perhaps a priest, of either Apollo or Cybele, though the evidence may not be reliable [Antti Marjanen, "Montanism: Egalitarian Ecstatic 'New Prophecy,'" in *A Companion to Second-Century Christian "Heretics,"* ed. Antti Marjanen and Petri Luomanen (Leiden: Brill, 2008), 189]. The Acts story of Simon Magus (8:9–24) suggests that the conversion of individuals of some religious status was at least conceivable, though perhaps the story carries a note of warning about such conversions too.

48. MacMullen, *Christianizing the Roman Empire*, 26–29; 59–67; 107–113.

49. Although pagans might seek recourse in the aid available from such encounters with the divine, they also recognized that fraud and harmful magic might also be at play, so one had to be on one's guard. Indeed, pagan and Christian emperors alike outlawed what was considered harmful magic, and sorcerers (*maleficii*) were always under suspicion and at risk. Pagan critics of Christianity often addressed these kinds of practices within Christianity, accusing Christians of practicing magic and using trickery and deception. One such attack used the story of Jesus' flight to Egypt as a child to link Jesus to training in the magical arts of Egypt. See Hans Josef Klauck, *Magic and Paganism in Early Christianity: The World of the Acts of the Apostles*, Brian McNeil, trans. (Minneapolis: Fortress, 2003).

50. Origen, *Cels.* 1.6; 1.7.

need and desperation, sought Christian aid and as a result experienced some recovery of health or a regaining of hope from the Christian god, the barrier would have been broken and the individual's own testimony could have become a further tool in enhancing the reputation and attraction of the Christian movement. This would have been true of city or country.

MacMullen has detailed the importance of these aspects of Christian proclamation and practice in the majority of Christian conversions after Constantine, a period for which we have the bulk of evidence. Although the evidence from the earlier period is more spotty, there is nothing in the pre-Constantinian mentality that would have rendered these tools less effective, and certainly nothing in the rural mentality that would have made the Christian case impossible.

Linguistic Barriers

Somewhat related to the assumption of the conservative nature of the countryside is the assumption that outside of the walls of the Greek cities, native languages not only dominated but also threw up an effective linguistic barrier that the Christian message, which seemed more designed for Greek hearers and readers, was unable to break through.[51] This is one of the points that Meeks makes in support of his urban thesis.[52] But that view seems to exaggerate the nature of the linguistic barrier, as we will see.

Evidence for Christian Worship in the Rural Vernacular

Various considerations weaken the hypothesis that linguistic barriers prevented Christian penetration into the countryside. Such barriers, at best, apply only to certain areas. Surely in the areas of Achaia, the Aegean islands and the coast of Ionia, where Greek was largely the language of city

---

51. Bruce M. Metzger, *The Early Versions of the New Testament* (Oxford: Clarendon Press, 1977), 5. For a survey of native languages, see Ramsay MacMullen, "Provincial Languages in the Roman Empire," *AJP* 87.1 (1966): 1–17; and A. H. M. Jones, *The Greek City: From Alexander to Justinian* (Oxford: Clarendon Press, 1940), 281–295. The most linguistically diverse area seems to have been around the eastern part of the Black Sea. Strabo, *Geogr.* 11.2.16, is prepared to accept that some seventy different tribal languages were spoken in the port of Dioscurias (Sukhumi) but dismisses claims that some 300 languages were spoken there. Pliny the Elder (*Nat.* 6.5) notes that Timosthenes spoke of 300 languages there and that translators of 130 languages were available for conducting business. It was largely a ghost town in Pliny's time. Clement of Alexandria, *Strom.* 1.21 comments that Euphorus and other historians speak of seventy-five languages.

52. Meeks, *The First Urban Christians*, 15.

and countryside, Christianity was not disadvantaged by its adoption of Greek language and idiom. Similarly in Armenia (the first nation to adopt Christianity), Christianity would not have faced a greater linguistic barrier in reaching into the countryside than into the city, since both spoke the same language.[53]

Much the same situation would seem to be the case for areas of Syria, where the church adopted the native language as early as the second century, reflected in the writings of Syriac authors such as Tatian (c. 110–180 C.E.) and Bardesanes (c. 154–222 C.E.), and by a Syriac translation of the Hebrew Bible and a Syriac version of the gospels.[54] In Egypt, a similar situation may have held. The church there was quite willing to appropriate Coptic, the native language, quite early, though we cannot be as specific about when that happened.[55]

Thus, we have evidence of Christians using languages other than Greek for their literature as early as the second century. A reasonable assumption would be that use of a language in literature presupposes the use of that language more widely, in oral liturgical and non-liturgical contexts.

For other native languages, we must be cautious not to conclude that the church never gained a linguistic facility in such languages or that it never ventured to use these languages in a liturgical context. A lack of Christian texts in such languages tells us nothing, for many (if not most) of the native languages did not have a written script. Even for those that did, we cannot expect surviving evidence of the full linguistic diversity of early Christianity, which may have reached even to tribal languages.[56]

---

53. Vrej Nerses Nersessian, "Armenian Christianity," in *The Blackwell Companion to Eastern Christianity*, ed. Ken Perry (Oxford: Blackwell, 2007), 23–46.

54. The church at Edessa and two individuals, Tatian and Bardesanes, were the primary forces that promoted Syriac in the eastern church. Mani (210–276 C.E.) also wrote in Syriac (MacMullen, "Provincial Languages in the Roman Empire," 5–7). For a summary of the arguments about whether the original *Diatessaron* of Tatian was in Syriac or Greek, see William L. Petersen, *Tatian's* Diatessaron: *Its Creation, Dissemination, Significance, and History in Scholarship* (Leiden: Brill, 1994).

55. MacMullen, "Provincial Languages in the Roman Empire," 7, places the first translation of part of the New Testament into Coptic in the second century. See Roger S. Bagnall, *Early Christian Books in Egypt* (Princeton: Princeton University Press, 2009) for a broad discussion of Christian writings in Egypt.

56. For languages that had a script, we must recognize that very few artifacts of these written scripts survive, and where there are artifacts, generally these are inscriptions. We cannot say that such scripts would never have been used for Christian writing simply because we have no extant evidence, for we know from Syriac and Coptic writings that Christians did

Various comments by ancient Christian writers address the matter. About the middle of the second century, Justin commented:

> There is not a single race of human beings, barbarians, Greeks, or whatever name you please to call them, nomads (ἀμαξοβίων) or vagrants (ἀοίκων καλουμένων) or herdsmen living in tents (ἐν σκηνα ῖς κτηνοτρόφων εὐχαὶ), where prayers in the name of Jesus are not offered up.[57]

His point is that Christians can be found everywhere (from the rising of the sun to its setting, as he says), in contrast to the Jewish people, for there were nations in which Jews have never dwelt. Whatever we make of Justin's claim, it is hardly likely that the world of Christianity, as he understands it, was clustered in small enclaves in Greek-speaking urban centers. Justin seems to view Christianity as linguistically diverse, already having gained converts outside of Greek-speaking communities. One might say that Justin is exaggerating, or (more kindly) that he simply using a descriptive technique to say that Christianity is considerably widespread, but it is difficult to dismiss Justin's comment as having no merit at all, particularly when other writers around the same time also comment on the linguistic diversity of the Christian community, which is concretely confirmed by the existence of early Christian texts in a variety of languages.

Irenaeus is our most explicit witness to the linguistic diversity of early Christian communities, well beyond the use of Aramaic, Greek, Latin, Coptic, Armenian, and Syrian (languages concerning which there is no dispute about Christian use). Although Irenaeus' purpose is to argue for the uniformity of the Christian message and the faithful transmission of the Christian tradition, he does so in the context of the linguistic diversity of the peoples who have received the Christian message. He states:

> For although the languages of the world are varied, yet the meaning of the Christian tradition is one and the same. There is no whit of difference in what is believed or handed down by the churches

---

use written languages other than Greek quite early. That many texts have not survived would not be surprising. Such is a reality for most ancient texts, even for Greek and Latin ones. See Bagnall, *Early Christian Books in Egypt*, 16–21.

57. Justin, *Dial.* 117.

planted in Germany or in Iberia or in Gaul or in the East or in Egypt or in Libya or in the central region of the world.[58]

It is clear that Irenaeus is saying more than that the Christian message, though found in widely scattered places, is nonetheless uniform. Had he only said that, the Christian church, though widespread, could have been unilingual, centered in Greek-speaking or Latin-speaking immigrant communities established in areas where a native tongue was nonetheless dominant. But he said more than that. He said that the meaning of the Christian message was uniform, even though it was expressed in the varied languages of the world, and he reinforces that comment by listing specific areas where native languages were known to be spoken, or would be assumed to be spoken.[59]

However much we might feel justified in dismissing Irenaeus' assertion that Christianity had managed to maintain a uniformity in its belief over such a wide expanse of the empire,[60] Irenaeus' comments about the linguistic situation of the church deserve less skeptical treatment. He was a firsthand witness to the situation in Gaul, and he spoke of the church planted there functioning in the native language and of his use of that language himself.[61] Of other areas, he may have had less reliable

---

58. Irenaeus, *Haer.* 1.10.2. According to Chrysostom writing two centuries later, the Christian message is known by Persians, Indians, Scythians, Thracians, Sarmatian, and Moors (*Hom. Matt.* 80.2).

59. Thomas C. Oden, *Early Libyan Christianity* (Downers Grove, IL: IVP Academic, 2011), 63–64, makes the case that Irenaeus, in reference to Africa, was not referring only to the Latinized cities of North Africa, but to the native languages of the tribes settled more in the interior of the area.

60. The traditional view proclaimed by the early fathers of a unified and uniform church from the beginning has been widely rejected in the modern period. But that should not obscure the fact that the early church did manage to create a remarkable uniformity and unity in the context of their world, where religion was generally much more localized. The church, by developing creedal statements, a canon, councils at various levels, and an authoritative and tradition-bound clergy (especially the bishop), created tools that fostered unity and uniformity over a wide area. And they knew that they had done that. When they say that the Christian tradition "is one and the same everywhere," they are not unaware of Christian groups that are not part of that unity and uniformity; they are simply unwilling to accept these as a valid part of the considerable unity and uniformity that they had managed to create. Some may now find it distasteful that these Christians dismissed other Christian interpretations as heretical, but we should not at the same time dismiss the considerable unity and uniformity that the church managed to create—whether we like that kind of uniformity and unity—or not.

61. Irenaeus, *Haer.* 1. Preface 3; 1.10.2. How successful this mission was is another matter. Robert M. Grant, *Irenaeus of Lyons*, Early Church Fathers (London: Routledge, 1997), 5, stated

knowledge, but he was a well-traveled and informed church leader, who was respected by other church leaders as one of their more competent colleagues. Irenaeus certainly does not leave us with a sense that Christianity encountered insurmountable linguistic barriers when it left its urban, Greek-speaking environment—or even that the urban environment was always Greek-speaking.

It is perhaps important to note that where a script had already been developed for a language (as with Greek, Latin, Syriac, Coptic, and Aramaic), early Christians did not hesitate to record their message in written form in these languages. But we know that most of the tribes and peoples within or bordering the empire did not have a written script for their language.[62] For cultures without a written language, communication would have taken place orally, as indeed would have been the case for the most part even where a culture had a written script. Given that it is certain that early Christians appropriated the written script of diverse languages in order to communicate their message to non-Greek-speaking peoples, it is difficult to imagine any hesitation on the part of Christians to communicate the Christian message in languages lacking a written script. This conclusion is well supported by a variety of comments from ancient church leaders that suggest a linguistically diverse Christianity. Again from Irenaeus, we read:

> What if even the apostles had not left us writings? Would it not be necessary for us then to follow the course of that tradition which

---

that "The Celtic population remained resolutely non-Christian," pointing out that the names of martyrs in the area in 177 are largely Greek, some Latin, and none Celtic, and he calls attention to the involvement of the local barbarians in the persecution in the report on the matter from the sixth-century Gregory of Tours, details of which Gregory apparently gleaned from Eusebius (*Hist. eccl.* 5.1.57–58). This is a bleak beginning for the church there. Irenaeus tells a different story. He became bishop after the persecution and apparently lived there until his death perhaps twenty-five years later. And on his own account, he normally spoke the local language and at least some native Celtic speakers appear to have converted. That Irenaeus seems to have spoken Celtic in the context of the Christian assembly suggests that the assemblies in Lyons and Vienne were not constituted entirely of Christian immigrants from Asia Minor and Rome but had native members as well. It may also suggest that some (if not most) immigrant Greek-speaking or Latin-speaking members of the church had facility in the local language, unless separate meetings were held for the linguistically diverse groups, a situation that could be easily accommodated in a household-church setting.

62. William V. Harris, *Ancient Literacy* (Cambridge, MA: Harvard University Press, 1989), 177–193; Maryline Parca, "Local Languages and Native Cultures," in *Epigraphic Evidence: Ancient History from Inscriptions*, ed. John P. Bodel (London: Routledge, 2001), 57–72. There are examples of Greek characters being used in inscriptions that use the Phrygian language, and the Coptic script was developed from Greek characters.

they bequeathed to those in whose care they left the churches?—a course adhered to by many nations among the barbarians who believe in Christ, having salvation written in their hearts by the Spirit, without ink or paper.[63]

As we might expect of Irenaeus, the primary concern is with the uniformity of the Christian message throughout the world, and in this particular passage he has made a point about the written texts that form a basis for that unity.[64] Then he raises a hypothetical situation. Suppose the apostles had not left writings. Could there be uniformity? His answer is "yes." And how can he be so sure? He notes that there are Christians among the various barbarian nations who do not have the gospel message in written form in their language but they do have that message written in their hearts (*sine charta vel atramento scriptam habentes per Spiritum in cordibus suis salute*). For our purposes here, it appears that the Christian message had already penetrated to cultures whose language was not Greek, and it seems that some Christian communities conducted their Christian worship in the vernacular. I will not press that point here, since it is not the primary point that Irenaeus is attempting to make, but his argument is weakened if the situation he described was never encountered.

If we had only one comment about the linguistic diversity of early Christian communities, we might be tempted to set it to the side as an anomaly. But we have a number of comments from well-traveled and informed Christian leaders who speak quite naturally about the linguistic diversity of Christian communities, though these writers could have made their primary point in some other way. And, as we have already seen, we know of several languages in which Christianity functioned (both in written and spoken form) prior to Constantine. It would seem, then, that the matter of linguistic diversity of Christian communities was a widely shared assumption in the ancient church to which appeal could be made to support arguments regarding other matters. Any theory that native languages threw up an insurmountable barrier against the penetration of the Christian message into the countryside should be set aside or heavily qualified.

---

63. Irenaeus, *Haer.* 3.4.2.

64. Irenaeus is credited with developing the concept of apostolic succession as a principle of unity and uniformity (*Haer.* 3.3.1–3.5.3.

The theory that Christianity grew by attracting newly arrived rural residents in cities comes into play here. Such connections give the church an exposure to these surrounding native languages that other kinds of community groups, such as collegia and synagogues, would be less likely to have had.[65] I am assuming here that collegia would have consisted of members of similar backgrounds—perhaps ethnic and linguistic—and that an individual collegium normally would not have had affiliation with a larger network of collegia.[66] Much the same would have been the case with synagogues, for whatever the proportion of proselytes in the membership,

---

65. Explaining the local church in terms of collegia became trendy about two decades ago, though the idea has been around since the 1800s. While some of the parallels may be helpful and while the church may have used a recognized structure in society to facilitate their common assemblies, a number of matters weaken the comparison. The following is a short list. (1) Collegia generally met monthly; Christians met weekly (and maybe more often). (2) Collegia were generally associations of men; the church had a mixed membership. (3) Collegia tended to be independent and local, without a larger network; the church understood itself to be translocal, and each small assembly understood itself to be a member of a much larger universal church (a point I argue below). Robin Lane Fox, *Pagans and Christians* (New York: Alfred A. Knopf, 1987), 325, points out a number of other differences (size and inclusion of slaves), though in regard to size Lane Fox is considering the whole body of Christians in a city, not the individual house-churches. See, too, Wayne Meeks, "Social and Ecclesial Life of the Earliest Christians," in *The Cambridge History of Christianity*, vol. 1, *Origins to Constantine*, ed. Margaret Mary Mitchell and Frances Margaret Young (Cambridge: Cambridge University Press, 2006), 151–153. Some have contended that synagogues, too, were structured as collegia, but the parallel may not be entirely compelling for some of the same reasons [E. Mary Smallwood, *The Jews under Roman Rule: From Pompey to Diocletian* (Leiden: Brill, 1976), 133–136].

66. My position is at odds with Richard S. Ascough, "Translocal Relationships among Voluntary Associations and Early Christianity," *JECS* 5.2 (1997): 223–241, who has attempted, on the one hand, to show translocal connections of some collegia and, on the other hand, to minimize the translocal sense that local Christian groups had. Although Ascough provides a useful review of the debate, the overall weakness of his position is that he attempts too much with too little. Certainly it is a stretch to take the hesitation of some in Paul's churches to support the Jerusalem collection as suggestive of a lack of translocal consciousness (237). On another matter, we do know that by the second century Christian leaders were coming together from wide areas to work out their common interests. We know, too, that many Christian writers wrote against what they judged to be peculiar forms of Christianity. Such action reflects some interest beyond their local assembly and some identity with others more distant who could be considered within the broadest orbit of Christianity. Other writers reflect a similar sense of association with churches at some distance and expect these churches to have similar sensibilities. See, for example, the letters of Ignatius to various churches (Ephesus, Magnesia, Tralles, Philadelphia, Smyrna, Rome), and Ignatius' expectation that these churches (and others, *Phld.* 10.2) will make contact with (by letter or visit) or pray for his church in Antioch (Ign. *Phld.* 10.1–2; *Smyrn.* 11.2–3; *Pol.* 7.1–3; *Eph.* 21.2; *Magn.* 14.1; *Trall.* 13.1; *Rom.* 9.1). Also, these letters reflect translocal connections among the churches in Asia that had hosted or had visited with Ignatius (*Magn.* 14.1; *Trall.* 13.1; *Phld.* 11.1–2; *Smyrn.* 12.1), as well as connections to other churches

synagogues would have had a significant ethnic Jewish component already in place, and in most areas of the empire, Greek would have been the functioning language of the synagogue.

The Christian church was different. Even in urban areas, it would likely have had a greater mix of the local languages if it drew many of its members from the class of recently arrived rural immigrants or immigrants from abroad.[67] Further, churches, unlike synagogues, would not have had a countering balance to this new linguistic element that the synagogue would have had.[68] This would have challenged concepts of ethnic and linguistic identity and would have helped to develop views within Christianity of what was foreign and outside one's circle. If any urban group was likely to have some positive connections to rural residents and an ability to overcome whatever barriers the languages of the countryside may have presented—which is our concern here—it seems that the Christian church was a better candidate than most urban groups, given the possibility, if not likelihood, of a somewhat greater linguistic and cultural mix in their membership.

(*Pol.* 8.1). Further, we have a striking passage of translocal Christian connections in the first century that Ascough passes over in silence. The author of Colossians (2:1; 4:13–16) speaks of churches in three towns and assumes connections and communications among them (Colossae, Laodicea, and Hierapolis). That, of course, does not mean that Christian assemblies could not have passed as collegia at the local level. As for translocal connection of non-Christian and non-Jewish collegia, we might well expect immigrants of like language and locale to group together and even to maintain some links to their homeland, particularly if they were traders, but unless most collegia were made up of immigrants with common background and resources, who came together to maintain distant links and traditions, what we determine about such collegia should not be offered as a template for the typical collegium in cities, which would not have consisted mainly of immigrants. For more comprehensive work on associations, see Philip A. Harland, *Associations, Synagogues, and Congregations: Claiming a Place in Ancient Mediterranean Society* (Minneapolis: Fortress, 2003).

67. Migrants from the nearby countryside would have shared a common native and local language, but immigrants from more distant areas would have brought a wider diversity.

68. It is possible that some house-churches may have reflected a particular cultural or linguistic background, especially given the household setting of most of the early Christian communities, where a family residence was used for meetings. There the core membership would have probably consisted of individuals associated with that household—family members, servants, and clients or others external to the family but in some way associated with it. I suspect that it would have been possible to find the occasional house-church conversing in a language other than Greek, even in cities dominated by the Greek language. Yet, even if some house-churches—or even most—had some mark of ethnic or linguistic identity, members of these small household units would have had a sense that they had a broader and more primary identity as members of the *Church*. This gave Christians a different sense of their identity than members of most collegia would have had.

Some contend that native languages were a vehicle of dissent, heresy, and nationalism, particularly for North Africa and Egypt.[69] The observation may have some merit, though both A. H. M. Jones and Ramsay MacMullen have shown how problematic the theory is in specific cases.[70] From a completely different angle, over a century ago Karl Holl, one of the leading German historians of early Christianity, argued that inhabitants of the countryside could find themselves alienated from the empire, and some were thus attracted to Christianity, particularly in Africa, Egypt, and Phrygia.[71] He also argued that Greek was not as dominant as had been thought, pointing to evidence for the late survival of native languages. Frank Trombley dismisses Holl's conclusions except for Africa.[72] But for our purposes, the primary question is whether Christianity was able to overcome linguistic barriers. It does not matter whether such success happened everywhere, or whether a normative or schismatic form of Christianity had success in the countryside, for if the linguistic barrier was breached in some places by some Christian groups, then the case is at least made that it could happen, and the possibility of early Christian penetration into the countryside cannot, then, be simply dismissed out of hand. If native languages came to be used by Christians (even dissenting or heretical ones), then the Christian message, in one form or another, had managed to overcome whatever barrier the linguistic differences had presented.[73]

Bilingualism

Further, the supposed linguistic barrier between city and countryside would have been far less serious in areas where bilingualism was widespread, and a number of recent studies have focused on that matter. Warren Treadgold points out that Greek was gradually making progress

---

69. See chapter 8.

70. A. H. M. Jones, "Were Ancient Heresies National or Social Movements in Disguise?" *JTS* 10.2 (1959): 280–298; MacMullen, "Provincial Languages in the Roman Empire," 13–15.

71. Karl Holl, "Das Fortleben der Volksprachen in Kleinasien in nachchristlicher Zeit," *Hermes* 43 (1908): 240–254.

72. Frank Trombley, "Overview: The Geographical Spread of Christianity," in *The Cambridge History of Christianity*, vol. 1, *Origins to Constantine*, ed. Margaret Mary Mitchell and Frances Margaret Young (Cambridge: Cambridge University Press, 2006), 312.

73. I argue later that the attempt to dismiss rural Christianity as abnormal or antagonistic to urban Christianity is problematic at various levels (chapter 8).

into some rural areas, and he offers a map of the areas where Greek was either the dominant language or widely spoken.[74] J. N. Adams notes that bilingualism was thought to be more common than monolingualism, and he provides the first extensive study of bilingualism in the Roman Empire.[75] Mark Janse offers a detailed study of bilingualism, showing that as Greek increasingly became dominant, some languages died out, though others managed to survive. Janse examines a number of passages where natives spoke Greek (sometimes with a heavy accent), as well as their native tongue.[76] E. G. Clark rejects the assumption that "someone leaving the city walls entered a different language environment."[77] Donald Engels argues that native speakers did not resist Greek language or culture, pointing out that farmers not only came to the city to sell their produce but had sufficient surplus to buy goods too, at least in the centuries of our concern.[78] Further, Macedonian and Greek soldiers frequently married local women,[79] and Roman soldiers, though forbidden to marry while in active service, often established families with native women, and settled with their families upon their discharge from the army.[80] These alliances would have weakened to some degree any linguistic barrier originally in place.

---

74. Warren T. Treadgold, *A History of the Byzantine State and Society* (Stanford, CA: Stanford University Press, 1997), 5–7. Although Treadgold's map is for a date around 284 C.E. (selected because that is when he starts his history), it is clear that the map applies as well to an earlier period. There is nothing in the crisis of the third century that would account for a rapid rise in the spread of Greek. Greek had been in the area as the language of the rulers and the elite for about six hundred years stemming from the conquests of Alexander, and some communication in that language would have been necessary from the start.

75. J. N. Adams, *Bilingualism and the Latin Language* (Cambridge: Cambridge University Press, 2003), 1.

76. Mark Janse, "Aspects of Bilingualism in the History of the Greek Language," in *Aspects of Bilingualism in the History of the Greek Language*, ed. J. N. Adams, Mark Janse, and Simon Swain (Oxford: Oxford University Press, 2002), 332–390.

77. E. G. Clark, "Pastoral Care: Town and Country in Late-Antique Preaching," in *Urban Centers and Rural Contexts in Late Antiquity*, ed. Thomas S. Burns and John W. Eadie (East Lansing: Michigan State University Press, 2001), 268.

78. Donald W. Engels, *Roman Corinth: An Alternative Model for the Classical City* (Chicago: University of Chicago Press, 1990), 132. For a more detailed discussion of the urban–rural relationship, see Dennis P. Kehoe, *Law and the Rural Economy in the Roman Empire* (Ann Arbor: University of Michigan Press, 2007).

79. A. H. M. Jones, *Cities of the Eastern Roman Provinces* (Oxford: Clarendon Press, 1937), 313.

80. Richard Alston, *Soldier and Society in Roman Egypt: A Social History* (London: Routledge, 1995); Sara Elise Phang, *The Marriage of Roman Soldiers (13 B.C.–A.D. 235): Law and Family in the Imperial Army*, Columbia Studies in the Classical Tradition 24 (Leiden: Brill, 2001).

Some have noted the bilingualism of special areas. For example, the case has been made for considerable bilingualism for many areas of Syria.[81] Some think a case can be made for widespread bilingualism in North Africa.[82] And in Egypt we find Greeks living in Egyptian towns and villages.[83] The reality was that the urban and the rural areas had a dependency on each other, and communication of some kind had to be established. The easiest way to bridge any linguistic barrier was to learn the necessary language for exchange. In other words, some people would have needed to be bilingual, and in so far as such ability was a key to more successful exchange, the more likely that a greater number of people would have been bilingual.

Some level of bilingualism seems to be assumed by the author of Acts for cities in the orbit of Paul's mission. According to the author, Barnabas and Paul visited a number of the cities of Lycaonia.[84] In one of these, Lystra, the crowd was stirred by the apostles' preaching and resulting miracle and responded in their native dialect. Whatever one makes of the historicity of the story, the author, who seems relatively informed about his world, speaks of residents of a city able to converse both in Greek (the language of Paul's preaching) and in their native dialect. For our purposes, this story is helpful in pointing out that bilingual speakers of native languages could have had access to the Christian message even if the Christian message had not been ported over to their native tongue. Further, if native languages were retained along with Greek by residents of towns and cities (as is suggested by the Acts story), then the language barrier that supposedly prevented the spread of the Christian message to the countryside simply would not have existed in many areas. Even were we to take the Lystra situation portrayed in Acts as somewhat of an anomaly or a fictional creation of the author, it is unlikely that there is no correspondence to the reality on the ground.[85] Whatever the

81. Fergus Millar, *The Roman Near East* (Cambridge, MA: Harvard University Press, 1993), 232–234.

82. In North Africa, Latin would have been the dominant language of government and culture, but also a language used to some degree by the native population as well [Peter Brown, "Christianity and Local Culture in Late Roman Africa," *JRS* 58 (1968): 85–95].

83. Jones, *Cities of the Eastern Roman Provinces*, 308–309. That does not mean that there would have been widespread facility in Greek throughout the Egyptian countryside, but it does show that the links between language and locale were not without nuance.

84. Acts 14:6–20.

85. Dean P. Béchard, "Paul among the Rustics: The Lystran Episode (Acts 14:8–20) and Lucan Apologetic," *CBQ* 63 (2001): 84–101, has treated the Lystra episode in detail, seeing it

author's purpose for including the Lystra episode, there is some sense that the rural empire or at least the non-Greek-speaking element is as much a domain of Christian interest as the urban Greek-speaking empire.

Perhaps a similar sentiment is expressed elsewhere in Acts, in the account of Peter's sermon on the feast of Pentecost. The author lists some fifteen territories where Jews then living in Jerusalem once had lived, and he assumes that such Jews would have understood the native language of these diverse areas. However much the author may have been driven by his theological interest to make the linguistic event on the feast of Pentecost as sweeping as possible, the author betrays no sense of a linguistic barrier that separated diaspora Jews from the native tongues in regions where they had settled. He, at least, thinks his story makes sense.[86]

Sang-Il Lee has made an extensive study of bilingualism in the period and has concluded that both Jews and Christians often had proficiency not just in Greek or Aramaic but in vernacular languages as well.[87] Peter Brown has made the case that bilingualism was widespread in North Africa, with Christianity helping to spread Latin literacy throughout the area.[88] Such wide evidence for bilingualism would put the Acts accounts, however fictional or shaped to the author's needs, into an intelligible, real world of Christian experience, where bilingualism was not abnormal.

W. H. C. Frend has worked with an interesting and rare rural inscription that may shed some light on the bilingualism of villages in Phrygia, one area where Christianity had considerable rural success.[89] The inscription deals with a legal decision regarding a dispute between two villages concerning their obligations to supply transportation for the imperial post.

---

as the author's attempt to set the Christian message in two quite different environments that one might encounter in the Hellenistic world: that of intellectual and cultured Athens and that of the remote and rustic hinterland of Lycaonian settlements. Luke Timothy Johnson, *The Acts of the Apostles*, Sacra Pagina 5 (Collegeville, MN: Liturgical Press, 1992), 247–248, speaks of the reference to the native dialect serving a "dramatic function" for the author. It could serve as that (and, no doubt, did), but that it has no correspondence to the linguistic realities of areas of the empire is unlikely.

86. Acts 2:6–11. Whatever the controversies about this passage, multiple intelligible languages are featured.

87. Sang-Il Lee, *Jesus and Gospel Traditions in Bilingual Context: A Study in the Interdirectionality of Language* (Berlin: Walter de Gruyter, 2012); G. H. R. Horsley, "The Fiction of 'Jewish Greek,'" *NewDocs* 5 (1989): 5–40.

88. Brown, "Christianity and Local Culture in Late Roman Africa," 85–95.

89. W. H. C. Frend, "A Third-Century Inscription Relating to Angareia in Phrygia," *JRS* 46 (1956): 46–56.

The inscription records both Latin and Greek parts of the proceedings. Frend sees the inscription providing evidence that the language of these villagers was Greek.[90]

Phrygia brings another kind of evidence of bilingualism, where there exists a wealth of epitaphs, many in Phrygian and many in Greek.[91] Many of the Greek epitaphs bear the "Christians for Christians" inscription that has been associated with rural Phrygian Christianity[92] or perhaps more specifically with Montanism.[93] Village familiarity with Greek may also be reflected in Montanist use of Greek. At least, it does not appear that the first Montanists, village dwellers of Phrygia, could not use Greek or that they preferred to use some form of Phrygian.[94] So, too, with the village bishops in the area who were opposed to the Montanists.[95] Indeed, it may be that in some regions of Phrygia the native language had faded completely, as Greek took over.[96] In such areas, the linguistic barrier to the Christian message simply did not exist.

---

90. Frend, "A Third-Century Inscription Relating to Angareia in Phrygia," 56.

91. Only a few of the Christian ones are in Phrygian (using Greek characters). Gary J. Johnson, *Early-Christian Epitaphs from Anatolia* (Atlanta: Scholars Press, 1995), 1.

92. Trombley, "Overview: The Geographical Spread of Christianity," 312, notes that many of these inscriptions are of urban residents whose burial is in the countryside. He recognizes the difficulty of estimating the number of rural Christians, which he counts as a "small minority, perhaps 5–10 percent." But even those numbers would give 2.6 to 5.1 million rural Christians in an empire that had, supposedly, only 6 million Christians in total. This "small minority" of the rural area would constitute an "overwhelming majority" of the Christians in the empire, a matter that Trombley does not note or address.

93. William Tabbernee, "Asia Minor and Cyprus," in *Early Christianity in Contexts: An Exploration across Cultures and Contexts*, ed. William Tabbernee (Grand Rapids, MI: Baker Academic, 2014), 271, cautions about accepting the widespread view that such inscriptions were Montanist, pointing out that nothing locates Montanists to the area of these inscriptions.

94. Christine Trevett, *Montanism: Gender, Authority and the New Prophecy* (Cambridge: Cambridge University Press, 1996), 18. William Tabbernee, *Montanist Inscriptions and Testimonia: Epigraphic Sources Illustrating the History of Montanism*, North American Patristic Society Patristic Monograph Series 16 (Macon, GA: Mercer University Press, 1997), provides a near-exhaustive list of possible Montanist inscriptions. Even the earliest Montanist inscriptions from Phrygia are in Greek (51–104).

95. Zoticus of Cumane and Julian of Apamea (Eusebius, *Hist. eccl.* 5.16.17). The language of these bishops is not stated, but given the overwhelming evidence that Montanism in small towns and villages used Greek from the start, it is reasonable to assume that non-Montanist bishops from neighboring villages used Greek too, thus removing at least for this area a linguistic barrier to Christian expansion into the countryside. On the other hand, if these bishops spoke some dialect of the native language of the area, the linguistic barrier for Christianity would seem to have been overcome.

96. Trevett, *Montanism*, 18.

In further support for links of communication between Greek and the native languages spoken in the countryside is that, as we have seen, many ancient cities (if not most) required a regular influx of dwellers from the countryside in order to maintain a stable population in the city, which would otherwise have been in deficit.[97] If this is indeed the case, then we must be cautious when we speak of the urban character of the city as somehow void of rural sensibilities and enclaves or that there was an effective linguistic barrier between the city and the countryside. Although such newcomers to the city would have needed to adapt to their new environment, much of their rural character would have remained intact, including the retention of their native language. Indeed, it is likely that the rural influx into the city would have helped to open a channel of exchange between Greek and the native languages, as rural newcomers gained some greater facility in Greek from the influence of their urban environment.

Rather than speaking of a linguistic barrier that separated city from countryside and which posed an obstacle to Christian mission, we should recognize the opposite—a linguistic highway (or a donkey trail, at any rate) that would have been created as rural folk moved to the cities, quite apart from those farmers who had always lived in cities while tending their land beyond the walls. If any of these newcomers converted to Christianity, such individuals could have provided potentially strong and effective links to the countryside for Christianity. These new city residents, recently arrived from the countryside, would have shared in both worlds, the urban and the rural, and many would have maintained some links with their families in the country. Indeed, some of these rural dwellers who had taken up residence in the city may well have returned at some point to the countryside. Converts with these kinds of connection to the countryside could have provided a powerful link for the church to extend its reach. Whether Christianity took advantage of such links is another matter, but the supposed barrier that prevented such penetration cannot be simply asserted.

Further, whatever we make of the bilingualism of specific areas, widespread bilingualism is not required for Christian success in the

---

97. See section "Supplying the Cities with People" in chapter 5 for more detailed discussion. See, too, Willem Jongman, "Slavery and the Growth of Rome: The Transformation of Italy in the Second and First Centuries BCE," in *Rome the Cosmopolis*, ed. Catharine Edwards and Greg Woolf (Cambridge: Cambridge University Press, 2006), 106–109. Although Jongman examines Rome, in particular, he sees the situation being similar for most large cities, due to the higher urban mortality rates in cities.

countryside. All that is really necessary is one zealous bilingual convert, who can then proclaim the Christian message in his or her native tongue.

In light of these various observations, the hypothesis of linguistic obstacles preventing Christian advance into the countryside has merit, at best, only for particular areas of the empire. It is not, even remotely, a general condition. The oft-repeated pronouncement that the language of the early church was Greek needs to be more carefully stated, for it is usually connected to the contention that early Christianity was almost exclusively an urban movement and that Hellenistic Greek-speaking cities were the primary locale of the movement. The matter clearly is considerably more nuanced than that.

Urban Dislocation and Religious Conversion

Another erroneous assumption behind the "urban thesis" is that new religious movements need the dislocation created by the city in order to germinate and thrive. Meeks mentions the alienation and "status inconsistency" that members of Paul's community would have experienced in the city.[98] Stark and his followers develop this idea in various ways.[99] Stark points out that "a very considerable proportion of the population consisted of recent newcomers—Greco-Roman cities were peopled by strangers."[100] Many of these newly arrived people from the countryside would have lost essential social networks as a result of their move, according to Stark. This loss would have left newcomers to the city alienated and alone in the midst of impersonalized urban throngs, making the recently arrived ripe for the picking by a religious movement such as Christianity or Judaism. It is out of this dislocation of the city—whether experienced by newcomers (Stark) or by longtime residents of ambiguous or undervalued status (Meeks)—that Christianity drew its converts.

Although there may be merit in seeing opportunities for Christian mission in the dislocations of the city, such dislocation should not be taken as a *necessary* factor for conversion in the city, and it certainly should not be taken to exclude the likelihood of conversions in the countryside, where

---

98. Meeks, *The First Urban Christians*, 55, 191.

99. Stark, *The Rise of Christianity*, particularly in chapter 7: "Urban Chaos and Crisis: The Case of Antioch," 147–162. Stark recognizes the significance of Meeks' reconstruction to his own focus on Christianity as an urban movement.

100. Stark, *The Rise of Christianity*, 156.

other factors might have played a role in conversion. At best, urban alienation and dislocation might account for a higher rate of conversion in the
urban environment compared to a supposedly more tightly knit countryside, though even that would need to be established, not merely assumed.

Further, the unfavorable portraits of city life upon which theories of
urban dislocation and alienation depend can be easily exaggerated, especially in light of our modern expectations and sensitivities, a point that
Bruce Malina and Jerome Neyrey made specifically against Meeks' work.[101]
Along similar lines, I have criticized Stark and Zetterholm for their bleak
assessment of life in ancient Antioch.[102]

One of the problems of reconstructions like that of Stark is that he
fails to note how self-defeating his argument is to his overall thesis of a
largely urban church. If cities needed to be repopulated constantly with
an influx from the countryside, a large element of the urban population
would have had considerable links with the rural world. Stark's scenario
in which Christians were particularly successful among recent newcomers to the city creates a situation in which the Christian mission would
have had natural, obvious, and exploitable networks into the countryside.[103] Although Stark is happy to exploit Christian use of networks when
they provide links to Jewish communities,[104] he fails to note the considerable networks that must have linked Christianity to the countryside, if,
as he claims, large numbers of urban converts were recent arrivals from
the countryside. Such rural contacts make Stark's urban portrait of early
Christianity appear inadequately nuanced, though Stark is correct to call
attention to rural newcomers in the urban mix.

Conscious of this rural/urban mix, Stark makes one small qualification
to his overall view that the early church did not make serious efforts to convert the rural peasantry for several centuries. He admits that "many [rural
inhabitants] were converted by friends and kinfolk returning from urban
sojourns."[105] This is an important point, but Stark does not follow through

---

101. Bruce J. Malina and Jerome H. Neyrey, *Portraits of Paul: An Archaeology of Ancient Personality* (Louisville, KY: Westminster/John Knox Press, 1996), 14.

102. Thomas A. Robinson, *Ignatius of Antioch and the Parting of the Ways: Early Jewish-Christian Relations* (Grand Rapids, MI: Baker Academic, 2009), 62.

103. See, too, John H. Elliot, *Home for the Homeless: A Social-Scientific Criticism of I Peter, Its Situation and Strategy* (Minneapolis: Fortress, 1990), 48.

104. Stark, *The Rise of Christianity*, 49–71.

105. Stark, *Cities of God*, 26.

on what these networks and links might mean for Christian growth in rural areas. For someone who has built much of his thesis regarding the expansion of early Christianity on the importance of networks, Stark had a vehicle for exploring Christian growth in the countryside that he failed to use.

Meeks' use of status inconsistency is focused on urban life and aspirations, and Meeks thinks that the Christian church provided a world in which such status inconsistency might be reduced or resolved, though within a smaller circle. The problem of that view is that the Christian movement in its early period would have magnified status inconsistency rather than muted it, as critics of Meeks have pointed out.[106] At best, Meeks' theory might explain why some people who were raised in the Christian movement remained in the church. Meeks' theory cannot explain why people of status inconsistency joined the Christian movement prior to Christianity itself gaining status within the larger society.

Urban Views of Rural Inhabitants

Stark quotes with approval the dismissive views of Richard Fletcher, who had contended that urban Christians would have viewed the rural world beyond their walls as subhuman and would have taken little or no interest in the conversion of the dwellers there, for that, supposedly, was the view that all ancient urban dwellers had.[107] Granted, the attitude of urbanites to the rustics of the countryside may well have reflected a disdain and a sense of superiority.[108] Ramsay MacMullen colorfully describes the urban view of the rustic: "clumsy, brutish, ignorant, uncivilized."[109] And Fletcher is equally colorful in his depiction of the urban perception of rustics: "They were dirty and smelly, unkempt, inarticulate, uncouth, misshapen by toil, living in

---

106. Bruce W. Longenecker, "Socio-economic Profiling of the First Urban Christians," in *After the First Urban Christians: The Socio-Scientific Study of Pauline Christianity Twenty-Five Years Later*, ed. Todd D. Still and David G. Horrell (London: T & T Clark, 2009), 54–58.

107. Richard A. Fletcher, *The Barbarian Conversion: From Paganism to Christianity* (New York: H. Holt and Co., 1998; Berkeley: University of California Press, 1999), 16; Stark, *Cities of God*, 26. Note that Fletcher does express some caution about the sharp line often drawn by scholars between city and countryside, particularly in the eastern provinces (15–16). Stark does not recognize that Fletcher exempted the eastern empire from such a marked dichotomy, the very area where Stark needed it to work.

108. Fletcher, *The Barbarian Conversion*, 16.

109. MacMullen, *Roman Social Relations*, 15.

conditions of unbelievable squalor, as brutish as the beasts they tended."[110] Paul Erdkamp captures a slightly less dismissive attitude of the town folk toward rural inhabitants: they were "boorish and ignorant simpletons, at best as naïve and unspoiled."[111] And rustics would have had their own contempt for the affectations of city folk: "baffling, extortionate, arrogant," in MacMullen's words.[112] Whether the classic tale of the country mouse and the city mouse provides some evidence of links and attitudes between city and rural people or just between rodents, I leave to the judgment of others.[113]

But such stark lines between city and countryside or between the attitudes expressed by the inhabitants of these domains probably were somewhat more nuanced. Although the urban and rural worlds were often presented as antithetical, it was not always the city that was viewed as superior.[114] Indeed, cities were filled with urban rabble, and this throng offered no more delight to the urban elite than did country rustics.[115] And comments in the ancient literature that seem to be dismissive of rural culture often appear to be more of a foil against which to mock some perceived deficiency in an urban comrade or competitor. Consider Catullus' dismissal of Suffenus, who, though urban, wrote atrocious poetry. He is described as "stupider than the stupid countryside" (*idem infaceto est infacetior rure*).[116] Even the polished city-dweller might appear a little rustic if he made some slip in grammar.[117] And there is the flip side of that urban image of the

---

110. Fletcher, *The Barbarian Conversion*, 16.

111. Paul Erdkamp, "Urbanism," in *The Cambridge Companion to the Roman Economy*, ed. Walter Scheidel (Cambridge: Cambridge University Press, 2012), 241.

112. MacMullen, *Roman Social Relations*, 15.

113. The story, originally told by Aesop, was retold by Horace, *Sat.* 9.6.79–117 (in Latin) and by Babrius (in Greek).

114. See Penelope J. Goodman, *The Roman City and Its Periphery: From Rome to Gaul* (London: Routledge, 2007), 9–10. MacMullen, *Roman Social Relations*, 28–32, notes that Greco-Romans writers could express contradictory views of the countryside from one writing to another, and he judges the praise of the countryside reflected in these writers as somewhat idealized.

115. For a review of views of city life from the perspective of some of the writers of the time, see chapter 11 of John E. Stambaugh, *The Ancient Roman City* (Baltimore, MD: Johns Hopkins University Press, 1988), 183–197.

116. Catullus, *Carmen* 22.14.

117. MacMullen, *Roman Social Relations*, 30–32, points to a few passages where how one spoke was an important marker of the true urbanite. One did not want to ever sound rustic. MacMullen points further to a number of ancient comments about the ridiculousness of

rural. As Wallace-Hadrill points out, the rustic was both mocked *and* ideal-ized, for there was a prominent strain in Roman sensibilities that elevated rustic morals over that of the city and that traced traditional Roman moral values back to the countryside.[118]

In many ways, the distinction made between urban and rural is more often misleading than it is helpful. It would perhaps be much more ac-curate, and considerably more significant, to speak of the distinction be-tween the urbane and the rustic, both of whom might be found in the countryside or in the city. MacMullen draws a similar line, pointing out that the cleavage that counted was "a matter not of place...but of civiliza-tion...of culture."[119] And, of course, there would be a middle ground, or as Strabo calls them, the "semi-rustics."[120]

My attempt to argue for some rustic coloring in the Christian member-ship is not an attempt to specify the primary complexion of the Christian church, where proposals have run the gamut from the poor, to a supposed "middle class," to "the connected."[121] My more minimalist effort here is simply to try to remove the urban/rural barrier that has marked much of scholarship. The matter of the social status of early Christians will con-tinue to be debated, but what should not be a matter of much debate is that there would have been many of rustic character in the urban church, for that is the kind of resident that made up a sizeable segment of cities—not just of the countryside. Certainty we must exercise caution when we use

a farmer trying to pass himself off as an urbanite, where speech and grace would betray him (30–31). MacMullen also mentions that when Cicero wanted to dismiss his enemies, he called them "rustic and country folk" (30).

118. Andrew Wallace-Hadrill, "Elites and Trade in the Roman Town," in *City and Country in the Ancient World*, ed. John Rich and Andrew Wallace-Hadrill (London: Routledge, 1991), 244–249.

119. MacMullen, *Paganism in the Roman Empire*, 8.

120. Strabo, *Geogr.* 13.1.25, following ideas of Plato, notes the three types: τῶν ἀγροίκων καὶ μεσαγροίκων καὶ πολιτικῶν, based on whether they lived in the mountains, foothills, or plains, and particularly on the plains near the sea, or on islands. H. L. Jones, LCL, translates this as "rustic and semi-rustic and civilized." MacMullen, *Roman Social Relations*, 31, trans-lates the phrases "rustics, semi-rustics, and the inhabitants of cities."

121. Many have spoken of a shift in the scholarly view of the complexion of the Christian movement, from one emphasizing the poor to one seeing a broad cross-section of society (often with an emphasis, it seems, on a middle class). See, for example, Meeks, *First Urban Christians*, 52–53, and Rodney Stark, *The Rise of Christianity* (Princeton: Princeton University Press, 1996), 29–33. But Steven J. Friesen, "Poverty in Pauline Studies: Beyond the So-Called New Consensus," *JSNT* 26 (2004): 323–361, challenges such a sketch of the supposedly chang-ing view in scholarship by setting these modern comments and concerns in their modern

the difference between city and countryside and the attitudes of each to the other as near-insurmountable barriers to Christian attempts to spread its message to the countryside. For one thing, however much the typical Greco-Roman urbanite may have looked down on rural dwellers, we cannot assume that Christians shared this dismissive attitude, or if they shared it, that such an attitude was not challenged within the Christian community. As Gerald Downing reminds us: "whatever the tensions generally between town and country there is no sign of any hard cultural barrier among Christians."[122]

That is not to say that some urban Christians did not share an elitist view of the urban over the rural.[123] We know that Christianity did not challenge everything about their culture—they were not, for the most part, anarchists and revolutionaries. But the Christian message itself did constitute, at some level, a challenge to the attitudes and actions of the wider populace. Christians were critics of the world in which they lived, and they modified or were encouraged to modify their conduct in light of

---

historical context. Longenecker, "Socio-economic Profiling of the First Urban Christians," 36–59, reviews the matter and argues against Meeks downplaying the poor in the Pauline assemblies (41); see, too, Longenecker, "Good News for the Poor: Jesus, Paul and Jerusalem," in *Jesus and Paul Reconnected*, ed. Todd D. Still (Grand Rapids, MI: Eerdmans, 2007), 37–66. As to the upper echelons of society ("the connected"), many now argue that Paul did have connections to the ruling elite. See, for example, Andrew Clarke, *Secular and Christian Leadership in Corinth: a Socio-historical and Exegetical Study of 1 Corinthians 1–6* (Leiden: Brill, 1993). The matter is complicated by talk of a "middle class," which Meeks sometimes does, and which was done even earlier by H. Hill, *The Roman Middle Class in the Republican Period* (Oxford: Basil Blackwell, 1952). This is roughly what Friesen, "Poverty in Pauline Studies," 341, labels ES4 on his seven-part scale. John Barclay, "Poverty in Pauline Studies: A Response to Steven Friesen," *JSNT* 26 (2004): 363–366, dismisses some of what Friesen has to say but recognizes the importance of the effort. Many are quite cautious about positing a middle class. See MacMullen, *Roman Social Relations*, 88–120; Peter Garnsey and Richard Saller, *Roman Empire: Economy, Society and Culture* (London: Gerald Duckworth & Co., 1987), 45, 116. For a brief review of the issues, see Emanuel Mayer, *The Ancient Middle Classes: Urban Life and Aesthetics in the Roman Empire 100 BCE–250 CE* (Cambridge, MA: Harvard University Press, 2012), 1–21. For a detailed discussion of the urban poor, see L. L. Welborn, "The Polis and the Poor: Reconstructing Social Relations from Different Genres of Evidence," in *The First Urban Churches*, vol. 1, *Methodological Foundations*, ed. James R. Harrison and L. L. Welborn (Atlanta: SBL Press, 2015), 189–243.

122. F. Gerald Downing, *Cynics and Christian Origins* (Edinburgh: T & T Clark, 1992), 93.

123. MacMullen, *Roman Social Relations*, 31, points out that Gregory of Nazianzus, *Oration* 2.29, recognized the considerable difference between those of the city (ἀστικοί) and those of the countryside (ἀγροικία). But, in context, Gregory's comment need not be seen as a dismissal of the countryside, as must Strabo's comment, quoted by MacMullen in the same discussion. Gregory points to several differences: between the married and the unmarried; between the anchorite and the cenobite; between men of business and men of leisure, among various other pairings. That one element of each pairing must be negative is not clear; it need only be different.

their new sensibilities. Certainly it seems too hasty to conclude that the urban church would have had no interest in the countryside, as Fletcher asserts:

> The peasantry of the countryside were beyond the pale, a tribe apart, outsiders. Such attitudes underpinned the failure of the urban Christian communities to reach out and spread the gospel in the countryside. We might regard this lack of initiative as negligent. But such an accusation would probably have bewildered the urban Christians. For them the countryside simply did not exist as a zone for missionary enterprise. After all, there was nothing in the New Testament about spreading the Word to the beasts of the field.[124]

Fletcher surely is exaggerating, perhaps for effect.[125] But his statement has too much hyperbole to be helpful. Granted, we cannot simply assume that Christian teaching affected the views of urban members regarding the countryside, changing the attitudes of urban Christians from a haughty contempt of rustics to a bond of friendship—if, indeed, that had been the negative view that every urbanite carried. But neither can we simply assume an unchallenged, deep-seated contempt for peasants and villagers within the urban church either. Indeed, if Stark is correct that Christianity drew many of its members from rural newcomers to the city, one might point to the constitution of the church's membership as evidence that the attitudes of at least some urbanites had changed, as they were willing to have rustics join with them in a common assembly and brotherhood. Again, a comment by Gerald Downing is worth noting: "urban Christian communities receive as authoritative rural Christian tradition and, presumably, welcome migrant rural country people into their fellowship ... by and large stories of a rural Jesus preserved by rural congregations make good enough sense with their discernible rustic flavour largely intact, among Greek-speaking city-dwellers."[126] But it was not just in story that urban Christians would have encountered rural followers of Jesus; they encountered rustics in substance too, within their own assemblies.

---

124. Fletcher, *The Barbarian Conversion*, 16. Stark is impressed with Fletcher's comment here and quotes it at length in his *Cities of God*, 26.

125. Fletcher, *The Barbarian Conversion*, 15, does recognize some rural Christian presence.

126. Downing, *Cynics and Christian Origins*, 93.

We get a glimpse of the consciousness of a realignment of social boundaries in many of the early Christian texts, from comments such as Paul's that "there is no longer Jew or Greek,"[127] which is repeated and expanded by the author of Colossians to "there is no longer Greek and Jew . . . barbarian, Scythian,"[128] and, in the second century, to a claim that Christians were a third race—made by both Christians and non-Christians.[129] Of course, as is often pointed out, these revolutionary statements are set in a series of revolutionary statements, such as "neither slave nor free," and "neither male or female," and a breakdown of these categories clearly was not the reality of early Christian experience. As Martin Goodman points out, "in practical terms the existing social structure was taken for granted."[130] Yet, however idealized these early Christian statements might have been, we do know that Christian leaders did see the Christian faith changing the relationship between master and slave and between husband and wife in positive ways. That there was also a positive adjustment in the attitude to the rustic and the barbarian is probable, and, given the likelihood of rustics within the church, indeed seems almost certain and necessary.[131]

In fact, some Christian writers made the Christian interest in the poor and the uneducated a noble quality rather than a discrediting one. Responding to Celsus' criticism of the lack of literary merits of Christian writings compared to the writings of Greek philosophers, Origen stands the value system for judging literature on its head. He comments that it is the literature that can be understood by the simple person that has the most merit, noting the contrast between Christian preachers and pagan philosophers:

> Now we maintain, that if it is the object of the ambassadors of the truth to confer benefits upon the greatest possible number, and, so far as they can, to win over to its side, through their love to men,

---

127. Gal 3:28.

128. Col 3:11.

129. For a discussion of some of the issues, see Denise Kimber Buell, *Why This New Race: Ethnic Reasoning in Early Christianity* (New York: Columbia University Press, 2005).

130. Martin Goodman, *The Roman World 44 B.C.–180 A.D.* (London: Routledge, 1997), 322.

131. Phlm 1:16; Eph 5:33; 6:9; Col 4:1; Ign. *Pol.* 4.3; 5.1; *Did.* 5.10; *Barn.* 19.7, to list but a few. More important are the numerous direct and uncompromising orders to show generosity to the poor and the needy and to the widows and orphans (Jas 1:27; *1 Clem.* 8.4, 15.6, 38.2; Ign. *Smyrn.* 6.2; Pol. *Phil* 6.1; ; *Barn.* 20.2; Herm. *Sim.* 1.27; Justin, *1 Apol.* 67) along with

every one without exception—intelligent as well as simple—not Greeks only, but also Barbarians (and great, indeed, is the humanity which should succeed in converting the rustic [ἀγροικοτάτους] and the ignorant [ἰδιώτας]), it is manifest that they must adopt a style of address fitted to do good to all, and to gain over to them men of every sort. Those, on the other hand, who turn away from the ignorant as being mere slaves, and unable to understand the flowing periods of a polished and logical discourse, and so devote their attention solely to such as have been brought up amongst literary pursuits, confine their views of the public good within very strait and narrow limits.[132]

Even were we tempted to dismiss these comments as mere rhetoric—on what grounds is not clear—such kinds of comments would have had some effect, softening somewhat Christian attitudes to the rustic and the downtrodden.

The Christian church did seem to attract some, and perhaps many, of the socially insignificant into their membership. One routine criticism of the Christian community was the number of uneducated rustics who were attracted to Christianity.[133] While such language possibly was little more than an attempt to discredit Christians by slinging mud at them, it is likely that there was some substance to the criticism, particularly if newly arrived country residents made up a segment of the membership of most city churches. Christian authors themselves certainly did not try to counter the charge by denying the accusation that rustics were part of their membership. Indeed, somewhat the opposite. For Origen, the mixed complexion of the membership of Christian churches was a reality, and he never disparaged members whose understanding or education might be judged deficient by critics. He willingly concedes that the number of the simple and ignorant Christians outnumber the more intelligent. That, he says, is how things are in the larger society.[134] He challenges Celsus that it is not the wicked who are won over to the Christian side but, rather, "the more

commands not to be haughty (Gal 5:26; Jas 4:6; 1 Pet 5:5). That does not mean that snobbery did not raise its head within Christian assemblies. We know that it did. But we also know that church leaders tried to check this behavior, and though it is unlikely that everyone complied, the mere addressing of the problem by church leaders would have had some effect.

132. Origen, *Cels.* 6.1.

133. Minucius Felix, *Oct.* 12.

134. Origen, *Cels.* 1.27; 29; 3.55–58; 4.10, 49, 50, 52; 5.15, 19; 6.1, 14; 7:41, 59; 60.

simple class of person, and, as many would term them, the unpolished."[135] And he points out that, depending on the composition of the audience, the Christian preacher or teacher would modify their talk to the level of the hearers, even if that meant a simple exposition, or what he calls "milk."[136] Although some of Origen's defense of the simple is really a defense of the unpolished language of the Christian scriptures, it is difficult to set these passages aside as unreflective of the makeup of the Christian assembly.

Conclusion

In the next chapter, we will see that most scholars allow for the beginning of Christian success in the countryside in the latter half of the third century. If the Christian message was able to win converts at that time among the supposedly conservative countryside, there would seem to be no compelling reason not to allow the same receptiveness to the Christian message earlier. As we have seen in this chapter, the factors often presented as obstacles to a rural mission cannot carry the weight put on them.

---

135. Origen, *Cels.* 3.78. The word used here is (κομψοί), which, in context, must be an error, and the intended word the opposite (ἀκομψοι) (3.52). On another matter, besides the dismissal of the rustic character of members of the Christian churches, it appears that critics sometimes dismissed Christianity because its founder was born in a village to a poor, working woman (1.29). But there was another side of the story. In the conclusion, I point to Origen's admission that there were people of previous wicked behavior who have joined the church and had been, to a greater or lesser degree, reformed.

136. Origen, *Cels.* 3.52.

7

The Pre-Constantinian Evidence

Finding Evidence

We know far more about urban life in the Roman Empire than about rural life. That is not because the empire was largely urban—it was not. It is because the literary elite were urban, and no matter how much they might have enjoyed escaping from the overpowering stench, clamor, and crush of the city to their airy rural estates, their writings generally reflect an urban sensibility. We know less about the rural empire because less was written about it and less survived from it. The same might be said for rural Christianity, if, of course, we can establish that there was a rural Christianity.

Other matters further limit our data. Most of Christian growth in the first three centuries occurred in the eastern part of the Roman Empire and in lands to the east of the empire, but it was not an even growth. Christianity's success varied, being spotty in some places and sweeping in others. Thus, in many ways ancient evidence available often depends on chance finds, as the Dead Sea Scrolls and Nag Hammadi materials remind us, and we cannot extrapolate from what we have found—nor from what we have not found—as to what the larger situation must have looked like. Further, the various kinds of evidence used in reconstructing the ancient world is more limited for Christianity, for almost nothing remains of early Christian buildings and little of early Christian art for the period of our study.[1] Somewhat more material comes from inscriptions,

---

1. The church at Dura Europos is the only clearly identifiable Christian building before the year 300 for which we have archaeological remains. See Graydon F. Snyder, *Ante Pacem: Archaeological Evidence of Church Life before Constantine*, 2nd ed. (Macon, GA: Mercer University Press, 2003), 128–209. We know that there were other church buildings before Constantine, since the Edict of Milan orders the return of Christian assembly places that had

most of which are epitaphs, and for the pre-Constantinian period concentrated in one small area.[2] Little of this tells us much about Christianity in the countryside—or in the city, for that matter. Further complicating our investigation, much of archaeological interest has been in the urban landscape and with monumental structures, which benefits neither the countryside and its less durable remains, nor the areas of cities where urban Christians might have resided and assembled.

What we do have in some quantity are literary remains. It is here that we find clear evidence for Christianity in the pre-Constantinian world. A few documents are from pagan writers; most of the literature, however, is from Christian sources. Although those sources are extensive, such material was hardly designed to tell us where Christianity was located, even indirectly. Most of the sources are for internal consumption, dealing with issues of theological import or community behavior, though some are perhaps for external use too, directed sometimes at Judaism and sometimes in defensive mode against slander from the larger society. It would be an arduous task to sort through all of this material for the occasional comment about the urban or rural dimension of Christianity.

Fortunately, such a task has already been done over a hundred years ago by Adolf Harnack, one of the leading historians of early Christianity. Harnack provided a detailed listing of all references that in some way indicated the spread of Christianity in the Roman Empire prior to Constantine.[3]

---

been confiscated. L. Michael White, *The Social Origins of Christian Architecture*, vol. 1, *Building God's House in the Roman World: Architectural Adaptation among Pagans, Jews and Christians* (Valley Forge, PA: Trinity Press, 1990), 127–139, discusses the building boom in Christian churches *prior to* Constantine's conversion, where larger assembly halls were constructed from the ground up or substantially renovated from older structures. One such structure, set among some large (and wealthy) houses, was visible from Diocletian's imperial palace in Nicomedia. But it could be destroyed "in a few hours," which White takes to indicate that it was not approaching anything like the basilicas that were shortly to come (130). Except for the house-church at Dura Europos, which was preserved because it was located along the walls of the city and came to be buried in an effort to strengthen the city's defenses, any other church buildings that may have existed prior to Constantine were unlikely to have been substantial enough or distinctive enough to have survived as identifiable Christian artifacts.

2. Roderic L. Mullen, *The Expansion of Christianity: A Gazetteer of Its First Three Centuries* (Leiden: Brill, 2004), 2–4, discusses the kinds of evidence available. Recognizing that the primary evidence is literary, Mullen points also to papyri, inscriptions, and archaeological materials. But such evidence is not massive for the pre-Constantinian period and almost nonexistent for the years before 250 C.E.

3. Adolf Harnack, *The Mission and Expansion of Christianity in the First Three Centuries*, trans. and ed. James Moffatt, 2nd ed. (London: Williams and Norgate, 1908), 2.1–32. Note that in the first edition (1905), the corresponding pages are numbered 147–182. This material is part

Such a compilation of the evidence had not been done before, and Harnack's effort still stands as the primary reservoir of such material.[4] That evidence has been updated and sometimes corrected by the recent works of Roderic Mullen and William Tabbernee.[5] In many ways, however, Harnack's work is still the best introduction into the field, since he provided each text in its original language (Greek or Latin), accompanied by an English translation. And Harnack provided a judicial reading of these texts, carefully sorting through what had clear rhetorical exaggeration. His judgment on the significance of each passage shows a mind sharply aware of the need to read the sources with a certain skepticism at times, recognizing how the need of the moment may have conditioned what each author said, a caution we all need to be reminded of from time to time, although it is interesting how selective we can be in finding exaggeration.[6]

---

of what is called "book 4," which is part of volume 2 of the German original. The entire book 4 (over three hundred pages) is a rich resource for evidence of the presence and spread of Christianity up to 325.

4. For a judicial treatment of Harnack's contribution and a defense of Harnack against some of the recent criticism, see Jan N. Bremmer, *The Rise of Christianity through the Eyes of Gibbon, Harnack and Rodney Stark*, 2nd ed. (Groningen: Barkhuis, 2010), 24–47. See, too, Ian H. Henderson, "Mission and Ritual: Revisiting Harnack's 'Mission and Expansion of Christianity,'" in *The Changing Face of Judaism, Christianity and Other Greco-Roman Religions in Antiquity*, ed. Ian H. Henderson and Gerbern S. Oegema, Studien zu den Jüdischen Schriften aus hellenistisch-römischer Zeit 2 (Gütersloh: Gütersloher Verlagshaus, 2006), 34–56. Henderson discusses Meeks and Stark too.

5. Mullen, *The Expansion of Christianity*; William Tabbernee, ed., *Early Christianity in Contexts: An Exploration across Cultures and Continents* (Grand Rapids, MI: Baker Academic, 2014).

6. Harnack, *The Mission and Expansion of Christianity*, II.1–22, offered scores passages from ancient documents that speak in some way to the size or spread of the Christian population up to the time of Constantine. He then explored the rhetorical context of those passages, particularly those he felt that must be used with more caution (II.22–32). He did so to show that many of the comments about early Christian success are too sweeping and exaggerated. Ludwig Friedländer, *Roman Life and Manners under the Early Empire*, vol. 3, trans. J. H. Freese (London: George Routledge & Sons, 1908–1913), 206, writing the original German version of his work a few years before Harnack, shared with Harnack a sense of the exaggerated claims put forward in some of these ancient passages. But, as Friedländer pointed out regarding Origen's comment that Christians were "very few" in terms of their proportion of the population of the empire, an author could exaggerate "in the other direction." And Bremmer, *The Rise of Christianity through the Eyes of Gibbon, Harnack and Rodney Stark*, 65, notes that this one comment of Origen is often focused on, disregarding the various other comments Origen made to the contrary. Granted, most scholars are skeptical of the comments made by early Christian writers about the success and extent of Christianity, for these early Christian writers generally either simply assumed that Christianity was widespread or wished to present Christianity as widespread. There is certainly wisdom in taking some of these ancient comments with a grain of salt.

Harnack's collection of sources relates to the presence of Christianity in the empire, whether urban or rural. I will not examine each passage listed by Harnack, since I am interested only in those passages that might illuminate the state of Christianity in the countryside prior to Constantine. Even some passages that may be relevant to Christianity in rural areas need to be set aside or used with considerable qualification, such as passages that simply state that Christianity had spread throughout the empire. Although the author may have understood Christianity as having both rural and urban presence, such comments are too general to be a basis for asserting a rural Christian presence. It is probable, however, that some of the authors of such comments did intend to include a rural element in their view, a likelihood suggested by the existence of a number of passages from the period that state explicitly that Christianity was present in both rural and urban areas. It is to these more explicit passages that we now turn, though the more general passages should not be dismissed as having no value.

The primary problem of the evidence is how little of it addresses the matter of interest in this present study. Although we have a vast quantity of Christian literature prior to Constantine, its purpose is not to provide a list of all the places in which Christianity had established itself, and certainly not to provide—even as an aside—a list of rural settlements. Such information, when provided, is generally peripheral to the main purpose of the writing and leaves us only with a scant and coincidental sketch of the presence of Christianity, even for urban centers, where attention has often been focused. Even so, Harnack is able to list about a thousand districts, cities, towns, and villages where some reference to Christianity can be found by the early 300s. Most of these sites are within the Roman Empire. Many of the locales are identified because of the mention of a church official, generally a bishop, who was associated with the place, or a martyr identified by his or her hometown. The lists of bishops in attendance at some of the early councils also add to our knowledge of Christian presence

---

But we can become too cautious, failing to note that even writers with a clear intention to make a point may well have had some bases for the point being made. Further, to dismiss such statements outright, particularly when we have similar kinds of statements made when there is no particular intent by the writer to address the extent of Christianity, seems to reflect an overzealous skepticism in regard to our ancient sources. That point is strengthened further when we note that Christian literature often takes it as a given that pagan neighbors have a similar sense of the presence of Christians in both city and countryside.

in the empire.[7] In addition, the names of a good number of the locales identified by Harnack are drawn from the work of ecclesiastical historians of the period or slightly later, such as Eusebius (*c.* 260–*c.* 340), Socrates (*c.* 380–*c.* 440), Sozomen (*c.* 400–*c.* 450), and Theodoret (*c.* 390–*c.* 460).

The Great Divide: 250 *C.E.*

Although it is common to speak of Christianity as an urban movement prior to Constantine, most scholars who study the period in depth recognize that a rural Christianity was already present by the time of Constantine's ascension to power, and present in significant numbers. As we will see, evidence of Christian congregations in rural areas comes from throughout the empire by the early 300s. What almost every scholar does with this evidence is to assert that this rural Christianity was a recent phenomenon, taking root in the countryside no earlier than the middle of the third century. By restricting the establishment of Christianity in the countryside to this late period, the first two centuries of Christianity can still be spoken of as almost fully urban. Although I will criticize reconstructions that place the origin of rural Christianity in the middle of the third century, I recognize that such theories are considerably more nuanced and insightful than the view one often hears expounded that delays the initial Christian effort in rural areas largely to the reign of Constantine or later.

Claims that rural Christianity was not established until some two hundred years after the birth of Christianity must be examined closely, for such assertions provide the crucial structure upon which the urban thesis depends. Richard Fletcher, although following the trend to place the rise of rural Christianity in the third century, admits that the reasons for Christian efforts to convert the countryside in the third century have never been satisfactorily answered.[8] Perhaps there is a reason for that. Maybe rural Christianity did not begin in the third century—but earlier—a matter that has been given almost no attention in scholarship on the expansion of early Christianity.

---

7. See Mark Humphries, "The West (1): Italy, Gaul, and Spain," in *The Oxford Handbook of Early Christian Studies*, ed. Susan Ashbrook Harvey and David G. Hunter (Oxford: Oxford University Press, 2008), 285–289, for a cautious reflection on how such kinds of evidence should be used (and not used) in reconstructing the spread of Christianity in the early period.

8. Richard A. Fletcher, *The Barbarian Conversion: From Paganism to Christianity* (Berkeley: University of California Press, 1999), 37.

W. H. C. Frend has been a major player in discussions regarding the rise of rural Christianity. He offers, on the one hand, strong statements in support of the "urban thesis" and, on the other, a wide range of evidence for a considerable rural Christian population prior to Constantine. Frend even argues that it is largely because of the Christian success in the countryside *prior to Constantine* that the church was able to survive the Great Persecution.[9] He is able to maintain both positions by placing the Christian success in the countryside in the latter half of the third century[10]—or the last two decades of that century as he says in one place.[11] Prior to that, the "urban thesis" would hold, according to Frend.

In the discussions following, I will examine the theories of Frend and others that have been offered as explanations of the beginnings of a Christian presence in the countryside in the latter half of the third century. I contend that each reconstruction raises more questions than it answers. If the current explanations for the late establishment of Christianity in the countryside fail, then we will be forced either to seek other late roots for rural Christianity or to look for the roots of rural Christianity in an even earlier period.

Theories of the Origins of a Rural Christianity
Imperial Crises and the Weakening of Paganism

In one work, Frend pinpoints the time of the change of Christianity's fortunes in the countryside. It was the Decian persecution that supposedly marked a "watershed." Frend claimed that "Christianity had been slow to make an impact on the rural population of the empire,"[12] but success came because of a general weakening of traditional paganism in the third century as the empire was shaken by crisis after crisis.[13] Such a world of

---

9. W. H. C. Frend, "The Failure of the Persecutions in the Roman Empire," in *Studies in Ancient History*, ed. M. I. Finley, Past and Present Series (London: Routledge and Kegan Paul, 1974), 276–277; 285–286.

10. W. H. C. Frend, "The Winning of the Countryside," *JEH* 18 (1967): 5.

11. W. H. C. Frend, "Town and Countryside in Early Christianity," in *The Church in Town and Countryside*, ed. Derek Baker (Oxford: Basil Blackwell, 1979), 39.

12. W. H. C. Frend, *The Rise of Christianity* (Philadelphia: Fortress, 1984), 421.

13. The matter of a third-century crisis, or a series of crises, was once widely accepted and one still finds the idea routinely repeated in general works on the Roman Empire. But a number of historians of the ancient period are expressing reservation and offering more nuanced

insecurity supposedly made people largely disillusioned with the traditional gods, and the Christian message became an easier sell to those experiencing a religious void and discontent. The theory of religious discontent was most prominently espoused by E. R. Dodds in his short book *Pagan and Christian in an Age of Anxiety: Some Aspects of Religious Experience from Marcus Aurelius to Constantine.*[14] Many adopt Dodds' explanation, finding some degree of Christian success in the crises in the empire.[15]

Such a characterization of a debilitated paganism or of an empire in crisis recently has been challenged by scholars such as Ramsay MacMullen and others.[16] MacMullen has offered a portrait of a vital and revered paganism well into the 300s, explaining away what had been offered as evidence of a dying paganism. MacMullen is particularly dismissive of Franz Cumont and Dodds. MacMullen mocks Cumont's assessment of the third century: "what sense does it make to assign a single character to so long an era?—as if one were to say, 'in Italy, Switzerland, the low countries, Britain, France and Spain between about 1400 and 1600, people were tense and worried.' "[17] With only slightly more restrained dismissal, Peter Brown

---

assessments of the period. See Olivier Hekster, Gerda de Kleijn, and Daniëlle Slootjes, *Crises and the Roman Empire: Proceedings of the Seventh Workshop of the International Network Impact of Empire* (Leiden: Brill, 2007); Pat Southern, *The Roman Empire from Severus to Constantine* (London: Routledge, 2001). Thomas S. Burns and John W. Eadie, eds., *Urban Centers and Rural Contexts in Late Antiquity* (East Lansing: Michigan State University Press, 2001), xiv, speak of the crises as "far more ephemeral than contemporary literature would have us believe." For the counter-view that the crisis had wide impact, see Lukas De Blois, "The Crisis of the Third Century A.D. in the Roman Empire: A Modern Myth?" in *The Transformation of Economic Life under the Roman Empire*, ed. Lukas De Blois and John Rich (Leiden: Brill, 2002), 204–217. For a summary of the debate, see Wolf Liebeschuetz, "Was There a Crisis of the Third Century," in *Crises and the Roman Empire*, ed. Olivier Hekster, Gerda de Kleijn, and Daniëlle Slootje (Leiden: Brill, 2007), 11–20. For other recent works on the subject, see Adrin Goldsworthy, *How Rome Fell* (New Haven: Yale University Press, 2009), 48n3.

14. E. R. Dodds, *Pagan and Christian in an Age of Anxiety: Some Aspects of Religious Experience from Marcus Aurelius to Constantine* (Cambridge: Cambridge University Press, 1965).

15. For example, Stephen Mitchell, *Anatolia: Land, Men, and Gods in Asia Minor* (Oxford: Clarendon Press: 1993), II.55–56, uses somewhat dramatic language to describe the third century: "strains and stresses to which the empire was subject," "the troubled years of the third century," and "the collapse of local civic life."

16. Frend, "The Failure of the Persecutions in the Roman Empire," 277–279. For a review of the history of the discussion, see Philip A. Harland, "The Declining Polis? Religious Rivalries in Ancient Civic Context," in *Religious Rivalries in the Early Roman Empire and the Rise of Christianity*, ed. Leif E. Vaage (Waterloo, ON: Wilfrid Laurier University Press, 2006), 28–35.

17. Ramsay MacMullen, *Paganism in the Roman Empire* (New Haven: Yale University Press, 1981), 123.

takes on Dodds and Frend for their use of the "anxiety" thesis.[18] Drawing similar conclusions, Averil Cameron comments that "nearly all the individual components of the concept of 'third-century crisis' have been challenged in recent years." She concludes: "if the crisis was less severe than had been thought, then the degree of change between the second and the fourth centuries may have been less exaggerated too."[19]

That is not to deny that there were crises in this period. But it is clear that the impact of the crises did not hit with the same intensity everywhere. Christianity prospered quite well during the third century in North Africa, an area of the empire largely spared of such crises—quite contrary to what would be expected under the "anxiety" thesis.[20] The same seems to hold for areas of Asia Minor. Rural communities in Asia Minor, too, were "relatively untouched" by these crises, Stephen Mitchell argues, speaking specifically of regions of Phrygia, another area where Christians prospered.[21] Such gains of adherents in these areas run counter to the general kind of explanation that Frend, Dodds, and others have offered for the Christian success in the countryside, where conversions supposedly were produced by crises. However probable such theories might seem, the reality on the ground seems to run counter to the expectations.

Further, the impact of these third-century crises on any rural population must not be exaggerated.[22] At least, we should not merely assume that there would have been a change to the conditions of rural life of sufficient dimension to suddenly make Christianity attractive to the countryside, so that rustics flooded into the church in mass. Rural life was hard enough at the best of times. Little that was controllable lay between hunger and harvest. Fate was fickle, and good fortune did not regularly visit one's door. Life would have been lived largely from year to year, if not for many from

---

18. Peter Brown, "Approaches to the Religious Crisis of the Third Century A.D.," *EHR* 83 (1968): 542–558.

19. Averil Cameron, *The Later Roman Empire* (Cambridge, MA: Harvard University Press, 1993), 3.

20. David J. Mattingly and R. Bruce Hitchner, "Roman Africa: An Archaeological Review," *JRS* 85 (1995): 176, state that the military crises in third-century Africa has been overstated. Also see Leslie Dossey, *Peasant and Empire in Christian North Africa* (Berkeley: University of California Press, 2010), though much of that work is focused on the fourth and fifth centuries.

21. Mitchell, *Anatolia*, 1.239.

22. Mitchell, *Anatolia*, 1.239, argues that "the decline or 'crisis' of the third century was primarily an urban phenomenon, which did little to trouble the country districts."

day to day. If it were crises that made Christianity attractive to rustics, rustics should have been lining up to join at almost every period in the history of the early Christian movement. A series of decade-long crises would not have been necessary to provoke such a move.

Finally, we must be careful not to assume that increased worries and an increased level of insecurity would have driven people to seek another religious option. Indeed, a crisis might well have caused an individual or a community to intensify its devotion to the traditional gods, thus dislike and suspicion of Christianity might actually have intensified in times of crises. Tertullian put the matter bluntly:

> If the Tiber rises so high it floods the walls, or the Nile so low it doesn't flood the fields, if the earth opens, or the heavens don't, if there is famine, if there is plague, instantly the howl goes up, "The Christians to the lion!" What, all of them? to a single lion?"[23]

Rather than making Christianity look more attractive to pagan neighbors, crises could, at least according to Tertullian, bring Christians under suspicion and attack. If the Christian community felt the brunt of such response, such crises far more likely would have produced flight *from* the church than a flood *into* the church.

Persecution

But what of Tertullian's famous assertion that the blood of martyrs is seed, causing the church to grow? This may have been more a reflection of hope than of reality, though Tertullian was not the only one to hold that view.[24] Yet for every pagan who joined Christianity as a result of viewing some martyrdom, there may have been scores who fled from the church in terror, making far more ex-Christians than fresh Christians, for we do have clear evidence of significant apostasy during persecutions but few stories of conversions.[25]

---

23. Tertullian, *Apol.* 40.

24. Tertullian, *Apol.* 48–50.

25. The problem of apostasy under persecution is most fully documented in Cyprian, *On the Lapsed*, where he deals with results from the Decian persecution. The problem arose again after the Great Persecution of Diocletian. See Graeme Clarke, "Third-Century Christianity," *CAH*, vol. 12, *The Crisis of Empire, A.D. 193–337* (Cambridge: Cambridge University Press,

There is another way to approach the matter of persecution as an agent of church growth, and this has allowed some scholars to use the experience of persecution to explain the establishment of a rural Christian presence in the empire prior to Constantine. In connecting rural Christianity to persecution, a church in the countryside can still be delayed to the middle of the third century, when more organized and empire-wide persecutions were initiated.

Marilyn Dunn, for example, has offered persecution as a key factor in the establishment of a rural Christian presence in Egypt. She suggests that it was the Decian persecution that was most responsible for placing Christians in rural areas, through deportation.[26] But Dunn's explanation for the origin of a rural Christianity in Egypt seems neither early enough nor necessary. For one thing, exile would not have brought Christians into contact with the countryside for the first time. As we have seen, city and countryside flowed into one another, and the countryside was never a domain isolated from urban contact. Therefore, there is nothing radically new about Christians having contact with non-urban areas.

Further, exile would have been largely disruptive to the ones exiled, if the befuddlement of Bishop Dionysius is any indicator.[27] The Decian persecution seems to have caught the church off guard, and the response of the church was largely disorganized and chaotic.[28] Although some stood firm and suffered execution or exile, many apostatized, and many in cities fled in fear to the countryside to hide. It is hardly likely that such Christians—not forced into exile for confessing Christ but fleeing the city to escape any jeopardy from such a confession—would have suddenly become bold, preaching the gospel in their places of retreat and concealment in the countryside. The new hostile environment of exile and displacement hardly seems a likely setting from which to launch a rural mission if more settled and day-to-day contacts with the countryside had never prompted a rural concern. Further, although the place of exile was not always remote, we have evidence that leaders, at least, were sometimes

2008), 634–635; Stuart George Hall, "Ecclesiology Forged in the Wake of Persecution," in *The Cambridge History of Christianity*, vol. 1, *Origins to Constantine*, ed. Margaret Mary Mitchell and Frances Margaret Young (Cambridge: Cambridge University Press, 2006), 415–433.

26. Marilyn Dunn, *The Emergence of Monasticism: From the Desert Fathers to the Early Middle Ages* (Oxford: Blackwell, 2000), 5–6.

27. Eusebius, *Hist. eccl.* 6.40.

28. Eusebius, *Hist. eccl.* 6.42.

sent to desolate and distant places, hardly the place from which a rural mission could spread broadly.[29]

Finally, the persecution was brief, about one year.[30] Thus, many exiles may have been able to return to their homes within a few weeks or months of having been deported, providing little time to get their bearings in the countryside, let alone establish enduring rural and Coptic Christian assemblies. While some converts were made from such contacts, nothing suggests an explosive success of Christian advance in the countryside stemming from these kinds of persecution.[31]

Imperial Toleration

Frend points to another factor for the rural success of Christianity: the tolerant position taken toward the church by Emperor Gallienus in 260, who restored church property and gave the church a *religio licita* status.[32] But Frend expects too much from this new imperial attitude. A new toleration for the church can explain, at best, a more rapid conversion of the *urban* populace, where a successful mission already had been established. It cannot account for an *initial* rural success, for there is nothing in any pre-Constantinian imperial toleration of Christianity that would have inspired or propelled such rural transformation. Only if the rural populace already had been attracted to Christianity but dissuaded from joining because of fear of persecution would the end of persecution have created a wave of rural conversions. A mere imperial disinterest in Christianity, or a toleration of it, simply does not have the power to explain a transformed attitude of the countryside to the Christian option. Such disinterest in and toleration of Christianity by the authorities existed at most times in the empire, with fierce persecution being the exceptional and generally quite localized situation that Christians only sometimes encountered, whether in urban areas or rural.

---

29. Dionysius was first exiled to a town a short distance from Alexandria (Eusebius, *Hist. eccl.* 7.11.5), but Dionysius and two companions ended up in a remote settlement: "a lonely, parched spot, a three-day journey from Paraetonium," which itself was about 300 km from Alexandria (7.11.14–17).

30. Clarke, "Third-Century Christianity," 627–628. Persecution was perhaps a little longer in Egypt than elsewhere (Eusebius, *Hist. eccl.* 6.41.1).

31. Dionysius mentions a few converts (*Hist. eccl.* 7.11.13–14), but there is no hint that he suddenly saw in such conversions a new rural horizon of mission.

32. Frend, "The Failure of the Persecutions in the Roman Empire," 275.

Increasing Social Status of Bishops

As an explanation of a new Christian interest in the countryside, Richard Fletcher suggests that as bishops came to be elected from more wealthy or influential members of the society, possibly some of these bishops took an interest in the peasantry on their rural estates. Others in the church may then have been inspired by such examples to cultivate a similar concern for the rural population.[33]

But if we assume that bishops had that kind of interest in their rural workers, any wealthy Christian with rural holdings might have a similar interest—without the bishop's initiative. If wealthy Christians could have that kind of interest, poorer Christians, with family connections to the countryside, might have had similar concerns. If it is argued that wealthy bishops had both the means and the authority to shape the first successful rural missions, we would need to explain the rural successes that do not have such connections, particularly when some rural Christian groups have, according to some scholars, an anti-urban or at least an anti-establishment mood.[34]

Even granting Fletcher's reconstruction, the question might be raised whether we have a sufficient contingent of such bishops, with both land and interest, to account for rapid expansion of the church into rural areas in the latter half of the third century, when even defenders of the urban thesis generally admit a rural Christian presence. Further, the examples of bishops with rural interests that Fletcher puts forward come from the late fourth century and later (Chrysostom, Augustine, Martin of Tours).[35] This is too late to explain third-century rural success.

Making Romans out of Rurals

Fletcher also offers another possible motivation for the beginnings of a Christian interest in the countryside in the third century. He argues that there was a near-identification within Christianity of *Romanitas* with *Christianitas*. In fact, such identification is somewhat a mantra for Fletcher. It is not simply Christianity's alliance with the empire that Fletcher notes;

---

33. Richard A. Fletcher, *The Barbarian Conversion: From Paganism to Christianity* (Berkeley: University of California Press, 1999), 38.

34. See chapter 8.

35. Fletcher, *The Barbarian Conversion*, 39–40.

it is the related but reverse exclusion of the barbarians that is, supposedly, part of this Christian–Roman identity.[36]

According to Fletcher, only when Emperor Caracalla widely extended Roman citizenship to all free men in 212 C.E. did Christians (who apparently identified closely with Rome) supposedly become interested in the countryside now populated with newly minted Roman citizens.[37] If this kind of explanation has any merit at all, it would seem a far better explanation for a fourth-century Christian interest in the countryside, when the empire and Christianity are much more formally linked. But that would be too late as an explanation for the initiation of rural missions in the third century, which is the explanation we need here.

Further, that the expansion of Roman citizenship had much (if anything) to do with creating a Christian interest in the countryside is rendered unlikely for at least two reasons. One, early Christians had a variety of senses of their citizenship: they were a third race, they were strangers and pilgrims in the present world, they were the true or new Israel, they were citizens of heaven.[38] That they sensed themselves to be Roman above all else does not strike one as the most obvious identity they drew to themselves. And, two, whatever alliance or affinity that may have developed between the church and the empire from Constantine onward, even then the Church would have been forced to think of itself as encompassing an expanse greater than the empire or it would have had to redefine the empire to take into account the lands not formally subject to Rome.[39]

---

36. Fletcher, *The Barbarian Conversion*, 39–40. See, too, Mark W. Graham, *News and Frontier Consciousness in the Late Roman Empire* (Ann Arbor: University of Michigan Press, 2006), 159–163; E. A. Thompson, *Romans and Barbarians: The Decline of the Western Empire* (Madison: University of Wisconsin Press, 1982), 240–250.

37. Fletcher, *The Barbarian Conversion*, 37.

38. See Denise Kimber Buell, *Why This New Race: Ethnic Reasoning in Early Christianity* (New York: Columbia University Press, 2005).

39. By extending the Church into areas beyond the empire, any linking of the Church with the world of Rome would require a modification of the definition of what was Roman. David S. Potter, *The Roman Empire at Bay AD 180–395* (London: Routledge, 2004), 445–446, speaks of a new category of "extraimperial 'Roman.'" According to a story preserved by Eusebius, Constantine expresses a sense that the Church existed beyond the empire, and he took an interest in the welfare of Christians beyond his own territories, writing to the Sassanian emperor Shapur II about the matter almost immediately after uniting the Roman Empire under his rule (Eusebius, *Life of Constantine*, 4.9–13). Whether the story is rooted in reality is debated, but it at least reflects the view of a highly placed bishop.

Failed Explanations

The various theories addressed above seem to be solutions that arise not from the evidence but from an assumption that Christian missions to the countryside did not occur until the third century. Having adopted that assumption, it was then necessary to explain what situation in the third century could have sparked a rural mission. My sense is that none of these explanations is very compelling, and some do not even remotely rise to that level.

If, however, we allow for early Christian interest in the countryside from the beginning, then the growth of a Christian presence among the rural population in the third century would not appear abnormal or puzzling, though I think the wisest position is to step back from neat divisions between the rural and the urban altogether. Such divisions either do not work or are sufficiently flawed to be of much use for our question.

Evidence for a Rural Church (50 C.E.–250 C.E.)

As we have seen, most who admit a pre-Constantinian rural Christianity restrict it to the latter half of the third century, though on close examination those explanations appear unconvincing.[40] The failure to prove that the origins of rural Christianity did not take root until the latter half of the third century presents a serious obstacle to the urban thesis, for if the origins of rural Christianity can be traced back into an earlier period—say, into the second century—we are getting too close to the origins of Christianity itself to speak meaningfully of a period of purely urban Christianity. Although I am not comfortable with Stark's numbers (or any concrete numbers), I would point out to those who are prepared to work with such numbers that Stark lists only slightly over 200,000 Christians by the year 200 and only about 40,000 fifty years earlier.[41] It would not take many rural Christians at all to make rural Christians a significant contingent of the Christian movement in these years. We do know that some rural Christians can be found in this earlier period, for there are a number of matter-of-fact comments in the early literature that assume a Christian presence in the countryside, as we will see.

---

40. See chapter 8.

41. Stark, *The Rise of Christianity*, 7.

Early General Evidence

Before examining individual passages, however, two more general matters require attention. First, a rural environment is the setting for many of the stories of Jesus' activities. Some scholars have made much of this rural character for earliest Christianity,[42] and some have noted that even well after the first generation of the Palestinian church, the leaders of this church (relatives of Jesus) were still rural-based.[43] With the common tongue being Aramaic in town and countryside, there would have been no linguistic barrier to overcome in Palestine, though that would not necessarily have led to the success of Christianity there, for other factors may have been at play.[44] Further, since these stories became part of the church's primary literature, even urban Christians would have some familiarity with a rural dimension of Christianity.

The second general point for granting an early Christian presence in the countryside is that the case has been made for the rural provenance of some of the early Christian writings,[45] including some of the gospels.[46]

---

42. That is not to say that Jesus' activities were exclusively rural, for the stories have Jesus as familiar with town as with countryside. Yet a prominent rural dimension of early Christianity likely did exist, as is argued in the works of Gerd Theissen [particularly *Sociology of Early Palestinian Christianity*, trans. John Bowden (Philadelphia: Fortress, 1978)] and by John Dominic Crossan [*The Birth of Christianity: Discovering What Happened in the Years Immediately after the Execution of Jesus* (New York: HarperCollins, 1998) and *The Historical Jesus: The Life of a Mediterranean Jewish Peasant* (New York: HarperCollins, 1991)]. See Bernard Aubert, *The Shepherd-Flock Motif in the Miletus Discourse (Acts 20:17–38) against Its Historical Background* (New York: Peter Lang, 2009), 45–49, for a brief review of the use of rural imagery and the question of urban or rural provenance.

43. Richard Bauckham, *Jude and the Relatives of Jesus in the Early Church* (Edinburgh: T & T Clark, 1990), 94–106. The information comes from Hegesippus, through Eusebius, *Hist. eccl.* 3.19.1–3.20.7.

44. Christian success in rural Palestine is a matter of dispute. See Doron Bar, "The Christianisation of Rural Palestine during Late Antiquity," *JEH* 54 (2003): 401–421.

45. In particular, it is generally accepted that the *Didache* was set in rural environs (Huub Van De Sandt and David Flusser, *The Didache: Its Jewish Sources and Its Place in Early Judaism and Christianity* (Minneapolis: Fortress, 2002), 52, 344–346). The date is less certain, though according to Van De Sandt and Fusser, a growing consensus of a date around 100 C.E. seems to be forming. A case has been made for a rural setting of the *Infancy Gospel of Thomas* (Reidar Aasgaard, *The Childhood of Jesus: Decoding the Apocryphal Infancy Gospel of Thomas* (Cambridge: James Clarke, 2010).

46. For a review of the debate over the provenance of the Gospel of Mark, see Brian J. Incigneri, *The Gospel to the Romans: The Setting and Rhetoric of Mark's Gospel* (Leiden: Brill, 2003), 70–78. A rural provenance for the *Gospel of Thomas* has been proposed. See Simon J. Gathercole, *The Gospel of Thomas: Introduction and Commentary* (Leiden: Brill, 2014),

Although determining the exact milieu of documents is often, at best, inconclusive, arguments of greater or lesser merit point to a possible active rural Christianity in the early period. Without claiming that any of this kind of witness establishes a wide rural presence in early Christianity, when concrete statements for Christianity's presence in the countryside in the first two centuries of the movement are added to the evidence, a readiness to factor in some kind of early rural Christian presence seems fully in order. It is to such explicit statements of a rural Christian presence that I now turn.

Specific Statements Regarding the Rural Situation

For the most part, ancient comments that address a rural dimension of the Christian movement are routine and unfeigned. No one is trying to argue the point that there were Christians in the countryside, against widespread opinion that Christians were found only in the cities. And where comments are rhetorical, they are no more rhetorical when speaking of the country than of the city. These numerous, natural references to Christians in the countryside suggest that there were rural as well as urban Christians in the early period, and that no one thought this unusual or surprising.

The following collection of comments comes not only entirely from pre-Constantinian sources, but, more importantly, from sources before 250 C.E. The importance of this date is that many scholars admit that Christianity began to spread into the countryside in the second half of the third century, and numerous passages witness to a rural presence of Christianity by this time, obvious from Harnack's near-exhaustive collection of sources. But the passages that I cite below come from a time when, according to most scholars, rural Christianity simply did not exist, except for an occasional Montanist.

103–111. But it is one thing to locate a document's origin in the countryside; it is quite another to make that document definitive of the character of rural Christianity in some sweeping way. Take the gospels, for example. Some may have a rural provenance; all have numerous stories set in a rural milieu, perhaps reflecting to a greater or lesser degree memories of incidents in Jesus' career, or even of later compilers. But these rural touches do not seem to have given the gospels a more warm appeal in the countryside. The reality is that the gospels became the most prominent part of the liturgy of the *urban* churches, and thus whatever the rural texture of the gospels, they functioned effectively in an urban context. This may suggest that the world of the urban and of the rural church had much in common.

In the mid-90s, Clement of Rome spoke of the apostles preaching "throughout the countryside (χώρας) and in the cities (πόλεις)."[47] Fifteen years later, the Roman governor Pliny noted that Christianity had spread not only to cities (*civitates*), but also into villages (*vicos*) and country districts (*agros*).[48] These comments provide some evidence of a rural Christian presence around the end of the first century and the beginning of the second— or at least a perception of a rural Christian presence. Around this time, and perhaps earlier, the author of the *Acts of the Apostles* describes Paul's message spreading throughout the whole countryside (δι' ὅλης τῆς χώρας).[49]

By the middle of the second century, as Christianity entered its second century, Justin Martyr made several comments about the situation. In his *Dialogue with Trypho*, Justin stated:

> there is not a single race of human beings, barbarians, Greeks, or whatever name you please to call them, nomads (ἀμαξοβίων) or vagrants (ἀοίκων καλουμένων) or herdsmen living in tents (ἐν σκηνα ῖς κτηνοτρόφων εὐχαὶ) where prayers in the name of Jesus are not offered up.[50]

In his *First Apology*, Justin speaks of the meetings of Christians taking place on Sunday in cities (πόλεις) and villages (ἀργοὺς μενόντων).[51] While one might try to dismiss the comment in the *Dialogue* because Justin is trying to make the point that Christianity has spread widely, the comment in the *Apology* does not suggest anything but a report of the situation. The matter of whether there were Christians in the countryside is not at issue, and Justin does not seem to be trying to make Christianity more widespread or significant than it was.

About the end of the second century, Clement of Alexandria spoke of Christianity pouring out over the whole world among both Greeks and barbarians, in nation (ἔθνος), village (κώμην), and city (πόλιν).[52] Not much

---

47. *1 Clem.* 42.4.

48. Pliny, *Ep. Tra.* 46.

49. Acts 13:49 (my translation). Most English translations read "region" rather than countryside. The Greek is χώρας.

50. Justin, *Dial.* 118.

51. Justin, *1 Apol.* 67.

52. Clement of Alexandria, *Strom.* 6.18.167.

later, Tertullian offered a similar assessment of the Christian presence in the empire. He warned the opponents of Christianity: "we have filled every place among you—cities (*urbes*), islands (*insulas*), fortresses (*castella*), towns (*municipia*), market-places (*conciliabula*), the very camp (*castra ipsa*), tribes (*tribus*), companies (*decurias*), palace (*palatium*), senate (*senatum*), forum (*forum*)—we have left nothing to you but the temples of your gods."[53] At the opening of the same document, Tertullian made a similar comment: "The outcry is that the State is infested with Christians—that they are in the fields (*agris*), in the citadels (*castellis*), in the islands (*insulis*)."[54] Further, in his *Adversus Judaeos*, Tertullian spoke of the extent of Christians among barbarian lands, and though he did not mention villages explicitly, he leaves the impression that Christians could be found in the remotest corners.[55]

Tertullian also comments on the range of occupations of Christians, asserting that Christians have not withdrawn from society but work alongside the larger population in most places of labor and life: the forum, the meat market, the bath, the workshop, the inn, the weekly market, and other places of commerce. Christians sail, fight, and till the ground (*rusticamur*) with the rest of the population.[56] The main points for our purposes here are the references to the weekly market and to farming, or at least life in the country.[57]

Of course, Tertullian is, it seems, almost by nature an exaggerator, or, more kindly, we might say that he can carry rhetoric almost to its

---

53. Tertullian, *Apol.* 37. Harnack's translation reads: "cities, lodging-houses, villages, townships, markets, the camp itself, the tribes, town councils, the palace, the senate, and the forum." *Insula* can be translated either as island or lodging-house. Harnack uses lodging-house both here and in the note below.

54. Tertullian, *Apol.* 1. Harnack's translation reads: "The cry is that the State is infested with Christians, in the fields, in the villages, in the lodging-houses."

55. Tertullian, *Adv. Jud.* 7. Origen was perhaps more realistic about the extent of the Christian reach. In his commentary on Matthew, discussing passage 24:14, Origen admitted that most of the far reaches of the various barbarian groups had not heard the Christian message. At other times, however, Origen spoke in sweeping terms about the extent of Christianity, which, he said, "reaches to every soul under the sun" (*Cels.* 1.27; cf. 5.62).

56. Tertullian, *Apol.* 42. The reference to fighting (*militamus*) indicates military service, though that matter is one that provoked considerable controversy within the early Christian movement. See George Kalantzis, *Caesar and the Lamb: Early Christian Attitudes on War and Military Service* (Eugene, OR: Cascade Books, 2012), for discussion and English translations of every relevant text.

57. The word *rusticor* can mean to farm or to live in or visit the countryside.

breaking point in order to give sting and storm to his argument. In the citations above, Tertullian is interested in making a point of how widespread Christianity was in the empire and even beyond, and he does this by listing just about every place of habitation he can name and almost every occupation. His mention of fields, farming, and the market may be simply a matter of filling out his list as much as possible. Yet, one gets no sense from these passages that Tertullian had any other view of the situation than that which he expresses here, where Christians are to be found in rural as well as urban areas. Possibly he was mistaken about Christian presence outside of the urban centers, but that is not the most natural reading of his comments, however exaggerated they might be.

A short time after Tertullian, Origen spoke of Christian preachers who have "made it their business to itinerate not only through cities (πόλεις), but even villages (κώμας), and country houses (ἐπαύλεις), that they might make converts to God."[58] To demonstrate how much the urban thesis controls the current reading of texts, note Richard Fletcher's dismissive treatment of Origen's comment. "This was certainly an exaggeration," Fletcher says.[59] Nothing in Origen's comment, however, suggests anything more than that some Christian preachers had made rural areas part of their mission. Origen is replying to Celsus' charge that "if all men wanted to be Christians, the Christians would not want them." Origen probably could have responded in a variety of ways to refute Celsus' charge. To Origen, the extent of the church's mission seems a sufficient and obvious challenge to Celsus' odd complaint. Nothing in Origen's response suggests that he was backed into a corner by Celsus' comment and that he had to be inventive to get out of it, or that his simple comment about some Christian mission in the countryside is an exaggeration.[60]

In another place, Origen challenged Celsus' elitist view of access to the truth,[61] commenting that the aim of the Christian message is to engage both Greeks and barbarians, and even the rustic (ἀγροικοτάτους)

---

58. Origen, *Cels.* 3.9.

59. Fletcher, *The Barbarian Conversion*, 34.

60. Fletcher finds it odd that Origen made this kind of comment as an appropriate response to the point of Celsus' polemic (*The Barbarian Conversion*, 34). It is not odd if it is true.

61. Origen speaks of the truth (τά τῆς ἀληθείας), playing off the title Celsus gave to his work, λογός ἀληθῆ, the *True Word*.

and the ignorant (ἰδιώτας) so as to convert people "of every sort."[62] And in another passage, Origen states: "not only rustic (ἀγροίκους) and ignorant individuals (ἰδιώτας)" were won by Jesus, but also "not a few of those who were distinguished by their wisdom."[63] The impression created by such comment is that the rustic character of the Christian congregation was obvious. It was the presence of the more well-off that might escape notice.

Origen also recalled the passage from Matthew's gospel that "the Gospel shall be preached throughout all the whole world" (24:14), and then he claimed that this was indeed already true.[64] While it is possible that Origen meant nothing more than that Christians could be found in various cities throughout the Roman Empire, it is unlikely that he intended only that, for he consciously connected the Christian growth to Jesus' own mission, which, as Origen pointed out, "overlooked not only no city, but not even a single village (κώμην), of Judea."[65] Perhaps some passage from the Gospel of Matthew came to his mind, such as in 9:35: "Then Jesus went about all the cities (πόλεις) and villages (κώμας), teaching in their synagogues, and proclaiming the good news of the kingdom, and curing every disease and every sickness."[66] Or Matthew 10:11: "Whatever town (πόλιν) or village (κώμην) you enter, find out who in it is worthy, and stay there until you leave."[67] Those verses, from the church's most used gospel, would have reminded not just Origen but anyone reading or hearing the text of the broad and inclusive scope of Christian mission.

Origen's comments seem to suggest a fairly aware observation about a rural Christian mission.[68] Origen assumes the presence of rural elements

---

62. Origen, *Cels.* 6.1.

63. Origen, *Cels.* 1.29.

64. Origen, *Cels.* 2.13.

65. Origen, *Cels.* 2.38.

66. John Chrysostom, *The Gospel of Matthew,* Homily 32.3, commented on this passage, stating that Jesus went everywhere "not overlooking a single village."

67. The NRSV renders πόλιν as "town." For our purposes, it is the word κώμας (villages) that is important.

68. A similar account of village activity can be found Mark 6:56: "And wherever he went, into villages (κώμας) or cities (πόλεις) or farms (ἀγροὺς ἐν ταῖς ἀγοραῖς), they laid the sick in the marketplaces, and begged him that they might touch even the fringe of his cloak; and all who touched it were healed."

or those with rural connections or rustic character in the Christian movement, and his various comments indicate that some early Christian thinkers of influence did reflect on a broad mission.

Hippolytus (c. 170–236 C.E.), in his review of the deaths of the apostles, indicated that some died in what appear to be insignificant towns; others died in larger urban centers.[69] Whatever we make of the reliability of the traditions of Hippolytus, we can at least conclude that a Christian writer in the first part of the third century saw no difficulty in placing major disciples in towns rather than in thriving urban areas.

In the above collection of passages, I have attempted to show that explicit references to rural Christianity appear in a variety of early Christian writings and settings before the middle of the third century, leaving no trace that pagans or early Christians themselves saw Christianity as distinctly urban. The existence of rural Christianity is assumed or mentioned in a natural, unfeigned way. To the passages mentioned above could be added numerous more that speak of Christians being "everywhere," or words to that effect, without specifically mentioning the countryside.[70] At the end of the third century, when Eusebius looked back over Christian history, he betrayed no sense of a largely urban Christianity. By his time, the church was established in the countryside, and he showed no hint that this rural presence was a recent thing.[71]

Although some of these comments considered above are tainted with exaggeration and generalization, the overall impression is sufficient to raise some caution concerning sweeping assertions about Christianity being almost exclusively an urban religion in the first three centuries. I turn now to the more concrete evidence of early rural Christianity that might lend support to the more general statements that dot the literature from this period.

---

69. Hippolytus, *On the Twelve Apostles* 6, 7.

70. See Harnack, *The Expansion of Christianity in the First Three Centuries*, 1–32, for a comprehensive list of such passages.

71. Eusebius, *Hist. eccl.* 2.3.2. Many of his comments assume a rural mission from the beginning of the church (though he is certainly not a firsthand witness to anything earlier than the situation in the latter part of the 200s). For example, Eusebius claims that as a result of the preaching of the apostles "in every city (πόλεις) and village (κώμας) arose churches crowded with thousands of men." Although this is an obvious exaggeration, Eusebius' comment is somewhat useful in establishing that by his time both city and village have had successful Christian missions. Eusebius betrays no hint that this was a recent phenomenon for the countryside.

Asia Minor

The earliest evidence of Christianity in Asia Minor comes only two decades after the execution of Jesus. In the 50s, Paul wrote several letters that were later incorporated into the Christian canon. Most of these letters were written to areas west of Asia Minor, though from comments in them we are able to reconstruct some of Paul's activities in Asia Minor.[72] Further, Acts supplies many stories of Paul's activities in Asia Minor, which, whether reliable or not in their details, certainly fit the general sketch of Paul from what we can learn in his authentic letters.

Not only do we have very early evidence of Christianity in Asia Minor, we have very early evidence of Christianity in rural areas of Asia Minor. Our source is pagan. Pliny the Younger, a governor, confronted the Christian problem in Pontus[73] (c. 112 C.E.) when he was sent there by Emperor Trajan to put the area on a firmer financial footing. We know about the situation only because Pliny wrote to Trajan for advice, and his letter and Trajan's reply came to be preserved in a collection of Pliny's letters. Pliny's report is important for a number of reasons, the most obvious being that it is the earliest firsthand pagan reference to the existence of Christianity.[74] More than that, it is particularly rich in detail.

The letter tells us that Christianity, at least of the kind that Pliny encountered, was largely (or perhaps solely) made up of pagan converts, not Jewish ones.[75] And it tells us that Christianity was made up of rural as well as urban members: as Pliny reports, Christianity had "penetrated not the cities

---

72. Taking only the undisputed letters of Paul written to churches (Romans, 1 and 2 Corinthians, Philippians, 1 Thessalonians, Galatians), five of the six are to areas west of Asia Minor. Only Galatians is addressed to Asia Minor, though some of the more disputed letters and letters addressed to individuals have areas of Asia Minor as their destination (Ephesians, Colossians, Philemon, 1 and 2 Timothy, and Titus, the last to Crete). Specific reference to churches in Asia Minor in Paul's undisputed letters at found at Rom 16:5; 1 Cor 15:32, 16:8, 19; 2 Cor 1:8.

73. MacMullen, *Christianizing the Roman Empire*, 135n26, points out that Sherwin-White blamed a comment by Harnack for the widespread error that the Christian situation addressed by Pliny affected Bithynia as well as Pontus.

74. Pliny the Younger, *Ep.* 10.96.

75. If the Christianity encountered by Pliny had been heavily Jewish in either its membership or its complexion, it is almost certain that Pliny would have become aware of this in his investigations. There is not a hint of this in Pliny's comments. Christianity is seen as a new movement and no association with Judaism is made. Further, if the Christianity that Pliny encountered largely consisted of Jewish converts and proselytes, there would have been no impact on the economy of the pagan temples, for such individuals would not have been supporters of the temple economy before their conversion to Christianity. Yet, Pliny sees Christianity as having significantly reduced the demand for sacrificial victims and in

(*civitas*) only, but the villages (*vicos*) and country (*agros*)."[76] In both matters—
the pagan and the rural element of Christianity—far too little attention has
been given in current scholarship on early Christianity, which generally has
asserted that early Christianity was heavily Jewish in its complexion and
urban in its membership. As we have seen earlier, a few decades after Pliny
and in reference to the same area, the satirist Lucian of Samosata, in his
story of *Alexander the Oracle-Monger*, provides evidence pointing to the likelihood of Christianity's continuing presence in the countryside.[77]

In Phrygia, a territory in the west-central part of Asia Minor, the situation seems to have been much the same. This territory was part of the
Roman provinces of Asia and Galatia at the time. Douglas Edwards points
to the Christian presence in this area as early as the mid-second century,
and he notes that the editors of *MAMA* 10 concluded that the widely held
view of an almost totally urban Christianity is challenged by the evidence
from Phrygia.[78] As for the urbanization of this area, Peter Thonemann
describes it as a "paper-thin façade."[79]

Montanism is the best-known evidence for Christianity's early presence in the countryside of Phrygia, where it had established itself in some
of the small towns of the area.[80] But, far too often, Montanism is treated
as though it were the only example of early rural Christianity in the area,
and then it is dismissed because of its "unusual" or "deviant" character.[81]

---

causing the temples to lie largely deserted, however exaggerated these comments may be.
For a shift in religious loyalty to have affected the temple economy, the best interpretation of
the evidence is that Christianity had attracted a significantly large number of pagans.

76. Pliny the Younger, *Ep.* 10.96.9.

77. Lucian, *Alex.* 25. See section "The Case of Alexander, the 'Oracle-Monger,'" in chapter 6.

78. Douglas R. Edwards, *Religion and Power: Pagans, Jews, and Christians in the Greek East*
(Oxford: Oxford University Press, 1996), 162n101. The evidence comes from gravestones
that are dateable to the mid-second century. William Tabbernee, *Montanist Inscriptions and
Testimonia: Epigraphic Sources Illustrating the History of Montanism*, North American Patristic
Society Patristic Monograph Series 16 (Macon, GA: Mercer University Press, 1997), 61–99,
provides a detailed discussion of ten relevant inscriptions from Phrygia dated between 180
and 224 C.E.

79. Peter Thonemann, "Phrygia: An Anarchist History, 950 BC–AD 100," in *Roman
Phrygia: Culture and Society*, ed. Peter Thonemann (Cambridge: Cambridge University
Press, 2013), 3.

80. I have dealt with the linguistic character of Montanism and Phrygia in chapter 6.

81. For example, various scholars have called attention to the rural and abnormal character
of Montanism but have failed to note the rural and *orthodox* character of bishops in the area
who opposed Montanism. See chapter 8.

The evidence strongly suggests that Montanism was neither the first nor the only form of rural Christianity in the area. Consider this. Two of the bishops who opposed Montanism were from small towns or villages, according to Eusebius: Zoticus, from the village of Cumane in Pamphylia or from the village of Otrous near Hieropolis,[82] and Julian, from Apamea, thought to have been perhaps a village near the border with Pisidia.[83] Montanus himself was a convert from the village of Ardabav, near the Mysian/Phrygian border.[84] Presumably there was a church there when he converted. Further, Eusebius tells us that Montanus selected two small towns[85] in Phrygia (Pepuza and Tymion) to be called "Jerusalem."[86] Although there is no proof that Christian churches had existed in these latter towns prior to Montanus, Montanus' selection of these towns makes an earlier Christian presence likely, particularly when other settlements in the area mentioned by Eusebius have churches.

These various matter-of-course comments suggest the presence of rural, non-Montanist Christians prior to Montanism. If Eusebius' information about the rise of Montanism is correct, then Christian churches had been established in a number of rural settlements probably at least by the mid-second century, before Montanus converted. Further, it seems that rural opposition to Montanism on the one hand and the presence of a non-Montanist Christian movement on the other hand continued to exist in the area of Montanism's origin, in spite of the success of Montanism there.[87] Indeed, in the early days of Montanism, it would be difficult to account for any great success of Montanism outside the circle of those

---

82. Eusebius, *Hist. eccl.* 5.16.5, 17.

83. Eusebius, *Hist. eccl.* 5.16.17; Roderic L. Mullen, *The Expansion of Christianity: A Gazetteer of Its First Three Centuries* (Leiden: Brill, 2004), 89.

84. Eusebius, *Hist. eccl.* 5.16.7, described Montanus' hometown of Ardabav as a village (κώμη), and he uses the same term for the hometowns of two bishops from the area who opposed Montanus: Zoticus of Cumane and Julian of Apamea (5.16.17), though possibly the term "village" was intended only for Cumane, the first mentioned.

85. Apollonius, Eusebius' source, calls these "small cities" (μικραὶ πόλεις) in contrast to the villages (κώμη) mentioned in the footnote above. The phrase is better translated as "small towns" rather than "small cities," as most translators of Eusebius appear to have recognized.

86. Eusebius, *Hist. eccl.* 5.18.2. For a discussion of the probable location of these towns, see Christene Trevett, *Montanism: Gender, Authority and the New Prophecy* (Cambridge: Cambridge University Press, 1996), 19–24.

87. We must not assume that Montanism drove out the orthodox church in the area, though it seems certain that it did provide it with stiff competition.

already converted to Christianity. Montanus' message seems to be an intra-Christian one; its peculiar twist makes sense largely against a Christian background. Who outside the Christian church would have been concerned, intrigued, or even remotely interested in the question of whether the Paraclete had returned or whether the New Jerusalem was about to be established? The Montanist claim assumes the conceptual world of the Christian church and seems to be directed at hearers who could have understood those nuances. Thus, it seems, a pre-Montanist rural Christianity is likely, and perhaps even necessary, to explain the Montanist perspective and success.

That is not to rule out entirely the possibility of Montanism being the first form of Christianity in the area. The message of Montanism, with its apocalyptic flavor, was not so strangely different from much of early Christian preaching, so if a non-Montanist version of Christianity could take hold, perhaps a Montanist version, even colored by an intra-Christian debate, could also take hold. Yet that cuts both ways. If Montanism could establish itself there, other forms of Christianity could have sold their message among the rustics of the countryside, too, for all shades of Christianity would have appeared roughly the same to an outsider.[88] Given the rural Christian opposition to Montanism, a pre-Montanist rural Christian presence seems the more likely option.

Other evidence of rural Christian success comes from the "Christians for Christians" inscriptions in the area. Although some see these as evidence of Montanism, Stephen Mitchell points out that little requires such identification.[89] Further, he contends that Christians outnumbered non-Christians "well before the end of the third century" in the upper Tembris Valley of Phrygia, a region and a Christianity that he describes as rural.[90]

We should note that we might not have known about the existence of rural Christianity so early in this area had not controversy with Montanism provoked response and comment. The same can be said of the situation related to Pliny's investigation. For Asia Minor, we have stark and irrefutable evidence of rural-based Christianity in the second

---

88. Pauline Christianity, often connected to cities, has a rich apocalyptic flavor. And the Apocalypse, whose recipients reach into Phrygian territory, carry similar expectations. In fact, early Christianity in most of its forms is marked by some apocalyptic fervor.

89. Stephen Mitchell, *Anatolia: Land, Men, and Gods in Asia Minor* (Oxford: Clarendon Press: 1993), II.40, 104.

90. Mitchell, *Anatolia*, II.40.

century. But it is serendipitous. Had there not been some controversy of sufficient import to provoke response, such rural Christianity may have left no record for the modern investigator, save for the "Christians for Christians" inscriptions.

If Phrygia, where Montanism started, had non-Montanist village churches by the mid-second century, and Pontus had a rural Christian presence in the second decade of the second century and perhaps even much earlier,[91] why would we assume these to be exceptions to the rule? These should serve as a warning about any conclusion regarding the presence or lack thereof of Christians in areas for which we have no data.

Egypt

Before we even start to examine the Christian population of Egypt, we run into a debate among demographers regarding the total population of the province. The numbers range from 3 million to 9 or 10 million, largely based on comments made by two ancient historians writing about a century apart. Diodorus Siculus provided the low number; Josephus provided the basis for the high number.[92] Although most historians still opt for the higher number, or a number near that, a case has recently been made for the lower number.[93]

In addition to the question of the total population, there is the question of the percentage of that population that can be considered urban. Bruce Frier opts for 30%, which would make the province one of the most highly urbanized areas of the Roman Empire. Alexandria itself may have had a population of a million. The population of Alexandria alone could account for 17% of the population for Egypt, according to Frier, and he adds about another three-quarters of a million residents in other urban

---

91. Pliny's investigations revealed that some had been Christians twenty-five years earlier (the 80s, C.E.) but were no longer. It is not clear that these were rural Christians, but nothing requires that they not be.

92. Diodorus Siculus, *Bibliotheca historica* 1.31.8. There is some disagreement regarding the original reading. Most manuscripts read 3 million, but many editors think that this is an error and that the proper reading would not conflict with the figure of 7 million that Diodorus Siculus had offered earlier; Josephus, *J.W.* 2.385 gives the number of 7.5 million, excluding the population of Alexandria.

93. D. W. Rathbone, "Villages, Land, and Population in Graeco-Roman Egypt," *Proceeding of the Cambridge Philological Society* 36 (1990): 123–124, thinks that the population fluctuated between 3 and 5 million.

centers of Egypt.[94] Based on these numbers, Alexandria, then, would account for about 60% of Egypt's urban population, and the remainder of Egypt would reflect about a 15% urbanization, a number in line with that often given for the urban proportion of the empire as a whole.

The Macedonians and Greeks who settled in Egypt as a result of Alexander's conquest formed a minority and were largely resident in Alexandria. By far the majority of the population consisted of native Egyptians. A substantial Jewish population is found in Egypt too, perhaps with a concentration in Alexandria, but with a presence in other urban centers and even in rural settlements.[95] There is some suggestion, however, that as a consequence of the revolt by Jews in Egypt in the years 115–117 C.E., the Jewish community in Alexandria (and perhaps in other parts of Egypt) was decimated—whether by slaughter or exile, or more likely, by both.[96] If that was the case, there must have been some recovery at least by the latter part of the 300s when Jewish-Christian tensions resulted in riots in Alexandria and an expulsion of Jews, who by that time seem to have become again a somewhat significant element in that city.[97]

Tracing the origins of Christianity in Egypt is difficult. Early in the twentieth century, B. H. Streeter had described the early history of Christianity in Alexandria, the main city of Egypt, as "darkness itself."[98] By the end of

---

94. Bruce W. Frier, "More Is Worse: Some Observations on the Population of the Roman Empire," in *Debating Roman Demography*, ed. Walter Scheidel (Leiden: Brill, 2001), 140–141, has a brief review of some of these matters. Earlier, R. S. Bagnall and Bruce Frier, *The Demography of Roman Egypt* (Cambridge: Cambridge University Press, 1994), 56, note an urbanization of 37% according to one method of measuring, though they sense that this "seems high," and they speak of a third of the population as likely to have "lived in cities." But if a large percentage of urban populations were farmers, as many contend, then the boundaries between what is urban and what is rural and who should be counted as which become fuzzy.

95. Aryeh Kasher, *The Jews in Hellenistic and Roman Egypt: The Struggle for Equal Rights*, Texte und Studien zum Antiken Judentum 7 [Tübingen: J. C. B. Mohr (Paul Siebeck), 1985], 26; Sang-Il Lee, *Jesus and Gospel Traditions in Bilingual Context: A Study in the Interdirectionality of Language* (Berlin: Walter du Gruyter, 2012), 152n64.

96. Kasher, *The Jews in Hellenistic and Roman Egypt*, 28. The matter is discussed in the Talmud (*T.J. Sukkah* V 55b; *T.B. Gittum* 57a).

97. Jewish and Christian mobs slaughtered each other in riots in 415 C.E. under the tenure of Cyril, Patriarch of Alexandria (412–444 C.E.). In the end, Jews were expelled from the city. See Socrates, *Hist. eccl.* 7.13. Socrates comments that Jews had lived in Alexandria since its founding and that when Jews were forced out by Cyril, the governor Orestes was concerned about the loss of a significant portion of the population of the city.

98. B. H. Streeter, *The Primitive Church* (London: Macmillan, 1929), 233.

that century, little had changed. Wilfred Griggs describes early Christianity in Egypt as "veiled in obscurity."[99] Compared to other areas of the Roman Empire, Egypt lacks the kind of data scholars have depended on to reconstruct Christianity, and this situation holds for nearly the first two centuries of early Christianity there.[100] But we know that Christianity was in Egypt early, or we can reasonably assume that. The Christian movement, born and shaped in Judaism, is unlikely to have had no presence there, given that Egypt was one of Palestine's closest neighbors and a large contingent of Jews lived there—perhaps the largest outside of Palestine itself.[101]

Whatever Egypt might lack in some kinds of evidence, it is not without evidence entirely. The earliest extant manuscripts of the New Testament are of an *Egyptian* provenance, written in *Greek* language. Perhaps more surprising, and most relevant to the subject of the present work, these manuscript fragments come from a *rural* environment. Based on such evidence, Philip Comfort concludes that Christian churches existed in rural Middle Egypt as early as 125 c.e.[102] On the other hand, as Alan Bowman has pointed out, until about 300 there is little Christian literature in Coptic, the native language of Egypt.[103]

99. C. Wilfred Griggs, *Early Egyptian Christianity from Its Origins to 451 c.e.* (Leiden: Brill, 1991), 1.

100. C. H. Roberts, *Manuscripts, Society, and Belief in Early Christian Egypt*, The Schweich Lectures of the British Academy for 1977 (London: Oxford University Press, 1979), 1; Birger A. Pearson, "Earliest Christianity in Egypt: Some Observations," in *The Roots of Egyptian Christianity*, ed. Birger A. Pearson and James E. Goehring (Philadelphia: Fortress, 1986), 132. Such problems have long been noted. Walter Bauer, *Orthodoxy and Heresy in Earliest Christianity*, R. A. Kraft, et al., trans. and ed. (Philadelphia: Fortress, 1977), 44. Also A. F. J. Klijn, "Jewish Christianity in Egypt," in *The Roots of Egyptian Christianity*, ed. Birger A. Pearson and James E. Goehring (Philadelphia: Fortress, 1986), 161–175. See, too, Helmut Köster, *Introduction to the New Testament*, vol. 2, *History and Literature of Early Christianity* (Philadelphia: Fortress, 1982), 219.

101. Egypt was near Palestine. As the largest center of diaspora Judaism, contacts between Jerusalem and Alexandria must have been considerable. The earliest Christian evidence offers only passing note of Egypt, largely because the earliest Christian literature that offers much of a glimpse of the diaspora (Paul's letters and the Acts of the Apostles) is focused on Paul, whose home and area of mission had Syrian, Asia Minor, Macedonia, and Achaean connections. The only hints of possible Christian presence in Egypt in this literature is in Acts 2:10; 6:9 and 18:24, and the story in Matthew's gospel of Jesus and his parents fleeing to Egypt to escape Herod's sword. Pearson offers a cautious examination of these passages and other literature that may point to an early Christian presence in Egypt ("Earliest Christianity in Egypt: Some Observations," 132–156).

102. Philip W. Comfort, "Texts and Manuscripts of the New Testament," in *The Origin of the Bible*, ed. Philip W. Comfort (Carol Stream, IL: Tyndale House Publishers, 2003), 204.

103. Alan L. Bowman, *Egypt after the Pharaohs: 332 b.c.–a.d. 642* (Berkeley: University of California Press, 1986), 129.

What does this say about whether Christianity had penetrated the countryside or, perhaps more to the point, whether Christianity had gained converts from among the rural Coptic-speaking communities? Perhaps some of the observations of Roger Bagnall have relevance here. Although Bagnall follows the standard view of earliest Christianity as an urban phenomenon, he does describe the population of the countryside as "partly bilingual, partly Egyptian-speaking,"[104] and he argues for the considerable influence of Greek, Hellenism, and urbanism in the Coptic world.[105] He does not reflect on what this might say about the presence of Christianity in rural areas, however, but given the partly bilingual character of the average town and rural village, it would seem that links to the native Egyptian rural population were available, if Christians wanted to exploit them. Further, given that the Jewish community was widely spread throughout Egypt and seems to have been able to function in the countryside, whether in Greek or with some bilingual ability, Christians may have had the same kinds of facility for communication.[106] And if, as many now think, early Christianity in Egypt was heavily Jewish, then Christianity may have had some success in rural communities that had a Jewish component, though it is another matter whether such contacts with the Jewish community would have linked easily to the native Coptic rural population.[107]

What, then, of the claim of Frank Trombley that Christianity was a largely urban phenomenon in Egypt, with little interest in the Egyptian countryside until the end of the fourth century, when Coptic monks successfully "appealed to the rustics' sense of outrage at their economic

---

104. Roger S. Bagnall, *Egypt in Late Antiquity* (Princeton: Princeton University Press, 1993), 322, notes that third-century Egypt was "essentially without a written vernacular." Even when a Coptic script is developed, such writing should not be thought of as rural, according to Bagnall. Rather, Coptic is an expression of bilingual urbanism linked to Christianity.

105. Bagnall, *Egypt in Late Antiquity*, 322–323. MacMullen, "Provincial Languages in the Roman Empire," 7, points to Coptic translation of scripture in the second century, and in that context states that the Church had been established by that time and "perhaps even conspicuous, in Egypt."

106. Lee, *Jesus and Gospel Traditions in Bilingual Context*, 150–162. His position is not the dominant one, and he cites Martin Hengel and C. Wilfrid Griggs as scholars who deny Jews spoke the native language (151n60). See, too, G. Horsley, "The Fiction of 'Jewish' Greek,'" *New Docs* 5:5–40.

107. One of the primary problems of connecting Christian expansion to the links it had to Jewish communities is that the Jewish communities in Egypt may have been largely annihilated or forced to flee after the revolt of 115–117 C.E. Bagnall, *Egypt in Late Antiquity*, 275–277, argues for a considerable destruction of Jewish life in Egypt after the revolt. Joseph Mélèze Modrzejewski, *The Jews of Egypt: From Rameses II to Emperor Hadrian*, trans. Robert Cornman

exploitation by the landed magnates"? And what of Trombley's suggestion that a sense of ethnic differentiation possibly played a role, with a distinction between Copts and their landlords, who were often Hellenes in religion as well as culture?[108]

Too many problems make this an unlikely scenario. For one thing, if a Christian mission to the countryside did not begin until the late fourth century, how was Christianity an attractive option for the exploited rural population? By this time, Christianity, as the religion of the empire, would have been more prominently identified with the elite and the powerful than ever before. It is much more likely that Christianity would have presented itself as an ally against exploitation much earlier, prior to Christianity's promotion to imperial power and influence. Further, it is unlikely that by the late fourth century many landlords would have stood out as Hellenes in religion rather than Christian, as Trombley suggests. The religion of the elite was likely Greco-Roman religion prior to Constantine, shifting then to the Christian religion during and after Constantine. From that time on, it is unlikely, then, that Christianity would have been an obvious ally for the Copts. Coptic monastics may have presented a viable religious option against elitist urban exploitation *for those Copts who were already Christian,* but it would have been quite another matter for non-Christian Copts to convert to the religion of their abusive Christian overlords, even with a Coptic monastic buffer.

Against general kinds of objections to an early rural Christianity in Egypt are matters that seem to point to a rural Christianity prior to 250, the time that many posit as the beginnings of a rural mission. Note the conflict between Bishop Dionysius of Alexandria (in office from 248 to his death in 264 or 265) and the teaching of a bishop by the name of Nepos. Dionysius, as bishop, had to deal with a rise in millennial interests in some of the churches of his diocese. He journeyed to a rural area where the problem had surfaced and called together presbyters and teachers and other Christians interested in the matter from the villages (κώμαις) affected by the teaching.[109] The millennial beliefs had been inspired by

---

(Princeton: Princeton University Press, 1995), 227–231, argues that since Christians were so closely identified with Judaism there, the Christian community may have suffered the same fate as the Jewish community after the revolt of 115–117.

108. Frank R. Trombley, *Hellenic Religion and Christianization c. 370–529*, vol. 2 (Leiden: Brill, 1995), 206–207.

109. Eusebius, *Hist. eccl.* 7.24.6.

a work titled *The Refutation of the Allegorists*,[110] written by Nepos, a well-loved bishop,[111] whose church—or at least whose influence—appears to have been in the area of Arsinoë, a rural district about 300 kilometers up the Nile from Alexandria.[112]

Eusebius alone offers an account of Nepos, largely by quoting now lost material written by Dionysius, who challenged Nepos' teachings. Neither Eusebius nor Dionysius provides a date for Nepos, although several matters suggest that Nepos had died at least by the middle of the third century, if not many years before that. For one thing, Dionysius died in 264/5, and he had time after the incident with the churches of Arsinoë to write a work against Nepos' millennialism, though we do not know how long before his death he wrote that.[113] Whatever the case, Nepos lived well before the intervention of Dionysius in the affairs of the churches of Arsinoë. By that time, Nepos was dead, and probably had been for some years. Dionysius mentioned that the hymns of Nepos had cheered many "to the present" (μέχρι νῦν),[114] which suggests that these hymns had been around for some time.

---

110. Nepos' work, otherwise unknown, attacked those who allegorized the Apocalypse. The early church was of two minds on this matter, with credible voices on both sides. See Bernard McGinn, "Turning Points in Early Christian Apocalypse Exegesis," in *Apocalyptic Thought in Early Christianity*, ed. Robert J. Daly (Grand Rapids, MI: Baker Academic, 2009), 81–105.

111. Dionysius was careful not to offend the admirers of Nepos by any hint of an attack on the deceased bishop. Indeed, Dionysius mentions Nepos in the most glowing of terms, praising him for his work, his study of the Scriptures, and his hymnody, which had become popular (Eusebius, *Hist. eccl.* 7.24.4).

112. We know nothing of Nepos other than for what Eusebius mentions (in quoting works of Dionysius of Alexandria) about the outbreak of millennialism in Arsinoë in Egypt, during and likely before the reign of Bishop Dionysius. The rare references to Nepos in modern literature refer to him as Bishop of Arsinoë in Egypt. Everett Ferguson, "Dionysius of Alexandria," *Encyclopedia of Early Christianity*, speaks of Nepos as Bishop of Arsinoë; J. Gribomont, "Nepos," *Encyclopedia of the Early Church*, calls Nepos bishop of Arsinoë, and suggests that he may have been the first bishop. Gribomont is uncertain whether Nepos' hymnody was in Greek or Coptic. Johannes Quasten, *Patrology* (Utrecht: Spectrum, 1950) II.104, speaks of Nepos as bishop of Arsinoë. Although such is the general consensus, we cannot say with certainty that Nepos was even from this area. All we can say with certainty is that Nepos' millennialist writing had become popular in the area of Arsinoë and that his hymns were known there and loved. According to Eusebius, Nepos was a "bishop of the Egyptians," though it is not clear that Eusebius had specific information in this regard or simply assumed that to be the case from Dionysius' account. Dionysius' information provides grounds for concluding that Nepos was popular in the area of Arsinoë; it does not require that Nepos resided in that area, or indeed even in Egypt, for that matter, though he may well have (Eusebius, *Hist. eccl.* 7.24.9).

113. After his meeting with the churches in the Arsinoë area, Dionysius published a work against the views of Nepos in two volumes, titled *A Treatise on the Promises*.

114. Eusebius, *Hist. eccl.* 7.24.4.

Further, Dionysius stated that the teachings of Nepos "had long been prevalent" (πρὸ πολλοῦ τοῦτο ἐπεπόλαζεν τὸ δόγμα).[115] That does not necessarily mean that Nepos died a long time before this, but it certainly suggests that his hymns were written much earlier, which would place his presence or influence well before 250. One other matter that may push back Nepos' date even earlier is that Dionysius seems to suggest that someone named Coracion had introduced the millennial beliefs of Nepos into the area, not Nepos himself, thus seeming to separate Nepos even farther from the time of the intervention of Dionysius.

The more important question for our purposes is not when millennialism was introduced in this area but when churches were first established there. It is hardly likely that the churches in the Arsinoë area were *recent* plants in the countryside by the urban Alexandrian-based Christianity. These churches simply do not reflect the Alexandrian character when we first meet them, for they already have a millennialist character not characteristic of the church in Alexandria, and, according to Dionysius, these churches had held such eschatological beliefs for a long time. That forces us to one of two conclusions: the Arsinoë churches were planted independently of the Alexandrian church, and Alexandria was now trying to assert and extend its authority, or the churches were established under Alexandrian sponsorship some time earlier, and the present millennialism reflected a departure from the original beliefs of these churches.

The latter seems much more likely. Dionysius spoke of "schism (σχίσματα) and defections (ἀποστασίας) of whole churches,"[116] and he described a man by the name of Coracion as the "leader (ἀρχηγός) and introducer (εἰσηγητής) of this teaching."[117] The terms used for Coracion seem to recognize the substantial role that Coracion played in introducing or promoting Nepos' doctrine in the churches of the Arsinoë area. Had Nepos been bishop (or leader of some sort) of these churches, or their founder, it seems strange to use such substantial terms for Coracion if he was merely the current leader of the group or the successor of Nepos. These statements fit better the context of already established churches coming under the sway of a new teaching than of

---

115. Eusebius, *Hist. eccl.* 7.24.6.

116. Eusebius, *Hist. eccl.* 7.24.6.

117. Eusebius, *Hist. eccl.* 7.24.9.

new churches distinguished by this teaching being established in places where churches had not existed beforehand. Further, it seems that Dionysius did not view his visit to Arsinoë as a missionary foray into new areas or an exploratory discussion of common interests between two independent bodies. Rather, it is a recovery operation, aimed at churches once in Alexandria's orbit but now separated. This is an important point, for it would give these churches a longer history, well before the middle of the third century, and it would serve as evidence of Christianity in a rural and small-town environment.

The Decian persecution offers further evidence of the presence of Christianity in the countryside. Eusebius quotes Dionysius, the bishop of Alexandria at the time of the persecution, who, after describing in gruesome detail the torture and execution of various Christians in Alexandria, states: "And many others throughout the cities and villages (κώμας) were torn in pieces by the heathen."[118] This is a contemporary witness to the Decian persecution by the leading churchman of the area. There is nothing to suggest that these village congregations were only recently established, and we should not simply assume that they were. Further, of some relevance to the question of a rural Christian presence is that most of extant *libelli* (34 of 46) issued during the Decian persecution were found in a village, though what that evidence means is more open to dispute.[119]

Other stories connected to Dionysius speak to a rural setting of at least some Christian activity. In one story, set during the Decian persecution, Dionysius fled from Alexandria but was captured by soldiers who took him to Taposiris, a city about 25 kilometers from Alexandria. Dionysius was rescued by a rural wedding party, which was probably Christian.[120] The story is quite entertaining—though it does not seem that Dionysius

---

118. Eusebius, *Hist. eccl.* 6.42.1.

119. Thirty-four of the forty-six extant Decian *libelli* come from the village of Theadelphia (Kharabet Ihrit), and none was issued to anyone who was clearly a Christian. See H. Idris Bell, "Evidences of Christianity during the Roman Period," *HTR* 37 (1944): 205; Malcolm Choat, et al., "The World of the Nile," in *Early Christianity in Contexts: An Exploration across Cultures and Continents*, ed. William Tabbernee (Grand Rapids, MI: Baker Academic, 2014), 194; Clarke, "Third-Century Christianity," 629.

120. Eusebius, *Hist. eccl.* 6.40. While the story does not explicitly identify the wedding party as Christian, the quick response of the party in spite of personal danger and the treatment they render Dionysius suggest that they were either Christians or sympathetic to Christians. As to their rural character, the term χωριτῶν is used. Eusebius here is quoting from Dionysius' own firsthand report.

told the story for that reason, since he comes off looking rather befuddled. For our purposes here, the story provides one more account that, in quite unintended ways, witnesses to a likely rural Christian presence already established by the year 250 C.E. in Egypt. Further material from Dionysius' account hints at, if not a rural Christianity, at least some success of Christianity among the native Egyptian population. Various martyrs of the Decian persecution are specifically identified by Dionysius as Egyptian.[121]

A rural environment is encountered a second time in Dionysius' story. Dionysius was exiled to Cephro, a village in Libya near the desert, which he said he had hardly heard of, let alone known its location. There were no Christians there, other than people who came with him or who later joined him from Egypt, though after some opposition, some locals did convert.[122] After that, Dionysius was sent to the district of Colluthion, an even more bleak place of exile. Although the area was part of Egypt and closer to Alexandria in miles, it was a rougher and more Libyan-like place than the Libyan village in which Dionysius had begun his exile. This second place was said to be "without brethren or persons of good character."[123] At first glance, this might look like evidence that Christianity had not yet penetrated the countryside of Egypt and Libya by the mid-200s. But the text may not show that at all. It is clear that both areas were remote and the settlements were villages, and that these places of exile were chosen for that reason. Thus, they are not typical rural settlements that would have dotted the Egyptian and Libyan landscape. Further, Dionysius reported on the absence of Christians prior to his arrival in Cephro and mentioned that he had heard about the lack of Christians in the district of Colluthion. If the countryside was largely void of a Christian presence until after this time, then there would have been little need to state the obvious. What strikes Dionysius as worthy of note about both areas is that they did not have Christians.

Other evidence of an early rural Christian presence in Egypt may be found in monasticism, though the information here has been read in various ways, leaving the roots and rural character of monasticism a matter of

---

121. Eusebius, *Hist. eccl.* 6.41. Only Hero, Ater, and Isodore are identified as Egyptian, but Dioscorus, a boy of about fifteen years, was with them. Most likely, he was an Egyptian as well. In another passage, the martyr Nemesion is identified as an Egyptian (6.41.21).

122. Eusebius, *Hist. eccl.* 7.11.10–15.

123. Eusebius, *Hist. eccl.* 7.11.14–16.

controversy.[124] Some, such as Peter Brown, make much of the rural aspect of the monastic movement.[125] Others, however, have pointed out that the rural dimension may have been too starkly drawn, and the traditional association of monastics with the desert has been challenged by some recent studies.[126]

Perhaps the attempt to resolve the urban and rural complexities of monasticism is bound to fail, being based on the defective schema of a clear urban/rural divide. Whether we call Antony's birthplace a village (κῶμη) as Athanasius does in his *Vita Antonii* or a town (*municipium*) as the anonymous Latin translation renders it several decades later,[127] the sources agree that Antony's family was Coptic and they lived in what appears to be a Coptic community. That Antony's family owned considerable land would have set them somewhat apart from the rural rabble, but as farmers they were connected to the land, and as Coptic they attended a church in their village where the liturgy was probably in Coptic.[128]

---

124. A number of surveys of the issue are available, though often offering only a sketch of the roots of monasticism: Derwas James Chitty, *The Desert a City: An Introduction to the Study of Egyptian and Palestinian Monasticism under the Christian Empire* (Oxford: Blackwell, 1996); Marilyn Dunn, *The Emergence of Monasticism: From the Desert Fathers to the Early Middle Ages* (Oxford: Blackwell, 2000); Douglas Burton-Christie, *The Word in the Desert: Scripture and the Quest for Holiness in Early Christian Monasticism* (New York: Oxford University Press, 1993).

125. Peter Brown, "The Rise and Function of the Holy Man in Late Antiquity," *JRS* 61 (1971): 80–101; Reprinted in Peter Brown, *Society and the Holy in Late Antiquity* (Berkeley: University of California Press, 1982), 103–152; Brown, "Town, Village and Holy Man: The Case for Syria," in *Assimilation et résistance à la culture gréco-romaine dans le monde ancient*, ed. D. M. Pippidi (Bucharest: Editura Academiei, 1976), 213–220.

126. Averil Cameron, *The Mediterranean World in Late Antiquity* A.D. 395–600 (London: Routledge, 1993), 73–75; David Brakke, *Athanasius and the Politics of Asceticism* (New York: Oxford University Press, 1995); Lois Gandt, "A Philological and Theological Analysis of the Ancient Latin Translations of the *Vita Antonii*," Ph.D. diss., Fordham University, 2008; James E. Goehring, *Ascetics, Society, and the Desert: Studies in Early Egyptian Monasticism* (Harrisburg, PA: Trinity Press International, 1999); Goehring, "Withdrawing from the Desert: Pachomius and the Development of Village Monasticism in Upper Egypt," *HTR* 89.3 (1996): 267–285. Other reasons might be given too. Some have argued that economic crises drove some to the desert.

127. See Gandt, "A Philological and Theological Analysis of the Ancient Latin Translations," 94.

128. Athanasius does not provide the name of Antony's birthplace. The name first appears in a source long after Antony's death, in Sozomen's (*c.* 400–*c.* 450) writings. He calls the birthplace Coma (*Hist. eccl.* 1.13). Coma (the modern village of Kemn-el Arouse) was a town about 360 kilometers (225 miles) upriver from Alexandria. Gandt, "A Philological and Theological Analysis of the Ancient Latin Translations," 92–95, argues for a less rural environment for Antony on the basis of Coma's proximity to Heracleopolis Magna, the third largest city in Roman Egypt, which she argues makes Coma more likely a "substantial town"

Antony has recently been rehabilitated from illiterate country bumpkin to a competent leader who could correspond easily by letter with others.[129] Such remaking of Antony can lead the discussion of monasticism in quite different directions. On the one hand, the roots of monasticism may appear more urban. On the other hand, the character of the countryside may appear less rustic, or at least the supposed gap between the urban and rural worlds may appear more linked or linkable. Athough the recent tendency has been to associate monasticism more with the urban environment, that may reflect more the unnecessary (and flawed) urban/rural dicotomy that had overshadowed the discussion of much of early Christian monasticism and of early Christianity itself.

Even if monasticism is to be located nearer to urban centers than had been the customary portrait, the Coptic character of early monasticism seems a part of the portrait that is less easily dismissed. And that is perhaps a more important point than where to locate monasticism physically. Consider Antony's parents. They were Christian and Coptic. When they became Christian is not stated, but Antony seems to have been raised as a Christian from childhood.[130] Further, Antony's parents were neither the first nor the only Christians in the area; some older Christian men had already started monasteries nearby. As Derwas J. Chitty has pointed out, Antony was not "the first in the field."[131] Certain men had already taken up an asceticism that marked them off as distinctive from the rest of the Christian community there. Although Athanasius mentions that there were not many monasteries before this time, there were some. In fact, the ascetic who caught Antony's attention was old when Antony became attracted to asceticism at about the age of twenty. That man had been an ascetic from a young age himself, pushing back well before 250 evidence for an ascetic Coptic presence in the area. Further, when Antony opted for asceticism, there was already a group of virgins nearby with whom Antony

---

than a "small rural village" (94). Although it is possible that Sozomen had an older source that provided the name of the birthplace, the only source we are certain that was available to Sozomen about Antony was Athanasius' *Vita Antonii*, which does not name the birthplace but does call it a village (κώμη) (2–3).

129. Samuel Rubenson, *The Letters of St. Antony: Monasticism and the Making of a Saint* (Minneapolis: Fortress, 1995), 141–144.

130. The Greek and Latin versions of the *Life of Antony* agree on most details, including these details about Antony's parents. See Carolinne White, *Early Christian Lives* (London: Penguin Books, 1998), for an English translation of one of the two Latin versions.

131. Chitty, *The Desert a City*, 2.

trusted the care of his young sister. At least, these are the details presented by Athanasius.[132]

But the most important point for our question here is not that there were rural ascetics prior to Antony;[133] it is that there were rural Christians prior to Antony who were *not* ascetic—Antony's own parents being an example. That Antony's parents were the only couple or the first who were Christian and non-ascetic is not even remotely suggested by the evidence. It seems likely that at least some areas of Egypt had *both* ascetic and non-ascetic expressions of rural Christianity somewhat before the middle of the third century, when Antony was born.

Whatever we make of Antony, two things stand out. He is part of a Coptic community and he is a monastic. Too often, however, the establishment of monasticism is used as an approximate date for the establishment of rural, Coptic-based Christianity itself. For example, Frend, the leading

---

132. There is a question of how reliable the information is that we have about Antony, the main details of which come from what has been traditionally known as Athanasius' *Life of Antony*. Some debate has arisen about the authorship of the Greek *Life of Antony* as well as the possibility of a more primitive Coptic version [T. D. Barnes, "Angel of Light or Mystic Initiate? The Problem of the 'Life of Antony,'" *JTS* n.s. 37 (1986): 353–368. Barnes is challenged by Rubenson, *The Letters of St. Antony*, 128–129]. But whether Athanasius or another person who knew Antony well is the author, as Barnes believes (p. 357), or whether Athanasius, as author, used an earlier biography of Antony, none of this should obscure the fact that the author declares in his introduction that he is only telling details that he is certain about, and he encourages his readers to put aside the various stories in circulation that he thinks are less reliable. Even supposing this is no more than a standard literary trope to assert the reliability of the author's story (and thus, for the historian, of no use for determining the reliability of the details in that story), some details of the story may carry their own likelihood. In particular, I would place here details that are somewhat incidental (though that is a judgment in itself). For example, the comment that Antony's parents were Christian and that there were ascetics near the Coptic villages would seem to qualify unless it can be shown how the invention of these details would advance the author's purposes. So, too, for Antony's death at an old age. One comment in *Vita Antonii* speaks of his teeth being worn down to the gums. Even if the old age of Antony is exaggerated (and it need not be), Antony must have died at what was taken to be a considerably old age, for *Vita Antonii* comes out shortly after Antony's death, and any gross misrepresentation of Antony's age would have been challenged by many who themselves knew Antony or knew of him. Indeed, given how Athanasius presents himself as truthful and certain about details he presents, it would hardly help his effort to be mistaken about Antony dying at a considerably old age. If Athanasius is correct on that detail, then Antony's birth should be dated somewhat near the middle of the third century. And if Antony was attracted to asceticism around age twenty by a man already then elderly and who had himself become an ascetic at an early age, then a Coptic monastic presence in rural Egypt might be pushed back to the early 200s, though the size of the movement and its growth during the first half of the third century could not be determined from that.

133. I am calling these ascetics rural because that seems to be how Athanasius presents them. They are connected to villages. They are not urbanites.

scholar on the question of rural Christianity, claims that between Paul and the beginnings of monasticism, Christianity was an urban religion.[134] Such a connection is too hastily drawn. Nothing about the rise of monasticism requires a late date for the rise of rural Christianity in Egypt. In fact, everything in Antony's story points in the opposite direction.

A crucial matter is whether it is likely that a rural Christian monasticism would have developed without prior *rural* Christian roots. If not, that would date the presence of a rural non-ascetic form of Christianity *prior* to the rise of monasticism, and this would challenge theories that put monasticism forward as the oldest form of rural Christianity or that delayed the establishment of rural Christianity until the latter half of the third century. It is difficult to envision a situation where *rural* Coptic monasticism would have arisen from urban Christianity without such rural monastics having had an intermediate or transitional environment within a rural non-monastic Coptic Christianity. That is to say: it is easier to envision a Christian rustic opting for a monastic life than a pagan rustic opting for that way of life, for monasticism was Christian in its origin, character, and purpose.

If it is unlikely that the rise of a rural Christian monasticism would have occurred outside of a preexisting rural non-monastic Christianity, it seems that we can then somewhat confidently conclude that rural Christianity is likely to have existed in the first half of the third century in Egypt. And, further, if native, rural Egyptians were converting to Christianity in the earlier part of the third century, we might speculate that some rural Egyptians may have converted to Christianity in the second century as well, there seeming to have been no significant shift in rural sensibilities between the second and third centuries that would have made any particular form of Christianity more attractive than the others.

North Africa

It is widely accepted that North Africa had a considerable Christian population by the time of the conversion of Constantine. What is more debatable is when Christianity came to North Africa, from what center it came, what its initial character was, and most importantly whether there was a

---

134. Whether Frend is correct in drawing stark lines between city and countryside, as he set out to do in his article, his evidence does point to the existence of a rural Christianity in the pre-Constantinian period and of the roots of monasticism in a rural environment.

substantial difference between the native cultures and that of the Roman transplants, and whether any such difference is reflected in the makeup of the Christian community.[135]

As to Christianity's first presence in North Africa, the New Testament itself mentions Cyrene, the province in North Africa just to the west of Egypt.[136] We have little evidence for the situation between that time and the time of Tertullian (*c.* 200 C.E.), however,[137] though such evidence does tell us something about that intermediate period. By Tertullian's time, the general population of the area was aware of the Christian presence and had some understanding—even if a poor understanding—of it. The cases of the Scillitan martyrs and the martyrdom of Perpetua and her companions have gotten the most attention.[138] But Christians were already regularly enough the victims of execution by Tertullian's time that the pagan society had coined nicknames for Christian martyrs: "faggot fellows" and "half-axle men."[139] The terms relate to the wood chips for the fire and the stakes upon which the victims were bound. Further, the terms seem to have been applied specifically to Christians.[140] Such terms are not the kinds of labels that Christians would have coined for themselves. Tertullian's use of these

---

135. For a summary of the various positions, see Geoffrey D. Dunn, *Tertullian* (London: Routledge, 2004), 13–15; David Wilhite, *Tertullian the African: An Anthropological Reading of Tertullian's Context and Identities.* Millennium Studies 14 (Berlin: Walter de Gruyter, 2007), 31–35.

136. In addition to Simon of Cyrene (Mk 15:21; Mt 27:32; Lk 23:26), mention of people connected with Cyrene occurs in the story of the day of Pentecost (Acts 2:10) and further in Acts at 6:9, 11:20, and 13:1. In the Pentecost story, apart from Egypt, Cyrene is the only area of Africa mentioned in the list of fifteen different areas.

137. Dunn, *Tertullian*, 9, points out that if Apuleius' reference in *Metamorphoses* 9.14 is to Christians, then Christianity must have been established in North Africa by the middle of the second century. Vincent Hunink, "Apuleius, Pudentilla, and Christianity," *Vigiliae Christianae* 54 (2000): 80–94, makes a case for Apuleius' knowledge of and opposition to Christianity, though as a well-traveled person, such familiarity need not suggest that Apuleius had encountered Christians in Africa.

138. Brent D. Shaw, "The Passion of Perpetua," *Past and Present* 139 (1993): 3–45.

139. Tertullian, *Apology* 50.3. The Latin terms are *sarmenticios* and *semaxos*. *Sarmenticios* means twigs and *semaxios* is a half-axle post, part of the axle of a chariot that was used as a stake to which the victim would be tied. Tertullian plays with the idea, making the seemingly ignoble death of the martyr into a victory celebration of a chariot-riding general. See Robert D. Sider, *Christian and Pagan in the Roman Empire: The Witness of Tertullian* (Washington, DC: The Catholic University Press of America, 2001), 69n163.

140. Tertullian is the only writer to record the use of these terms. The terms may have had only local currency among pagans in Tertullian's immediate locale. Even so, they suggest an environment of recurring persecution. This is not a one-off thing.

terms would seem to require a general familiarity by the wider public with these terms in the specific context of Christian executions, and that would suggest that Christians have been executed in sufficient numbers to make some impression on the locals, and to prompt the coining of mocking labels for Christian martyrs. It might even be argued that these terms should be treated as more convincing evidence for the frequency of persecution than even several accounts of an occasional martyrdom.[141]

It is one thing to show that there was an early Christian presence in North Africa; it is quite another to determine whether Christianity had penetrated the countryside. That matter is somewhat tied to the broader question of the relationship between the native cultures of North Africa and the Latin culture of the Roman overlords. The matter is complicated at various levels. For one thing, there is not just one native culture in North Africa; there are many, though often these are simply referred to as Berber, a term that does not occur until after the period we are examining. In addition to the Berber culture (or what some prefer to call the Libyan), there was a more recent transplanted "native" culture, the Punic, which was established by the Phoenicians, who settled in the area in the 800s B.C.E. and established their capital at Carthage. These settlers developed into the dominant naval power in the Mediterranean but lost that position to the Romans, who in a series of wars from 264 to 146 B.C.E. conquered the Carthaginians and destroyed their capital. The Romans then settled the area and governed for the next six hundred years.

Heated debates have been a feature of modern scholarship on North Africa, largely around the question of "Resistance" or "Romanization," with sharp disagreement whether the native cultures adopted Latin culture thoroughly or only as a thin veneer, under which lay a determined

---

141. For example, Dunn, *Tertullian*, 12, uses the word "sporadic" in describing Christian persecution in North Africa during the reign of Septimius Severus. I think terms like "regular" or "frequent" might better describe the situation where specific mocking vocabulary had been coined for victims of persecution, unless these terms had currency more widely for any victim of the arena, Christian or otherwise, which does not seem to have been the case. At least, we know these terms only in the context of Christian executions. Further, these terms seem specifically suited for burning at the stake or being tied there as victims for the beasts, but only in the account of Perpetua and her companions do the martyrs face this type of death. The Scillitan martyrs were beheaded. This hints at far more frequent incidents of persecution than we have preserved reports, for if the generally accepted dates are correct for Tertullian's *Apology* (197 C.E.) and for Perpetua's death (203 C.E.), the mocking terms were coined earlier than Perpetua's death and earlier than Tertullian's *Apology*, suggesting a number of early and unrecorded victims of this kind of execution. A later persecution took place in 212 C.E. in Mauretania and Numidia (Tertullian, *Ad Scapulam*).

resistance to Roman culture and a staunch defense of native culture.[142] Some see the present scholarly disagreement tied up in the modern postcolonial debates over empire.[143]

The issue is an important one, for it affects how Christianity in North Africa is understood, which will have implications regarding our question of an early rural Christianity. Two leading historians of the early church have taken different sides on the issue. W. H. C. Frend, who made North Africa the focus of much of his study, drew lines sharply between Roman and native culture and, on the basis of such division, interpreted the entire Donatist schism.[144]

But Peter Brown pointedly rejects Frend's assessment.[145] He argues that Christianity did not foster native traditions; rather, it made Latin available to a wider circle.[146] Rather than having Donatism marked by a Punic language and a rural character, as Frend had argued for, Brown argued that Donatists functioned in the same language as the Catholics and they operated in cities as well as in the countryside.[147] Further, Brown also rejected Frend's assessment of Donatism as rural in character, concluding rather that the conflict was "not between 'town' and 'country' but, perhaps, between two layers of the aristocracies of the towns."[148] Brown builds on

---

142. David J. Mattingly and R. Bruce Hitchner, "Roman Africa: An Archaeological Review," *JRS* 85 (1995): 169–170. See Wilhite, *Tertullian the African*, for a detailed study reflecting a postcolonial perspective. For a challenge to both the "Resistance" and "Romanization" theories, see Greg Woolf, "Beyond Romans and Natives," *World Archaeology* 28.3 (1997): 339–350.

143. Wilhite, *Tertullian the African*, 1–11.

144. W. H. C. Frend, *The Donatist Church: A Movement of Protest in Roman North Africa* (Oxford: Clarendon Press, 1952).

145. Peter Brown, "Religious Dissent in the Later Roman Empire: The Case of North Africa," *History* 46 (1961): 83–101; *Religion and Society in the Age of Saint Augustine* (London: Faber & Faber, 1972), 237–259; "Religious Coercion in the Later Roman Empire: The Case of North Africa," *History* 48 (1963): 293–297; *Augustine of Hippo: A Biography* (London: Faber and Faber, 1967), 217 and 227–230; "Christianity and Local Culture in Late Roman Africa," *JRS* 58 (1968): 85–95.

146. Brown, "Christianity and Local Culture in Late Roman Africa," 90–91, describes this Latin as a clerical language, with the "simplicity and uniformity" that allowed it to be a vehicle of literacy—even if it did not meet the approval of the "educated pagan."

147. For a summary and analysis of the two general positions and of Frend and Brown's interpretations, see Mattingly and Hitchner, "Roman Africa: An Archaeological Review," *JRS* 85 (1995): 165–213. Mattingly and Hitchner favor Brown's view. They speak of Frend's major work as "an influential, but ultimately misleading book" (208n439).

148. Brown, "Christianity and Local Culture in Late Roman Africa," 92.

the work of others, particularly A. H. M. Jones' short but classic critique of Frend.[149]

From a slightly different perspective, F. W. Walbank comments:

> it is easier to identify elements in provincial culture as being of local origin and resistant to Romanisation than it is to assess how far such survivals indicate conscious opposition to Rome and genuine nationalist feeling. Much depended in the attitude of the Romans themselves toward native culture, and in general this tended to be tolerant. Native, non-Roman cults and language were something to be left alone, not (with few exceptions) eradicated or ironed into uniformity.[150]

Whatever the North African resistance to Romanization, certainly Christianity had been established well before the end of the second century since a group of Christians were tried and beheaded in Carthage in 180 C.E. for practicing Christian rites and refusing to participate in rites related to the imperial cult. What is perhaps more significant is that these victims appear to have been rural. The Christians were from the village or town of Scillium (Scilli). Frend speaks of "small settlements of Scilli,"[151] thought to be in the vicinity of Carthage, though no particular village has been identified in modern investigations. Some scholars consider this as evidence that Christianity had extended its reach into the countryside of North Africa early.[152] Éric Rebillard concludes that, given that our knowledge of African cities is "fairly good" and that we know nothing about the location of Scilli, Scilli was likely "a (very) small" settlement. He concludes from this that Christianity was already present in the countryside by 180.[153] Tertullian, writing only a few years later, seems to confirm the

---

149. A. H. M. Jones, "Were the Ancient Heresies National or Social Movements in Disguise?" *JTS* n.s. 10.2 (1959): 280–295.

150. F. W. Walbank, "Nationality as a Factor in Roman History," *HSCP* 76 (1972): 155.

151. Frend, *The Rise of Christianity*, 290.

152. Thomas C. Oden, *Early Libyan Christianity: Uncovering a North African Tradition* (Downers Grove, IL: IVP Academic, 2011), 39–40, 65, 270. Another execution of Christians took place in 202 in Carthage [Thomas A. Heffernan, *The Passion of Perpetua and Felicity* (New York: Oxford University Press, 2012)].

153. Éric Rebillard, "The West (2): North Africa," in *The Oxford Handbook of Early Christian Studies*, 304.

soundness of this conclusion, for he noted that there had been complaints that Christianity was already in the countryside and villages.[154]

Regarding another piece of evidence, Frend notes that a synod convened by Cyprian in 256 had representatives of "up-country" bishoprics, which he takes as evidence that Christianity had begun to spread into the North African countryside.[155] If Frend is correct in that conclusion, then one would assume that a mission to the countryside must have started somewhat earlier, and perhaps considerably earlier, well before the middle of the third century.[156] One is unlikely to find bishops where there are no Christians; indeed, one would expect a fair number of conversions would have first occurred in order for there to have been a need for a bishop.[157] Further, we have no way to ascertain whether there had been bishops in these areas even before the bishops who attended the synod of 256. There is nothing that demands that these were the first bishops in these areas or that rural Christianity was, therefore, a recent phenomenon.

In spite of that, Frend contends that when Diocletian became emperor, the church was still "overwhelmingly urban," and he thinks that the strength of the rural Christian movement in North Africa and Egypt was not recognized until the Great Persecution.[158] Somewhat strange is Frend's seemingly contradictory assertion that Christianity was able to survive Diocletian's persecution because of the strength of that rural Christianity. But such strong rural Christian presence would require a rapid and resolute swing to Christianity in rural areas that until this time had apparently paid little attention to Christianity. Such meteoric success of Christianity in the countryside would need explanation. Frend argues

---

154. Tertullian, *Apol.* 1.7.

155. Frend, *The Rise of Christianity*, 424.

156. Clarke, "Third-Century Christianity," 609n62, finds evidence for rural Christians as early as the 230s in the correspondence of Firmilian (Cypr. *Ep.* 75.10): "unum de presbyteris tusticum item et alium diaconum."

157. Some think the Donatists and Catholics were in such a race to be first to establish bishops in settlements that they sometimes placed a bishop in settlements where there were yet no Christians. Brent D. Shaw, *Sacred Violence: African Christians and Sectarian Hatred in the Age of Constantine* (Cambridge: Cambridge University Press, 2011), 580, points out that in the argument between Donatists and Catholics, charges and countercharges were made: against the Donatists, that many of their places were merely farms where bishops had been appointed; against the Catholics, that where they had bishops, their churches had almost no members. The question is how much of that rhetoric reflects reality.

158. Frend, *The Rise of Christianity*, 424.

that the "Romanization" of the chief native god Baal-Hamon may have led some natives to reject their god, who now, as Saturn, appeared too much in the dress of their Roman conquerors.[159] As a result of this disillusionment, native North Africans supposedly were prepared to accept the Christian god as a reasonable substitute. But Frend so cautiously states his case that one wonders whether there is a case to be made here at all. Frend says:

> Clearly, one cannot say without irrefutable literary or archaeological evidence that the Romanization of their chief god alienated some of his worshipers and made them think of a Christian alternative, but subject peoples have been known to reject violently the deliberate modernization of traditional religious practices by their conquerors.[160]

But too much of Frend's explanation for a *late* success of Christianity into the countryside depends on this supposedly native disillusionment with the Romanization of their chief native god. Whatever we make of such disillusionment, it is unlikely that the native North Africans, in resisting Romanization of their cult, would have turned to Christianity, for the Christian god could hardly have seemed an attractive replacement for North Africans' somewhat Romanized native god. It is unfounded speculation to maintain that somehow the Christian Jesus in any wrapping would have appeared more authentically native to the rural North Africans than their traditional god, however fully wrapped that god had become in Roman garb. Furthermore, the Christian Jesus hardly strikes one as a particularly Semitic deity at any stage of the Christian mission.

Syria

The matter of Christianity in Syria is complicated. Regarding language, there was the western region, where Greek dominated in the cities, in particular in Antioch (though Syriac would have been spoken there too[161]); to the east, there was Edessa and beyond, where Syriac dominated. Regarding

---

159. Frend, *The Rise of Christianity*, 348.

160. Frend, *The Rise of Christianity*, 348.

161. Harnack, *Expansion of Christianity*, 134, notes that Syriac would have been spoken by the lower classes in Antioch itself, with much the same situation in other Greek towns.

politics, the west was part of the Roman Empire, the east was generally part of the Parthian Empire, and Edessa, somewhat in the middle, was a small independent kingdom until 214 C.E.

Our question in the present examination is the possibility of a rural Christianity, and in this matter Syria is far less complicated than some of the other areas. I have already addressed the linguistic question for Syria earlier.[162] Whatever case can be made for Greek being a barrier to Christian expansion into the countryside (assuming a non-Greek countryside, where native languages survived in daily discourse), the linguistic problem evaporates for areas where the dominant language of the city was also the language of the countryside. Such is the situation for the Syriac church—urban or rural, particularly in the eastern part. Granted, our earliest evidence is for Christianity in urban environments, and we cannot assume Christianity's early presence in rural areas. Yet a primary barrier often thrown up in arguments against the possibility of a rural Christianity—the linguistic barrier—is simply not relevant for most of Syria.

Other Areas within the Empire

Although I am primarily interested in the eastern part of the empire, where we are most likely to find evidence of rural Christianity prior to 250 C.E., a few passages from other locales are worth some mention. In Italy, for example, during the Decian persecution, a controversy broke out between the Roman bishop, Fabian, and Novatian, another claimant to the office. The critics of Novatian are colorful but not kind, and we would be wise not to take the motives assigned to Novatian too readily, if at all. Yet, even biased comment may offer useful, unintended insight. In arguing that Novatian's election as bishop was a sham, Cornelius (later to become the recognized successor to Fabian), reports that Novatian brought back three bishops from "a small and very insignificant part of Italy."[163] These men are described as "rough and simple men" (ἀγροίκους καὶ ἁπλουστάτους), where "rustic" or "rural" would be as good a translation as "rough." Whether Cornelius exaggerated the lack of qualifications of these three bishops or whether the story as a whole is a fabrication does not matter for

---

162. See chapter 6.

163. Eusebius, *Hist. eccl.* 6.43.

our purposes here. The point is that a prominent member of the Roman clergy could speak of bishops in remote areas of Italy and refer to such bishops as rustics. This is in the year 250 C.E., and there is no indication that the churches served by these bishops were only recently established. Indeed, it is likely that Cornelius can speak of these bishops as rustics or rurals because such bishops were commonplace enough for that part of the story not to raise suspicions about its veracity.

Farther to the west, in Britain, Peter Salway contends that "the old notion of urban Christianity and rural paganism certainly cannot be maintained."[164] That may have been because the society was more villa-based. Whatever the case, we do have here an example of rural mission and some level of success largely independent of the urban church, though both were spotty enough, according to Salway.[165]

Beyond the Empire

We now turn to the Christian missions to the barbarians. Our interest here is not to review or describe that mission so much as it is to see whether aspects of that mission may throw some light on Christian attitudes to rustics and cultures less influenced by Greek language and sensibilities. In other words, does the Christian approach to barbarian tribes tell us anything about the likelihood of a Christian mission to dwellers in the rural areas of the Roman Empire?

Some scholars think the church took little interest in the barbarian tribes until after the church became linked with the empire through the conversion of Constantine,[166] and, indeed, some think that, even then, the Church had little interest in the barbarians. Largely, the debate revolves around the issue of how closely the church identified itself with the empire, and whether such identification tended to restrict the church's vision of mission or to expand their vision of empire.

We have seen earlier how the church adopted a range of languages, including those of barbarian cultures, and we do know that by the early 300s, a number of bishops were associated with remote Christian

---

164. Peter Salway, "Roman Britain (c. 55 BC–c. AD 440)," in *The Oxford History of Britain*, 2nd ed., ed. Kenneth O. Morgan (Oxford: Oxford University Press, 2010), 47.

165. Salway, *The Oxford History of Britain*, 47–49.

166. Carole M. Cusack, *Conversion among the Germanic Peoples* (London: Cassell, 1998), 38.

settlements beyond the Roman Empire. Some attended the Council of Nicea.[167] A hundred years before that council, Tertullian, though clearly boasting, gives no hint that Christians had no interest or success beyond the borders of the Roman Empire, as he lists off the places of Christian presence:

> Parthians, Medes, Elamites, and they who inhabit Mesopotamia, Armenia, Phrygia, Cappadocia, and they who dwell in Pontus, and Asia, and Pamphylia, tarriers in Egypt, and inhabiters of the region of Africa which is beyond Cyrene, Romans and sojourners, yes, and in Jerusalem Jews, and all other nations; as, for instance, by this time, the varied races of the Gaetulians, and manifold confines of the Moors, all the limits of the Spains, and the diverse nations of the Gauls, and the haunts of the Britons—inaccessible to the Romans, but subjugated to Christ, and of the Sarmatians, and Dacians, and Germans, and Scythians, and of many remote nations, and of provinces and islands many, to us unknown, and which we can scarce enumerate?[168]

Although Tertullian does not mention rural areas specifically, many of these areas lack the urbanization of the Roman Empire. They could be counted as rustic as one might find anywhere.

Problems for the Urban Thesis

When we explore the possible origins of rural Christianity in the period before 250 c.e., we are faced with a difficult situation. As we have seen, the surviving evidence is meager and random, and Christians, even in the cities, were few. But given how few Christians there were anywhere, we might ask what kind of evidence we need in order to establish that there was a rural Christian presence, particularly considering that it would take few rural Christians to make the Christian church as rural as it was urban, at least in terms of raw numbers. We need not show massive Christian missions, sweeping whole villages and valleys into the church, though we

---

167. Richard A. Fletcher, *The Barbarian Conversion: From Paganism to Christianity* (New York: Henry Holt, 1998), 66.

168. Tertullian, *Adv. Jud.* 7.

know that such did happen and could be appealed to.[169] We are talking about nothing more than one Christian convert or perhaps a whole family here and there, some towns with a few more; and most with none.

Looking specifically at the year 200, Stark, followed by Hopkins, thinks that there were about 200,000 Christians in the empire.[170] A rural Christian population of only 100,000, or one-fifth of one percent of the total rural population, would provide as many rural Christians as urban Christians. Such a tally of rural Christians is not unrealistic, particularly given what appears to be considerable success in rural Phrygia, only one area for which some evidence of early Christian presence in the country-side can be found. Whatever we make of the peculiar Christian character of the church in Phrygia, whether Montanist or a mix of Montanist and non-Montanist Christians, we must grant a sufficient number of rural Christians in this area by 200 to account for what appears to be a largely Christianized area there by the time of Constantine—if, indeed, perhaps much earlier.[171]

Even the numbers offered by Stark for the year 250 require only slightly more than 500,000 rural Christians for half the membership of the Christian church to have been rural. This is less than 1% of the rural population. And Stark's numbers for the year 300 actually demand that a large number of rural Christians be included in that count, though Stark fails to recognize this. He concludes that there were slightly over 6 million Christians by the year 300. As we have seen, if most Christians were urban at this time, then *a significant majority* of the population of all urban areas within the Roman Empire would need to be Christian, a highly unlikely—indeed, impossible—reconstruction of the religious situation at the time

---

169. Just after Constantine conquered the eastern empire, the village of Orcistus in Phrygia appealed to him for a favor, reporting that everyone in the town was Christian [W. M. Calder, *MAMA*, vii, No. 305 (Manchester: Manchester University Press, 1956), xxxviii]. Another town in the same area seems to have been put to the sword during the Great Persecution because it was considered to be fully Christian (Eusebius, *Hist. eccl.* 8.11.1; Lactantius, *Inst.* 5.11). Whether the latter is fictional matters little for our purposes here; the story is apparently believable to writer and reader at the time [Kenneth W. Harl, "From Pagan to Christian in Cities of Roman Anatolia," in *Urban Centers and Rural Contexts in Late Antiquity*, ed. Thomas S. Burns and John W. Eadie (East Lansing: Michigan State University Press, 2001), 320n28].

170. Stark, *The Rise of Christianity*, 7, uses the number 217,795. Hopkins, "Christian Number and Its Implications," 195, rounds off the number.

171. If the area is largely Christianized by Constantine's time, it is unlikely that it had just become so. The period immediately before Constantine involved the Great Persecution, and Phrygia seems to have suffered in particular. These are hardly the conditions under which

of the beginning of the Great Persecution of the church under the Roman Empire.[172] Even if we were to say that one-third of the urban population was Christian by the year 300, itself a remote possibility at best only for the most Christianized cities of the eastern empire, then over half of the total Christian population would need to be rural, if the commonly accepted number for the total Christian population in the empire is correct.[173] Stark and others give no consideration to this as they confidently declare the urban character of early Christianity.

As we have seen, most scholars who have studied the early centuries in depth recognize that Christianity made significant advance into the countryside in the latter half of the third century. The problem is this. If the Christian message was able to win rural converts in the latter part of the third century among the supposedly conservative countryside, there would seem to be no compelling reason for not allowing the same receptiveness to the Christian message earlier, unless we could account for a significant shift in rural sensibilities or a significant change in rural conditions. But, as we will see in the next chapter, no explanation for any such shift is really compelling, or even slightly so.

The impression of Christian cities in the midst of a pagan countryside is mainly that—an impression, created not by the raw numbers of Christians in each area but by the percentage of the population of urban areas that became Christian compared to the percentage in rural areas. That tells us nothing of the numerical strength of urban Christians compared to rural Christians, though that is generally how the numbers have been taken.

To summarize the situation we have just examined: we could maintain that cities were more Christianized than the countryside; we could not maintain, however, that the church was dominantly urban—as is often asserted. The two matters are not the same. Given equal numbers of Christians in urban and rural areas, the rural areas will look more pagan,

---

there would have been a spurt of Christian growth. Thus, if Phrygia was largely Christian by the year 300, we must push back the date for substantial Christian success in this area even earlier. The evidence from Phrygia challenges Stark's thesis bluntly. The Christianity there is rural, at least in part, and the rate of conversion must have been considerably higher than Stark has argued if Christianity had not established itself in rural areas early.

172. See Appendix B.

173. Christians in the empire: 6 million; total urban population of empire: 9 million; one-third of urban population Christian: 3 million. Conclusion: half the Christian population must have been rural.

and be more pagan, simply by reason of the proportion of the population in the empire that was rural. The countryside, then, can look considerably more pagan than the city without that requiring that the church, in terms of raw numbers, be largely urban. Indeed, if the rural and urban areas had equal *proportions* of their respective populations Christianized, rural Christians would have outnumbered urban Christians by almost seven to one.[174]

And, of course, there will always be the question hanging over any of these kinds of investigations whether we have such neat divisions between urban and rural that would allow us to talk in any meaningful way of distinct identities. As we have seen, the boundaries are hardly clearly defined in the scholarship on the issue—indeed, the boundaries are very likely impossible to define. What we can say is this: there is adequate evidence of an early Christian presence beyond city walls (which, of course, never really separated the rural and the urban) and beyond urbanite sensibilities.

---

174. See Table 3.2, chapter 3. When 50% of urban areas are Christian, only 8.8% of rural areas need to be Christian to have equal numbers of urban and rural Christians. With 100% of the urban areas Christianized, only 17.6% of the rural population needs to be Christianized to have a balanced urban/rural membership.

8

Dismissing the Evidence
of Christianity in the Countryside

ALL SCHOLARS ADMIT a rural Christian presence after Constantine, usually connecting that success to an imperial-sponsored church, which had the resources to force the supposedly more traditional and conservative countryside into line. One searches hard to find a book on early Christianity that does not assume or comment on the urban character of early Christianity and a late rural mission.

But such a view needs to be considerably more nuanced. Even the most vigorous promoters of the urban thesis are forced by the evidence to admit a Christian presence of some note in at least some rural areas (such as Phrygia and North Africa, and most likely Egypt and Syria) well before Constantine's conversion. Generally, however, scholars who have admitted the presence of a rural Christianity prior to Constantine have downplayed this evidence as too insignificant to challenge the urban thesis. This downplaying of a pre-Constantinian rural Christianity is done in several ways, usually by scholars without particular agenda and quite unconscious that something more may be at stake. In this chapter, I examine the ways scholars who admit a pre-Constantinian rural Christianity have downplayed its significance. Such downplaying has put the thesis of an early Christian presence in the countryside at a distinct disadvantage.[1]

---

1. My interest here is to determine whether the various reconstructions offer a reasonably convincing account of the origins of rural Christianity, and whether these reconstructions offer, as well, a fair assessment of that rural Christianity when it is found. I point primarily to weaknesses in reconstructions that have been proposed. The large question of the origins and development of rural Christianity will be answered only by extensive examination of all areas of the Mediterranean and by a willingness among investigators to consider the possibility, at least, of an early rural presence.

Restricting Rural Christianity
to the Late Third Century

The willingness to admit a rural Christianity in the half-century prior to Constantine, which many scholars concede, is taken to have little consequence for the overall reconstruction of early Christian expansion and development as an urban religion, for that still leaves two centuries in which Christianity might be classed as an urban religion. But dating rural Christianity prior to Constantine, even if only in the half-century before his rule, is of critical import. Most profoundly, it challenges the primary assumptions of the urban thesis: that is, that the countryside was largely immune to Christian mission and largely neglected in Christian interest until the age of Constantine, when cities became Christianized and attention might then be turned to rural areas, and when the church had the resources of imperial will and weight to force the stubborn pagan traditionalists in the countryside into line. If, however, there was Christian success in rural areas before Constantine, and if not in one region but in many, we would seem to have evidence that Christianity could and did overcome whatever barriers a rural mission confronted, and that it was able to do this without the aid of the imperial power of persuasion. And if Christians had success in the countryside prior to Constantine, why restrict rural Christianity to the latter part of the third century? Second-century Montanism—and its more orthodox rural opponents—will always be a reminder of the possibility of an even earlier rural Christian presence.

Treating Rural Christianity as Abnormal

The second way the evidence of an early rural Christianity has been downplayed in the overall scheme of the urban thesis is that such Christianity is treated as non-representative and abnormal, largely composed of schismatic or heretical groups.[2] This generally means that, with few exceptions,

---

2. Chris C. Park, *Sacred Worlds: An Introduction to Geography and Religion* (London: Routledge, 2002) reviews approaches to geography and religion over the centuries and offers a substantial contribution to the field. He addresses the question of urban and rural relationships and diffusion of ideas and movements from city to countryside or vice versa in largely modern, and often North American, situations. But the modern and ancient contexts of Christianity are so starkly different to require caution in drawing parallels. For example, using patterns of religious settlement in the United States as a framework or a helpful parallel to explain either the spread or the character of Christianity in the Roman Empire is fraught with difficulties, particularly as we are primarily talking about patterns of immigration in Park's example rather than religious spread through conversion. That is not to say that no useful parallels

rural Christianity developed late, after some crisis had led to a schism and the formation of a distinctive identity.[3] Montanists, Donatists, Novatians, and sometimes monastics are pointed to as groups that were rural (at least to some extent) and non-representative.[4] A frequent associated assumption is that no orthodox form of Christianity existed in rural areas where these deviant fringe groups had residence. Such a conclusion allows for a dismissal of rural Christianity, or the relegating of rural Christianity into a remote corner.

Frend is a good example of this position. He says:

> We find the same pattern repeated elsewhere, particularly in North Africa where the Donatists drew their strength from the countryside ... In Asia Minor, the Novatianists of the late third and early fourth centuries were also strong among the rural populations. Significantly, like the Montanists and the African Donatists, their bishops often represented villages and not towns.[5]

Frend comments further: "If any conclusion may be drawn from this evidence, it would seem to be that rural Christianity in the East seldom fitted any accepted canon of orthodoxy."[6] In another article, where Frend deals with the pre-Constantinian situation, he provides considerable evidence for the existence of rural Christianity prior to 300 C.E., but his judgment there is the same regarding the deviant character of rural Christianity: "Meletianism in Egypt, Donatism in Africa and Novatianism

---

can be found between pre-Constantinian Christianity and modern western Christianity, but I doubt that insight will have much to do with urban/rural distinctions or our concern here.

3. That is not to say that orthodoxy was the original form of Christianity, and all heresies were later deviations, as Irenaeus and other early Christian writers argued. Without getting into the debate sparked by Walter Bauer's consensus-changing *Orthodoxy and Heresy in Earliest Christianity*, R. A. Kraft, et al., trans. and ed. (Philadelphia: Fortress, 1977), it can be said that those forms of Christianity that are identified as rural happen to be later than the developing catholic church, and such forms are often clearly schisms from what becomes the Great Church.

4. For example, Karl Holl, "Das Fortleben der Volksprachen in Kleinasien in nachchristlicher Zeit," *Hermes* 43 (1908): 253. For a challenge to the idea that there existed some correspondence between mother tongue and heresy, see A. H. M. Jones, "Were Ancient Heresies National or Social Movements in Disguise?" *JTS* n.s. 10 (1959): 280–297. See, too, Speros Vryonis, Jr., "Problems in the History of Byzantine Anatolia," *Ankara Univ. D.T.C. Fakültesi Tarih Arastirmalari Dergisi* 1.1 (1963): 120–121.

5. Frend, "The Winning of the Countryside," *JEH* 18 (1967): 6.

6. Frend, "The Winning of the Countryside," 9.

in Asia Minor ... all represent the same primarily rural Christianity."[7] We might add the Montanists of Phrygia to Frend's list of rural deviants, whose rural character he mentions elsewhere.[8]

Frend's position has been challenged because it exaggerates the rural character of these groups.[9] For one thing, each of these movements had an urban side as well, and some started in cities. Montanism, born in small towns, had success in cities.[10] Novatianism started in Rome—in the very leadership of the church there.[11] Meletianism, though stronger along the Nile outside of Alexandria, got its start by the bishop Meletius ordaining presbyters in Alexandria during the Diocletian persecution.[12] As for Donatism, the founder (Majorinus) was from Carthage. The leader after that, Donatus, though from a settlement on the edge of the North African desert, became a rival bishop of Carthage, the leading city of North Africa.[13] Indeed, as we have seen, it perhaps is not possible to draw a line between the rural and the urban, and even if it were possible, it would probably be impossible to do so for groups that cross into both spheres, in so far as such spheres can be distinguished. Peter Brown has taken issue with Frend's kind of assessment of native cultures and rural Christianity, as has A. H. M. Jones.[14] Most believe that Brown and Jones have effectively answered Frend.[15]

---

7. Frend, "The Failure of the Persecutions in the Roman Empire," in *Studies in Ancient History*, ed. M. I. Finley, Past and Present Series (London and Boston: Routledge and Kegan Paul, 1974), 283. An early proponent of this view was Edward Rochie Hardy, *Christian Egypt: Church and People: Christianity and Nationalism in the Patriarchate of Alexandria* (Oxford: Oxford University Press, 1952).

8. Frend, *The Rise of Christianity*, 256.

9. R. A. Markus, "Christianity and Dissent in Roman North Africa: Changing Perspectives in Recent Work," in *Schism, Heresy and Religious Protest*, ed. Derek Baker, Studies in Church History 9 (Cambridge: Cambridge University Press, 1972), 21–36.

10. Christine Trevett, "Montanism," in *The Early Christian World*, ed. Philip F. Esler (London: Routledge, 2000), II.936.

11. James L. Papandrea, *Novatian of Rome and the Culmination of Pre-Nicene Orthodoxy*, Princeton Theological Monograph Series 175 (Eugene, OR: Pickwick Publications, 2011).

12. Hardy, *Christian Egypt: Church and People*, 53.

13. W. H. C. Frend, *The Donatist Church: A Movement of Protest in Roman North Africa* (Oxford: Clarendon Press, 1952).

14. Peter Brown, "Christianity and Local Culture in Late Roman Africa," *JRS* 58 (1968): 85–95; Jones, "Were Ancient Heresies National or Social Movements in Disguise?" 280–297.

15. See Ramsay MacMullen, "Provincial Languages in the Roman Empire," *AJP* 87.1 (1966): 1–17, for a discussion of the matter, particularly as it relates to the use of native languages.

Yet Brown is not so different from Frend in seeing the countryside as home for less than orthodox forms of Christianity. He states that "it was in the countryside that many of the most radical forms of Christianity took root,"[16] and he points to an odd assortment of monastics and to the villager Mani, who founded, as Brown says, "the first new religion to emerge out of Christianity."[17] Even in the 500s, the countryside, according to Brown, "remained the Cinderella in a recognizably 'Roman' Christian order that still looked to the bishop and his city as the center of 'high density' Catholicism."[18] Tabbernee, too, makes rural areas a haven for less "mainstream" versions of Christianity both prior to and after Constantine.[19] Robin Lane Fox has a slightly different spin. He thinks that many of the urban Christian schismatic groups withdrew to the countryside "to keep their sect alive," but the two passages he offers (both from Eusebius) illustrate the opposite.[20] The passages speak of those who have fled to the desert specifically during persecution in order to save their lives, most of whom were not able to achieve even that. There is nothing to suggest that the flight to the desert was to keep any sect alive, as Lane Fox states, nor is there anything in these passages that suggests that it was schismatics who were involved, though Lane Fox makes that the context.

Some attempts have been made to argue that the forms of Christianity that developed in rural areas adopted or reflected aspects that would have meshed more with the character of the countryside. J. B. Lightfoot pointed out that Phrygia was "the mother to Montanist enthusiasm, and the foster-mother of Novatian rigorism. The syncretist, the mystic, the devotee, the puritan would find a congenial climate in these regions of Asia Minor."[21] Many agree with Lightfoot's assessment, noting the rigor, asceticism, and

---

16. Brown, *The Rise of Western Christianity*, 41.

17. Brown, *The Rise of Western Christianity*, 42.

18. Brown, *The Rise of Western Christianity*, 96.

19. William Tabbernee, "Asia Minor and Cyprus," in *Early Christianity in Contexts: An Exploration across Cultures and Continents*, ed. William Tabbernee (Grand Rapids, MI: Baker Academic, 2014), 267.

20. Robin Lane Fox, *Pagans and Christians* (New York: Alfred A. Knopf, 1987), 280. Lane Fox only refers to Eusebius, *Hist. eccl.* 6.42.2–4; 7.11.23.

21. J. B. Lightfoot, *St. Paul's Epistles to the Colossians and to Philemon*, rev. ed. (London: Macmillan & Co, 1875), 98. Trevett, *Montanism*, 19, citing the third edition of Lightfoot's text, speaks only of the mystic, the devotee, the puritan, though Lightfoot's text did include the syncretist there too.

strict morality of the Phrygians. For example, Stephen Mitchell comments that Phrygia and Lycaonia were regions "where the traditional morality of the rural population provided a solid foundation for the development of the rigorist Novatian Church."[22] Further, Mitchell, quoting Socrates, links Novatian success in rural Asia Minor to the "natural puritanism of the conservative country people."[23] Barbara Levick, too, points to the Phrygian character to explain the success of Christian movements such as Montanism and Novatianism in the area.[24] But do we know enough about Phrygia to determine beforehand that this area would have been especially suited for syncretists, mystics, devotees, and puritans—or for anyone else, for that matter?[25] These are slippery slopes to be playing on.

And does Socrates' comment about the Phrygian character really explain anything?[26] Socrates attributes a distinctive and definitive character to various peoples, a strategy that encourages (and generally requires) exaggeration. Our concern here is whether rurals would have more readily converted to rigorous forms of Christianity. That is not Socrates' concern. He speculates about why *churches* in the areas of Paphlagonia and Phrygia were open to the rigorous Novatian position. The important point is that he assumes that there are churches already in these rural areas, which requires that a non-Novatian and pre-Novatian Christian perspective was already present, and had been able to win converts. Thus, Socrates' "observation" cannot serve as a basis for explaining the origin of a Christian success in the countryside but only perhaps why some *Christian* groups would have come to favor a Novatian option, and even that is not a necessary conclusion from Socrates' comment.

Others have played with the idea of distinctive and more radical ideas developing in rural environs. Brian Sowers sees a "drastic difference" in the use of the Thecla story in Alexandria and in the countryside, one promoting an urban-based chastity and the other promoting transvestite behavior,

---

22. Mitchell, *Anatolia*, I.10.

23. Mitchell, *Anatolia*, II.97.

24. Barbara Levick, "In the Phrygian Mode: A Region Seen from Without," in *Roman Phrygia: Culture and Society*, ed. Peter Thonemann (Cambridge: Cambridge University Press, 2013), 53–54.

25. See Levick, "In the Phrygian Mode: A Region Seen from Without," 41–54, for a review of the ancient portrait of the Phrygians.

26. Socrates, *Hist. eccl.* 4.28.

which flips the general contention on its head that rural Christianity was more rigorous in its morality.[27] This complicates rather than clarifies the nature of rural Christianity if that document is put to such a purpose. A better approach is not to use any document for such sweeping conclusions.

But even if a rural character of these supposedly deviant groups could be established, we would need to be quite cautious about grouping these as forms of Christianity with a similar character, as is sometimes done. Frend, for example, states explicitly that the various forms of schismatic groups "all represent the same primarily rural Christianity."[28] Usually a more rigorous lifestyle or less accommodating engagement with the larger culture is pointed to as a common feature,[29] but we must be careful not to make these kinds of links more substantial than they are. In some ways, such links or parallels are quite superficial. It is not as though there were a hundred options available, in which case similarities might then be worthy of note. Rather, we should recognize that there are three basic options in determining similarities and differences among groups. In regard to asceticism, for example, one group is more ascetic, less ascetic, or similar to the main group to which the comparisons are being made. That any two groups might be described as "ascetic" in this kind of setting tells us nothing about the relationship of the two "ascetic" groups. That they have anything more in common other than being more ascetic than the primary group cannot be assumed. Their "asceticism" may have arisen from quite different causes, and the asceticism of each group may have attracted a different kind of individual (if we can assume that it was asceticism, rather than some other feature or a whole cluster of features, that drew people to the group). Further, the interpretation of the practice of asceticism may have differed substantially, or, even when agreeing, may not suggest any closer infinity than reflection on the same biblical passages. The same can be said for almost any other trait—parallels and similarities

---

27. Brian Sowers, "Thecla Desexualized: The Saint Justina Legend and the Reception of the Christian Apocrypha in Late Antiquity," in *"Non-canonical" Religious Texts in Judaism and Early Christianity*, ed. Lee Martin McDonald and James H. Charlesworth (London: T & T Clark, 2012), 232–233. Sowers builds on the works of John Anson, "The Female Transvestite in Early Monasticism: The Origin and Development of a Motif," *Viator* 5 (1974): 1–32, and Stephen J. Davis, "Crossed Texts, Crossed Sex: Intertextuality and Gender in Early Christian Legends of Holy Women Disguised as Men," *JECS* 10 (2002): 1–36.

28. Frend, "The Failure of the Persecutions in the Roman Empire," 283.

29. Mitchell, *Anatolia*, I.10.

may indicate little about common roots, associations, or even sensibilities. Thus, to speak of rural Christianity as having a particular character, as is often done, may be creating a perception of the situation that would never have occurred to anyone "on the ground." Unless we can find clear evidence of the association of such groups, it seems best to treat each as a separate phenomenon than as instances of a more general rural phenomenon and religious sensibility.

More seriously, there is something suspicious about any reconstruction that asserts a successful rural mission by fringe or schismatic groups while denying to the orthodox church either an interest in the countryside or an ability to appeal to rural sensibilities. The nub is this. Nothing in the message of the schismatic groups was particularly directed to a rural pagan audience and nothing in their message would have had created a special rapport with rural sensibilities to any greater degree than the general Christian message itself. In fact, the messages of these supposedly fringe Christian groups appear to be driven by issues that would have had little intelligibility outside the larger Christian church. Schismatic and heretical groups were much more likely to be directing their dialogue and their mission to those already within the church. The issues driving these groups were internal matters of Christian discipline or doctrine, and it was against a broadly shared Christian background that these debates raged—a background unintelligible to rural pagans, or to urban pagans, for that matter. To the rural or urban pagan, the competing Christian groups would have all looked largely the same, at best appearing as different shades of the same color. If one Christian group could appeal to rural folk, there is little reason why another could not have done so too, for the large and unique world common to all Christian groups was what defined Christianity for the non-Christian, not some debate over second baptisms or the return of the Paraclete. These intra-Christian differences would have been meaningless to anyone but an insider.

Neither can we conclude much from the fact that it was the rural Montanist or the rural Donatist or the rural Novatianist that seems to be the focus in literature that mentions the countryside. Even were that the case, it certainly would not follow that there were no rural orthodox Christians. It simply would indicate that heretics and schismatics, whether rural or urban, frequently provoked comment in the Christian literature, as might well be expected.

Further, it cannot be argued that people in the countryside would have thrown their lot with the Christian schismatics and heretics as an expression of protest against the Roman order, as Frend has suggested.[30] The problem is this. If country dwellers joined these fringe Christian groups as a protest against the Roman order, with Christianity appearing as their ally because it was persecuted by the Roman authorities, then any form of Christianity would have provided that bond. It is only well after the conversion of Constantine that the church and empire would appear to be linked, at which time heretical Christian groups might perhaps appear to be opposed to the Roman order in contrast to the main Christian group, which supported the empire. Possibly, then, these fringe groups might begin to appear as potential allies in any opposition to Rome—rural or otherwise. But, even then, we could not simply assume that rural pagan discontent with Rome would develop such an alliance as a reasonable and obvious route of protest. Most pagans, surely, would still have seen even fringe Christian groups as primarily Christian rather than primarily anti-Roman. Thus, such schismatic groups likely would not have been much more attractive than more orthodox forms of Christianity.

Further, even supposing that these "heretical" Christian groups found their refuge in the countryside, we cannot simply assume that they would have been interested in converting the countryside. Indeed, not only is there no evidence for such an interest, such an interest is not even likely. The uncompromising and stern position of these rigorous Christian groups that caused them to separate from their supposedly lax Christian brethren suggests that these groups would have confronted rural paganism with disdain and dismissal—not with arms wide open. Whatever the supposedly rigorous nature of traditional rural morality, it is hardly a good mesh with what drove the rigorous schismatic groups within Christianity, where things like celibacy, second marriages, and rejection of the lapsed defined them. But even supposing that these rigorous schismatic groups would have been willing to admit rural pagans into membership, it is quite another thing to expect that rural pagans would have wanted to join these groups. They may have shared a rigor, but it is a stretch to say that they shared a morality.

Treating Christianity in Rural Areas as Urban

A third way by which the evidence of a rural Christian presence is dismissed or muted is to contend that what looks like rural Christianity was

---

30. Frend, "The Winning of the Countryside," 6.

really a segment of urban Christianity that had fled to the country for some reason or other, though persecution is the most common explanation for that migration. It can then be argued that such Christianity really is not rural in character. Unless such Christianity successfully engaged its new neighbors in the countryside, there would be no need to treat this kind of Christianity as rural, and even if it did win members from the countryside, that church would not be rural in an unqualified way.

Take Robin Lane Fox's approach, for example. He is more friendly than many to the idea of a rural Christianity, admitting the presence of Christians in the countryside[31] and offering a range of evidence for Christian use of languages other than Latin and Greek, an indication that the church may have been advancing into less Hellenized areas.[32] But he makes a distinction between "a rural mission and a rural presence."[33] He thinks that empire-wide persecutions, begun under Decius in the middle of the third century, forced many Christians to flee the cities, and it is here that we may get our first Christian communities in the countryside. Once in the countryside, these groups supposedly engaged in missionary activity.

No doubt, there were some urban Christians who fled to the countryside to escape persecution. Perhaps there were many. We know of at least some who did.[34] But such stories should not be used as evidence for the beginning of Christianity in the countryside. That the countryside was perceived to offer refuge may suggest that there was already a Christian presence in the countryside where Christians in flight might be sheltered. Further, even if such flight to the countryside represented the first presence of Christianity in rural areas, we would need to be cautious about marking that as the beginning of a rural church, for as we have seen, it is likely that when a persecution ended—generally after a few brief months—those who had fled would have returned to their urban homes. Certainly that was the case for Cyprian and many in his church who had fled to the countryside.[35]

---

31. Fox, *Pagans and Christians*, 280–293.

32. Fox, *Pagans and Christians*, 282–287.

33. Fox, *Pagans and Christians*, 288.

34. Such stories of a flight to the countryside to escape persecution appear as early as Polycarp (*Mart. Pol.* 5–7). Cyprian, a century later, directs his church from a hiding place in the countryside (*Ep.* 14).

35. J. Patout Burns Jr., *Cyprian the Bishop* (London and New York: Routledge, 2002), 12–24.

The Pagan Countryside

This study has largely focused on the evidence for the presence of Christianity in the countryside in the second and third centuries, unlike most studies of this period, which focus on the church in urban settings. The fourth century serves as a dividing line, for it is in that century that a massive religious shift takes place in the Roman Empire, with the pro-Christian dynasty of Constantine and its successors promoting Christianity at the expense of paganism. By the end of that century, paganism was officially outlawed[36]—or at least the public practice of paganism was outlawed, which is largely the extent of the practical reach of law in matters where private faith and practice are less easily detected or more easily hidden. On the surface, at least, the Roman Empire looked quite Christianized by the end of the 300s. According to Ramsay MacMullen, that view was held by just about every scholar until the 1980s. But, says MacMullen, they were wrong.[37] A considerable number of scholars would now agree with MacMullen: the image of a largely Christianized empire is a false one, particularly for the countryside. The Christianization of the empire was more show than substance.

Various studies regarding the nature of the Christianization of the countryside have been offered and various conclusions proposed.[38] Some scholars argue that the countryside had, at best, a Christian veneer, beneath which the world of paganism survived. Others have noted that the countryside was Christianized, but that the Christianity there was often out of step with the Christianity of urban areas. Peter Brown, for example, notes that by 550 C.E., Christianity was present throughout the countryside. It was

---

36. Some have argued that the legislation against Greco-Roman religious rites was not as sweeping as is often proposed; rather, it had either a more specific target, or if a more comprehensive target, one that the legislators had no intention, will, or need to enforce. See, for example, Testa, "When the Romans Became Pagans," 46–48, in regard to Emperor Gratian's terminating rights of pagan priesthoods, or as Testa reads it, of the Vestal Virgins.

37. Ramsay MacMullen, *Christianity and Paganism in the Fourth to the Eight Centuries* (New Haven: Yale University Press, 1997), 5. MacMullen deals with the condition of paganism in the Roman Empire, arguing against the then near-consensus that paganism (in its classical Greco-Roman form) had become decrepit and debilitated [*Paganism in the Roman Empire* (New Haven: Yale University Press, 1981). In his most recent work, MacMullen, *The Second Church*, 101–111, discusses how the label "Christian" should be applied, and he leaves the countryside with only a 3% Christian element well after the age of Constantine (112).

38. Stephen McKenna, *Paganism and Pagan Survivals in Spain up to the Fall of the Visigothic Kingdom*, The Catholic University of America Studies in Mediaeval History, New Series, 1 (Washington, DC: Catholic University of America, 1938); James J. O'Donnell, "The Demise

not against paganism that the bishops had to fight, it was against "varieties of 'home grown' Christianity," according to Brown.[39] The most recent and thorough analysis of the matter is that of Ramsay MacMullen. He divides the church into the elite and the masses, the urban and the largely rural, the 5% and the 95%, a matter I take up in Appendix A.

It is not my intention here to probe deeply into this matter, though I am not particularly comfortable with attempts to determine things such as the thinness of the veneer that supposedly marked rural Christianity. Nor do I find much to be gained by looking at every practice not approved by the church or that was a carryover from a pagan past as proof of a significant surviving paganism or a lack of Christian devotion. I think these kinds of questions, though interesting at one level, can miss a primary point when it comes to trying to determine Christian or pagan identity. Brown points out that bishops often had to decide whether a practice should be classified as *pagan*, and thus suppressed, or simply treated as "innocent survivals, devoid of religious meaning."[40] Robert Markus discusses the question of what should count as pagan survivals and what as simply "non-religious, secular institutions and traditions."[41] And Wolfgang Liebeschuetz notes the accommodation of early Christianity to the world of the classical tradition until the collapse of the western empire in the 400s and, in the east, until the rise of Islam.[42] Not every aspect of the Greco-Roman world had to

---

of Paganism," *Traditio* 35 (1979): 45–88; Frank R. Trombley, "Paganism in the Greek World at the End of Antiquity: The Case of Rural Anatolia and Greece," *HTR* 78 (1985): 327–352; Frank R. Trombley, *Hellenic Religion and Christianization c. 370–529*, Religions in the Graeco-Roman World, 115/1,2. 2 vols. (Leiden: Brill, 1993, 1994); Timothy E. Gregory, "The Survival of Paganism in Christian Greece: A Critical Essay," *AJP* 107 (1986): 229–242. Stephen Mitchell, *A History of the Later Roman Empire AD 284–641: The Transformation of the Ancient World*, Blackwell History of the Ancient World (Oxford: Blackwell, 2007), 225–300.

39. Brown, *The Rise of Western Christendom*, 147. Brown notes the different attitudes toward the survival of pagan elements between Christians in the east and those in the west (147–150). In contrasting himself to Ramsay MacMullen, Brown states: "Whether everything that average Christians did was automatically 'pagan' and a 'survival of pagan practice' is less certain for me than it is for Professor MacMullen" (letter exchange between Brown and MacMullen, "The Tenacity of Paganism," *The New York Review of Books*, June 9, 2011).

40. Brown, *The Rise of Western Christendom*, 149–150. Brown also points out that the borrowing of practices did not simply go in one direction. Pagans borrowed Christian rituals (153).

41. R. A. Markus, *The End of Ancient Christianity* (Cambridge: Cambridge University Press, 1990), 9. Markus' introductory chapter, "Secularity," provides a useful review of the use and usefulness of terms such as "paganism," and in particular the terms "secular" and "sacred" (1–17).

42. Wolfgang Liebeschuetz, "Pagan Mythology in the Christian Empire," *International Journal of the Classical Tradition* 2 (1995): 193–208.

be rejected. The fundamental question is the degree to which the customs of ancient life were neutralized, and thus rendered benign, by one's alignment with Christianity.

In regard to the significance of aspects of pagan practice, I would ask whether individuals, in immediate response to crisis, routinely turn in hope to Jesus, the saints, a priest, or the church and do they self-identify as Christians. Or, to bring it down to the most basic and telling indication of trust, I would ask: "When they want their mommy, to whom do they go?" If it is to Jesus, they are Christian. If it is to the Christian priests, they are Christian. If it is to the Christian martyrs and saints, they are Christian. And I would hold that view, regardless of whatever other techniques and talismans they might turn to in addition to their entreaty of the Christian God—and however much bishops might have preached against some of these elements. To disqualify a Christian convert because he or she had retained some aspect of their pagan past is to propose some highly idealized template for what is Christian that even the strictest bishops would have known was not the reality on the ground. Thus, when MacMullen points out the 95% of Christians whose Christianity may not have measured up to the standards desired by the bishop,[43] that should not be seen as either unexpected or disturbing—save to the bishops, and even then only to the most unreasonably idealistic of them.

The Term "Pagan"

It was not until Emperor Valentinian I (364–375 C.E.) that non-Christian religions, with the exception of Judaism, began to be designated as *paganus* in Christian literature, using the term much as it is now popularly understood to identify non-Jews and non-Christians in the Roman world. Alan Cameron has found over six hundred examples of this kind of use over the writings of fifteen authors during the period from *c.* 360 to 420.[44]

Two main views are offered for the meaning of the term. Both go back many centuries.[45] One view, made popular by Harnack, was that the term

---

43. MacMullen, *The Second Church*, 109.

44. Alan Cameron, *The Last Pagans of Rome* (Oxford: Oxford University Press, 2011), 16. Note the title of Orosius' work *History against the Pagans* (*Historiarum adversum paganos*), written in 417.

45. Cameron, *The Last Pagans of Rome*, 14–15.

distinguished between the civilian and the soldier, which Christians used (as soldiers of Christ) to distinguish themselves from the non-converted.[46] The alternative view was that the term came to be used to describe the old polytheism as a peasant-religion because that religion was almost extinct in the cities and was hanging on as "only a decrepit and obscure existence in retired villages," as Philip Schaff put it.[47] It is that latter use that is of particular importance to the present study.

Not every scholar today would take Schaff's description of the polytheism of the countryside as so debilitated or the polytheism of the cities as almost extinct. Many, such as MacMullen, would argue that polytheism continued to thrive, at least in the countryside. But almost everyone would agree with Schaff that the word pagan, supposedly meaning country folk, came to be used for the old polytheism because the countryside remained largely unconverted even after the cities had been Christianized.[48]

The debate over the degree to which paganism survived in cities and the countrysides may need to be rethought as a result of Cameron's recent re-reading of the evidence in his massive *The Last Pagans of Rome*.[49] Certainly the common association of the word "paganism" with country dwellers and the conclusion that the use of the term reflected the continued loyalty of the rural folk to the old polytheism need the kind of close examination that Cameron has provided. Too much has been made of the rural implications of the word "pagan" (*paganus*) and the supposed religious character of the countryside, based on dual questionable assumptions: (1) that the countryside was more conservative and thus slower to convert and (2) that the term *paganus* meant "rural." These assumptions still have currency. We find this idea repeated frequently in modern surveys of early

---

46. Adolf Harnack, *Militia Christi: The Christian Religion and the Military in the First Three Centuries*, David McInnes Grade, trans. (Philadelphia: Fortress, 1981). German original: *Militia Christi. Die christliche Religion und der Soldatenstand in den ersten drei Jahrhunderten* [Tübingen: J. C. B. Mohr (Paul Siebeck), 1905].

47. Philip Schaff, *History of the Christian Church*, rev. ed. (New York: Charles Scribner's Sons, 1884), 3.61.

48. See, for example, Rodney Stark, *Cities of God: The Real Story of How Christianity Became an Urban Movement and Conquered Rome* (New York: HarperCollins, 2006), 2.

49. Cameron's work has elicited the highest praise and the sharpest criticism. For criticism, see the collection of various papers from Italian scholars in Rita Lizzi Testa, ed., *The Strange Death of Pagan Rome* (Turnhout, BE: Brepols, 2013). See, in particular, Testa, "When the Romans Became Pagans," 31–51. Most reviewers have been more generous, even if cautious about some of Cameron's conclusions.

Christianity,[50] perhaps to some considerable extent because the influential works of Rodney Stark promote this view.[51]

It may well be that the countryside retained older, pre-Christian religious practices and attitudes longer than did urban areas, though Cameron argues that what survives in the countryside was not necessarily Greco-Roman religion but rather ancient and local religious practices that predated Greco-Roman religion.[52] If that is the case, then the collapse of Greco-Roman religion might still be dated early, marking a significant religious revolution, in spite of whatever elements of that religion that might have survived and whatever elements of the even older and localized religious sensibilities that might have continued to offer some comfort—or disquiet.

Even if the countryside retained some elements from their religious past, it does not follow that the word "pagan" was adopted as a label for the "non-Christian" because of a more rural character that marked those who had not fully embraced Christianity. Following are four considerations that weaken the commonly accepted association of the word "pagan" with the rural environment.

First, there is considerable debate what the word pagan implies in a rural and religious context.[53] The first use of the term to describe religious practice was in the legislation of Emperors Valens and Valentinian in 370 C.E., where the term referred to the revival of Hellenistic religion under Julian.[54] Why the word was chosen here is unclear, though the term does not have a rural connotation in this context. Julian's reforms and successes were as much urban as they were rural. About seventy years later, the word was used in Theodosian legislation for Hellenistic religious practice,[55] though other words were also used for Hellenistic religion in

---

50. As noted by Cameron, *The Last Pagans of Rome*, 1, who finds that view expressed as far back as medieval writers.

51. See, for example, Rodney Stark, *The Rise of Christianity* (Princeton: Princeton University Press, 1996), 10; *Cities of God*, 2; *The Triumph of Christianity* (New York: HarperOne, 2011), 262.

52. Cameron, *The Last Pagans of Rome*, 788–789.

53. Peter Brown, *The Rise of Western Christendom: Triumph and Diversity, A.D. 200–1000*, 2nd ed. (Oxford: Blackwell, 2003), 35–36.

54. *Cod. theod.* 16.2.18.

55. *Cod. theod.* 16.5.4; 16.5.6.

other places in the Code.[56] There, too, no rural/urban distinction seems intended.

Second, the word *paganus* is not the most common or natural word to use if one wished to make a clear rural connection. Rather, *rusticus* is likely to have been used, and it was commonly used by Christians themselves for rural or rustic people.[57] That the choice of *paganus* was made because it reflected a rural condition seems neither compelling nor even likely.

Third, the word *paganus* works best in a western, Latin context, though even here it should be noted that Latin writers tended to adopt Greek words for the non-Christian world, and these words did not denote a rural connection.[58] Although the Latin word *paganus* was transliterated into Greek (παγανός), it was not used to denote a rural person in that language.[59] Rather, terms such as ἀγρότης and χωρίτης were used in Greek to specify a rural person. Yet Greek-speaking Christians did not use either of these Greek words that identified a rural environment or character to describe polytheistic religions. Rather, they used terms such as ἕλλην (hellene) or ἔθνη (nations),[60] terms that have no special link at all to the countryside. Whether this indicates that we may be dealing with two substantially different environments in terms of Christianity's extension into the countryside in the eastern and the western empires is more difficult to say. Peter Brown thinks so.[61] But he also thinks that, even when examining the west, the "sharp dichotomy between 'town' and 'country,' 'Christian' and 'pagan' does not do justice to its nuances."[62] Cameron, in his attempt to disassociate the word "pagan" from a rural rustic identity, notes that "it would be paradoxical if western Christians had called pagans by a name symbolizing lack of culture when eastern Christians called them by a name symbolizing culture itself ('hellene')."[63]

---

56. *Cod. theod.* 9.16; 16.10.

57. See section "The Rustic Element" in chapter 10 for rustics in the Christian community. Cameron, *The Last Pagans of Rome*, 14, points to the use of the word *agrestis* for the unpolished country person, similar in meaning to the word *rusticus*.

58. Cameron, *The Last Pagans of Rome*, 16. Cameron lists: *gentes, nations, ethnici,* and *infidels*.

59. Cameron, *The Last Pagans of Rome*, 14.

60. Cameron, *The Last Pagans of Rome*, 16–18.

61. Brown, *The Rise of Western Christendom*, 148–150.

62. Peter Brown, *The Cult of the Saints* (Chicago: University of Chicago Press, 1981), 119.

63. Cameron, *The Last Pagans of Rome*, 15.

Fourth, even if the term "pagan" was used to indicate the rural polytheism of the empire (which Cameron has quite convincingly shown to be mistaken[64]), such use could tell us only that the majority of the countryside was non-Christian—not that all of it was. As we have seen, given the proportion of the empire that was rural, the countryside would have reflected a pagan character even when rural Christians considerably outnumbered urban Christians, as most certainly must have been the case by the time of Valentinian I, when the term *paganus* began to be used.

Conclusion

The various ways that evidence of an early rural Christianity has been downplayed need to be reconsidered and much more cautiously stated. I suggest that a more reasonable position is that Christianity had natural links to the countryside from the beginning, and that the church had some presence there early, not just in the form of deviant or schismatic groups but in groups that fit what an urban bishop's church would have counted as normal and part of their alliance. The efforts to dismiss or diminish in some way the evidence for a Christian presence in the countryside is neither necessary nor helpful.

---

64. Cameron, *The Last Pagans of Rome*, 14–25.

9

The Country Bishop

The Chorepiscopos

Another phenomenon relevant to the discussion of an early rural Christianity is the office of the country bishop or what is referred to as a *chorepiscopos* (χωρεπίσκοπος[1]) in Greek literature. The word is transliterated into Latin for the technical term in that language.[2] The exact nature and origin of the office of country bishop are open to debate.[3] Some think that the establishment of this office indicates that rural Christianity did not develop until the latter half of the third century or early in the fourth century, for it is at that time that the term seems to have been coined, or at least when we first encounter the term in the surviving literature.[4] Others

---

1. An *episcopos* (bishop) of a *chora* (country place).

2. The two main sources of early information about the country bishop are canons of early church councils (mainly in the 300s) and from letters written by Basil of Caesarea from the same period, and from a few other scattered references.

3. The matter has been dealt with extensively in the scholarly literature of a century ago—and even earlier—but little attention is given it today. A still useful survey is that of the brief article in *The Seven Ecumenical Councils*, NPNF 2–14, 21–23, covering the debates of the 1800s, which is when most of the "modern" discussion of *chorepiscopoi* has taken place. For the first half of the 1900s, see E. Kirsten, "Chorbishof," *RAC* 2 (1954): 1105–1114. For the *chorepiscopos* later in the western church, see Jörg Müller, "Gedanken zum Institut der Chorbischöfe," in *Medieval Church Law and the Origins of the Western Legal Tradition*, ed. Wolfgang P. Müller and Mary E. Sommar (Washington, DC: Catholic University Press of America, 2006), 77–94.

4. John McDowell Leavitt, "Suffragans," *AQCR* 23 (1871): 394–410; W. H. C. Frend, "The Winning of the Countryside," *JEH* 18 (1967): 13–14. John Zizioulas viewed the *chorepiscopos* as an office functioning as early as the second century, with full status as a bishop [Demetrios Bathrellos, "Church, Eucharist, Bishop: The Early Church in the Ecclesiology of John Zizioulas," in *The Theology of John Zizioulas: Personhood and the Church*, ed. Douglas H.

think the office resulted from the successful effort of urban bishops to bring their fellow bishops in rural areas under their control. Thus, country bishops would have been fully bishops, equal in status and rights to the urban bishops until a redefinition of the role of bishops in country areas, which included the coining of a new term, *chorepiscopos*, to distinguish the rural bishops from their urban counterparts. In this case, evidence for the presence of Christianity in rural areas might be extended back farther into the third century and even into the second.

I will not attempt to address every aspect of the phenomenon here. I am interested primarily to show that the office does not provide evidence of a late rural Christianity, as many scholars have contended, but rather the opposite: the office points to an early rural Christianity.

First Mention and Earliest Evidence

Much of the discussion has focused on the time of the first known occurrence of the Greek term *chorepiscopoi*. From this, the conclusion is drawn that the office was created around this time, and then a further conclusion is drawn about the lack of a rural Christian presence prior to this time. But there is a methodological problem with that approach. If Christianity developed both in the city and in the countryside, however unevenly, from the first century onwards, then it is possible, if not likely, that the primary Christian leader of a Christian assembly in any settlement would have been simply considered the bishop, or overseer, whether that assembly was in a city, a town, or a village, for we do know of individuals from small towns who bear the title of bishop as early as the second century.[5] If leaders of churches in small towns originally bore the title of bishop, then the use of the term *chorepiscopos* could be a later attempt to distinguish degrees of rank within the highest office, as bishops became more numerous with the growth of the church. Thus, the introduction of a distinctive

Knight (Aldershot: Ashgate Publishing, 2007), 134–135]. See, too, John Meyendorff, *Imperial Unity and Christian Division* (Crestwood, NY: St. Vladimir's Seminary Press, 1989), 42–44.

5. Zoticus, an opponent of Montanism and leader of the church in the village of Cumane, is called a bishop (Eusebius, *Hist. eccl.* 5.16.17). Eusebius' source is Apollinarius, bishop of Hierapolis, who lived during the time of Marcus Aurelius and the rise of Montanism. Cumane is thought to have been close to Apamea, from which Julian, another anti-Montanist bishop, came. Apamea is a short distance to the northeast of the Hierapolis–Laodicea–Colossae triangle.

term could be evidence of a redefinition of the office rather than the establishment of the office. That likelihood should become more obvious as we explore various aspects of the evidence.

There are hints in the literature that rural bishops existed before the first extant use of the term *chorepiscopos*. For one thing, the text in which the term first occurs has nothing to do with the establishment of the office. It assumes that the office exists. The concern of the text is to restrict some of the rights these individuals had been exercising in their role as bishops. Thus, the first occurrence of the term is proof of a somewhat earlier existence of the office.

Chorepiscopoi and the Early Councils

The earliest uses of the term *chorepiscopoi* in the surviving literature are found in the decrees of the early councils and in the record of the attendees of these councils. Not only do numerous *chorepiscopoi* attend the councils, they have full voting rights and cast votes of equal weight to that of the city bishops. It is clear that in the hierarchical scheme, *chorepiscopoi* were considered to rank with the bishops, not with the lower clergy, such as the presbyters, with whom often they are wrongly associated in modern discussions.

The first occurrence of the word *chorepiscopoi* is in canon 13 of the Council of Ancyra (Ankara), held in 314 C.E. It reads: "It is not lawful for *chorepiscopoi* to ordain presbyters or deacons, and most assuredly not presbyters of a city, without the commission of the bishop given in writing, in another parish."[6] No effort is made to clarify the title of *chorepiscopos* in the canon. Clearly the office is not viewed here as an innovation. Further, the canon does not list the duties of the office; it simply prohibits the *chorepiscopoi* from doing some of the things they had been doing. Indeed, the range of authority that these country bishops apparently claimed for themselves suggests either that they functioned as bishops or, if they had been appointed as agents of the urban clergy, that they aspired to rights they saw being exercised by bishops in rural areas. Granted, there is an attempt to restrict the activities of the *chorepiscopoi* or to define their authority more

---

6. Various attempts have been made to emend the text. See Charles Joseph Hefele, *A History of the Christian Councils*, 2nd ed., William R. Clark, trans. (Edinburgh: T & T Clark, 1883), 212–213. Cyril C. Richardson, "The Riddle of the 13th Canon of Ancyra," *CH* 16 (1947): 32–36, argues that no change is needed.

narrowly, but such restriction appears to be a revision to practices already in place, as we will see.

What was it, then, that sparked the discussion of this office at the Council of Ancyra? While it is possible that a single incident prompted the deliberation of the council, one would have thought that if *chorepiscopoi* were staff of or under the supervision of city bishops, then a rogue *chorepiscopos* simply would have been brought to heel by his bishop. Although we do not know any details of the situation beyond what the canon offers, we do know that other canons from various councils in the 300s tried to restrict the authority of *chorepiscopoi*,[7] which suggests that rights and responsibilities of rural bishops had some ambiguity. It is not clear why that was the case. It could be that rights assumed to be traditional were being challenged. It could be that new rights were being asserted. What we do know is that the councils, which (according to the lists of attendees) were controlled by urban bishops, were taking action to limit the activities of country bishops and to place them clearly under the authority of city bishops.

One canon from the Council of Laodicea (380 C.E.) sets forth the following policy: "Bishops must not be appointed in villages (κώμαις) or country districts (χώραις), but visitors (περιοδευτάς); and those [bishops] who have been already appointed must do nothing without the consent of the bishop of the city. Presbyters, in like manner, must do nothing without the consent of the bishop."[8] This is curious, largely because of its late date. Bishops were still being appointed in some rural settlements, it seems, even though that practice had been addressed and significantly qualified or prohibited by earlier councils. In spite of that, these more recently appointed rural bishops apparently retained their position, though they were forbidden from taking action without the consent of the city bishop. Further, these bishops were not appointed as *chorepiscopoi*; they were bishops in the full sense—without qualification.

As we have noted, scholars have read the references to *chorepiscopoi* in the canons of early councils in quite different ways, either seeing bishops

---

7. Council of Ancyra (Ankara) (314 C.E.): Council of Neocaesarea. (314 C.E.?): canon 14 (note: many manuscripts combined canons 13 and 14), canon 13; and Council of Nicea (325 C.E.): canon 8. Council of Antioch (341 C.E.): canon 10; Council of Serdica (Sofia) (343 C.E.): canon 6; Council of Laodicea (380 C.E.): canon 57.

8. For the Greek text, see Charles Joseph Hefele, *Histoire des Conciles d'après les Documents Originaux* 1.2 (Paris: Letouzey et Ané, 1907), 1024.

in the countryside merely continuing to exercise traditional rights but with some urban effort to restrict those rights, or seeing a new office for the first forays into the countryside by the Christian movement.[9] Although the canons might be read in either way, I think the stronger case can be made that these canons were intended to restrict powers that bishops from rural areas had always possessed as bishops. Certainly it is not obvious from the early canons that *chorepiscopoi* had been exercising authority beyond their jurisdiction, though that may be how the urban bishops sought to portray the matter (and we cannot be sure even of that). It is possible, and perhaps likely, that the *chorepiscopoi* did not consider that they had overstepped their rights, and that the restrictions now being placed on these individuals required some delicacy and sensitivity to that fact. There is, curiously, a considerable degree of deference shown by the councils to the *chorepiscopoi*. Such individuals were clearly to be treated as superior to presbyters, and their duties were of an episcopal nature. Indeed, it appears that when we first encounter *chorepiscopoi* in our literature (at the early councils), they are granted the same voting rights as urban bishops. No mere staff appointee of bishops had such rights.

Such deference seems strange if the *chorepiscopoi* were—from the beginning—appointees of the city bishop who now had started to overstep roles assigned to them by their bishop. Why such deference to the *chorepiscopoi* if these recently appointed clergy were disregarding the duties assigned to them by the bishop who appointed them and who now were attempting to enhance their own position at the expense of the bishop? On the other hand, the deference shown by the councils to the *chorepiscopoi* makes good sense if an attempt was being made to restrict the traditional episcopal rights of rural bishops by the urban bishops. The status as these rural office holders as bishops is not challenged, nor are these individuals

---

9. Robert D. D. Rainy, *The Ancient Catholic Church: From the Accession of Trajan to the Fourth General Council (A.D. 98–451)* (New York: Charles Scribner's Sons, 1902), 307; Hamilton Hess, *The Early Development of Canon Law and the Council of Serdica* (Oxford: Oxford University Press, 2002), 154–157; Charles Gore, *The Church and the Ministry*, rev. ed., ed. C. H. Turner (London: Longmans, Green and Co., 1919), 96, 327–332; Franz Gillmann, *Das Institut der Chorbischöfe im Orient* (Munich: Lenter, 1903); Peter L'Huillier, *The Church of the Ancient Councils: The Disciplinary Work of the First Four Ecumenical Councils* (Crestwood, NY: St. Vladimir's Seminary Press, 1996), 61. L'Huillier thinks that the subordination of the rural bishops to the urban hierarchy had taken place by the middle of the 200s, but he does not explain how he reached that conclusion. He does recognize that "it is difficult to follow in time the unfolding of this process." If the subordination of rural bishops by urban bishops had occurred by the mid-200s, does it not follow that there were such rural bishops in the period before that?"

removed from episcopal rank, even though they are brought more closely under the supervision of the urban bishops.

The Spread and the Range of the Office

Another factor about the *chorepiscopoi* that inclines me to conclude that the office—but not necessarily the term[10]—was instituted early is that the office is fairly widespread. If the office was just being introduced shortly before we have first evidence of it—more an experiment than anything else—and if the office seemed to be almost immediately abused, requiring restrictive legislation and a replacement of it with the περιοδευτάς, it is surprising that it would have gained such wide dispersion. One would have expected little new adoption of the office, since even in our first encounter with it, the office seems to have caused problems and required canonical legislation to control its holders. Thus, the more widespread we find the office after its first mention in restrictive canons of councils, then the more likely an office of this kind (by whatever name) had existed for quite some time prior to its first mention.

Although we do not have evidence of the office of *chorepiscopos* in every corner of the empire where Christianity was established, the office was clearly widespread in the 300s. As we have seen, the first evidence comes from western Asia Minor at the Council of Ancyra and other councils in Asia Minor. Ramsay MacMullen mentions in passing that even a village might have a bishop, but he does not develop this idea, other than to say that we know this from the subscriber-lists of councils.[11] Adolf Harnack used the list of attendees at the Council of Nicea (325 C.E.) to determine the spread of Christianity in particular areas, and he commented on the presence of *chorepiscopoi* as well as bishops.[12] Two *chorepiscopoi* from

---

10. I make this qualification because it is possible that country bishops were recognized simply as *bishops* of country places, with a title developing later to reflect the location.

11. Ramsay MacMullen, *The Second Church: Popular Christianity* A.D. *200–400* (Atlanta: Society of Biblical Literature, 2009), 12.

12. Adolf Harnack, *The Mission and Expansion of Christianity in the First Three Centuries*, 2nd ed., trans. and ed. James Moffatt (London: Williams and Norgate, 1908), 190. Harnack recognized that one must exercise caution in reading from the presence or lack of *chorepiscopoi* at Nicea as indicative of the presence or strength of Christianity in the countryside (117, 122, 135, 137, 181), but then when he notes that twenty-two bishops and two *chorepiscopoi* attended from Coele-Syria, he hints that this may say something about the lack of Christianity in rural Coele-Syria (135, 137) and ponders whether the lack of Palestinian *chorepiscopoi* representation at Nicea indicates that Christianity had not yet penetrated into the Palestinian countryside (117, 122).

Coele-Syria attended the Council of Nicea,[13] but none from Palestine or Phoenicia.[14] One *chorepiscopos* came from Cilicia, along with nine bishops.[15] Four *chorepiscopoi* and thirteen bishops came from Phrygia, the same numbers as from Isauria.[16] Five *chorepiscopoi* and seven bishops attended from Cappadocia.[17]

Turning to Egypt, we have our first comment about the *chorepiscopoi* there in a work of Athanasius, written about 357 C.E., in which Athanasius argued against Ischyras, who had attempted to become a bishop in a town a short distance from Alexandria.[18] Athanasius gave various reasons for rejecting Ischyras, but the main point seems to have been that there was simply no need for bishops in small towns. As Athanasius says: "The Mareoti ... is a country district (χώρα) of Alexandria, in which there has never been either a Bishop or a Chorepiscopus; but the Churches of the whole district are subject to the Bishop of Alexandria, and each Presbyter has under his charge one of the largest villages, which are about ten or more in numbers."[19] In this case, presbyters from Alexandria handled the needs of the villages, though Athanasius clearly was familiar with the office of *chorepiscopos*. What is intriguing about the situation is that Athanasius appears to have anticipated that his readers might have expected such areas to be served by a *chorepiscopos* (or even a bishop), for he appears to have sensed that he needed to counter an argument that a *chorepiscopos* or a bishop should be appointed in the area. This suggests two things. One, *chorepiscopoi* were probably to be found in other towns and rural areas of Egypt itself, for Mareoti, in lacking *chorepiscopoi*, seems to be an exception. Two, both Athanasius and the people of the Mareoti district were familiar with the office of *chorepiscopos*, though we cannot say how informed they were or where they learned of it. Certainly Athanasius does not argue that

---

13. Harnack, *The Mission and Expansion of Christianity*, 135, 137.

14. Harnack, *The Mission and Expansion of Christianity*, 117, 122.

15. Harnack, *The Mission and Expansion of Christianity*, 181.

16. Harnack, *The Mission and Expansion of Christianity*, 192, 227.

17. Harnack, *The Mission and Expansion of Christianity*, 192n4, seems to use this number and ratio to conclude that the chorepiscopate was strongest in Cappadocia and Isauria, and to argue for "how deeply Christianity had permeated the population of the country" (192). Basil of Caesarea (c. 329–379 C.E.) had fifty *chorepiscopoi* under him.

18. Athanasius, *Defence against the Arians*, largely recounts Athanasius' clashes with Ischyras.

19. Athanasius, *Apol. sec.* 85.

chorepiscopoi are unthinkable—not even for the area of Mareoti—though he does point out that *chorepiscopoi* have never been appointed there and are unnecessary, given that presbyters were able to provide whatever religious services are needed.

One further point regarding Athanasius' comment: Athanasius argued that the district of Mareoti did not need either a bishop or a *chorepiscopos* because the churches there were subject to the bishop of Alexandria. That comment would make little sense if the office of *chorepiscopoi* had been established by urban bishops principally to create subordinates who could be appointed to do the bishop's bidding in rural areas under the bishop's domain. From Athanasius' standpoint and probably from the standpoint of Athanasius' readers, *chorepiscopoi* seem to have been normally viewed as independent of the bishop.

Chorepiscopoi are to be found in Syria, too, if Sozomen is correct about the title of Mareabdes, who was martyred, along with two hundred fifty of his clergy, by the Sassanid king Shapur I about 260 c.e.[20] And in Armenia, *chorepiscopoi* can be found too. We know of one named Daniel from the first half of the 300s.[21]

As important as it is to establish the use and range of the term *chorepiscopos*, it is more important to establish the use and range of the concept. In other words, when and where were there bishops in country churches, by whatever name they might have been called. I am assuming here the possibility and even the likelihood that the individual in a position of bishop in a rural area (i.e., a country bishop) was at first simply referred to as "bishop." Only later would a technical term be considered necessary to distinguish between bishops of more significant centers and those from less significant centers. How the distinction was to be made cannot have been clear from the beginning. Although the term implies distinction and when first encountered reflects an effort to restrict the rights of that office, no attempt is made to withhold or withdraw a recognition of episcopal status from the holders of this office. That is perhaps the key to unraveling the puzzle.

---

20. Sozomen, *Hist. eccl.* 2.13.

21. R. A. Markus, "Country Bishops in Byzantine Africa," in *The Church in Town and Countryside*, ed. Derek Baker (Oxford: Blackwell, 1979), 1–15, covers the period up to the Muslim conquest and takes issue with Frend's read on the situation. Also see Harnack, *The Mission and Expansion of Christianity*, 201n2, who cites Faustus of Byzantium, regarding Daniel, the *chorepiscopos*.

The North African countryside was particularly rich in bishops, and they appear to have shared equal rank with the urban bishops.[22] Indeed, these bishops in rural settlements seem to have been referred to simply as bishops, without a qualifying label such as *chorepiscopos* that might have diminished their episcopal status somewhat. And rural bishops appear early in Phrygia, where they opposed the Montanist movement. That there could be bishops in rural communities is certain, then, well before a distinctive term was coined to try to distinguish these bishops from those in urban areas, and even after the coining of such a term, some areas appointed bishops to rural settlements and used the title "bishop" without qualification, as in the case of North Africa.

Determining the Origins

The view that the office of *chorepiscopos* was established in the latter part of the third century is not so much a conclusion drawn from the evidence as it is an assumption based on the time of the first occurrence of the term, and then that assumption being tied to the hypothesis that Christianity had no rural presence to speak of until after 250 c.e. Neither assumption can carry that weight.

Perhaps the crucial question is why the office rose at all. In the early 300s, efforts were made to reduce the power of the *chorepiscopos* office, and in many ways the office could be replaced simply by appointing a presbyter to assume the duties of ministry outside the city, as was to become a common practice. If a presbyter was able to reasonably meet the needs of the rural areas, one must ask why that would not have been the obvious solution a few decades earlier—supposing that rural Christianity did not develop until the latter half of the 200s and that the mission in the

---

22. Brent D. Shaw, *Sacred Violence: African Christians and Sectarian Hatred in the Age of Constantine* (Cambridge: Cambridge University Press, 2011), 354, notes that there were about 500 dioceses in North Africa by 411 c.e. Even a settlement so small that it was called merely a farm might have a bishop. How early this was a reality is less clear. Such a multitude of rural bishops give some scholars pause. Leslie Dossey, *Peasant and Empire in Christian North Africa* (Berkeley: University of California Press, 2010), 128, states: "it is probably safe to say that few villages or estates had bishops during the third century." But it is not clear from the evidence Dossey presents that this was the case, and Dossey herself introduces the quote above with the qualification "despite these caveats." We can at least say that given the considerable success of Christianity throughout North Africa well before Constantine, small settlements would have had a Christian presence and most likely their leaders would have been called simply "bishops," that being the term used for leaders of small settlements later.

countryside was initiated by the urban church. The later we posit the intro-duction of an office of *chorepiscopos*, the more difficult it is to explain why it was introduced at all, seeing that, almost immediately upon instituting it, lower clergy were viewed as the more appropriate leaders for the church's functioning in the countryside.[23]

Further, if the country bishop was an office instituted by the urban power structure, established to help the urban church to extend its author-ity as the church expanded into the countryside, then why would the urban church have used the term "bishop" as part of this term, particularly when the title of "bishop" was coming to be so closely guarded, serving as the mark of the one legitimate authority in an area? But, in our first glimpse of the office of *chorepiscopos*, country bishops do not seem to be a tool of the urban clergy at all, nor do they appear to reflect dependence upon the urban bishop or submission to him. They certainly do not appear as ad-ministrative or liturgical assistants to the urban bishop.

The problem with the hypothesis that the country bishop arose within the urban bishop's hierarchy is that when we first meet the office in the literature, the country bishop seems to possess considerable autonomy, which church councils wish to limit to the benefit of the city bishops. If the country bishop were clearly an appointee and delegate of the city bishop, one would expect to find the bishop himself regulating his subordinate's activity. The question is how the country bishop gained an authority roughly parallel to the city bishop if the country bishop was—and always had been—a mere agent of the city bishop. Further, and more baffling, why was such deference shown to a group that had so overstepped their authority?

The matter is difficult to settle, for the evidence is scarce, but there are enough questions about the development of the country bishop to weaken it as a basis for asserting that rural Christianity did not begin until roughly the time of Constantine or only slightly earlier.

---

23. James Barnett, *The Diaconate: A Full and Equal Order*, rev. ed. (Harrisburg, PA: Trinity Press, 1995), 100, referring to canon 8 of the Council of Nicea, has argued that the Council saw "little, if any, difference" between rural bishops and presbyters. That may well be what they hoped to achieve in the end, but it is clear that the Council did not believe that such was the present state of affairs. Country bishops were clearly held in greater esteem than the presbyters, and the Council itself shows a certain deference to the episcopal status of holders of the *chorepiscopos* office that it does not recognize for presbyters.

10

Conclusion

ON A NUMBER of grounds I have contested the widely held hypothesis that early Christianity was largely urban. One, the numbers usually put forward do not work; major adjustments would need to be made to current calculations about the expansion of Christianity if a rural component is not factored in. Two, the definition of what is to count as urban and what as rural varies so widely within scholarship that the terms become almost meaningless, particularly when the definition of what an urban area is seems largely arbitrary and idiosyncratic, both in the ancient world and, more troubling, in modern scholarship. Three, inhabitants of the countryside flowed into the city and rustics constituted a significant part of the city's residents, so much so that it becomes misleading to think of urban centers as devoid of or immune to some considerable rustic complexion. Fourth, the "urban thesis," at best, is a skewed perception, based more on the ratio of Christians in the respective urban and rural populations than of actual numbers.

I see my work primarily as an attempt to dismantle what I perceive to be a defective consensus view. Such dismantling, even if only partly successful, will require a fresh analysis of the complexion of early Christian communities. My sense is that such a rethinking of early Christianity's portrait and place in the Roman world must have at least a bit more rustic coloring in its complexion and a bit more rural territory in its reach.

But I recognize that dismantling is the easier task, and thus I submit my work as a necessary but hardly a complete contribution to that effort. Any major reimagining of the complexion of the early Christian movement as a result of the dismantling or revising of the urban thesis will be a long-term and multifaceted effort from the pens of many—scholars who are convinced either by parts of the present critique of the urban thesis or by fresh descriptions of rural/urban relationships in the empire, and who then find ways to incorporate some of these reflections into fields in which they have expertise.

The Numbers

I started out by pointing to two prominent scholars in recent debates about the expansion of early Christianity. Both insisted that it was important to put numbers to things. On that point I agree. But I have not been comfortable with the numbers that either of these scholars offered, or for that matter with any numbers offered anywhere. The most hopeful success for a reasonably secure number is for the population of the Roman Empire as a whole, since there are various methods by which that might be determined, though still with a considerable margin of error. Even here the proposals are fairly wide-ranging.

But supposing some consensus could be reached about the size of the population of the Roman Empire, that number would be of little help—actually no help—in determining the fundamental question for early Christian studies: the *proportion* of Christians in the empire at any given time, for that number hinges on the *size* of the Christian population. But the size of the Christian population is at best a fairly wild or arbitrary guess, and probably must always remain so, for there is no way to measure the number of Christians by the mechanisms used to determine the population of the empire as a whole. For the size or the proportion of the Christian population of the empire, then, we are left with impressions, and such impressions vary widely.

Because of this, impressions must be tested. We must at least attempt to visualize what the empire must have looked like on the framework of the various numbers that have been proposed. That has not been done, and as we have seen, sometimes we have been carried, quite unaware, into supporting reconstructions that are not simply unlikely but, in fact, impossible and absurd. The numbers must be made real. We must populate the streets of these ancient cities with the full contingent of people we have proposed. What does the city look like? Can it carry the population we have placed there? Can we read ancient literature and examine archaeological remains and confirm that in our calculation of numbers we have populated these streets with some degree of probability? Ramsay MacMullen has tried an exercise of this kind for the number of people that might be accommodated within the space of urban church architecture.

The usefulness of such visualization may be more in its corrective and cautionary function than in its ability to construct a new portrait of early Christianity, but even that would be of considerable value given the kinds of impossible scenarios that have been presented as convincing and accepted as certain. Had such an attempt at visualization been done with the numbers proposed by Rodney Stark, the need for substantial revision or complete discarding of his now highly popular and widely propagated numbers would have been obvious from the start.

Must we abandon all attempts at specifying raw numbers or percentages of Christians or of Jews in the Roman Empire? I think we must. We are confronted, it seems, by the necessity of numbers and the impossibility of numbers. This is not a good position to be in, but it is a better situation than being wrong about numbers that we have accepted as reliable. Yet we cannot free ourselves completely from some notion of the size of the early Christian movement. Such a sense arises quite unconsciously from various impressions left by the scattered literature and by the crumbling ruins that each investigator has encountered, leaving one person with the sense that Christianity was sizable and another person with an equally strong sense that Christianity was barely on anyone's radar. Such an unsettled state has probably made us too willing to cling in hope to anything that seems to offer something more grounded, whether MacMullen's mere 1% based on architectural space or Stark's near-saturation based on Mormon growth rates. I am not convinced that we are better off with either of these seemingly more concrete efforts than we are with mere impressions.

On one point we can have certainty. If there was a rural component in the early Christian movement, we are freed from the near-impossible scenarios that the urban thesis forces us into: either an insignificantly small Christian movement in the empire or an urban population overly saturated with Christians—neither of which seems to pass the visualization test. The question, of course, is whether a case has been made for a rural element in the early Christian movement. I submit that there is enough suggestive comment in the ancient literature to lead us in that direction.

The Rural Element

The most blunt and baffling matter that needs correction is the assumption that there could have been a significant Christian presence in the empire without a sizeable rural component in the Christian membership.

A largely urban Christian movement constituting about 10% of the empire around the year 300 cannot be made to work by any mental or mathematical gymnastics, yet that has been a widely accepted reconstruction—indeed, the most widely accepted. And that impossible reconstruction is made even more impossible when a substantial component of diaspora urban-centered Jews is added to the equation.

In part, the placement of Christians (and Jews) in urban areas of the empire has come about from the flawed perception that the urban and rural domains represented alien and mutually exclusive worlds, and that, for Christians, nearly insurmountable barriers faced any effort to take their message to the countryside and to those of rural and rustic attachments. But such a view is challenged by almost everything we know about how the rural and urban domains meshed with and depended on each other—if, indeed, we can even speak of these as clearly distinguishable domains in terms of the kinds of people who lived there. Perhaps the more significant categories would be the urbane and the rustic, but even these concepts are more caricatures than portraits and are used by the ancients as such.

As to the presence of Christianity in the countryside, if Christians represented even a small minority in the Roman Empire (say, 5%), then some element, and perhaps a substantial element of the Christian movement, almost certainly would have been rural-based. Simply to increase the degree of urbanization in the empire in order to accommodate a larger number of Christians (even if that were a credible motivation) does not lessen the likelihood of a rural Christian presence; rather, it may increase it. Urban areas generally depended on an influx of rural people to keep their population stable, and the more rural people who made urban areas their home, the more rustic the urban areas would have felt and been. Further, a web of links to acquaintances and relatives still in the countryside would have been created by that kind of influx, a network that the Christian movement could have exploited.

Supposing, then, that it is likely—or at least possible—that Christian assemblies existed in rural areas throughout most of the early history of the movement, can we determine what these churches might have been like? The once common view of the countryside as an abode of protest, fringe, or schismatic movements, devoid of Christian groups of a more orthodox flavor, must be set aside. It is unlikely that such groups would have had any greater appeal to a rural audience than would more orthodox forms of Christianity. Indeed, these movements were generally marked by a moral rigor that would have made them far less likely open to rustics—and rustics far less likely open to them.[1]

There is really no reason to suspect that urban and rural churches would have been inherently starkly different from each other. Their leaders may have met together regularly, and it is possible that some rural Christians made their way into nearby towns for common assembly or even that urban Christians joined believers in a gathering in a village, perhaps reflecting family connections, longtime friendships, or patron/client relations. The situation probably differed in various degrees from location to location and from individual to individual. Certainly given the natural and routine interchanges between urban and rural areas, nothing requires that urban and rural Christian assemblies be of a significantly different theological orientation or communal practice. More likely would be the case of largely shared beliefs and practices by urban and rural members of an area, perhaps under the influence of a particularly dynamic or devout personality. Such churches, if differing at all, may have differed more from churches in other territories than from each other. And whatever diversity Christianity came to express, it is at least as likely that each group had both urban and rural followers than that a theological position or point of practice was distinctively and exclusively urban or rural.[2]

It is at this point that Ramsay MacMullen's "second church" thesis seems inadequate and too narrowly drawn. MacMullen says: "While the hierarchy were preoccupied with such abstract matters as the Trinity and the interrelationship of its personae, the masses expressed its religious impulses in the cemeteries."[3] But MacMullen gives insufficient credit to the theological reflections of the simple, the ordinary, and the common—the non-intellectual who identified with the Christian movement. Take,

---

1. This includes groups such as the Montanists, the Novatians, the Donatists, and the Meletianists, and in some presentations of this kind of reconstruction, with monasticism included too. The case for the rural character of these groups has never been strong, since whatever their rural component, they had an urban component as well, with perhaps only the Montanists originating in the countryside (see the section "Treating Rural Christianity as Abnormal" in chapter 8).

2. For example, both sides in the Donatist controversy had rural and urban adherents. Modern attempts to read the Donatist movement as rural have failed. See Peter Brown, "Christianity and Local Culture in Late Roman Africa," *JRS* 58 (1968): 85–95; A. H. M. Jones, "Were Ancient Heresies National or Social Movements in Disguise?" *JTS* 10.2 (1959): 280–298.

3. Ramsay MacMullen, *The Second Church: Popular Christianity* A.D. 200–400, (Atlanta: Society of Biblical Literature, 2009), 50.

for example, the well-known quote of Gregory of Nyssa who was in Constantinople in 381 for the famous council there. He commented:

> The whole city is full of it, the squares, the market places, the cross-roads, the alleyways; old-clothes men, money changers, food sellers: they are all busy arguing. If you ask someone to give you change, he philosophizes about the Begotten and the Unbegotten; if you inquire about the price of a loaf, you are told by way of reply that the Father is greater and the Son inferior; if you ask "Is my bath ready?" the attendant answers that the Son was made out of nothing.[4]

This suggests that the common person—the butcher, the baker, the candlestick-maker kind of folk—shared in at least some of the theological exertions that the elite found compelling. And there is nothing to indicate that sides in the theological fisticuffs marked off the elite from the rabble. Each side would have drawn loyalists from both segments of the membership, for it was not city walls nor rustic sentiment that would have separated the sides in these theological disputes. We could step back fifty years from Gregory's experience in Constantinople to Arius in Alexandria and find there a similar situation. Arius had composed songs championing his theology, set to popular tunes, it seems, and these were sung by sailors, millers, and travelers,[5] much as Augustine was to do later, attempting to link some element of the masses with anti-Donatist sentiments in his area.[6]

Granted, such rural and urban theological bonds must remain speculation for most areas, but such relationships have as much probability as a reconstruction that posits a fundamentally different complexion of urban and rural Christianity of the kind Ramsay MacMullen has proposed.[7] And that leads to the second significant adjustment that needs

---

4. Gregory of Nyssa, *Deit.* (PG 46:557). The English translation used above is found in Timothy Ware, *The Orthodox Church*, 2nd ed. (London: Penguin Books, 1997), 35.

5. Mentioned by Philostorgius in his *History of the Church*, 2.2; preserved in the epitome of that work by Photius. Athanasius mentions something similar in regard to Arius in two places (*C. Ar.* 4–5, and *Syn.* 14–15).

6. Cited by MacMullen himself, "Provincial Languages in the Roman Empire," *AJP* 87.1 (1966): 14. Such actions would seem to link MacMullen's two churches.

7. For a discussion of MacMullen's proposal, see Appendix A.

to be made to the urban thesis. Not only was there a *rural* element in the early Christian movement, there was a *rustic* element too. And that element would likely have constituted a significant component of even the urban church.

The Rustic Element

Rustics could be found in urban areas as well as in rural areas. Some had always lived in the city, going out each morning to tend nearby fields. Others had abandoned their rural homes for the promise and the allure of the city. Still others moved back and forth, players in a market economy. And many, whether born in the city or an immigrant from the countryside, constituted the mass of the urban poor, who lived from day to day, praying with hope and desperation that some benefactor (or a father—perhaps in heaven) would give them bread for the day. In this motley environment, one certainly did not need to leave the city to find rustics in considerable numbers.

Early critics of Christianity pointed dismissively to this rustic element in the church, and apologists did not attempt to challenge this characterization, as they were at pains to do when baseless accusations were made against the Christian movement. Rather, in regard to the lower-class complexion of the Christian movement, the apologists accepted the charge, pointed out that such people were not the only ones associated with the Christian assembly, and then neutralized the charge by showing that the church's interest in those of low status pointed to the value and veracity of the Christian message—not to its worthlessness, and that the change in behavior of such rustics and wretches proved Christianity's virtue.[8]

Yet the presence of rustics in the early Christian movement has been dismissed for the countryside and downplayed for the city under the sway of efforts to portray or at least highlight the urban middle class, a socially

---

8. Celsus is a good witness to how some outsiders (and probably most) were viewing the Christian movement in the latter part of the second century, and Origen, in his response to Celsus about fifty years later, is a good witness to the Christian movement not only for the time in which Origen wrote but also for the half-century between the two authors. Unlike a writing that may provide a useful portrait for a movement at one point in time and place, Origen's *Contra Celsum*, by giving near-verbatim copy of Celsus' criticism followed by Origen's own response, provides a much more sweeping portrait of the Christian movement over considerable time and place. The rustics are part of that movement during Celsus' time, and they appear to have remained so, for they are clearly still a significant element in the church fifty years later when Origen wrote.

pretentious and connected element in the Christian movement.[9] This trend has provoked a sharp rebuke from Steven Friesen, who specifically points to the "disappearance of the topic of poverty" in modern discussions of the complexion of the Christian movement.[10] Meeks, for example, while recognizing that the church would have had a cross-section of the urban population, emphasizes what he takes to be the most active and prominent members—"upwardly mobile" people of "high status inconsistency." The "typical" Christian was a "free artisan or small trader," according to Meeks, and he explicitly omits the destitute, which for him encompasses "the hired menials and dependent handworkers, the poorest of the poor, peasants, agricultural slaves, and hired agricultural day laborers." These are absent "because of the urban setting of the Pauline groups," Meeks explains.[11] And herein lies the problem. The wretched, the rustic, and the rabble were very much part of urban life.

Meeks' portrait of the context and complexion of the early Christian movement is largely drawn from Acts and Paul's letters—and selectively at that. For clues to the social status of Christians in the second and third centuries, it might be wiser to turn away from Paul and Acts rather than toward them. Even if we could construct the social world of Paul and his earliest assemblies from the meager evidence we have,[12] we should not assume that such a complexion stayed intact for 250 years or more. For one thing, the encounter that occurs when a movement first presents itself to an audience will never again provoke the same kind of response in that

---

9. Rodney Stark, *The Rise of Christianity* (Princeton: Princeton University Press, 1996), 29–33, provides a brief sketch of how scholarship had changed its view of the social status of early Christians, from seeing early Christians as educated and well connected (Gibbon, Ramsay, Harnack), to the disadvantaged from the lower strata (Deissmann and Troeltsch), coming full circle to the "socially pretentious" with the underprivileged classes "largely untouched" (Judge, Grant, Malherbe, Theissen, Lane Fox, Meeks, and others). Steven J. Friesen, "Poverty in Pauline Studies: Beyond the So-Called New Consensus," *JSNT* 26 (2004), 323–337, calls into question whether scholarship over this period really reflected substantially different views.

10. Friesen, "Poverty in Pauline Studies," 332, 334–335, 336.

11. Wayne A. Meeks, *The First Urban Christians: The Social World of the Apostle Paul* (New Haven: Yale University Press, 1983), 73.

12. I speak of the Pauline corpus as meager because much of it is of little or no use in reconstructing the social complexion of Pauline communities. Note how the two letters to Corinth dominate the discussion of Paul's social world. It escapes me how that limited correspondence, written to a community just established and already fractured and only months—not decades—old, can be used to provide useful descriptions of the early Christian social world and the status of its members throughout the empire over two and a half centuries.

locale. On the introduction of a new message, individuals hear and come to a decision. Some may hesitate, but the more delayed the decision is, the less likely an individual will decide in favor. The point is that decisions for or against the movement are likely to be made early. The message is either compelling or at least intriguing or it is not. But a new crop of individuals is not minted each day who will, for the first time, hear the new option and make a decision either for or against it. Indeed, after a few months or years or perhaps decades (depending on the movement's success and visibility), the message becomes no longer attention-grabbing but rather more passé. The context of encounter has changed in significant ways. Those presenting the message, for example, may cease to be foreign visitors but residents of long standing, and the movement that could on first presentation offer itself without the baggage of a reputation now exhibits itself with the burden of judgments already made, either for or against it. The kinds of people who join a movement after it has been established and has become more a part of the public scene may be of a significantly different status or inclination from those who joined at first. That is why building a description of the social complexion of the church in the second and third centuries on the basis of Paul's circle or those identified with Jesus' ministry must be abandoned or at least more cautiously done, so that the voices of those of the rabble in the second- and third-century church are not drowned out by the welcomed discovery by modern researchers that Jesus and Paul had some socially respectable connections.[13]

However much we might feel wedded or welded to the middle class or socially well placed view of the membership of early Christian assemblies, too many references surface in the Christian literature of the first three centuries regarding the poor and the ignorant not to conclude that the lower social stratum was a significant element in the Christian movement. One wonders how Paul's statement (if Paul is to be appealed to at all) that there were *not many wise, not many powerful, not many noble* who were chosen by God has come now to be read (at least at the popular level) as *many quite wise, many fairly well placed, and most with middle-class status*. It is important to note that Paul continues his comments, pointing out that

---

13. Robin Scroggs, "The Sociological Interpretation of the New Testament: The Present Stage of Research," *NTS* 26 (1980): 171, suspected that some of the modern efforts to enhance the social level of the early Christian movement stemmed from the desire to find more respectable origins. Note the importance of Paul to Meeks' depiction of the social status of early Christian communities. See David A. Fiensy, *Christian Origins and the Ancient Economy* (Cambridge: James Clarke & Co., 2014) for a focus on Jesus' social connections.

most of those who were chosen were the stupid, the weak, the lowly, the despised, and the nothings of the world (τα μωρὰ, τα ἀσθενῆ, τα ἀγενῆ, τα ἐξουθενημένα, and τὰ μὴ ὄντα), words that indicate people of low or no status—whatever that would have loosely identified.[14]

A much more serious problem arises, however, for any portrait of an urban church largely devoid of the rustic and those of low status. That is the difficulty of finding a sufficient number of middle-class individuals to populate the Christian movement. Given that the middle class constituted only one segment of the urban population, with rustics and slaves making up a significant segment as well, even with a solid success among the middle class, the Christian slice of the urban pie would be quite small. Walter Scheidel and Steven Friesen have tried to give numbers to the size of the middle-class (or middle-income) group, proposing that between 5% and 10% of the population were of "middling" income, as they put it, and that about two-thirds of such people lived in urban areas.[15] They then calculate that this middle group would have made up one-eighth to one-quarter of the urban population. If we take Scheidel and Friesen's numbers for the urban middle class, we have the following scenario. Counting urbanization of the empire at 15%, the urban middle class would have a population of between 1.125 and 2.25 million. Even were we to set the Christian portion of the middle-class population at one-third (an optimistic and perhaps unrealistic high[16]), that would leave only 350,000 to 750,000 Christians in the empire of 60 million—well under or only slightly over 1% of the total population of the empire.[17]

But such numbers provide us with only 6% to 12% of the supposed 6-million-strong Christian movement so often put forward as reliable for the year 300 c.e. It would seem that the urban poor, the urban ignorant,

---

14. 1 Cor 1:27–28. My translation.

15. Walter Scheidel and Steven J. Friesen, "The Size of the Economy and the Distribution of Income in the Roman Empire," *JRS* 99 (2009), 84, 90. They increase the number of the "middling" to a range of 6% to 12% if soldiers are included.

16. Neither Celsus nor Origen gives any hint that a large segment of a "middle" class population converted to Christianity. Celsus may not have been keen to recognize such an element in the Christian movement, but it would have been a useful matter for Origen to have pointed out.

17. I have taken a total population of 60 million (as I have throughout this book); Scheidel and Friesen estimate 70 million, but that does not alter the percentages. Increasing urbanism to a high of 25% does not change the situation much: 625,000 to 1,250,000 Christians (calculated as one-third of the urban middle class).

and the urban rustic must be allowed back on the stage. I say "allowed back onto the stage" because, though most scholars recognize that the membership of the Christian movement included a cross-section of society (or at least of urban society), the poor are as marginal in modern discussions of the complexion of early Christianity as they were in real life in the empire. But the marginalized in the ancient world were not so marginalized in the early church. They formed a significant segment of the membership and they received a significant portion of the church's resources and concern. How such a large part of the church's membership has been kept in the shadows of modern discussions is baffling, for the poor and the ignorant are such essential constituents in a movement that makes the care of the poor and the instruction of the ignorant both an individual and a corporate responsibility. Without the poor and individuals of low estate, the Christian emphasis on charity and generosity, the exhortation to the wealthy, and the attention to the needy, both in word and action, would make no sense.[18] On the flip side, of course, is that without some members of substance in the congregational mix, the exhortations to charity would ring hollow and have results as shallow. The cross-section must be a truer cross-section. Meeks may have offered a useful, indeed brilliant, depiction of one section in the early Christian movement, but he has not offered a depiction of the "typical" adherent—even the typical urban adherent, let alone the sweeping rural reality that made up an extremely high percent of the population of the Roman Empire.

But even adding the rustic and the marginal as a component of the urban church does not resolve the problem of numbers, for unless

---

18. The issue of poverty in society and the poor in early Christian assemblies are unsettled matters. It is not my intention here to resolve the dispute or even to offer a description of the various issues. My concern is to determine whether the matter might have any implications regarding the existence of Christianity in the countryside or among the rustic and the poor. The Christian response to wealth and to poverty, though not uniform, leaves little doubt of an obligation to the poor and consequences to the rich who spend on grand houses, rich finery, and wasteful dinners while neglecting the orphan, the widow, and the poor. See Helen Rhee, *Loving the Poor, Saving the Rich: Wealth, Poverty, and Early Christian Formation* (Grand Rapids, MI: Baker Academic, 2012); Justo L. Gonzalez, *Faith and Wealth: A History of Early Christian Ideas on the Origin, Significance, and Use of Money* (New York: Harper & Row, 1990); Justin J. Meggitt, *Paul, Poverty and Survival* (Edinburgh: T & T Clark, 1998); J. A. McGuckin, "The Vine and the Elm Tree: The Patristic Interpretation of Jesus' Teaching on Wealth," in *The Church and Wealth*, ed. W. J. Sheils and Diana Wood (Oxford: Basil Blackwell, 1987), 1–14. For a treatment of wealth in the western church in the post-Constantinian period, see Peter Brown, *Through the Eye of a Needle: Wealth, the Fall of Rome, and the Making of Christianity in the West, 350–550 AD* (Princeton: Princeton University Press, 2012).

Christians saturated the urban Roman world, we would still fall far short of the 6 million number usually put forward. What the better option is at this point is unclear. We are left with impressions, and impressions vary widely on these matters. Perhaps Christians did number significantly under the 10% so often claimed, as MacMullen argues.[19] Perhaps Christians did come close to saturating the urban Roman world before the rise of Constantine. Or, perhaps the neglected countryside, making up 80% of the empire's population, needs to be part of the consideration of the growth of the Christian movement.

One thing seems certain. Whatever the description of the complexion of the Christian movement, the miserable and the marginal must be made part of the Christian mix—the poorest of the poor, the agricultural day worker, the hired menials, the peasant, the dependent handworker—though Meeks dismisses these.[20] If the Christian movement made charity a serious part of its responsibility, then those most in need of charity may have found their way into the Christian fold if for no other reason than mere survival. Origen is aware that some have joined the church for their physical welfare rather than their spiritual welfare, but he counters that reality by pointing to the host of marginal adherents whose conversion is genuine and whose conduct had been radically changed by the Christian message.[21]

The transformation of conduct from vile to virtuous that Origen speaks of may be crucial here for understanding the background and status of a noticeable segment of the Christian membership. It is unlikely that Origen has in mind the hard-working artisan of the middle

19. MacMullen, *The Second Church*, 101–112.

20. Meeks, *The First Urban Christians*, 72–73, says that there is "no specific evidence of people who are destitute ... There may have been members of the Pauline communities who lived at the subsistence level, but we hear nothing of them," and when commenting on one passage that speaks of the poor, Meeks states that we should not take it "too literally" (66), and in another place Meeks adds the word "relatively" in parentheses before the words "poor" and "rich" (68). Yet in a later work, Meeks recognizes that "many" could identify not just with the poor but with the poorest of the poor, the "destitute" [Wayne A. Meeks, "Social and Ecclesial Life of the Earliest Christians," in *The Cambridge History of Christianity*, vol. 1, *Origins to Constantine*, ed. Margaret Mary Mitchell and Frances Margaret Young (Cambridge: Cambridge University Press, 2006), 157]. The poor seem to have become more poor and more present in Meeks' later work.

21. Origen, *Cels.* 1.67. They have joined for food (βιωτικά) and other basic needs (χρείας), it seems. Origen does not mention how these individuals were identified as insincere or whether much effort was made to weed such people from the church's charity.

class. He more likely has in mind the class of people, who by character and conduct, both he and Celsus describe as sinners (ἁμαρτάνων).[22]
Indeed, according to one of the earliest Christian writers, some of the
first Christians *were* thieves, a matter concerning which the writer did not
hesitate to remind his readers: "You were taught to put away your former
way of life,....[T]hieves must give up stealing; rather let them labor and
work honestly with their own hands, so as to have something to share
with the needy (Eph 4:22, 28).

It is the transformation of the conduct of these kinds of individuals that speaks to the credibility of the Christian movement, according to Origen, though one might dismiss his suggestion that the worst
person in the Christian movement had been made better than the best
person outside of it.[23] If Origen is correct in seeing a significant aspect
of Christianity in the transformation of character, then this may serve
as further evidence that the Christian movement's slice of the urban
pie included somewhat more than a stable, hard-working middle class,
and that this kind of transformed lower-class individual was perhaps the
most visible element in the complexion of the movement, or at least
could be presented as a compelling point in the church's response to the
dismissive critic.

The question is how large this lower-class contingent might have
been. Origen had to deal with repeated charges that the Christian movement was largely made up of the ignorant and the rustic. His response
was clear and unequivocal. The majority within the Christian movement are individuals of the simple and the ignorant stratum. They
outnumber the more intelligent. But he turns the charge back. Those
who are ignorant and simple will always outnumber the others because
there are, quite simply, more of these in society.[24] Since the Christian
message is for everyone, it is neither surprising nor discrediting, then,
that the Christian movement has a majority of its members from the
ignorant and simple segments of society, and in terms of conduct, even
some who were the worst of sinners—"the most unholy and abandoned of men" and those who have committed "the most abominable

---

22. Origen, *Cels*. 3.65. Much of what Origen deals with over a considerable part of Book 3
relates to the rustic, the ignorant, and the sinner in the Christian membership (3.44–69).

23. Origen, *Cels*. 3.29–30.

24. Origen, *Cels*. 1.27.

sins"—transformed to a greater or lesser degree, of course."[25] Not that every member had been the worst of sinners. Origen does go on to point out that the churches did have a greater number of members who had been converted from not so very sinful lives. While they may not all have been very sinful, most would have been drawn from what would have a fairly marginal existence, if the church's membership reflected the cross-section of society, as Origen had asserted. According to Friesen, the urban population of the empire would have had 68% of its inhabitants at the level of mere subsistence or below it, and only 22% more at a stable existence, but at near-subsistence.[26] That would place about 90% of the urban population among the poor or close to it, hardly the portrait ones sees in most of the current scholarship on the early Christian movement. Friesen's calculation may well be problematic, yet even a critic of Friesen agrees that most of Paul's converts lived "at or near subsistence level."[27]

Even admitting a larger and dominant lower-class stratum in the Christian movement, it may be possible to retain the importance of a middle-class element in the configuration of early Christian assemblies. But it will not be by increasing the size of the middle-class element that its importance comes into play. Rather, it is in terms of the economic clout this group has by bringing resources into the church to enable the church to carry out its mission. Here, again, something along the lines of Scheidel and Friesen's analysis may be helpful. Given that the disposal income of the so-called middle class was significant,[28] it is possible that a middle-class component within Christianity could have made a marked impact on the plight of the poor. At least, the church could have functioned as an institution not only with a mission to the poor but with some means to

---

25. Origen, *Cels.* 3.65. Origen uses the words ἀνοσιστάτοι and ἐλωλεστάτοι. He also notes that various degrees of moral rigor (or lack thereof) can be found in the Christian assemblies (3.30).

26. Friesen, "Poverty in Pauline Studies," 347.

27. John Barclay, "Poverty in Pauline Studies: A Response to Steven Friesen," *JSNT* 26 (2004): 365–366. Barclay does make the important point that "habitually" living either slightly above or below subsistence made a significant difference—"the difference between life and imminent death!"

28. Scheidel and Friesen, "The Size of the Economy and the Distribution of Income in the Roman Empire," 88–89. These authors are looking at the distribution of income and note the economic clout that the "middling income" group would have. Such studies would then need to be carefully incorporated into the situation of the early church.

effect that mission. That may mean that the Christian movement would have attracted a greater slice of the contingent of the poor, driven for their survival to where they could find help. Such a slice would have included people with various attachments to the countryside. If such people with rural attachments or rustic character were attracted to the Christian movement (for whatever reason), there is little reason to expect that the countryside would have been immune to the Christian message or that the church and its adherents with such rural connections would have had no interest in the countryside.

Back to the Countryside

Scheidel and Friesen's work might suggest an additional route for Christian presence and success in the countryside. They calculate that about two-thirds of the middle class was urban.[29] This would locate a significant slice of the middle class in a rural environment. If Christianity attracted an element of the middle class (for whatever reason), an element of the *rural* middle class, too, may have joined the Christian movement and become its leaders and resource suppliers. Thus, a mission from urban churches would not be needed to account for a rural church. The same forces that allowed some urban middle-class, status-conscious people to find fulfillment within the church may have had similar attraction for some of the rural middle class. Further, whatever links connected a middle-class individual to other middle-class individuals may have linked rural and urban middle-class players together too. If so, then the urban and the rural churches may have not only looked similar but viewed themselves as part of the same community, sharing not only in the same future heavenly world but in the present world as well, linked as much through the natural links that kept city and countryside together as by the spiritual links that made them part of the same family.

Although the world of the rural church may be largely invisible to us now and must be inferred from scattered pieces of evidence, the weight of the evidence linking the urban and rural environments points to the likelihood of an early Christian presence in the countryside and a noticeable rustic complexion of the urban churches. If a rural and a rustic

---

29. Scheidel and Friesen, "The Size of the Economy and the Distribution of Income in the Roman Empire," 90.

element does not become a prominent factor in our reconstructions of early Christianity, we must revise almost every aspect of the urban portrait of the early Christian movement, which has failed badly both in terms of its use of numbers and in terms of its understanding of the relationships between the urban and the rural in the ancient world in which the Christian movement made its way.

APPENDIX A

The Numbers According to
Ramsay MacMullen

RAMSAY MACMULLEN HAS contributed so much to the field of early Christian studies that no one in the field is without some debt to him, and for most the debt is
considerable. His latest work, *The Second Church: Popular Christianity* A.D. *200–400*,[1]
is typical: thought-provoking, controversial, consensus-breaking—and, of course,
heavily documented. It builds upon conclusions MacMullen had reached in previous
works—regarding the nature of conversion, the kind of converts attracted to early
Christianity, the continued vitality of paganism well past the Constantinian era—
particularly in his 1989 article, in which the seeds for the present work can be seen.[2]

---

1. Ramsay MacMullen, *The Second Church: Popular Christianity* A.D. *200–400*, (Atlanta: Society
of Biblical Literature, 2009). One objection to MacMullen's method is that, by defining
his period of study as the 200s and 300s, MacMullen has grouped two markedly different
centuries and has treated these two periods as essentially the same, which they are not.
MacMullen's depiction of the early Christians, if accurate, is appropriate only for the period
of the 300s, not for the period of the 200s. We simply have too little to draw on for the
period of the 200s for the kinds of conclusions MacMullen offers, however compelling some
might find his analysis for the 300s. For example, the sermon material to which MacMullen
appeals is post-350, which would seem to compromise its use for describing the church in
the 200s. See the letter exchange between Robert L. Wilken and MacMullen [Robert Louis
Wilken, review of *The Second* Church, by Ramsay MacMullen, with response by MacMullen,
Conversations *in Religion and Theology* 8.2 (2010): 120–125. A second objection is that the
appeal to the physical dimensions of church structures is complicated by Constantine's massive church-building program, which divides the 200s from the 300s in a profound way
regarding the accommodations for Christian assembly.

2. Ramsay MacMullen, "The Preacher's Audience (AD 350–400)," *JTS* 40 (1989): 503–
511. E. G. Clark, "Pastoral Care: Town and Country in Late Antique Preaching," in *Urban
Centers and Rural Contexts in Late Antiquity*, ed. Thomas S. Burns and John W. Eadie (East
Lansing: Michigan State University Press, 2001), 265–284, takes issue with MacMullen's
argument in his 1989 article.

In his recent book, MacMullen divides Christian adherents into two groups: the elite and the masses. There is nothing particularly novel in this. Many have asserted that the average adherent to Christianity was markedly different from the individuals in leadership, and many have argued that the depictions of Christianity in early literature, largely preserved in writings of the elite, were more descriptive of what the leadership desired in the average member—not what the leadership observed. It was more a matter of rhetoric than of reality. More a matter of what was prescribed than what was practiced.[3]

What is novel in MacMullen's division is that not only does MacMullen contend that there were two kinds of Christianity, he thinks that the two groups did not even meet together. Many historians of the early church have felt that, mentally, the two groups did not meet together. MacMullen goes one step further: the two groups did not even meet together physically. MacMullen reaches this conclusion by examining the architectural remains of churches,[4] and from that making an estimate of the number of individuals that might physically meet in the space available.[5] He concludes that a vast number of individuals who might be tagged with the Christian label were unable (and, more importantly, unwilling) to meet in these churches. Rather, they were meeting independently in cemeteries. MacMullen describes the two churches: "one was the choice of the Establishment, principally the clergy, in-city; the other, for everyone else, including some part of the farming population, beyond the city walls."[6] And he

---

3. It has become popular to read ancient literature through the lens of rhetoric, often judging the portrait offered by these texts as an obscured and misleading reflection of the reality on the ground. I have offered some reasons for caution in the rush to separate reality and rhetoric in *Ignatius of Antioch and the Parting of the Ways: Early Jewish-Christian Relations* (Grand Rapids, MI: Baker Academic, 2009), 227–235. Surely some of the adherents of early Christianity followed their leaders' instruction with zeal. Of course, some did not, and preaching might be directed at them to improve conduct. But those who failed to measure up to the leaders' standards may have been a minority—even a small minority. That they had chosen to be part of this voluntary organization suggests that at some level they were attracted to what was being preached or provided. If the divergence between what was preached and what was practiced was stark, one would wonder why these people chose to remain, or were permitted to remain, part of the group. There must have been some fit between what was proclaimed and what converts chose to practice.

4. MacMullen, *The Second Church*, 101, notes the body of evidence on which his work is based: an impressive 255 churches in 155 towns and cities. A list of churches before 400 C.E. is provided on pp. 117–141. By MacMullen's calculations, these churches could have held only 1% to 8% of the local population.

5. That is not MacMullen's only argument. He points to the content of sermons in order to argue that the audience must have been drawn from the elite, as in his "The Preacher's Audience (AD 350–400)," but this argument is supplemental to his main argument that relates to the size of the Christian church structures. Note the criticism by Philip Rousseau, *Basil of Caesarea* (Berkeley: University of California Press, 1994), 42, regarding MacMullen's view of the audience of Christian preaching.

6. MacMullen, *The Second Church*, 107.

gives numbers to the two components: the 5% (elite meeting in the city churches) and the 95% (the masses meeting elsewhere, in the cemeteries).[7] Without such meetings "beyond the city walls," the number of Christians participating in any active way in the church would be scandalously low—in some cases, only 1% of the population.

I have already argued that the city was hardly the exclusive domain of the urbane. The poor, the uneducated, and the workers in the surrounding fields crowded within city walls and made their homes there—much like the modern city, where the sophisticate is one small slice of the urban pie. And that must be what MacMullen means when he uses the phrase "beyond the city walls"—a mental state rather than a physical location—unless MacMullen is simply referring to the location of cemeteries, which is hardly a point of contrast, since cemeteries were as much a part of the "city" as anything else, even though they lay beyond the city walls.

MacMullen's suggestions are provocative and have the potential to alter our view of the development of early Christianity significantly. But there are problems with MacMullen's radical picture of the structure (both physical and mental) of the early Christian community.

MULTIPLE PLACES OF ASSEMBLY

MacMullen contrasts two venues of Christian assembly: the basilica and the cemetery. But the basilica and the cemetery are only part of the story. During the three centuries before basilicas became widespread, Christians met in a variety of venues for their liturgical and social needs. Few of these venues would have housed more than a few dozen, and most probably far less. Some of these places of meeting may have been upscale,[8] but many were likely to have been quite shabby. Celsus actually used the shabbiness of Christian meeting places to dismiss the movement, calling attention to the houses of people who worked in wool and leather (some of the more menial of occupations, which could be found in rural or urban areas) and the dwellings of ignorant and rustic people. Origen did not deny this; indeed, he seems to recognize that such people may have even served as teachers for the people who met in their homes and workshops.[9]

---

7. MacMullen, *The Second Church*, 15.

8. It had generally been assumed that the accommodation would have belonged to one of the more wealthy members, who had a house of sufficient size to accommodate two or three dozen people. Paul Trebilco, *The Early Christians in Ephesus from Paul to Ignatius* (Tübingen: Mohr Seibeck, 2004), 98, put the size of house-churches in homes of the wealthy at 30–40. He thinks that many would have been smaller, given that not every unit would have had a wealthy patron. David G. Horrell, "Domestic Space and Christian Meetings at Corinth: Imagining New Contexts and the Buildings East of the Theatre," *NTS* 50 (2004): 349–369, points out that Christians met in a variety of venues, and he is particularly critical of Jerome Murphy-O'Connor's proposal of the villa accommodating between forty and fifty as typical of early Christian assemblies.

9. Origen, *Cels.* 3.56

A key question is what happened to the Christian congregation in a city when the accommodation provided by a house or workshop was no longer of adequate size for the growing membership. There seem to be two main options. One, the congregation could have looked for a larger space to accommodate the growing Christian community, or two, the congregation could have subdivided, finding a similar space and setting up a second meeting place in the home of another member who had sufficient space to accommodate a new assembly. Whether one option was more likely than the other may have depended on the situation of the local community. We have examples of both: a renovated house enlarged to accommodate a larger assembly and set aside for Christian use (what technically is called a *domus ecclesiae*), as well as multiple households accommodating Christian gatherings in a town.[10] The church at Dura Europos (in use until 256 c.e.) was a residential building that had a wall removed, and in so doing was able to accommodate a crowd double the size of the community simply meeting in a home.

But we cannot be sure that the common practice was to obtain a new and larger space to accommodate a growing assembly, for in spite of how much such discussions are overshadowed by the Dura Europos church, it is not clear that as the Christian assembly grew in a city, the members would have seen no other way to accommodate the situation than by creating a larger assembly room to hold everyone. Indeed, perhaps the more natural option would have been to have another member volunteering his or her space for the weekly and occasional meetings of a second Christian assembly, seeing that the Christian assembly would have already been familiar with that kind of venue for their meetings. Indeed, multiple house-churches in a city may have been a reality almost from the first presence of Christianity in a city, and may have been the dominant practice for decades or centuries.

It is even possible that in some cities the initial preaching created a substantial number of converts, who, on hearing the Christian message for the first time, found something in that message that met their religious stirrings. Even if that was not the case for every city, surely it was so in some cities. In such cases, perhaps that would have necessitated several ready-made Christian assemblies, comprised largely of the membership of these households: family members and household slaves, and a few close friends or clients. Under such a scenario, multiple Christian assemblies could have been the reality within the first few months of a Christian mission in a city. Indeed, if Christian assemblies were formed around a household, then the idea that all Christian adherents in a city must physically meet together may not have crossed anyone's mind in the early period.

---

10. L. Michael White, *The Social Origins of Christian Architecture*, vol. 1, *Building God's House in the Roman World: Architectural Adaptation among Pagans, Jews and Christians* (Valley Forge, PA: Trinity Press, 1990), 1.111–123.

Although only a few specific reports describe early Christian assemblies, there are some that coincidentally but unambiguously describe Christian meeting places and that point to multiple house-church–like assemblies. Such assemblies appear to have been the case in Rome in the 50s;[11] and for Corinth in Paul's time there could have been six such house gatherings.[12] Justin's reply to the Prefect Rusticus' question about where the Christians assembled reflects a similar situation. He stated quite simply: "where each one chooses and can: for do you fancy that we all meet in the very same place?" When the question was repeated, Justin claimed to know of no other place where Christians met than in his own accommodations.[13] Further, even where there might have been a larger assembly space, at times there could have been some danger in meeting in a common assembly, as Tertullian warned, advising his readers how to assemble under the watchful eye of persecutors, and suggesting Christians assemble in groups as small as three if need be.[14]

That is not to say that prior to Constantine's conversion, Christians always met in homes or workshops of one of their members. MacMullen points to the literary evidence for specialized pre-Constantinian church buildings, appealing to Christian witnesses (Clement of Alexandria and Eusebius of Caesarea) and pagan ones (Porphyry).[15] On the basis of such evidence, MacMullen claims that in at least a dozen cities of the eastern empire, specialized buildings designed for Christian worship existed. MacMullen's conclusion seems reasonable—indeed, even restrained.[16] Eusebius points to what appears to be a building boom in church construction just prior to the Great Persecution,[17] and at the end of the persecution the order for restitution of church property included both buildings and cemeteries.

But we can hardly think of these larger buildings approaching in majesty or size the basilicas that were to come. They were large enough and visible enough to be recognized by the public, who knew them as Christian property, but as White points out, even the Christian church described by Lactantius as a "lofty temple" (*fanum*

---

11. Romans 16:1–15 speaks of multiple households, with some specifically described as churches (16:1, 3–5, 10, 11, 14, 15).

12. So argues White, *The Social Origins of Christian Architecture*, 1.105–106.

13. *Ac. Just.*, 2. Whether Justin's reply was to protect other Christian meeting places is unclear.

14. Tertullian, *Fug.* 3.2; 14.1.

15. MacMullen, *The Second Church*, 146n23.

16. MacMullen, *The Second Church*, 9. On one point, MacMullen does seem to be asking for too much. He claims that the pre-Constantinian churches mentioned in the literature would have been related in size to the size of their cities as the Dura Europos church was to its city. There is, however, no way to establish that. White, *The Social Origins of Christian Architecture*, 2.33–120, has provided a useful collection of this literature, in the original languages and in translation.

17. Eusebius, *Hist. eccl.* 8.1.5.

editissimum), which stood within sight of the emperor's palace, could not have been a monumental building since it was torn down in a few hours.[18] How large these more visible structures were and how many of these buildings one might find in a city are matters much more difficult to determine. That they were comparable to Jewish synagogues and the accommodations used by various collegia and other voluntary associations is a reasonable conjecture, since it appears that synagogues and collegia, too, had largely used renovated residential space,[19] but such buildings would not have accommodated great crowds, as we shall see when we look at diaspora synagogues.

We need to recognize that we do not know how these larger purpose-built structures related, or were intended to relate, to smaller venues used for Christian gatherings, such as the home of a member or some other accommodation.[20] It would not seem that these enlarged spaces were designed to gather all Christians in the city into a common place, for it is unlikely that such buildings would have held more than a hundred or so people.[21] But by the time such renovated specialized buildings were coming to be used, the Christian group in a city even as small as 5,000 could not have been accommodated in such structures unless the Christian population of the city stood at only 2% or 3% (assuming that the structure could accommodate between 100 to 150, which may be generous). And such a structure would have held a considerably smaller segment of the Christian population of larger cities.[22] But such a small number of Christians, particularly when coupled with the urban thesis, would leave the Christian population of the empire at fewer than 200,000 by the year 300.[23] Little wonder that MacMullen calls this a *scandalon* and attempts to augment the numbers by appeal to the concept of a "second church."

Homes and shops that had been the common meeting places probably continued to function in a similar way alongside the enlarged specialized spaces, and even

---

18. Lactantius, *Mort.* 12.4–5; White, *The Social Origins of Christian Architecture*, 1.130. MacMullen, *The Second Church*, 146n24, in contrast to White, calls this church an "imposing building." That it was a visible irritant is clear. That it was imposing, in a era of grand, imposing civil buildings, is less clear.

19. White, *The Social Origins of Christian Architecture*, 1.26–101, provides the most detailed study of the accommodations of cultic groups and synagogues.

20. Horrell, "Domestic Space and Christian Meetings at Corinth," 349–369.

21. MacMullen, *The Second Church*, 3, thinks that the Dura Europos church could have accommodated only seventy-five people, and perhaps fewer. This is the only pre-Constantinian Christian structure we have.

22. Assuming that the structure could accommodate between 100 to 150, and that may be generous.

23. Using 2% to 3% of an urban population of 6 million (the number often offered for the urban portion of the empire) would provide only 120,000 to 180,000 for the number of Christians in the empire. Even an urbanization double that (20% of the empire) would number Christians in the empire between 240,000 and 360,000.

the enlarged renovated spaces may have continued along with the basilicas, compli-cating any effort to calculate the Christian population of a city based on the dimen-sions of a basilica or two. It is on that point that Jan Bremmer objects to MacMullen's reconstruction. House-churches continued to be places of Christian assembly well after Constantine, according to Bremmer.[24] Bremmer points to the 383 C.E. legis-lation regarding house-churches (*Codex Theodosianus* 16.5.11), and to Kim Bowes, who argues that for most of the fourth century, Christians met as they had in the third century, in house-churches rather than basilicas, pointing out that the boom in church building did not come as early as had been assumed.[25]

The weight of the evidence seems to suggest that in the early period Christians who gathered in these small household assemblies used cemeteries (or some other open space), rather than building some large physical structure within a city that could accommodate a more full assembly of Christians in the area.[26] If such was customary, then it is conceivable (and likely) that the practice of meeting in cemeter-ies would have continued even after the building of large Constantinian-era basilicas. Thus, such gatherings may not indicate an opposition to the new reality. Rather, these gatherings may simply reflect the continuation of a long-standing, familiar practice. In such a case, we may not have, as MacMullen puts it, a "second church" in the strong sense that he wishes to make it.

When basilicas are first introduced, they were hardly a minor or natural transi-tional stage in the development of Christian assembly places. Nor could they have been intended to accommodate all the Christians in a city. Although these basili-cas were considerably larger than any of the prior Christian buildings and could

---

24. Jan N. Bremmer, *The Rise of Christianity through the Eyes of Gibbon, Harnack and Rodney Stark* (Groningen: Barkhuis, 2010), 64.

25. Kim Bowes, *Private Worship, Public Values, and Religious Change in Late Antiquity* (Cambridge: Cambridge University Press, 2008), 73.

26. There is evidence that early Christians gathered for communal rites in cemeteries, and there is no sense that these belonged to different factions. Dionysius, *Letter* 10.5 (parallel in Eusebius, *Hist. eccl.* 7.11.10), indicates that at the time of Valerian, Christians were prohibited from holding assemblies or entering those "places called cemeteries" (τά καλούμενα κοιμητ ήρια). The word κοιμητήρια, from which the English word "cemetery" comes, simply means "sleeping places," a term that, when used by early Christians for burial grounds, seemed odd to Greek speakers. Apparently such use of the term was widespread among Christians, so much so that when official imperial orders involved such spaces, the Christian terminol-ogy was used rather than the term that would have normally been used for burial places. At least, when Eusebius offers a Greek translation of the imperial orders, he uses the phrase τά καλούμενα κοιμητήρια or τά τῶν καλουμένων κοιμητηρίων (*Hist. eccl.* 7.11.10; 7.13.1), but when he mentions cemeteries in the context of Christian use, he drops the word καλούμενα (*Hist. eccl.* 2.25.5; 9.2.1). This seems to suggest that Christian use of such space and the unique term they gave such space were familiar enough to non-Christians that the odd Christian term (sleeping places) was adopted, with the qualification "so-called," as Arthur C. McGiffert, the translator of Eusebius' *Church History* in NPNF series, rendered the phrase.

accommodate several of the earlier Christian assemblies, it is quite another matter to assume that they were intended to accommodate all the Christians of a city. As MacMullen points out, generally they could not have accommodated more than 1% of the population, not remotely a reasonable number for the Christian population of cities during the reign of Constantine as the empire shifted rather rapidly toward Christianity. Thus, the new experiment of the basilica could not have been intended to replace whatever structures were already in place as venues for regular Christian assemblies.

CALCULATING SPACE

MacMullen determines the number of worshipers a basilica could accommodate by measuring the floor space and granting a square meter for each person.[27] But MacMullen's fixing the size of membership on the basis of architectural space, even if generally sound, must take into account a number of other relevant factors than simply how many people could be comfortably assembled in a liturgical setting in the space available. First, were children and household slaves part of the regular assembly? If not, then the percentage of people in the city who were Christian or under Christian influence would need to be increased substantially. If, on average, there were two children in each family,[28] and each family had a few slaves (as would be true for most of the elite, the group MacMullen thinks formed the urban Christian audience), then we might easily multiply several times over the number of individuals who could be considered part of the Christian circle. Further, the elite would have been patrons to a number of clients, thus potentially extending Christian influence in the city even more widely.

Other matters make it difficult to calculate the number of Christians in a town from the size of the church structure. A number of people in some way connected to the Christian church would have been either prevented by personal circumstances or by church regulations from joining the assembled group. Origen notes that Christians are particularly concerned to prohibit from the assembly those not yet baptized as well as those who were baptized but judged to have failed in some way.[29] As well, illnesses, travel, and other matters of daily life would have prevented full attendance of the Sunday assembly, thus the architectural space would not have needed to accommodate every member, even were we to adopt MacMullen's method as valid.

---

27. MacMullen, *The Second Church*, 12. He calls the square meter a minimum (14).

28. Averil Cameron, *The Later Roman Empire, AD 284–430* (Cambridge, MA: Harvard University Press, 1993), 129, points out that Christian and pagan family size did not differ significantly. It seems that the number of children in a family was somewhere between two and three. See Mogens Herman Hansen, *The Shotgun Method: The Demography of the Ancient Greek City-State Culture* (Columbia: University of Missouri Press, 2006), 57–60.

29. Origen, *Philoc.* 18.22.

As well, the possibility of multiple services in each facility would again change the number that could be accommodated, though multiple services of a considerable order would be required to accommodate any sizeable slice of the urban population. Another point that should have been factored into MacMullen's calculations is that the comfortable capacity of physical space (which MacMullen emphasizes) is quite different from the crowded capacity of physical space. How often the basilicas would have been crowded rather than comfortable is another matter.

Yet even with all of these qualifications, MacMullen's thesis would only be somewhat blunted; it would not be overthrown. A large part of a city's population would still not have been accommodated by the space set aside for liturgical assembly in a basilica setting. The need for some revision of MacMullen's thesis arises from other matters.

THE COMPLEXION OF THE MEMBERSHIP

MacMullen's primary aim involves the use of architectural space to show how few Christians could be accommodated within the physical dimensions of the church buildings.[30] He then assigns a majority of Christians (the non-elite) to gatherings in the cemeteries, and he reduces the number of Christians overall in the empire below the figure that has been generally accepted for the time of Constantine.[31]

But if MacMullen's general observations hold, he might need to conclude that Christianity was stronger rather than weaker than previously thought. Take Dura Europos, for example. According to MacMullen, only about 1% of the population of that city could be accommodated within the identified Christian church building there.[32] But MacMullen's 1% does not tell the whole story. If the membership of the urban church was largely drawn from the elite, then it is possible that Christians could have made up 10% or more of the city's elite, for not all city residents were part of the elite. Indeed, the city would have been largely filled with the non-elite: the poor, slaves, and the masses trying to scratch out a living in the city, with perhaps only a small minority counted among the elite. And the percentage of Christians among the city's elite would rise even more if not all members of Christian families would have regularly been physically part of the assembled church. Thus, if MacMullen wishes to use Dura Europos as a model of the "second church" phenomenon, *the Christian segment of the city's elite* may have been 25% or more. I am not arguing for that number, but MacMullen's 1% is no less a play with very slippery assumptions.

---

30. MacMullen. *The Second Church*, 22, notes that Alexandria had some two dozen churches by 325 C.E., but based on the size of churches for which we have evidence, these churches could accommodate only 1% to 2% of the population, according to MacMullen.

31. MacMullen. *The Second Church*, 9–10. By the year 400, MacMullen speaks of only 7% Christians in cities, and only 3% in rural areas (111–112).

32. MacMullen. *The Second Church*, 3.

There are, of course, other ways of viewing the situation in Dura Europos. One could argue that the Christian elite who supposedly filled the Dura church were not necessarily part of the city's elite, but merely the elite among the Christian membership—a relative status, meaningful only within the Christian assembly itself. But that would mean that the Christian laity and leadership were of a much more common background and sensibility—more part of the urban masses than the privileged high-born. That scenario would seem not to require MacMullen's "second church" idea. In fact, it would speak against it. Or one might argue that the Christian assembly was more reflective of the makeup of the city itself: a few from the elite, but most from the diverse mass that made up the city, as Origen pointed out regarding the makeup of the Christian movement generally at about the time of the destruction of the Dura Europos church.[33] Again, this would work against MacMullen's "second church" recon-struction—at least for the 200s.

As well, as we have already seen, in theological controversies, sides drew their loyalists and partisans from both the rustic and the elite segments of the popula-tion, raising questions about the adequacy of a "second church" concept. Further, the rabble were not without some say in the election of their bishops—another connection between the elite and the ordinary.[34] And bishops could call on the sup-port of the masses. This suggests that the "two churches" view may not be quite adequate.[35]

MacMullen's "second church" thesis requires both a physical and a mental sepa-ration of the Christian community into the elite and the masses, the rustic and the urbane, the city-dweller and the inhabitants of the countryside. But, as the comments above suggest, the mental separation did not mark off rural from urban. The sides in theological debates and disturbances each could draw their urban and their rural partisans. Rustic people could think—and did think. And they did not all think the same thing. The observation of David Potter is worthy of some attention here. Potter comments:

> The lives of rural peoples, closely tied though they are to the earth, are not simply defined by agricultural technologies. The inhabitants of the coun-tryside had brains; they had emotional lives, aspirations, and beliefs that did not continue unchanged from the Stone Age to the advent of modern

---

33. Origen, *Cel.* 1.27.

34. Leslie Dossey, *Peasant and Empire in Christian North Africa* (Berkeley: University of California Press, 2010), 133–136.

35. A. H. M. Jones, *The Later Roman Empire, 284–602* (Oxford: Basil Blackwell, 1964), 2.917–920; Stephen Mitchell, *A History of the Later Roman Empire* A.D. *284–641* (Oxford: Blackwell Publishing, 2007), 272.

technologies. The rhythms of everyday life were not simply those of sowing, reaping, and reproduction.[36]

Further, on some matters, there must have been a widely shared sentiment that drew most Christian adherents to the same religious perspective, wherever they happened to live. Not every issue had to be disputed, disruptive, and divisive. In other words, some attention must be given to the stark fact that, whether urban or rural, these people had joined the same movement, one that stood out from other religious options in the marketplace. It would have been strange, then, if adherents from the country and from the cities shared few sentiments and attended no common celebrations. Indeed, the shared world may have most closely meshed at the very point that MacMullen finds separation—in regard to the novel ideas of death and resurrection, a focal point for Christianity. Cemeteries became sacred places. Granted, many converts may have continued some funeral and death practices from their past, such as pouring wine into libation holes. But pointing to the continuing practice of such customs as proof of a continuing paganism in Christianity or at least a departure from bishop-approved (and thus, supposedly, more genuine) Christian practice may miss the main point. What is crucial here is that these people have adopted significantly new attitudes toward death, particularly the expectation of eternal life, and these new ideas came to mark and motivate Christian converts. It is hardly likely that many joined the Christian movement but rejected the main component of Christian teaching—the resurrection of the dead and the promise of eternal life.

Perhaps in weighing the significance of religious belief and practice, more weight should be given to the *adoption* of new elements than the *retention* of old elements. The adoption of a new element generally requires a conscious and sometimes tortuous exercise of decision and resolve. The retention of old elements is for the most part a less deliberate act, perhaps only to be raised to a more conscious level if an issue is made of the matter.

THE SYNAGOGUE: A TEST CASE
Diaspora Synagogues

MacMullen misses an opportunity to test his thesis on a comparable structure for which we have somewhat more information for the period in question. That is the Jewish synagogue. Although there remains much that is unknown or uncertain

---

36. David S. Potter, *The Roman Empire at Bay: AD 180–395* (London: Routledge, 2004), 24. Potter is cautious, pointing out that the evidence comes more from village elites than from those at the subsistence level. But the evidence that I have cited above shows that a wide range of common people were caught up in theological controversies, That the common resident of rural communities reflected on nothing but food and fornicating is a false portrait of the rural world. Indeed, one might say that the urban elite reflected at least as much on the base aspects of life as did the rural peasant—and perhaps more so.

about ancient synagogues, enough is known to help us with our question.[37] We can say something about the size of at least thirteen diaspora synagogues, in addition to a number of Palestinian synagogues that have been excavated over the past century,[38] though White points out only six of the identified diaspora synagogues have been extensively excavated.[39]

Before we look at the dimensions of these synagogues, it is important to draw attention to an observation White made about the six excavated synagogues. All but the synagogue at Sardis (exceptional in so many ways) were renovated domestic spaces and each reflected the domestic architecture of its area.[40] Leaving aside the debate of how synagogue accommodation may have influenced Christian assemblies, we have at least the diaspora synagogue as one example of how a group not so dissimilar from Christians satisfied the need to meet regularly for religious and other common pursuits. And synagogues were not so different from the accommodations used by various cult groups and voluntary societies.[41] If Christian accommodations varied much from such kinds of structure, that might need some explanation.

It appears that diaspora synagogues, voluntary associations, and Christian churches largely followed the same pattern, either meeting in homes or renovating a house to accommodate a large crowd of about 140 on average, if we take the known synagogues as our guide and adhere to MacMullen's space requirements.[42] Both the Jewish synagogue (or house-synagogue) and the Christian house-church at Dura Europos would fit that kind of adaption of space. The telling question is whether such a space could have accommodated the entire Jewish (or Christian) population of the city.

But before we can answer that, we must first resolve whether MacMullen's figure of 1 square meter per person is too generous. The richest resource for determining

---

37. Dan Urman and Paul V. M. Flesher, eds., *Ancient Synagogues: Historical Analysis and Archaeological Discovery* (Leiden: Brill, 1994); Anne Fitzpatrick-McKinley, "Synagogue Communities in the Graeco-Roman Cities," in *Jews in the Hellenistic and Roman Cities*, ed. John R. Bartlett (London and New York: Routledge, 2002), 55–87.

38. Sometimes there is dispute whether a building should be identified as a synagogue. The number thirteen comes from Lee I. Levine, *The Ancient Synagogue: The First Thousand Years*, 2nd ed. (New Haven: Yale University Press, 2005), 250.

39. White, *The Social Origins of Christian Architecture*, 1.62.

40. White, *The Social Origins of Christian Architecture*, 1.62, points out that none of the synagogues was designed from the ground up as a synagogue, even the one at Ostia, which some had argued for (69). The synagogue at Sardis, though not a renovated domestic space, was nonetheless not designed as a synagogue. It had been a municipal building before coming into the possession of the Jewish community (73–74).

41. Peter Richardson, "An Architectural Case for Synagogues as Associations," in *The Ancient Synagogue from Its Origins until 200 C.E.*, ed. B. Olsson and M. Zetterholm (Stockholm: Almquist & Wiksell, 2003), 90–117. See, too, White, *The Social Origins of Christian Architecture*, 1.26–59.

42. Averaging the numbers for all synagogues under consideration here except for Sardis (Table A.1).

Table A.1 Size of Diaspora Synagogues[a]

City	Size in meters	Size in feet	Synagogue audience	Population of city	% Jewish
Aegina	13.5 × 7.6	44 × 25	103	5,375	1.9
Apamea (Syria)	15.5 × 9	51 × 30	140	[large]	
Bova Marina	17 × 8*	56 × 26	136	?	
Delos	16.9 × 14.4	55 × 47	243	20,000	1.2
Dura Europos	14 × 8.7	46 × 29	122	6,000–8,000	
Elche	10.9 × 7.55	36 × 25	82	?	
Miletus	18.6 × 11.6	61 × 38	216	14,550–24,250	1.5–1.0
Naro	9 × 5.25	30 × 17	47	?	
Ostia	15 × 12.5	49 × 41	188	40,000*	0.5
Phillippopolis*	14.2 × 13.5	47 × 44	192	?	
Priene	12.59 × 10.2[b]	41 × 33	128	4,000	3.2
Sardis	59 × 18	144 × 59	1,000[c]	53,400*	1.9
Stobi	13.3 × 7.9	44 × 26	105	?	

* Plovdiv

[a] A considerable problem for this kind of data is that the populations of these cities are difficult to determine at any time. The population figures in Table A.1 come from the following sources: Aegina [Mogens Herman Hansen, *Studies in the Population of Aigina, Athens and Eretria* (Copenhagen: Det Kongelige Danske Videnskabernes Selskab, 2006), 8; Apamea: clearly a large city, with one of the largest theaters in the Roman world (*The Oxford Companion to Archaeology*, vol. 1, 55; Dura Europos: MacMullen, *The Second Church*, 1; Miletus: J. W. Hanson, "The Urban System of Roman Asia Minor and Wider Urban Connectivity," in *Settlement, Urbanization and Population*, ed. A. Bowman and A. Wilson (Oxford: Oxford University Press, 2011), 254; Priene: Charles Gates, *Ancient Cities: The Archaeology of Urban Life in the Ancient Near East and Egypt, Greece, and Rome*, 2nd ed. (Abingdon, GB: Routledge, 2011), 263.

[b] The building is irregular, with the length running between 12.59 and 13.7 (Levine, *The Ancient Synagogue*, 266).

[c] Paul Trebilco, "The Jews in Asia Minor, 66–c. 235 CE," in *The Cambridge History of Judaism*, vol. 4, *The Late Roman-Rabbinic Period*, ed. Steven T. Katz (Cambridge: Cambridge University Press, 2006), 77.

the number of people who could be accommodated within the physical space of religious buildings is Chad Spigel's *Ancient Synagogue Seating Capacities: Methodology, Analysis and Limits*.[43] Over fifty towns are considered, and some synagogues are analyzed over various stages. Although Spigel's detailed work is focused on Palestine, not on the diaspora, some aspects of his study can be applied directly to Christian

---

43. Chad S. Spigel, *Ancient Synagogue Seating Capacities: Methodology, Analysis and Limits* (Tübingen: Mohr Siebeck, 2012).

church structures generally. The most immediate is that Spigel offers a lower calculation for the required space per person: 0.55 m² if standing and 0.70 m² if seated.
MacMullen suggests a square meter for each person. Thus, if we think of the congregation standing for the entire meeting, we might double the figures in the table
above, or if seated we could increase the number of people accommodated by about
a third.

Table A.1 provides the dimensions of the assembly hall of the synagogue, the
place where the whole congregation would have met together.[44] Since synagogues
often contained various other smaller rooms, the dimensions of the synagogue
building would have been greater. It is, however, the space for the assembled congregation that is important in throwing some light onto the kind of approach that
MacMullen has taken with Christian church buildings.

The information for Table A.1 is taken largely from works by Levine and
Kraabel.[45] I have calculated the audience as the largest possible number, with each
member having a reasonable but not excessive amount of space—the square meter
per person that MacMullen proposed—while recognizing the number might be
twice as high.[46]

What we seem to be confronted with is a situation where the size of the synagogue in city after city would not have accommodated the number of Jews who are
thought to have resided in these cities. Granted, it is impossible to establish how
many Jewish residents any city contained, but few scholars would be comfortable
with such low numbers as we would have if calculated on the basis of synagogue
space. For the purposes of our inquiry here, let us suppose that Jews made up 5%
of the population of the empire (considerably lower than Stark's 10% to 15%, for example). In a city of 100,000, Jews would number around 5,000. That number would
be unreasonably low, however, if diaspora Jews were mainly urban and eastern, as
most seem to think, for under that scenario the Jewish element in a typical eastern
city could rise at least several times over, even saturating some cities.

But the excavated synagogues of the diaspora do not have that kind of space. They
provide room for between 100 and 250 people (with the exception of the grand Sardis
synagogue). Unfortunately, the population of most of the diaspora cities in which
synagogues have been excavated is elusive, though these small synagogues would

---

44. Locales in bold type in Table A.1 are sites that White describes in detail in his two-
volume work, *The Social Origins of Christian Architecture.*

45. Levine, *The Ancient Synagogue*; A. T. Kraabel, "The Diaspora Synagogue: Archaeological
and Epigraphic Evidence since Sukenik," in *Ancient Synagogues: Historical Analysis and
Archaeological Discovery*, ed. Dan Urman and Paul V. M. Flesher (Leiden: Brill, 1994), 100.

46. MacMullen, *The Second Church*, 143n3. MacMullen refers to Robin Lane Fox's calculation of sixty people in a space that MacMullen has set at 60 square meters (12 x 5). That
allotment of space may be generous, and more may have been able to be accommodated in
the space available.

seem to be inadequate for a Jewish population of noticeable size.[47] And the strain of synagogue space would be even greater were we to add to the number of synagogue attendees a significant number of god-fearers and proselytes.[48] Even the large Sardis synagogue could not have accommodated the Jewish population of the city, assuming a city population of at least 50,000 and possibly much larger, and a significant Jewish population in the city.[49]

Few passages suggest anything more than one synagogue in each town or city.[50] And archaeological evidence does not assist in clarifying the matter, since we have only about a dozen excavated synagogues in the diaspora, and no two in the same

---

47. Perhaps for small cities such as Aegina and Priene, the one excavated synagogue would have been adequate, for even supposing a Jewish population of 10% (400–500 people, or so), the synagogue would have held a fifth to a third of the entire Jewish population, or all the adult males. But for larger cities, such as Ostia, Miletus, and Apamea, more than one synagogue would have been required given any significant Jewish population.

48. The thorny issue of the god-fearers has recently been given a new spin by Anna Collar, *Religious Networks in the Roman Empire: The Spread of New Ideas* (Cambridge: Cambridge University Press, 2013), 224–286. Collar connects the disappearance of god-fearers to the success of the new Hypsistos cult, where god-fearers moved away from the synagogue and attached themselves to a cult that was already in existence. She attributes that move to two things: the hardening attitude toward Gentiles by the rabbis and the *Fiscus Judaicus* that was imposed more vigorously in the latter years of the first century. Collar provides a good review of the evidence for god-fearers and modern treatments of the phenomenon, though her own reconstruction is itself unconvincing. For one thing, any effective influence by the rabbis on the Roman Jewish diaspora probably should be dated later, given that the Mishnah and Talmud are products of the late second through the fifth centuries and written in Hebrew (Mishnah) or Aramaic (Talmud) rather than Greek, the working language of Jews in that diaspora—a split diaspora [though see Fergus Millar, "A Rural Jewish Community in Late Roman Mesopotamia, and the Question of a 'Split' Jewish Diaspora," *JSJ* 42 (2011): 351–374]. As well, Collar provides no explanation why, when god-fearers began to turn to the Hypsistos cult, there was no sustained (or even minor) attack on the cult from Christianity, in spite of the fact that such a cult supposedly would have been Christianity's main competitor for converts from the god-fearer source.

49. The size of the population of Sardis is disputed. Hanson, "The Urban System of Roman Asia Minor and Wider Urban Connectivity," 258, is fairly conservative in his calculations, putting the population between 50,000 and 90,000, and rejecting much larger figures that had been offered. If the Jewish population of Sardis represented only 5% of the city's population, then it is possible that a synagogue accommodating one thousand might have been adequate, if largely serving the adult male community. But any reconstruction that makes Jews largely urban and eastern would put the Jewish population in Sardis considerably above 5%, making even such a large synagogue as that at Sardis seem inadequate.

50. Margaret H. Williams, *Jews in a Graeco-Roman Environment* (Tübingen: Mohr Siebeck, 2013), 134. There was perhaps more than one synagogue in Thessalonica, and Acts speaks of synagogues (plural) in Damascus (9:2, 20) and in Salamis (13:5), and perhaps in Corinth, where two men (Crispus and Sosthenes) are each referred to as *the* leader of the synagogue (Acts 18:8, 17). Whether this requires two synagogues or simply multiple leaders of the one synagogue is unclear. Even if the author of Acts is mistaken about multiple synagogues in Damascus and Salamis, this relatively informed writer from the period seems to have

town. Given the size of the synagogues that have been excavated and the supposed extensive Jewish population of the Roman Empire, it would seem that such synagogues could not have accommodated even a small part of the Jewish community.

How this matter is to be resolved is not clear. Perhaps there were far fewer Jews in the diaspora, or far fewer Jews who were urban. Or perhaps there were considerably more synagogues,[51] or fewer Jews who regularly attended the synagogue. Furthermore, given that synagogues would normally have been situated among residential buildings and not near the more public space that is of interest to excavators and tourists, we have no grounds for dismissing the possibility or even the likelihood of multiple synagogues designed to meet the needs of the Jewish population of the city as well as the needs of interested or curious Gentiles. Certainly it would be unwise to calculate the size of the Jewish population of a city based on the size of any excavated synagogue.

Palestinian Synagogues

Turning from the diaspora, we find that excavated synagogues in Palestine were generally somewhat larger than those in the diaspora, often being two to three times as large. If we compare the size of the towns of Palestine that have excavated synagogues, a case can perhaps be made that a single synagogue could have accommodated the entire Jewish community of some towns, and often even that of the

---

no sense that there could only be one synagogue in each city. Yet elsewhere in the New Testament (and in Acts itself), it seems that the writers speak as though there was only one synagogue in various cities mentioned. The term "synagogue" occurs numerous times in the gospels and Acts in the New Testament. In the gospels and Acts narrative, frequent comment is made that Jesus went into *the* synagogue or into *their* synagogue. Had there been multiple synagogues, perhaps one should expect the phrase to read simply "a synagogue," though if towns had a number of small synagogues along with a more grand, central one, perhaps it would be natural enough to speak of *the* or *their* synagogue when the main synagogue is intended. Elsewhere in the New Testament, the word occurs only three times: once in James (2:2), where it is used for the Christian assembly, and twice in Revelation (2:9; 3:9) in the phrase "the synagogue of Satan." The word is also used for Christian assemblies in some later Christian writings (Ignatius, Ign. *Pol.* 4.2; Irenaeus, *Haer.* 4.31.1–2). The situation may have been different for Palestine. Spigel, *Ancient Synagogue Seating Capacities*, 347–348, expects that cities over 10,000 "most likely had multiple synagogues," though perhaps that would have been the case for the diaspora, too, where we have far too little material to make that kind of determination.

51. It is more an assumption than a certainty that there would have been several or scores of synagogues in a typical city in order to accommodate the Jewish population, though many scholars are convinced that multiple synagogues are likely [Tessa Rajak, "The Jewish Community and Its Boundaries," in *The Jews among Pagans and Christians*, ed. Judith Lieu, John North, and Tessa Rajak (London: Routledge, 1992), 10–11]. Spigel, *Ancient Synagogue Seating Capacities*, 355–357, speaking of the Palestinian situation, dismisses the idea that house-synagogues would have solved the problem of accommodation of Jewish residents of large cities, pointing out that cities such as Tiberias and Sepphoris, for example, would have required hundreds of such assemblies.

surrounding countryside. But the case depends on determining the populations of the towns, which is often a matter of considerable dispute and such wide-ranging opinion that it seems at times that scholars cannot have been talking about the same site. For example, Jonathan Reed estimated the population of Capernaum to have been between 600 and 1,500 or 1,700 at the time of Jesus.[52] But others have opted for figures ten to twenty times as high.[53] One might feel safer to go with the lower numbers, since they have been offered by one of the principal excavators of Capernaum. But, even here, there is the uncertainty whether the population remained at that level over the next few centuries. If the low numbers are correct and the population remained stable, then the excavated synagogue (dating from the fourth or fifth century) would seem to have been adequate for the town's population of 1,500 to 1,700. The synagogue, with space for almost 400, would have accommodated every adult male, or some mix of men and women. Even if the expectation was that every pious Jew would attend, there would have been individuals who were ill, menstruating, or away from the town, and some who were simply sitting under the shade of a tree, quite happy in their version of piety, as neighbors passed by on the way to the synagogue.

Spigel breaks down the Palestinian situation reflected in the more than fifty synagogues available for study. One synagogue in this count could hold, at most, 100; seventeen could hold between 100 and 200; eleven between 201 and 300; nine between 301 and 400; nine between 401 and 500; nine between 501 and 741; and two between 1,247 and 1,399.[54] Spigel offers a careful assessment about what this might mean to his primary question: "whether or not most Jews could have worshiped in particular synagogues on a regular basis."[55] Spigel concludes that there is little correspondence between the size of the city and the size of the synagogue in Palestinian communities.

Where does that leave us? According to Spigel, towns in Palestine, at least, may have required only one synagogue, provided that the population of Palestine and its towns is kept quite low. Of course, these conclusions immediately go out the window

---

52. Jonathan L. Reed, "The Population of Capernaum," *Occasional Papers of the Institute of Antiquity and Christianity* 24 (1992): 1–19; Reed, *Archaeology and the Galilean Jesus* (Harrisburg, PA: Trinity Press International, 2000), 151–153. For both praise and criticism of Reed, see James H. Charlesworth, "Jesus Research and Near Eastern Archaeology: Reflections on Recent Developments," in *Neotestamentica et Philonica: Studies in Honor of Peder Borgen*, ed. David Edward Aune, et al. (Leiden: Brill, 2003), 38–44; Mark A. Chancey, *The Myth of a Gentile Galilee* (Cambridge: Cambridge University Press, 2002), 102n218.

53. See the discussion in Jonathan Marshall, *Jesus, Patrons, and Benefactors: Roman Palestine and the Gospel of Luke* (Tübingen: Mohr Soebeck, 2009), 73–76. Marshall points out that Meyers and Strange set the population at 15,000 and H. C. Kee at 25,000, considerably out of line with what Reed offers.

54. Spigel, *Ancient Synagogue Seating Capacities*, 345.

55. Spigel, *Ancient Synagogue Seating Capacities*, 339.

if it can be established that the population of a town like Capernaum was into the many thousands, as some contend.[56]

THE MOSQUE: A MODERN PARALLEL?

Perhaps a more modern example could provide a cautionary note as to the usefulness of using the size of Constantinian church structures as a tool for calculating the size of the Christian population of a town or city. Istanbul has 3,113 mosques and a population of 14.16 million residents.[57] This means that each mosque would need to accommodate about 4,500 people. Yet on the basis of MacMullen's calculations of 1 square meter for each worshipper,[58] even the grand Sultan Ahmet Mosque would be filled to capacity with such a crowd.[59] Most of the mosques of Istanbul are much smaller, and even many of the famous ones would not accommodate more than a few hundred. By whatever means we might wish to use to ease those numbers (for example, making most attendees male and adult or counting some exterior space), it is clear that we cannot look to the size and number of mosques in Istanbul to get a sense of the Muslim population of Istanbul or the orthodoxy of the population.

Perhaps the same caution should hold in using synagogues or basilicas to determine the size of the Jewish or the Christian community of a city.

---

56. J. L. Reed, *Archaeology and the Galilean Jesus: A Re-examination of the Evidence* (Harrisburg, PA: Trinity, 2000), 65n8. Anything built on the various comments of Josephus, such as that there were 204 villages in Galilee, the smallest of which had 15,000 residents, should be taken with a grain of salt, as, Brian McGing, "Population and Proselytism: How Many Jews Were There in the Ancient World?" in *Jews in the Hellenistic and Roman Cities*, ed. John R. Bartlett (London and New York: Routledge, 2002), 88–106, points out in criticism of Louis Feldman.

57. http://en.wikipedia.org/wiki/List_of_mosques_in_Turkey; population of Istanbul: http://www.citypopulation.de/php/turkey-istanbul.php.

58. More than a square meter per person may be needed for the mosque setting, where the formal prayer requires room for movement.

59. The mosque is 64 x 72 meters (4,608 m²).

The Numbers According to Rodney Stark

IN THE YEAR 250, all Christians were Jews. By the year 300, all Jews were Christians. No one would say that—surely! Yet in many ways that is the conclusion that could be drawn from Rodney Stark's various well-received books on early Christianity.[1] This appendix explores Stark's claims and the undisclosed conclusions that seem to follow.

Stark has become the most quoted recent authority on the expansion of early Christianity. Although I find Stark's work always interesting and at times quite rewarding, I find Stark, far more often than not, excessive in his claims, selective in his sources, and wrong in his conclusions.[2] Since Stark has made various claims about

---

1. Keith Hopkins, "Christian Number and Its Implications," *JECS* 6 (1998): 216, plays with the numbers, noting that if only 3% of Jews converted to Christianity by 175 C.E., then all Christians would have been Jews at that time, using a growth rate of 3.35% per annum, roughly the 3.42% that Stark uses.

2. Stark regularly opts for the highest or lowest number offered by historians, depending of what number better suits his theory, and sometimes he offers numbers beyond the extreme ranges that experts have offered. I deal with a number of specific matters in the body of this appendix; here I will point out a few other problems. Stark states that Paul "often took a retinue of as many as forty followers with him" [*Cities of God: The Real Story of How Christianity Became an Urban Movement and Conquered Rome* (New York: HarperCollins, 2006), 129], pointing to the works of E. A. Judge and Abraham Malherbe for this number. Stark misunderstood Malherbe, and it is clear he did not check the original statement in Judge. Judge merely states that there were forty people named in the New Testament as sometime travelers with Paul—not that all of them accompanied Paul at the same time, as Stark states. Judge finds one case where nine others were with Paul, but that seems like a special situation involving the Jerusalem offering. Since many read Stark and not his sources, Stark does a real disservice by not checking his sources more. Stark leaves an image of Paul traveling with a crowded busload, and he even states that Paul's retinue often was "sufficient to constitute an initial 'congregation'" (*Cities of God*, 129). Nothing in early Christian literature leaves that impression. At other times, Stark is simply and bafflingly wrong. For example,

matters that I take up in this book, and since Stark has had considerable influence in shaping current thinking on a number of these matters, it is important to dedicate a chapter solely to Stark's method and conclusions, even though his ideas are addressed at various places elsewhere in this book.

Here I quote Stark at length on his method and his concerns. I do so because I want my criticism of Stark to be largely based on what he has tried to do, and which many feel that he has successfully done—a conclusion I challenge.[3] I do not examine every assertion of Stark. I am particularly interested in his presentation of the expansion of Christianity in light of the urban and rural realities in which Christianity developed. Here is Stark describing his purpose and method:

> A major purpose of this book is to demonstrate that quantitative methods can help to resolve many debates about early church history. Even so, the heart of the book is not statistical, but theoretical and substantive. Hypotheses do not simply fall out of the sky; they ought to be derived from theories and theses; and these, in turn, must be situated in an adequate historical context if the subsequent hypothesis-testing is to be of intellectual significance. However, given adequate context, testing well-formulated hypotheses through quantitative analysis of adequate indicators will put

---

he says that Edessa is mentioned in Revelation 2–3 as "one of the places where Christian communities made an early appearance" (*Cities of God*, 40). It is not Edessa—it is Ephesus that is mentioned! Even a lay reader of the New Testament is likely to know that. This cannot be dismissed as a mere typo. It is intentional, functioning as an important part of a section dealing specifically with Edessa and Mesopotamia. Sometimes Stark, in order to strengthen his argument, will make statements no one would hold: for example, he states that "with the exception of *Acts*, the New Testament was written by Jews" (*Cities of God*, 136), a point easily contested by simply linking the authorship of the gospel of Luke with Acts. Or he describes Ignatius' journey to martyrdom as "long and leisurely," hardly Ignatius' own description, which reads: "From Syria to Rome, I have been fighting the wild beasts, through land and sea, night and day, bound to ten leopards, which is a company of soldiers, who become worse when well treated. But I am becoming more of a disciple by their mistreatment" (Ign. *Rom.* 5.1). There is the rare time that Stark chooses an extreme number that severely complicates his theory though he need not have chosen that number. In particular, his claim that the empire was only 5% urban makes his projection of Christian numbers by 300 c.e. look at least hasty, and more likely reckless, as we shall see.

3. Stark, *Cities of God*, 213, comments on a likely criticism of his book: "Many historians, especially those devoted to ancient history, will receive this book with the deepest of suspicions; and others of them, with enthusiastic contempt. Of course, I didn't write it for them. I wrote it for the general reader, for numerate scholars, and especially for graduate students in history, to tempt the latter to pursue more disciplined and sophisticated undertakings." In other words, Stark is telling graduate students to disregard their professors who disregard him. Stark's admission that follows these words—that these scholars are experts while he is not—hardly mutes the arrogance of his address to graduate students. That graduate students could learn from Stark is certain. That Stark's work should sometimes be treated with "deepest suspicions" and at times "enthusiastic contempt" is equally certain.

historical studies of the early church on firmer footing—even when the results show that what most historians believe about something is in fact true![4]

The final chapter of the book just quoted is titled by Stark: "Why Historians Ought to Count."

But it is on counting that Stark's reconstruction fails.[5] Perhaps that is, in part, because he depended too much on historians who thought they could count, or, as is more often the case, he chose extreme positions of those historians who did count. Although many agree with Stark on particular points (e.g., the urban environment of the early church and of diaspora Judaism as a continuing source for converts to Christianity), many are more cautious regarding some of his other points. Generally Stark does not examine the structure that he has built to determine whether it is likely to collapse in upon itself. If he can find a historian whose calculations match his own expectations or predictions, then he feels that his work has passed the litmus test. In the following pages, I examine details of Stark's theory that make his reconstructions improbable, and, in all too many cases, impossible.

JEWS IN THE ROMAN EMPIRE

Stark contends that Jews made up 10% to 15% of the Roman Empire—6 to 9 million people. Further, Stark thinks 90% of Jews in the empire lived *in cities* outside of Palestine.[6] The first thing to note about these numbers is that few—if any—historians would use these numbers without serious qualification, though Stark claims that this is the "best estimate," referring to Frend and Meeks as his authorities.[7]

Even using Stark's lower number of 10% of the population of the Roman Empire being Jewish, there would have been 6 million Jews in the empire. With 90% of Jews residing in cities outside of Palestine, diaspora Jews would have numbered

---

4. Stark, *Cities of God*, 22–23.

5. See Jack T. Sanders, "Christians and Jews in the Roman Empire: A Conversation with Rodney Stark," *Sociological Analysis* 53.4 (1992): 433–445, for a detailed criticism of Stark's use of numbers. Jan N. Bremmer, *The Rise of Christianity through the Eyes of Gibbon, Harnack and Rodney Stark*, 2nd ed. (Groningen: Barkhuis, 2010), 58, dismisses Stark's statistics as "totally built on quicksand."

6. Stark, *Cities of God*, 6.

7. Stark, *Cities of God*, 241n16. Meeks does say that 5 to 6 million Jews lived in the diaspora (*The First Urban Christians*, 34), and Frend says that "one-seventh of the population of the Mediterranean population of the Empire . . . may be taken as possible" for the Jewish population [*Martyrdom and Persecution in the Early Church: A Study of a Conflict from the Maccabees to Donatus* (Oxford: Basil Blackwell, 1965), 133]. But it is not clear what Frend means by this. What exactly would constitute "the Mediterranean population of the Empire"?

5.4 million. Yet if the empire was only 5% urban, as Stark also contends,[8] there would have been only 3 million urban dwellers in the entire empire—an impossible fit for the 5.4 million urban Jews. Even were we to double the size of the urban population of the empire to 10%, almost every urban resident of the empire (both east and west) must have been Jewish, based on Stark's assumptions—a completely unrealistic reconstruction. And this is giving Stark the benefit of doubt at every corner.[9] Were we to take Stark's most extreme numbers—the empire at 5% urban and 15% Jewish, we would have three times too many Jews to fit into the urban areas, and no room at all for pagans and Christians, if as Stark contends (and must contend[10]), Jews in the diaspora were largely urban. This is not a matter of the numbers possibly being a little lumpy here and there, as Stark is willing to admit.[11] Such numbers are simply unworkable and should never have been proposed.

THE PROBLEM OF RURAL CHRISTIANITY

Stark, like many others, admits the success of Christianity in the countryside in the latter half of the 200s. But Stark's reconstruction fails at its most vital point. Stark dismisses (with some delight) the numerous claims of scholars of the early church that the early Christian success reflected "large-scale conversions," "inconceivable rapidity," "astonishing expansion," or the "miraculous."[12] There is no need for such large scale conversions, Stark informs us, since the conversion in the empire required nothing more than a 40% increase each decade, a rate of growth that he had already demonstrated for Mormonism, the modern religious movement that Stark had studied extensively.[13]

But Stark failed to take into account the rural dimension of the problem. If Christianity did not begin a rural mission until the middle of the third century, Stark

---

8. If 65% of the population of the empire lived in the East, 39 million of the 60 million in the empire would be eastern. If the urban population of the empire was 5% (as Stark claims), then there would have been 1.95 million people in urban areas in the East. Stark places the urban population of the entire empire at 3 million (*Cities of God*, 60).

9. Since most of these Jews would have been eastern, we could reasonably guess that at least 4 million Jews lived in the eastern diaspora.

10. Stark builds much of his explanation of early Christian growth on the social dislocation that newcomers to the city often experience. Stark argues that new religions are able to exploit the alienation that urban residents encounter. It is the urban world that, for Stark, is the world of Christian mission and success.

11. Rodney Stark, *The Rise of Christianity* (Princeton: Princeton University Press, 1996), 11–12, recognizes there may be lumps and bumps, but he thinks his approach is cautious enough. He is referring specifically to the growth numbers of Christianity in the empire, but he may concede the same for his Jewish numbers.

12. Stark, *The Rise of Christianity*, 14.

13. Stark, *The Rise of Christianity*, 14.

cannot get more than a handful of rural Christians by the year 300 C.E., based on a 40% growth rate per decade. Note that Stark had made much of the small number of Christians in the early period. For the first sixty years of the church, according to Stark, only a trickle became Christian, an increase from 1,000 to a mere 7,530.[14] Stark's key point is that a mere 40% growth rate per decade,[15] though providing only low numbers at the beginning, would result in explosive growth after about 250 years of the process. But what Stark does not seem to note is that if he delays the introduction of Christianity into the countryside until about 250 and if he wishes to maintain his 40% growth rate that he insisted upon for urban areas of earliest Christianity— there would be a mere few thousand Christians in the countryside sixty years after Christianity's introduction into rural areas, roughly when Constantine converts, not the millions that Stark proposes. At least, one would assume the same unimpressive numerical growth would hold in the first sixty years of the rural mission as it did in the urban mission. On his theory, Stark has no way to account for more than a handful of Christians in the rural areas by the time of Constantine if Christianity did not begin in the countryside until 250 and if Stark wants to remain tied to his formula for Christian growth. Stark seems unaware that he has a problem here.[16]

Could one not argue that there might have been, for whatever reason, a more dramatic rate of conversion in rural areas than in urban areas? Not according to Stark, for he dismisses comments by historians who spoke of "successes en masse," or other such language.[17] Stark informs us that social scientists have relegated such ideas as herd instincts, mob psychology, mass hysteria "to the dustbin of useless concepts," and he offers four grounds for dismissing such a view of Christian growth.[18]

---

14. Stark, *The Rise of Christianity*, 6.

15. Stark, *Cities of God*, 67. This would calculate to 40% per decade.

16. If Christianity did not begin to establish itself in the countryside until about the middle of the third century (as Stark and most others assert), that would require the most astounding growth rate. Suppose we take Stark's number of 1,171,356 Christians in the empire in the year 250 (Stark, *The Rise of Christianity*, 7). Even were we to take a quarter of this number as rural (292,839), we would need a growth rate of over 200% per decade (rather than Stark's 40%) to bring the numbers to 5 million. But such a rate of growth would be contrary to everything that Stark set out to prove. And if we took only 10% of the Christian population to be rural in 250 (117,136), we would need a growth rate of many more times over to bring the numbers to 5 million.

17. Stark, *Cities of God*, 65.

18. Stark, *Cities of God*, 66. While it is possible that such explanations have been overused and inadequately tested, the dismissal of such concepts should not be taken as proof that mass conversions and shifts of group loyalty could not take place. At best it would show that we do not have adequate explanations for such dramatic shifts. Stark is confident that he does not need any events of mass conversion to account for the number of Christians in the empire by the year 300. He could show, he asserted, that a mere 3.4% growth a year would make the empire 10% Christian by the year 300. But Stark leaves 95% of the empire—the rural empire—outside of the equation until 250, for it is then that Christianity enters the

But that leaves Stark with no fallback position for the kind of growth he needs in the countryside.

Since Stark's scheme will not allow for many rural Christians by the time of Constantine, he must place most of the Christian population of the empire in the year 300 in urban areas, where, supposedly, his theory of exponential growth might still be maintained. But, as we have seen, that scenario is impossible, for Christians would have come to saturate the cities of the empire by the year 300—cities that Stark had already saturated with Jews, a matter that seems to have escaped him. Such double saturation of cities with Christians and Jews is a phenomenon unlike any for which a sociologist might suggest parallels—and it is a reconstruction that no historian remotely maintains or any mathematician could fix. Even were we to double the urban population of the empire, the problem remains. There is simply no room in the empire's urban centers for anyone but Jews and Christians, and this remains true even if we allow for a considerable number of Jews converting to Christianity. Indeed, even if we were to quadruple the urban component of the empire, Stark's estimate of the number of urban Jews and Christians would leave room for no more than a handful of pagans in cities.

Granted, the problem is not one faced by Stark alone, but Stark intensifies the problem by proposing an extremely low proportion for the urban population of the empire and then making Jews and Christians largely urban. Even were we to try to fix the problem by reducing the number of Jews and Christians, populating cities with one-third Christian, one-third Jewish, and one-third pagan—numbers which, though almost unthinkable, are still considerably more realistic than Stark's numbers—there could be only 1 million Christians in the urban areas, given an empire of 60 million and urbanization at 5%, as Stark contends. But if Christians made up 10% of the empire at this time, as in Stark's reconstruction, there would have been about 6 million Christians. That leaves 5 million Christians who must have lived in rural areas by the year 300, a matter that wrecks Stark's urban characterization of Christianity and a point that Stark seems to miss entirely. Stark even contends that for the year 312, Christians numbered about 9 million, or 15% of the empire, asserting that "even as late as the fourth century the overwhelming majority of Christians lived in cities."[19] But again Stark misses the obvious. Even if all cities were filled entirely with Christians, two-thirds of the Christian membership must have been rural, based on Stark's numbers.[20] Not a hint of a recognition of this problem surfaces in any of Stark's writing.

---

countryside according to Stark. Even had Stark used somewhat more than 5% for his calculation of the urban portion of the empire, the late arrival of Christianity in the rural parts of the empire remains devastating to his growth theory.

19. Stark, *Cities of God*, 68.

20. See the tables in chapter 3.

Further, Stark loses his essential tools to explain Christian growth when we move our examination to the countryside. The two crucial factors that Stark offered to explain Christian growth are the dislocation present in cities and the social network provided by Jews and exploited by Christians, both groups which are largely urban according to Stark.[21] But neither factor is applicable to the countryside where Stark (unknowingly) must find the vast majority of his Christian population. Stark leaves the matter of the factors for the Christian growth in the countryside unaddressed because he assumes that Christians were largely urban. At this point, it would do well to quote Stark:

> In the end, what quantification mainly contributes to historical discussions and disputes is discipline. To work with quantitative data, one must make systematic arguments and draw clear conclusions—no dancing about and having it both ways.[22]

But it is with regard to numbers that Stark's work lacks discipline—many times over.

While Stark delights to point to scholars whenever their numbers seem to support his, he makes no appeal to scholarly works and to scholarly consensus when these do not support his reconstructions. Stark would be hard-pressed to find any scholar who would assert, as Stark does, that Christianity "enjoyed substantial majorities in the cities," even by the time of Constantine's conversion.[23]

THE MORMONISM PARALLEL

But does Stark not have in Mormonism a concrete, verifiable example of how a religious movement could grow, and does this not parallel in point after point what scholars have been saying about the growth of early Christianity? Stark would have us think that, but Stark's example of Mormonism is neither compelling nor relevant.

A number of aspects of Stark's kind of presentation call for caution, and for treating Stark's reference to Mormonism as more smoke and mirrors than anything else. What Stark has in Mormonism is a mathematical parallel—an equation. It is not a parallel in any other way. Mormonism need not have been mentioned at all. All that Mormonism provides is an example of a rate of growth of about 4% per year, though Stark anticipated much more.[24]

---

21. Stark, *The Rise of Christianity*, chapter 3: "The Mission to the Jews: Why It Probably Succeeded," and chapter 7: "Urban Chaos and Crisis: The Case for Antioch."

22. Stark, *Cities of God*, 222.

23. Stark, *Cities of God*, 8. 71.

24. Stark declared that Mormonism had "sustained the most rapid growth of any new religion in American history [Rodney Stark, "The Rise of a New World Faith," *RRelRes* 26 (1984): 19]. Stark also believed that he was witnessing an "incredibly rare event: the rise of a new world religion" (18). Stark continued: "I shall attempt to demonstrate that the Church of Jesus Christ

First, Stark failed to note three importance differences. One, Mormon family size would have been generally larger than that of early Christian families, both because family size was larger in the general American population during the period of Mormonism's growth than in the ancient Roman population, and because early Mormons practiced polygamy, making family size often considerably larger than the already large American family size generally.[25] Contrast this to the opposite tendency in Christianity to celibacy and monogamy. Two, life expectancy is higher in the modern period than in the ancient. In fact, any Mormon member today will be counted in the overall yearly count of Mormon members three times as often than the typical individual member of the early church, who had a shorter life expectancy.[26] These two factors mean that the early Christian community must have had a much higher rate of conversion to make up the 40% growth rate per decade to get to the 6-million mark by the year 300.

If Stark wants to appeal to modern religions, he could add Seventh-day Adventists, Jehovah's Witnesses, and various Pentecostal groups to the mix, all of which have grown more rapidly than Mormonism.[27] But this would challenge his structure of

---

of Latter-Day Saints, the Mormons, will soon achieve a worldwide following comparable to that of Islam, Buddhism, Christianity, Hinduism, and the other dominant world faiths" (18). He continued to defend his view in Stark, "Modernization and Mormon Growth: The Secularization Thesis Revisited," in *Contemporary Mormonism: Social Scientific Perspectives,* ed. Marie Cornwall, Tim B. Heaton, and Lawrence A. Young (Champaign: University of Illinois Press, 2001), 1–23. One might question Stark's judgment in making Mormonism into a new religion rather than a Christian denomination, especially as Mormonism increasingly appears more like a denomination in its aspirations. Further, Stark should have recognized other Christian denominations that are growing even more quickly than Mormonism, but Stark's fixation on Mormonism as a new religion probably caused him to miss how similar Mormonism was to a number of new Christian groups that formed in the United States in the 1800s, and how many had even a faster growth rate. For a recent criticism of Stark, see Ryan T. Cragun and Ronald Lawson, "The Secular Transition: The Worldwide Growth of Mormons, Jehovah's Witnesses, and Seventh-day Adventists," *Sociology of Religion* 71.3 (2010): 349–373.

25. Tim B. Heaton, "Vital Statistics," in *Encyclopedia of Mormonism* (New York, Macmillan, 1992), 1.1523, figures 5 and 6.

26. The life expectancy in the Roman Empire has been estimated to have been between 22 and 25 years. That compares to a life expectancy in the United States in 2008 at 78 years. Thus each individual presently in Mormonism would be counted in three times the annual membership tallies than would have been the case for an individual in the early Christian community. Further, according to Bruce W. Frier, "Demography," *CAH,* vol. 11, 2nd ed., 796–797, there was a perception of aging and an exaggeration of age in the Roman population. This would perhaps make the Mormon numbers even more problematic for calculating rates of growth.

27. Jehovah's Witnesses started a half-century after Mormonism, yet with considerable setbacks and mass desertions, they have a membership roughly equal to that of Mormonism. Various Pentecostal groups, half the age of Mormonism, are larger, and some even many times larger than Mormonism. For example, the Assemblies of God counts a worldwide membership of over 66 million (compared to the 15 million for Mormonism) http://ag-churches.org/Sitefiles/Default/RSS/AG.org%20TOP/AG%20Statistical%20Reports/2012/Online%20Stats%202012.pdf.

growth that supposedly fit so well with the growth of early Christianity. If any appeal is to be made to modern religious groups for an understanding of the expansion of early Christianity, perhaps we should be speaking of considerably greater numbers of Christians in the empire in the year 300. Or, more wisely, we should simply admit that modern examples can be found for any scenario of early Christian expansion that we might wish to propose, leading us wherever we wish. Such playing with numbers must be set aside as easily and likely misleading.

JEWISH CONVERSION TO CHRISTIANITY

As I noted at the beginning of this appendix, it would be only a slight caricature of Stark's calculations to say that by the mid 200s, every Christian was a Jew and that by the time of Constantine every Jew was a Christian. Of course, Stark does not put it that way, but he makes the links with Judaism the substantial route by which converts came into Christianity.[28] He even points out that only one in five Jews had to convert to Christianity for the necessary Christian numbers to grow at a rate of 40% per decade.[29] No Gentile convert would be needed, though he adds he is not saying that there were no Gentile converts.

But Stark should not be permitted to make a point like this and then walk away from its implications. If Stark is correct that Jews made up a substantial part of the contingent of early converts to Christianity and that this resulted from the social networks that Stark proposes to lie beneath most conversions, then as more and more Jews joined the Christian movement, the web of networks that might lead to further conversions becomes increasingly substantial and converts from Judaism should continue to flow into Christianity. But Stark cannot have that happen, for under that scenario by the year 300 all Jews would have become Christian. Something must have happened to rapidly slow the rate of Jewish conversion to Christianity. Stark offers nothing to account for a downturn in conversion rates. Indeed, he does not even seem to notice that he has a problem. But if Stark is permitted to sell his scheme of interpersonal social networks as the major route for conversion and allowed to continue to tout the Jewish communities as the main source of converts to Christianity, he must indicate when and why this scheme no longer held. And he must explain why the scheme did not dramatically become more important (rather

---

28. Jack T. Sanders, "Christians and Jews in the Roman Empire: A Conversation with Rodney Stark," *Sociological Analysis* 53.4 (1992): 433–445, summarizes one of the fundamental problems of Stark's work: "both population and the presence of Judaism were irrelevant for the spread of early Christianity." See, too, Michael L. White, "Adolf Harnack and the 'Expansion' of Early Christianity: A Re-appraisal of Social History," *SecCent* 2 (1985–1986): 97–127. Bremmer, *The Rise of Christianity through the Eyes of Gibbon, Harnack and Rodney Stark*, 53–55, criticizes Stark on this matter.

29. Stark, *The Rise of Christianity*, 70.

than less) when the emperor adopted Christianity, making Jewish conversion into Christianity beneficial in a way it never was before Constantine's conversion.

There is no doubt that Stark has added to the discussion of the expansion of early Christianity—if more in the area of provocative ideas than of productive results. But in terms of numbers, Stark offers nothing more solid than what his more historically focused predecessors had offered. Stark's guesses, disguised as statistics, do not provide a stronger foundation nor do they give a more credible account.

This is not a matter of Stark being a little out here or there in terms of his numbers. Rather, it is a matter of impossible numbers, which when connected to Stark's theories of urban dislocation, Jewish networks, and Jewish urbanization leaves us with little more than a house of cards. Stark must do one of two things to get out of this quagmire: (1) reduce the number of Christians, or (2) reject the urban thesis and allow for substantial numbers of Christians in the countryside, which would defeat what he had set out to show—that urbanism provided the necessary conditions for Christian growth.[30] While a lower number of Christians in the empire is possible, it would cut away Stark's frequent appeal to numbers offered by early church scholars that seem to show—reassuringly, as Stark points out—support for his own numbers.[31]

More seriously disturbing, Stark's work obscures the profound problems that numbers present in any attempt to understand Christianity's progress and place in the larger Roman world. His work leaves us with the impression that the older works that had concluded that there were 10% Christians in the empire in the year 300 are now confirmed by scientific and statistical examination. Nothing is further from the truth. All Stark has offered is a mathematical formula. It does not ground previous work onto a more concrete base in historical, sociological, or statistical reality. Rather, Stark's work simply strengthens a false confidence in a weak structure.

---

30. Indeed, the urban factor is spotlighted in the title of one of Stark's books. The subtitle of his *Cities of God* is *The Real Story of How Christianity Became an Urban Movement and Conquered Rome.*

31. Stark, *The Rise of Christianity*, 11. On pages 4–11, Stark points to numbers offered by a range of scholars.

Bibliography of Works Cited

ABBREVIATIONS: ANCIENT SOURCES

AJP	*American Journal of Philology*
AQCR	*The American Quarterly Church Review*
BASOR	*Bulletin of the American Schools of Oriental Research*
CAH	*Cambridge Ancient History*
CBQ	*Catholic Biblical Quarterly*
CF	*Classical Folia*
CH	*Church History*
EHR	*English Historical Review*
HSCP	*Harvard Studies in Classical Philology*
HTR	*Harvard Theological Review*
JAJ	*Journal of Ancient Judaism*
JBL	*Journal of Biblical Literature*
JECS	*Journal of Early Christian Studies*
JEH	*Journal of Ecclesiastical History*
JRomArch	*Journal of Roman Archaeology*
JRS	*Journal of Roman Studies*
JSNTSup	*Journal for the Study of the New Testament*
JTS	*Journal of Theological Studies*
LCL	Loeb Classical Library
MAMA	*Monumenta Asiae Minoris Antiqua*
NewDocs	*New Documents Illustrating Early Christianity*
NICNT	New International Commentary on the New Testament
NovTSup	Novum Testamentum Supplements
NPNF	Nicene and Post-Nicene Fathers
PCPS	*Proceedings of the Cambridge Philological Society*
PG	Patrologia graeca
RAC	*Reallexikon für Antike und Christentum*
RRelRes	*Review of Religious Research*

SBLSP   *SBL Society of Biblical Literature*
SecCent *Second Century*
TAPA   *Transactions of the American Philological Association*
VC   *Vigiliae christianae*
WUNT   Wissenschaftliche Untersuchungen zum Neuen Testament

ABBREVIATIONS: ANCIENT SOURCES

Ac. John
  Acts of John
Ac. Just. *Acts of Justin and his Companions*
Archelaus
  Acts of the Disputation with Manes
Athanasius
  Apol. sec. *Apologia contra Arianos [Defense against the Arians]*
  C. Ar. *Orationes contra Arianos [Orations against the Arians]*
  Syn. *De Synodi [On the Councils of Athanasius concerning Theodorus]*
Barn. *Barnabas*
Catullus
  Carmen
Clement of Alexandria
  Strom. *Stromata [Miscellanies]*
Clement of Rome
  1 Clem. *1 Clement*
  Cod. theod. *Codex theodosianus [Theodosian Code]*
Cyprian
  Ep. *Epistulae [Letters]*
Did. *Didache*
Dio Cassius
  Historiae Romanae [Roman History]
Diodorus Siculus
  Bibliotheca historica [Library of History]
Dionysius of Halicarnassus
  Ant. Rom. *Antiquitates romanae [Roman Antiquities]*
Dionysius, Bishop of Alexandria
  Letter
Eusebius
  Hist. eccl. *Historia ecclesiastica [Ecclesiastical History]*
  Vit. Const. *Viat Constantini [Life of Constantine]*
  The Genuine Acts of Peter
Gregory of Nyssa
  Deit. *[On the Deity of the Son]*

Hermas
  Her. *Sim.* [Shepherd of Hermas, *Similitude*
Herodotus
  Hist. Historiae [Histories]
Horace
  Sat. Satirae [Satires]
Ignatius
  Ign. *Eph. [To the Ephesians]*
  Ign. *Magn. [To the Magnesians]*
  Ign. *Phld. [To the Philadelphians]*
  Ign. *Pol. [To Polycarp]*
  Ign. *Rom. [To the Romans]*
  Ign. *Smyrn. [To the Smyrnaeans]*
  Ign. *Trall. [To the Trallians]*
Irenaeus
  Haer. Adversus haereses [Against Heresies]
John Chrysostom
  Hom. Matt. Homiliae in Matthaeum [Homily on Matthew]
  Hom. Act. Homiliae in Acta apostolorum [Homily on the Acts of the Apostles]
Josephus
  Ag. Ap. [Against Apion]
  Ant. [Antiquities]
  J.W. [Jewish War]
Julian
  Misopogon
Justin
  1 *Apol. Apologia I [First Apology]*
  Dial. Dialogus cum Tryphone [Dialogue with Trypho]
Lactantius
  Inst. Divinarum institutionum [The Divine Institutes]
  Mort. De morte persecutorum [The Deaths of the Persecutors]
Libanius
  Or. Orationes [Oration]
Lucian
  Alex. Alexander (Pseudomantis) [Alexander the False Prophet]
  Mart. Pol. Martyrium Polycarpi [Martyrdom of Polycarp]
Minucius Felix
  Oct. Octavius
Origen
  Cels. Contra Celsum [Against Celsus]
  Philoc. Philocalia
Pausanius
  Descr. Graeciae description [Description of Greec]

Philo

     Confusion [On the Confusion of Tongues]

     Creation [On the Creation of the World]

     Decalogue [On the Decalogue]

     Embassy [On the Embassy to Gaius]

     Eternity [On the Eternity of the World]

     Flaccus [Against Flaccus]

     Heir [Who Is the Heir?]

     Names [On the Change of Names]

     Rewards [On Rewards and Punishments]

     Spec. Laws [On the Special Laws]

     Virtues [On the Virtues]

Philostorgius

     Hist. eccl. Historoia ecclesiastica [Ecclesiastical History]

Pliny the Elder

     Nat. [Naturalis Historia]

Pliny the Younger

     Ep. Tra. Epistulae ad Trajanum

Polycarp

     Pol. Phil. [Polycarp, To the Philippians]

Socrates

     Hist. eccl. Historia ecclesiastica [Ecclesiastical History]

Sozomen

     Hist. eccl. [Ecclesiastical History]

Strabo

     Geogr. Geographia [Geography]

Tertullian

     Nat. Ad nationes [To the Heathen]

     Adv. Jud. Adversus Judaeos [Against the Jews]

     Apol. Apologeticus [Apology]

     Fug. De fuga in persecution [Flight in Persecution]

     Virg. De virginibus velandis [The Veiling of Virgins]

Theophilus of Antioch

     Autol. Ad Autolycum [To Autolycus]

Aasgaard, Reidar. *The Childhood of Jesus: Decoding the Apocryphal Infancy Gospel of Thomas.* Cambridge: James Clarke, 2010.

Abd-el-Ghani, Mohammed. "Alexandria and Middle Egypt: Some Aspects of Social and Economic Contacts." In *Ancient Alexandria between Egypt and Greece*, edited by W. V. Harris and Giovanni Ruffini, 161–178. Leiden: Brill, 2004.

Adams, J. N. *Bilingualism and the Latin Language*. Cambridge: Cambridge University Press, 2003.

Alston, Richard. *Soldier and Society in Roman Egypt: A Social History*. London: Routledge, 1995.

Angus, S. *The Environment of Early Christianity*. New York: Charles Scribner's Sons, 1915.

Anson, John. "The Female Transvestite in Early Monasticism: The Origin and Development of a Motif." *Viator* 5 (1974): 1–32.

Applebaum, S. "The Organization of the Jewish Communities in the Diaspora." In *The Jewish People in the First Century*, edited by S. Safrai and M. Stern, 701–727. Assen and Maastricht: Van Gorcum; Philadelphia: Fortress, 1987.

Arterbury, Andrew. *Entertaining Angels: Early Christian Hospitality in Its Mediterranean Setting*. Sheffield: Sheffield Phoenix, 2005.

Ascough, Richard S. "Translocal Relationships among Voluntary Associations and Early Christianity." *JECS* 5.2 (1997): 223–241.

Askowith, Dora. *The Toleration and Persecution of the Jews in the Roman Empire*, vol. 1, *The Toleration of the Jews under Julius Caesar and Augustus*. Columbia University: New York, 1915.

Aubert, Bernard. *The Shepherd-Flock Motif in the Miletus Discourse (Acts 20:17–38) against Its Historical Background*. New York: Peter Lang, 2009.

Aune, David E. *Prophecy in Early Christianity and the Ancient Mediterranean World*. Grand Rapids, MI: Eerdmans, 1983.

Bagnall, Roger S. *Egypt in Late Antiquity*. Princeton: Princeton University Press, 1993.

Bagnall, Roger S. *Early Christian Books in Egypt*. Princeton: Princeton University Press, 2009.

Bagnall, Roger S., and Bruce W. Frier. *The Demography of Roman Egypt*. Cambridge Studies in Population, Economy and Society in Past Times 23. Cambridge: Cambridge University Press, 1994.

Bang, Peter Fibiger. *The Roman Bazaar: A Comparative Study of Trade and Markets in a Tributary Empire*. Cambridge: Cambridge University Press, 2008.

Bar, Doron. "The Christianisation of Rural Palestine during Late Antiquity." *JEH* 54 (2003): 401–421.

Barclay, John. "Poverty in Pauline Studies: A Response to Steven Friesen." *JSNT* 26 (2004): 363–366.

Barclay, John M. G. *Jews in the Mediterranean Diaspora: From Alexander to Trajan (323 BCE–117 CE)*. Edinburgh: T & T Clark, 1996.

Barnes, T. D. "Angel of Light or Mystic Initiate? The Problem of the 'Life of Antony.'" *JTS* n.s. 37 (1986): 353–368.

Barnett, James. *The Diaconate: A Full and Equal Order*, rev. ed. Harrisburg, PA: Trinity Press, 1995.

Baron, S. W. *A Social and Religious History of the Jews*. 2nd ed. New York: Columbia University Press, 1952.

Bathrellos, Demetrios. "Church, Eucharist, Bishop: The Early Church in the Ecclesiology of John Zixioulas." In *The Theology of John Zizioulas: Personhood and the Church*, edited by Douglas H. Knight, 133–146. Aldershot: Ashgate Publishing, 2007.

Bauckham, Richard. *Jude and the Relatives of Jesus in the Early Church*. Edinburgh: T & T Clark, 1990.

Bauer, Walter. *Orthodoxy and Heresy in Earliest Christianity*, translated and edited by R. A. Kraft, et al. Philadelphia: Fortress, 1977.

Béchard, Dean P. "Paul among the Rustics: The Lystran Episode (Acts 14:8–20) and Lucan Apologetic." *CBQ* 63 (2001): 84–101.

Becker, Jürgen. "Paul and His Churches." In *Christian Beginnings: Word and Community from Jesus to Post-Apostolic Times*, edited by Jürgen Becker, translated by Reinhard Krauss, 132–210. Louisville, KY: Westminster/John Knox Press, 1993.

BeDuhn, Jason. *Augustine's Manichaean Dilemma*, vol. 1, *Conversion and Apostasy, 373–388 C.E.* Philadelphia: University of Pennsylvania Press, 2010.

Bell, H. Idris. "Evidences of Christianity during the Roman Period." *HTR* 37 (1944): 185–208.

Beloch, Karl Julius. *Die Bevölkerung der griechisch-römischen Welt*. Leipzig: Verlag von Duncker & Humblot, 1886.

Benet, Francisco. "Sociology Uncertain: The Ideology of the Rural-Urban Continuum." *Comparative Studies in Society and History* 6 (1963): 1–23.

Bingham, Joseph. *Origines Ecclesiasticæ: The Antiquities of the Christian Church*, vol. 1. London: Henry G. Bohn, 1846.

Boatwright, Mary T. *Hadrian and the Cities of the Roman* Empire. Princeton and Oxford: Princeton University Press, 2000.

Bock, Darrell L. *Studying the Historical Jesus: A Guide to Sources and Methods*. Grand Rapids, MI: Baker Academic, 2002.

Boring, M. Eugene. *Revelation, Interpretation: A Bible Commentary for Preaching and Teaching*. Louisville, KY: John Knox, 1989.

Bowerstock, Glen W. "Beloch and the Birth of Demography." *TAPA* 127 (1997): 373–379.

Bowes, Kim. *Private Worship, Public Values, and Religious Change in Late Antiquity*. Cambridge: Cambridge University Press, 2008.

Bowman, Alan K. *Egypt after the Pharaohs. 332 bc–ad 642: From Alexander to the Arab Conquest*. Berkeley: University of California Press, 1986.

Bowman, Alan, and Andrew Wilson, ed. *Settlement, Urbanization, and Population*. Oxford: Oxford University Press, 2011.

Brakke, David. *Athanasius and the Politics of Asceticism*. New York: Oxford University Press, 1995.

Bremmer, Jan N. *The Rise of Christianity through the Eyes of Gibbon, Harnack and Rodney Stark*. 2nd ed. Groningen: Barkhuis, 2010.

Broshi, M. "The Population of Western Palestine in the Roman-Byzantine Period." *BASOR* 26 (1979): 1–10.

Brown, Peter. "Religious Dissent in the Later Roman Empire: The Case of North Africa." *History* 46 (1961): 83–101.

Brown, Peter. "Religious Coercion in the Later Roman Empire: The Case of North Africa." *History* 48 (1963): 293–297.

Brown, Peter. *Augustine of Hippo: A Biography.* London: Faber and Faber, 1967.

Brown, Peter. "Approaches to the Religious Crisis of the Third Century A.D." *EHR* 83 (1968): 542–558.

Brown, Peter. "Christianity and Local Culture in Late Roman Africa." *JRS* 58 (1968): 85–95.

Brown, Peter. *Religion and Society in the Age of Saint Augustine.* London: Faber & Faber, 1972.

Brown, Peter. *The Cult of the Saints.* Chicago: University of Chicago Press, 1981.

Brown, Peter. "The Rise and Function of the Holy Man in Late Antiquity." *JRS* 61 (1971): 80–101.

Reprinted in *Society and the Holy in Late Antiquity.* Berkeley and Los Angeles: University of California Press, 1982. pp. 103–152.

Brown, Peter. *Society and the Holy in Late Antiquity.* Berkeley and Los Angeles: University of California Press, 1982.

Brown, Peter. "Town, Village and Holy Man: The Case for Syria." In *Assimilation et résistance à la culture gréco-romaine dans le monde ancient,* edited by D. M. Pippidi, 213–220. Bucharest, 1976. Reprinted in *Society and the Holy in Late Antiquity.* Berkeley and Los Angeles: University of California Press, 1982. pp. 153–165.

Brown, Peter. *Poverty and Leadership in the later Roman Empire.* The Menahem Stern Jerusalem Lectures. Hanover, NH: University of New England Press, 2002.

Brown, Peter. *The Rise of Western Christendom: Triumph and Diversity, A.D. 200–1000.* 2nd ed. Oxford: Blackwell, 2003.

Brown, Peter. "The Tenacity of Paganism." *The New York Review of Books,* June 9, 2011.

Brown, Peter. *Through the Eye of a Needle: Wealth, the Fall of Rome, and the Making of Christianity in the West, 350–550 AD.* Princeton: Princeton University Press, 2012.

Browning, Robert. *The Emperor Julian.* Berkeley and Los Angeles: University of California Press, 1976.

Budge, E. A. W., trans. *The Chronography of Gregory Abu'l Faraj, The Son of Aaron, The Hebrew Physician Commonly Known as Bar Hebraeus Being the First Part of His Political History of the World.* London: Oxford University Press, 1932.

Buell, Denise Kimber. *Why This New Race: Ethnic Reasoning in Early Christianity.* New York: Columbia University Press, 2005.

Burns, J. Patout Jr. *Cyprian the Bishop.* London and New York: Routledge, 2002.

Burns, Thomas S., and John W. Eadie, eds. *Urban Centers and Rural Contexts in Late Antiquity.* East Lansing: Michigan State University Press, 2001.

Burton-Christie, Douglas. *The Word in the Desert: Scripture and the Quest for Holiness in Early Christian Monasticism.* New York: Oxford University Press, 1993.

Butcher, Kevin. *Roman Syria and the Near East.* London: The British Museum Press; Los Angeles: Getty Publications, 2003.

Calder, W. M. *MAMA*, vii, No. 305. Manchester: Manchester University Press, 1956.

Cameron, Alan. *The Last Pagans of Rome.* Oxford: Oxford University Press, 2011.

Cameron, Avril. *The Later Roman Empire.* Cambridge, MA: Harvard University Press, 1993.

Cameron, Avril. *The Mediterranean World in Late Antiquity ad 395–600.* London and New York: Routledge, 1993.

Carroll, James. *Constantine's Sword: The Church and the Jews: A History.* New York: Houghton Mifflin, 2001.

Caseau, Béatrice. "The Fate of Rural Temples in Late Antiquity and the Christianization of the Countryside." In *Recent Research on the Late Antique Countryside*, edited by William Bowden, Luke Lavan, and Carlos Machado, 105–144. Late Antique Archaeology 2. Leiden: Brill, 2004.

Chadwick, Henry. "The Role of the Christian Bishop in Ancient Society." In *Protocol of the Colloquy of the Center for Hermeneutical Studies in Hellenistic and Modern Culture* 35. Berkeley, CA: The Center for Hermeneutical Studies in Hellenistic and Modern Culture, 1980.

Chancey, Mark A. *The Myth of a Gentile Galilee.* Cambridge: Cambridge University Press, 2002.

Chaniotis, Angelos. "The Dynamics of Rituals in the Roman Empire." In *Ritual Dynamics and Religious Change in the Roman Empire*, edited by Olivier Hekster, Sebastian Schmidt-Hofner, and Christian Witschel, 3–29. Leiden: Brill, 2009.

Charlesworth, James H. "Jesus Research and Near Eastern Archaeology: Reflections on Recent Developments." In *Neotestamentica et Philonica: Studies in Honor of Peder Borgen*, edited by David Edward Aune, et al., 38–44. Leiden: Brill, 2003.

Chilton, Bruce. "Tolerance and Controversy in Classical Christianity: The Gospel According to Matthew and Justin Martyr." In *Religious Tolerance in World Religions*, edited by Jacob Neusner and Bruce Chilton, 133–152. West Conshohocken, PA: Templeton Foundation Press, 2008.

Chitty, Derwas James. *The Desert a City: An Introduction to the Study of Egyptian and Palestinian Monasticism under the Christian Empire.* Oxford: Blackwell, 1996.

Choat, Malcolm, et al. "The World of the Nile." In *Early Christianity in Contexts: An Exploration across Cultures and Continents*, edited by William Tabbernee. 18–222. Grand Rapids, MI: Baker Academic, 2014.

Christie, Neil. *From Constantine to Charlemagne: An Archaeology of Italy, AD 300–800.* Aldershot: Ashgate Publishing, 2006.

Clark, E. G. "Pastoral Care: Town and Country in Late-Antique Preaching." In *Urban Centers and Rural Contexts in Late Antiquity*, edited by Thomas S. Burns and John W. Eadie, 265–284. East Lansing: Michigan State University Press, 2001.

Clarke, Andrew D. *Secular and Christian Leadership in Corinth: A Socio-historical and Exegetical Study of 1 Corinthians 1–6*. Leiden: Brill, 1993.

Clarke, Graeme. "Third-Century Christianity." *CAH*, vol. 12, *The Crisis of Empire*, A.D. *193–337*. Cambridge: Cambridge University Press, 2008: 589–671.

Cohen, Shaye J. D. "The Place of the Rabbi in Jewish Society in the Second Century." In *The Galilee in Late Antiquity*, edited by Lee Levine, 157–173. Cambridge, MA: Harvard University Press, 1989.

Cohen, Shaye J. D. "'Those Who Say They Are Jews and Are Not': How Do You Know a Jew in Antiquity When You See One?" In *Diasporas in Antiquity*, Brown Judaic Studies 288, edited by Shaye J. D. Cohen and Ernest S. Frerichs, 1–45. Atlanta: Scholars Press, 1993.

Cohen, Shaye J. D. "The Rabbi in Second-Century Jewish Society." In *The Cambridge History of Judaism*, vol. 3, edited by W. D. Davies, Louis Finkelstein, William Horbury, and John Sturdy, 922–990. Cambridge: Cambridge University Press, 1999.

Collar, Anna. *Religious Networks in the Roman Empire: The Spread of New Ideas*. Cambridge: Cambridge University Press, 2013.

Comfort, Philip W. "Texts and Manuscripts of the New Testament." In *The Origin of the Bible*, rev. ed., edited by Philip W. Comfort, 185–214. Carol Stream, IL: Tyndale House Publishers, 2003.

Conzelmann, Hans. *Gentiles, Jews, Christians: Polemics and Apologetics in the Greco-Roman Era*. Minneapolis: Fortress, 1992.

Corbier, Mireille. "City, Territory and Taxation." In *City and Country in the Ancient World*, edited by John Rich and Andrew Wallace-Hadrill, 211–239. London and New York: Routledge, 1991.

Cragun, Ryan T., and Ronald Lawson. "The Secular Transition: The Worldwide Growth of Mormons, Jehovah's Witnesses, and Seventh-day Adventists." *Sociology of Religion* 71.3 (2010): 349–373.

Crossan, Dominic. *The Historical Jesus: The Life of a Mediterranean Jewish Peasant*. New York: HarperCollins, 1991.

Crossan, Dominic. *The Birth of Christianity: Discovering What Happened in the Years Immediately after the Execution of Jesus*. New York: HarperCollins, 1998.

Cusack, Carole M. *Conversion among the Germanic Peoples*. London: Cassell, 1998.

Daniélou, Jean, and Henri Marrou. *The Christian Centuries*, vol. 1, *The First Six Hundred Years*, translated by Vincent Cronin. London: Darton, Longman and Todd, 1964.

Davids, Peter H. *The First Epistle of Peter*. NICNT. Grand Rapids, MI: Eerdmans, 1990.

Davis, Stephen J. "Crossed Texts, Crossed Sex: Intertextuality and Gender in Early Christian Legends of Holy Women Disguised as Men." *JECS* 10 (2002): 1–36.

Davis, Stephen J. *The Early Coptic Papacy: The Egyptian Church and Its Leadership in Late Antiquity*. Cairo: The American University of Cairo Press, 2004.

De Blois, Lukas. "The Crisis of the Third Century A.D. in the Roman Empire: A Modern Myth?" In *The Transformation of Economic Life under the Roman Empire*, edited by Lukas De Blois and John Rich, 204–217. Leiden: Brill, 2002.

Delia, Diana. "The Population of Roman Alexandria." *TAPA* 118 (1988): 175–292.

Dey, Hendrik W. *The Aurelian Wall and the Refashioning of Imperial Rome, ad 271–855.* Cambridge: Cambridge University Press, 2011.

Dickson, John P. *Mission-Commitment in Ancient Judaism and in the Pauline Communities: The Shape, Extent and Background of Early Christian Mission.* WUNT 2, 159. Tübingen: Mohr Siebeck, 2003.

Dodds, E. R. *Pagan and Christian in an Age of Anxiety: Some Aspects of Religious Experience from Marcus Aurelius to Constantine.* Cambridge: Cambridge University Press, 1965.

Donaldson, Terence L. "'The Field God Has Assigned': Geography and Mission in Paul." In *Religious Rivalries in the Early Roman Empire and the Rise of Christianity*, edited by Leif E. Vaage, 109–137. Waterloo, ON: Wilfrid Laurier University Press, 2006.

Dossey, Leslie. *Peasant and Empire in Christian North Africa.* Berkeley and Los Angeles: University of California Press, 2010.

Downey, Glanville. "The Population of Antioch." *TAPA* 89 (1958): 84–91.

Downing, F. Gerald. *Cynics and Christian Origins.* Edinburgh: T & T Clark, 1992.

Downing, F. Gerald. *Cynics, Paul and the Pauline Churches.* London: Routledge, 1998.

Drinkwater, J. F. "Women and Horses and Power and War." In *Urban Centers and Rural Contexts in Late Antiquity*, edited by Thomas S. Burns and John W. Eadie, 135–146. East Lansing: Michigan State University Press, 2001.

Duncan-Jones, Richard. "City Population in Roman Africa." *JRS* 53 (1963): 85–90.

Duncan-Jones, Richard. *The Economy of the Roman Empire: Quantitative Studies*, 2nd ed. Cambridge: Cambridge University Press, 1982.

Duncan-Jones, Richard. "The Impact of the Antonine Plague." *JRomArch* 9 (1996): 108–136.

Dunn, Geoffrey D. *Tertullian.* London: Routledge, 2004.

Dunn, Marilyn. *The Emergence of Monasticism: From the Desert Fathers to the Early Middle Ages.* Oxford: Blackwell, 2000.

Edwards, Douglas R. *Religion & Power: Pagans, Jews, and Christians in the Greek East.* New York and Oxford: Oxford University Press, 1996.

Ehrman, Bart D. *The New Testament: A Historical Introduction to Early Christian Writings*, 3rd ed. New York: Oxford University Press, 2004.

Ehrman, Bart D. *Jesus, Interrupted: Revealing the Hidden Contradictions in the Bible (and Why We Don't Know about Them).* New York: HarperCollins, 2009.

Elliot, John H. *Home for the Homeless: A Social-Scientific Criticism of I Peter, Its Situation and Strategy.* Minneapolis: Fortress, 1990.

Ellis, Steven J. R. "The Distribution of Bars at Pompeii: Archaeological, Spatial and Viewshed Analyses." *JRomArch* 17 (2004): 371–384.

Elsner, Jaś, and Rutherford, I., eds. *Pilgrimage in Graeco-Roman & Early Christian Antiquity: Seeing the Gods.* Oxford: Oxford University Press, 2005.

Engelman, Uriah Zevi. *The Rise of the Jew in the Western World: A Social and Economic History of the Jewish People of Europe.* New York: Behrman's Jewish Book House, 1944.

Engels, Donald W. *Roman Corinth: An Alternative Model for the Classical City.* Chicago: University of Chicago Press, 1990.

Erdkamp, Paul. "Urbanism." In *The Cambridge Companion to the Roman Economy,* edited by Walter Scheidel, 241–265. Cambridge: Cambridge University Press, 2012.

Farina, William. *Perpetua of Carthage: Portrait of a Third-Century Martyr.* Jefferson, NC: McFarland, 2009.

Feldman, Louis H. *Jew and Gentile in the Ancient World: Attitudes and Interactions from Alexander to Justinian.* Princeton: Princeton University Press, 1993.

Feldman, Louis H. *Jewish Life and Thought among Greeks and Romans: Primary Readings.* London: Continuum, 1996.

Feldman, Louis H. *Judaism and Hellenism Reconsidered.* Leiden: Brill, 2006.

Feldman, Louis H., and Meyer Reinhold. *Jewish Life and Thought among Greeks and Romans.* Minneapolis: Fortress, 1996.

Ferguson, Everett. *Backgrounds of Early Christianity.* 3rd ed. Grand Rapids, MI: Eerdmans, 2003.

Ferguson, Everett. "Dionysius of Alexandria." In *Encyclopedia of Early Christianity,* 2nd ed., ed. Everett Ferguson (New York: Routledge, 1999), 333–334.

Feuer, Lewis S. "The Sociobiological Theory of Jewish Intellectual Achievement: A Sociological Critique." In *Ethnicity, Identity, and History: Essays in Memory of Werner J. Cahnman,* edited by Joseph B. Maier and Chaim I. Waxman, 93–123. New Brunswick, NJ: Transaction Publishers, 1983.

Fiensy, David A. *Christian Origins and the Ancient Economy.* Cambridge: James Clarke & Co., 2014.

Fitzpatrick-McKinley, Anne. "Synagogue Communities in the Graeco-Roman Cities." In *Jews in the Hellenistic and Roman Cities,* edited by John R. Bartlett, 55–87. London and New York: Routledge, 2002.

Fletcher, Richard A. *The Barbarian Conversion: From Paganism to Christianity.* New York: H. Holt and Co., 1998.

Foakes Jackson, F. J., and Kirsopp Lake. *The Beginnings of Christianity.* London: Macmillan and Co., 1920.

Fowden, Garth. "Review of Lane Fox." *JRS* 78 (1988): 173–182.

Fredriksen, Paula. "Christians in the Roman Empire in the First Three Centuries." In *A Companion to the Roman Empire,* edited by David S. Potter, 587–606. Oxford: Blackwell, 2006.

Frend, W. H. C. *The Donatist Church: A Movement of Protest in Roman North Africa.* Oxford: Clarendon Press, 1952.

Frend, W. H. C. "A Third-Century Inscription Relating to Angareia in Phrygia." *JRS* 46 (1956): 46–56.

Frend, W. H. C. *Martyrdom and Persecution in the Early Church: A Study of a Conflict from the Maccabees to Donatus.* Oxford: Basil Blackwell, 1965.

Frend, W. H. C. "The Winning of the Countryside." *JEH* 18 (1967): 1–14.

Frend, W. H. C. "The Failure of Persecutions in the Roman Empire." In *Studies in Ancient History,* edited by M. I. Finley, 263–287. London and Boston: Routledge and Kegan Paul, 1974.

Frend, W. H. C. "Town and Countryside in Early Christianity." In *The Church in Town and Countryside: Studies in Church History XVI,* edited by Derek Baker, 25–42. Oxford: Basil Blackwell, 1979.

Frend, W. H. C. *Town and Country in the Early Christian Centuries.* London: Varoirum Reprints, 1980.

Frend, W. H. C. "Early Christianity and Society: A Jewish Legacy in the Pre-Constantinian Era." *HTR* 76.1 (1983): 53–71.

Frend, W. H. C. *The Rise of Christianity.* Philadelphia: Fortress, 1984.

Friedländer, Ludwig. *Roman Life and Manners under the Early Empire,* vol. 3, translated by J. H. Freese. London: George Routledge & Sons; New York: E. P. Dutton, 1908–1913.

Frier, Bruce W. "Demography." In *The High Empire AD 70–192. CAH,* vol. 11, edited by A. K. Bowman, P. Garnsey, and D. Rathbone, 787–816. Cambridge: Cambridge University Press, 2000.

Frier, Bruce W. "More Is Worse: Some Observations on the Population of the Roman Empire." In *Debating Roman Demography,* edited by Walter Scheidel, 139–159. Leiden: Brill, 2000.

Friesen, Steven J. "Poverty in Pauline Studies: Beyond the So-Called New Consensus." *JSNT* 26 (2004): 323–361.

Gandt, Lois. "A Philological and Theological Analysis of the Ancient Latin Translations of the *Vita Antonii.*" Ph.D. diss., Fordham University, 2008.

Garnsey, Peter. *Famine and Food Supply in the Graeco-Roman World.* Cambridge: Cambridge University Press, 1988.

Garnsey, Peter. *Cities, Peasants and Food in Classical Antiquity: Essays in Social and Economic History.* Cambridge: Cambridge University Press, 1998.

Garnsey, Peter, and Richard Saller. *Roman Empire: Economy, Society and Culture.* London: Gerald Duckworth & Co., 1987.

Gates, Charles. *Ancient Cities: The Archaeology of Urban Life in the Ancient Near East and Egypt, Greece, and Rome.* 2nd ed. Abingdon, GB: Routledge, 2011.

Gathercole, Simon J. *The Gospel of Thomas: Introduction and Commentary.* Leiden: Brill, 2014.

Gibbon, Edward. *The Decline and Fall of the Roman Empire,* intro. by Antony Lentin and Brian Norman. Ware, Kertfordshire: Wordsworth Editions, 1998.

Gilbert, Gary. "The List of Nations in Acts 2: Roman Propaganda and the Lukan Response." *JBL* 121 (2002): 497–529.

Gillmann, Franz. *Das Institut der Chorbischöfe im Orient.* Munich: Lentner'schen, 1903.

Glanville, S. R. K. *The Legacy of Egypt.* Oxford: Clarendon Press, 1942.

Glick, Leonard B. *Marked in Your Flesh: Circumcision from Ancient Judea to Modern America.* New York: Oxford University Press, 2005.

Goehring, James E. "Withdrawing from the Desert: Pachomius and the Development of Village Monasticism in Upper Egypt." *HTR* 89 (1996): 267–285.

Goehring, James E. *Ascetics, Society, and the Desert: Studies in Early Egyptian Monasticism.* Harrisburg, PA: Trinity Press International, 1999.

Goldsmith, Raymond W. "An Estimate of the Size and Structure of the National Product of the Early Roman Empire." *Review of Income and Wealth* 30 (1984): 263–288.

Goldsworthy, Adrin. *How Rome Fell.* New Haven: Yale University Press, 2009.

Gonzalez, Justo L. *Faith and Wealth: A History of Early Christian Ideas on the Origin, Significance, and Use of Money.* New York: Harper & Row, 1990.

Goodman, Martin. "Nerva, the Fiscus Judaicus and Jewish Identity." *JRS* 79 (1989): 40–44.

Goodman, Martin. *Mission and Conversion: Proselytizing in the Religious History of the Roman Empire.* Oxford: Clarendon Press, 1995.

Goodman, Martin. *The Roman World 44 B.C.–180 A.D.* London: Routledge, 1997.

Goodman, Penelope J. *The Roman City and Its Periphery: From Rome to Gaul.* London and New York: Routledge, 2007.

Gore, Charles. *The Church and the Ministry*, rev. ed., edited by C. H. Turner. London: Longmans, Green and Co., 1919.

Graham, Mark W. *News and Frontier Consciousness in the Late Roman Empire.* Ann Arbor: University of Michigan Press, 2006.

Grainger, John D. *The Cities of Seleukid Syria.* Oxford: Clarendon, 1990.

Grant, Robert M. *Early Christianity and Society.* San Francisco: Harper & Row, 1977.

Grant, Robert M. *Irenaeus of Lyons.* Early Church Fathers. London and New York: Routledge, 1997.

Gregory, Timothy E. "The Survival of Paganism in Christian Greece: A Critical Essay." *AJP* 107 (1986): 229–242.

Grey, Cam. *Constructing Communities in the Late Roman Countryside.* Cambridge: Cambridge University Press, 2011.

Gribomont, J. "Nepos." *Encyclopedia of the Early Church*, ed. Angelo Di Berardino, trans. Adrian Walford (New York: Oxford University Press, 1992), 593.

Griggs, C. Wilfred. *Early Egyptian Christianity: From Its Origins to 451 C.E.* Coptic Studies 2. Leiden and New York: Brill, 1990.

Guy, Laurie. *Introducing Early Christianity: A Topical Survey of Its Life, Beliefs and Practices.* Downers Grove, IL: InterVarsity Press, 2004.

Haas, Christopher. *Alexandria in Late Antiquity: Topography and Social Conflict.* Baltimore: Johns Hopkins University Press, 1997.

Hall, Stuart George. "Ecclesiology Forged in the Wake of Persecution." In *Origins to Constantine,* edited by Margaret Mary Mitchell and Frances Margaret Young, 415–433. *The Cambridge History of Christianity,* vol. 1. Cambridge: Cambridge University Press, 2006.

Hansen, Mogens Herman. *The Shotgun Method: The Demography of the Ancient Greek City-State Culture.* Columbia: University of Missouri Press, 2006.

Hansen, Mogens Herman. *Studies in the Population of Aigina, Athens and Eretria.* Copenhagen: Det Kongelige Danske Videnskabernes Selskab, 2006.

Hanson, J. W. "The Urban System of Roman Asia Minor and Wider Urban Connectivity." In *Settlement, Urbanization and Population,* edited by A. Bowman and A. Wilson, 229–275. Oxford Studies in the Roman Economy 2. Oxford: Oxford University Press, 2011.

Hardy, Edward Rochie. *Christian Egypt: Church and People: Christianity and Nationalism in the Patriarchate of Alexandria.* Oxford: Oxford University Press, 1952.

Harl, Kenneth W. "From Pagan to Christian in Cities of Roman Anatolia during the Fourth and Fifth Centuries." In *Urban Centers and Rural Contexts in Late Antiquity,* edited by Thomas S. Burns and John W. Eadie, 301–322. East Lansing: Michigan State University Press, 2001.

Harland, Philip A. "Connections with Elites in the World of the Early Christians." In *Handbook of Early Christianity: Social Science Approaches,* edited by Anthony J. Blasi, Jean Duhaime, and Paul-André Turcotte, 385–408. Walnut Creek, CA: AltaMira Press, 2002.

Harland, Philip A. *Associations, Synagogues, and Congregations: Claiming a Place in Ancient Mediterranean Society.* Minneapolis: Fortress, 2003.

Harland, Philip A. "The Declining Polis? Religious Rivalries in Ancient Civic Context." In *Religious Rivalries in the Early Roman Empire and the Rise of Christianity,* edited by Leif E. Vaage, 28–35. Waterloo, ON: Wilfrid Laurier University Press, 2006.

Harnack, Adolf. *The Mission and Expansion of Christianity in the First Three Centuries,* translated and edited by James Moffatt. New York: Harper & Brothers, 1961.

Harnack, Adolf. *Militia Christi: The Christian Religion and the Military in the First Three Centuries,* translated by David McInnes Grade. Philadelphia: Fortress, 1981.

Harris, William V. *Ancient Literacy.* Cambridge, MA: Harvard University Press, 1989.

Harrison, James R. "The First Urban Churches: Introduction." In *The First Urban Churches,* vol. 1, *Methodological Foundations,* edited by James R. Harrison and L. L. Welborn, 1–40. Atlanta: SBL Press, 2015, 7.

Harrison, James R., and L. L. Welborn *The First Urban Churches,* vol. 1, *Methodological Foundations,* edited by James R. Harrison and L. L. Welborn. Atlanta: SBL Press, 2015.

Heaton, Tim B. "Vital Statistics." In *Encyclopedia of Mormonism*. New York, Macmillan, 1992. pp. 1.1518–1537.

Hefele, Charles Joseph. *A History of the Christian* Councils, 2nd ed., translated by William R. Clark. Edinburgh: T & T Clark, 1883.

Hefele, Charles Joseph. *Histoire des Conciles d'après les Documents Originaux* 1.2. Paris: Letouzey et Ané, 1907.

Heffernan, Thomas A. *The Passion of Perpetua and Felicity*. New York: Oxford University Press, 2012.

Hekster, Olivier, Gerda de Kleijn, and Daniëlle Slootjes. *Crises and the Roman Empire: Proceedings of the Seventh Workshop of the International Network Impact of Empire*. Leiden: Brill, 2007.

Hemer, Colin J. *The Letters to the Seven Churches of Asia in their Local Setting*. JSNTSup 11. Sheffield: JSNT Press, 1986.

Henderson, Ian H. "Mission and Ritual: Revisiting Harnack's 'Mission and Expansion of Christianity.'" In *The Changing Face of Judaism, Christianity and Other Greco-Roman Religions in Antiquity*, edited by Ian H. Henderson and Gerbern S. Oegema, 34–56. Studien zu den Jüdischen Schriften aus hellenistisch-römischer Zeit 2. Gütersloh: Gütersloher Verlagshaus, 2006.

Hengel, Martin. *Jews, Greeks and Barbarians: Aspects of the Hellenization of Judaism in the Pre-Christian Period*, translated by John Bowden. Philadelphia: Fortress, 1980.

Hess, Hamilton. *The Early Development of Canon Law and the Council of Serdica*. Oxford: Oxford University Press, 2002.

Hill, H. *The Roman Middle Class in the Republican Period*. Oxford: Basil Blackwell, 1952.

Hin, Saskia. *The Demography of Roman Italy: Population Dynamics in an Ancient Conquest Society 201 BCE–14 CE*. Cambridge: Cambridge University Press, 2013.

Hin, Saskia. "Revisiting Urban Graveyard Theory: Migrant Flows in Hellenistic and Roman Athens," In *Migration and Mobility in the Early Roman Empire*, edited by Luuk de Ligt and Laurens E. Tacoma, 234-263. Leiden: Brill, 2016.

Hinson, E. Glenn. *The Evangelization of the Roman Empire: Identity and Adaptability*. Macon, GA: Mercer University Press, 1981.

Holl, Karl. "Das Fortleben der Volksprachen in Kleinasien in nachchristlicher Zeit." *Hermes* 43 (1908): 240–254.

Hopkins, Keith. "Christian Number and Its Implications." *JECS* 6 (1998): 185–226.

Horbury, William. "The Jewish Dimension." In *Early Christianity: Origins and Evolution to AD 600*, edited by Ian Hazlett, 40–51. London: SPCK, 1991.

Horbury, William. "Jewish-Christian Relations in Barnabas and Justin Martyr." In *Jews and Christians: The Parting of the Ways A.D. 70 to 135*, edited by J. D. G. Dunn, 315–346. WUNT 66. Tübingen: J. C. B. Mohr, 1992. Reprint, Grand Rapids, MI: Eerdmans, 1999.

Horrell, David G. "Domestic Space and Christian Meetings at Corinth: Imagining New Contexts and the Buildings East of the Theatre." *NTS* 50 (2004): 349–369.

Horsley, G. H. R. "The Fiction of 'Jewish Greek.'" *NewDocs* 5 (1989): 5–40.

L'Huillier, Peter. *The Church of the Ancient Councils: The Disciplinary Work of the First Four Ecumenical Councils*. Crestwood, NY: St. Vladimir's Seminary Press, 1996.

Humphries, Mark. "The West (1): Italy, Gaul, and Spain." In *The Oxford Handbook of Early Christian Studies*, edited by Susan Ashbrook Harvey and David G. Hunter, 283–301. Oxford: Oxford University Press, 2008.

Hunink, Vincent. "Apuleius, Pudentilla, and Christianity." *Vigiliae Christianae* 54 (2000): 80–94.

Incigneri, Brian J. *The Gospel to the Romans: The Setting and Rhetoric of Mark's Gospel*. Leiden: Brill, 2003.

Janse, Mark. "Aspects of Bilingualism in the History of the Greek Language." In *Aspects of Bilingualism in the History of the Greek Language*, edited by J. N. Adams, Mark Janse, and Simon Swain, 332–390. Oxford: Oxford University Press, 2002.

Jeffers, James S. *Conflict at Rome: Social Order and Hierarchy in Early Christianity*. Minneapolis: Fortress, 1991.

Jeffers, James S. *The Greco-Roman World of the New Testament Era: Exploring the Background of early Christianity*. Downers Grove, IL: InterVarsity Press, 1999.

Jensen, Robin M., Peter Lampe, William Tabbernee, and D. H. Williams. "Italy and Environs." In *Early Christianity in Contexts: An Exploration across Cultures and* Contexts, edited by William Tabbernee, 379–432. Grand Rapids, MI: Baker Academic, 2014.

Johnson, Gary J. *Early-Christian Epitaphs from Anatolia*. Atlanta: Scholars Press, 1995.

Johnson, Luke Timothy. *The Acts of the Apostles*. Sacra Pagina 5. Collegeville, MN: Liturgical Press, 1992.

Jones, A. H. M. *Cities of the Eastern Roman Provinces*. Oxford: Clarendon Press, 1937.

Jones, A. H. M. *The Greek City: From Alexander to Justinian*. Oxford: Clarendon Press, 1940.

Jones, A. H. M. "Were Ancient Heresies National or Social Movements in Disguise?" *JTS* 10.2 (1959): 280–298.

Jones, A. H. M. *The Later Roman Empire, 284–602: A Social Economic and Administrative Survey*, vol. 2. Oxford: Basil Blackwell, 1964.

Jones, A. H. M. *The Decline of the Ancient World*. Holt, Rinehart and Winston, 1966.

Jones, A. H. M. *The Roman Economy: Studies in Ancient Economic and Administrative History*. Oxford: Blackwell, 1974.

Jones, Michael E. *The End of Roman Britain*. Ithaca, NY: Cornell University Press, 1996.

Jongman, Willem. "Slavery and the Growth of Rome: The Transformation of Italy in the Second and First Centuries B C E." In *Rome the Cosmopolis*, edited by Catharine Edwards and Greg Woolf, 100–122. Cambridge: Cambridge University Press, 2006.

Judge, E. A. "The Beginning of Religious History." *JRH* 15 (1989): 394–412.

Judge, E. A. "Was Christianity a Religion." In *The First Christians in the Roman World: Augustan and New Testament Essays*, Wissemschaftlich Untersuchungen

Zum Neuen Testament, edited by E. A. Judge and James R. Harrison, 404–409. Tübingen: Mohr Siebeck, 2008.

Juster, Jean. *Les juifs dans l'Empire romain: Leur condition juridique, économique et sociale.* Paris: Librairie Paul Geuthner, 1914.

Kahlos, Maijastina. *Debate and Dialogue: Christian and Pagan Cultures c. 360–430.* Aldershot and Burlington, VT: Ashgate Publishing, 2007.

Kalantzis, George. *Caesar and the Lamb: Early Christian Attitudes on War and Military Service.* Eugene, OR: Cascade Books, 2012.

Kasher, Aryeh. *The Jews in Hellenistic and Roman Egypt: The Struggle for Equal Rights.* Texte und Studien zum Antiken Judentum 7. Tübingen: J. C. B. Mohr (Paul Siebeck), 1985.

Kehoe, Dennis P. *Law and the Rural Economy in the Roman Empire.* Ann Arbor: University of Michigan Press, 2007.

Kelhoffer, James A. *Miracle and Mission: The Authentication of Missionaries and Their Message in the Longer Ending of Mark.* Tübingen: Mohr Siebeck, 2000.

Kerkeslager, Allen. "The Diaspora from 66 to c. 235 CE." In *The Cambridge History of Judaism*, vol. 4, *The Late Roman-Rabbinic Period*, edited by Steven T. Katz, 53–68. Cambridge: Cambridge University Press, 2006.

Klauck, Hans Josef. *Magic and Paganism in Early Christianity: The World of the Acts of the Apostles*, translated by Brian McNeil. Minneapolis: Fortress, 2003.

Klijn, A. F. J. "Jewish Christianity in Egypt." In *The Roots of Egyptian Christianity*, edited by Birger A. Pearson and James E. Goehring, 161–175. Philadelphia: Fortress, 1986.

Köster, Helmut. *Introduction to the New Testament*, vol. 2, *History and Literature of Early Christianity.* Philadelphia: Fortress, 1982.

Kirsten, E. "Chorbishof." *RAC* 2 (1954): 1105–1114.

Kraabel, A. T. "The Diaspora Synagogue: Archaeological and Epigraphic Evidence since Sukenik." In *Ancient Synagogues: Historical Analysis and Archaeological Discovery*, edited by Dan Urman and Paul V. M. Flesher, 95–128. Leiden: Brill, 1994.

Kyratatas, Dimiritus J. *The Social Structure of the Early Christian Communities.* Brooklyn, NY: Verso, 1987.

Lane Fox, Robin. *Pagans and Christians.* New York: Alfred A. Knopf, 1987.

Lapin, Hayim. *Rabbis as Romans: The Rabbinic Movement in Palestine, 100–400 C.E.* Oxford: Oxford University Press, 2012.

Launaro, Alessandro. *Peasants and Slaves: The Rural Population of Roman Italy (200 BC to AD 100).* Cambridge: Cambridge University Press, 2011.

Laurence, Ray, Simon Esmonde Cleary, and Gareth Sears. *The City in the Roman West c. 250 BC–c. AD 250.* Cambridge: Cambridge University Press, 2011.

Lavan, Luke. "A.H.M. Jones and 'The Cities' 1964–2004.' In *A.H.M. Jones and the Later Roman Empire*, edited by David M. Gwynn, 167–192. Leiden: Brill, 2008.

Leavitt, John McDowell. "Suffragans." *AQCR* 23 (1871): 394–410.

Lee, Sang-Il. *Jesus and Gospel Traditions in Bilingual Context: A Study in the Interdirectionality of Language.* Berlin and Boston: Walter de Gruyter, 2012.

Leithart, Peter J. *Defending Constantine: The Twilight of an Empire and the Dawn of Christendom.* Downers Grove, IL: InterVarsity Press, 2010.

Levick, Barbara. "In the Phrygian Mode: A Region Seen from Without." In *Roman Phrygia: Culture and Society*, edited by Peter Thonemann, 41–54. Cambridge: Cambridge University Press, 2013.

Levine, Lee I. *The Ancient Synagogue: The First Thousand Years*, 2nd ed. New Haven: Yale University Press, 2005.

Levinskaya, Irina. *The Book of Acts in Its Diaspora Setting: The Book of Acts in Its First Century Setting*, vol. 5. Grand Rapids. MI: Eerdmans; Carlisle, Cumbria: Paternoster Press, 1996.

Liebeschuetz, J. H. W. G. *Antioch: City and Imperial Administration in the Later Roman Empire.* Oxford: Clarendon Press, 1972.

Liebeschuetz, Wolf [Wolfgang]. "Pagan Mythology in the Christian Empire." *International Journal of the Classical Tradition* 2.2 (1995): 193–208.

Liebeschuetz, Wolf. "Was There a Crisis of the Third Century." In *Crises and the Roman Empire.* Impact of Empire 7, edited by Olivier Hekster, Gerda de Kleijn and Daniëlle Slootjes, 11–20. Leiden: Brill, 2007.

Lieu, Judith, John North, and Tessa Rajak, eds. *The Jews among Pagans and Christians in the Roman Empire.* London and New York: Routledge, 1992.

Lightfoot, J. B. *St. Paul's Epistles to the Colossians and to Philemon*, rev. ed. London: Macmillan & Co., 1875.

Lightstone, Jack N. "Urbanization in the Roman East and the Inter-Religious Struggle for Success." In *Religious Rivalries and the Struggle for Success in Sardis and Smyrna*, edited by Richard S. Ascough, 211–244. Waterloo, ON: Wilfrid Laurier University Press, 2005.

de Ligt, L. *Fairs and Markets in the Roman Empire: Economic and Social Aspects of Periodic Trade in a Pre-industrial Society.* Leiden: Brill, 1993.

Lindberg, Carter. "Through a Glass Darkly: A History of the Church's Vision of the Poor and Poverty." *Ecumenical Review* 31 (1981): 37–52.

Littman, R. J., and M. L. Littman. "Galen and the Antonine Plague." *AJP* 94 (1973): 243–255.

Lo Cascio, Elio. "The Size of the Roman Population: Beloch and the Meaning of the Augustus Census Figures." *JRS* 84 (1994): 23–40.

Lo Cascio, Elio. "The Impact of Migration on the Demographic Profile of the City of Rome: A Reassessment." In *Migration and Mobility in the Early Roman Empire*, edited by Luuk de Ligt and Laurens E. Tacoma, 23-32. Leiden: Brill, 2016.

Longenecker, Bruce W. "Good News for the Poor: Jesus, Paul and Jerusalem." In *Jesus and Paul Reconnected*, edited by Todd D. Still, 37–66. Grand Rapids, MI: Eerdmans, 2007.

Longenecker, Bruce W. "Socio-economic Profiling of the First Urban Christians." In *After the First Urban Christians: The Socio-Scientific Study of Pauline Christianity Twenty-Five Years Later*, edited by Todd D. Still and David G. Horrell, 36–59. London and New York: T & T Clark, 2009.

MacMullen, Ramsay. "Provincial Languages in the Roman Empire." *AJP* 87.1 (1966): 1–17.

MacMullen, Ramsay. "Market-Days in the Roman Empire." *Phoenix* 24.4 (1970): 333–341.

MacMullen, Ramsay. *Roman Social Relations*, rev. ed. New Haven: Yale University Press, 1974.

MacMullen, Ramsay. *Paganism in the Roman Empire*. New Haven: Yale University Press, 1981.

MacMullen, Ramsay. "Two Types of Conversion to Early Christianity." *VC* 37 (1983): 174–192.

MacMullen, Ramsay. *Christianizing the Roman Empire (A.D. 100–400)*. New Haven and London: Yale University Press, 1984.

MacMullen, Ramsay. "Conversion: A Historian's View." *SecCent* 5 (1985–1986): 67–81.

MacMullen, Ramsay. "The Preacher's Audience (AD 350–400)." *JTS* 40 (1989): 503–511.

MacMullen, Ramsay. *Christianity and Paganism in the Fourth to the Eight Centuries*. New Haven: Yale University Press, 1997.

MacMullen, Ramsay. *The Second Church: Popular Christianity A.D. 200–400*. Atlanta: Society of Biblical Literature, 2009.

MacMullen, Ramsay. "Christian Ancestor Worship in Rome." *JBL* 129 (2010): 597–613.

Maddison, Angus. *Contours of the World Economy, 1–2030 AD: Essays in Macroeconomic History*. Oxford: Oxford University Press, 2007.

Magda, Ksenija. *Paul's Territorial and Mission Strategy*. Tübingen: Mohr Siebeck, 2009.

Malherbe, Abraham J. *Social Aspects of Early Christianity*. 2nd ed. Philadelphia: Fortress, 1983.

Malina, Bruce J., and Jerome H. Neyrey. *Portraits of Paul: An Archaeology of Ancient Personality*. Louisville, KY: Westminster/John Knox Press, 1996.

Marjanen, Antti. "Montanism: Egalitarian Ecstatic 'New Prophecy.'" In *A Companion to Second-Century Christian "Heretics,"* edited by Antti Marjanen and Petri Luomanen, 185–212. Leiden: Brill, 2008.

Markus, R. A. "Christianity and Dissent in Roman North Africa: Changing Perspectives in Recent Work." In *Schism, Heresy and Religious Protest*, edited by Derek Baker, 21–36. Studies in Church History 9. Cambridge: Cambridge University Press, 1972.

Markus, R. A. "Country Bishops in Byzantine Africa." In *The Church in Town and Countryside: Studies in Church History* XVI, edited by Derek Baker, 1–15. Oxford: Basil Blackwell, 1979.

Markus, R. A. *The End of Ancient Christianity*. Cambridge: Cambridge University Press, 1990.

Marshall, Jonathan. *Jesus, Patrons, and Benefactors: Roman Palestine and the Gospel of Luke*. Tübingen: Mohr Soebeck, 2009.

Mattingly, David J., and R. Bruce Hitchner. "Roman Africa: An Archaeological Review." *JRS* 85 (1995): 165–213.

Mayer, Emanuel. *The Ancient Middle Classes: Urban Life and Aesthetics in the Roman Empire 100 BCE–250 CE*. Cambridge, MA: Harvard University Press, 2012.

McEvedy, Colin, and Richard Jones. *Atlas of World Population History*. Hammondsworth: Penguin Books, 1978.

McGing, Brian. "Population and Proselytism: How Many Jews Were There in the Ancient World?" In *Jews in the Hellenistic and Roman Cities*, edited John R. Bartlett, 88–106. London and New York: Routledge, 2002.

McGinn, Bernard. "Turning Points in Early Christian Apocalypse Exegesis." In *Apocalyptic Thought in Early Christianity*, edited by Robert J. Daly, 81–105. Grand Rapids, MI: Baker Academic, 2009.

McGown, C. C. "The Density of Population in Ancient Palestine." *JBL* 66 (1947): 425–436.

McGuckin, J. A. "The Vine and the Elm Tree: The Patristic Interpretation of Jesus' Teaching on Wealth." In *The Church and Wealth*, edited by W. J. Sheils and Diana Wood, 1–14. Oxford: Basil Blackwell, 1987.

McKechnie, Paul. *The First Christian Centuries: Perspectives on the Early Church*. Downers Grove, IL: InterVarsity Press, 2001.

McKenna, Stephen. *Paganism and Pagan Survivals in Spain up to the Fall of the Visigothic Kingdom*. The Catholic University of America Studies in Mediaeval History, New Series, 1. Washington, DC: Catholic University of America, 1938.

McLynn, Frank. *Marcus Aurelius: A Life*. Cambridge, MA: Da Capo Press, 2009.

Meeks, Wayne. A. *The First Urban Christians: The Social World of the Apostle Paul*. New Haven and London: Yale University Press, 1983. 2nd ed. 1993.

Meeks, Wayne. A. "Breaking Away: Three New Testament Pictures of Christianity's Separation from the Jewish Communities." In "'To See Ourselves as Others See Us': Christians, Jews, 'Others.'" In *Late Antiquity*, edited by J. Neusner and E. S. Frerichs, 93–115. Chico: Scholars Press, 1985.

Meeks, Wayne. A. *The Moral World of the First Christians: The Social World of the Apostle Paul*. Philadelphia: Westminster Press, 1986.

Meeks, Wayne. A. *The Origins of Christian Morality*. New Haven and London: Yale University Press, 1993.

Meeks, Wayne. A. "Social and Ecclesial Life of the Earliest Christians." In *Origins to Constantine*, edited by Margaret Mary Mitchell and Frances Margaret Young, 145–173. *The Cambridge History of Christianity*, vol. 1. Cambridge: Cambridge University Press, 2006.

Meeks, Wayne A., and Robert L. Wilken. *Jews and Christians in Antioch in the First Four Centuries of the Common Era*. Missoula, MT: Scholars Press, 1978.

Meggitt, Justin J. *Paul, Poverty and Survival*. Edinburgh: T & T Clark, 1998.

Merdinger, Jane. "The World of the Roman Empire." In *Early Christianity: Origins and Evolution to ad 600*, edited by Ian Hazlett, 17–27. London: SPCK, 1991.

Metzger, Bruce M. *The Early Versions of the New Testament*. Oxford: Clarendon, 1977.

Meyendorff, John. *Imperial Unity and Christian Division*. Crestwood, NY: St. Vladimir's Seminary Press, 1989.

Millar, Fergus. *The Roman Near East*. Cambridge, MA: Harvard University Press, 1993.

Millar, Fergus. *Rome, the Greek World and the East*, vol. 1, *The Roman Republic and the Augustan Revolution*, edited by Hannah M. Cotton and Guy M. Rogers. Chapel Hill: University of North Carolina Press, 2002.

Millar, Fergus. "A Rural Jewish Community in Late Roman Mesopotamia, and the Question of a 'Split' Jewish Diaspora." *JSJ* 42 (2011): 351–374.

Mitchell, Stephen. *Anatolia: Land, Men, and Gods in Asia Minor*. Oxford: Clarendon Press: 1993.

Mitchell, Stephen. *A History of the Later Roman Empire a.d. 284–641*. Oxford: Blackwell, 2007.

Modrzejewski, Joseph Mélèze. *The Jews of Egypt: From Rameses II to Emperor Hadrian*, translated by Robert Cornman. Princeton: Princeton University Press, 1995.

Morley, Neville. *Metropolis and Hinterland: The City of Rome and the Italian Economy, 200 B.C.–A.D. 200*. Cambridge: Cambridge University Press, 1996.

Morley, Neville. "Demography and Development in Classical Antiquity." In *Demography and the Graeco-Roman World: New Insights and Approaches*, edited by Claire Holleran and April Pudsey, 14–36. Cambridge: Cambridge University Press, 2011.

Moss, Candida R. *The Other Christs: Imitating Jesus in Ancient Christian Ideologies of Martyrdom*. New York: Oxford University Press, 2010.

Moss, Candida R. *Ancient Christian Martyrdom: Diverse Practices, Theologies, and Traditions*. New Haven: Yale University Press, 2012.

Mullen, Roderic L. *The Expansion of Christianity: A Gazetteer of Its First Three Centuries*. Leiden: Brill, 2004.

Müller, Jörg. "Gedanken zum Institut dec Chorbischöfe." In *Medieval Church Law and the Origins of the Western Legal Tradition*, edited by Wolfgang P. Müller and Mary E. Sommar, 77–94. Washington, DC: Catholic University Press of America, 2006.

Nersessian, Vrej Nerses. "Armenian Christianity." In *The Blackwell Companion to Eastern Christianity*, edited by Ken Perry, 23–46. Oxford: Blackwell, 2007.

Neusner, Jacob. "The Experience of the City in late Antique Judaism." In *Approaches to Ancient Judaism*, vol. 5, edited by William Scott Green, 37–52. Atlanta: Scholars Press, 1985.

North, John A. "The Development of Religious Pluralism." In *The Jews among Pagans and Christians in the Roman Empire*, edited by Judith Lieu, John North, and Tessa Rajak, 174–193. London: Routledge, 1992.

North, John A. "Religion and Rusticity." In *Urban Society In Roman Italy*, edited by T. J. Cornell and Kathryn Lomas, 141–156. London: UCL Press, 1995.

Novak, Michael. *The Universal Hunger for Liberty: Why the Clash of Civilizations Is Not Inevitable.* New York: Basic Books, 2004.

Novak, Ralph Martin. *Christianity and the Roman Empire: Background Texts.* Harrisburg, PA: Trinity Press, 2001.

Oakes, Peter. "Contours of the Urban Environment." In *After the First Urban Christians: The Socio-Scientific Study of Pauline Christianity Twenty-Five Years Later,* edited by Todd D. Still and David G. Horrell, 21–35. London and New York: T & T Clark, 2009.

Oden, Thomas C. *Early Libyan Christianity.* Downers Grove, IL: IVP Academic, 2011.

O'Donnell, James J. "Paganus." *CF* 31 (1977): 163–169.

O'Donnell, James J. "The Demise of Paganism." *Traditio* 35 (1979): 45–88.

Osborne, Robin. "Pride and Prejudice, Sense and Subsistence: Exchange and Society in the Greek City." In *City and Country in the Ancient World,* edited by John Rich and Andrew Wallace-Hadrill, 119–145. London and New York: Routledge, 1991.

Papandrea, James L. *Novatian of Rome and the Culmination of Pre-Nicene Orthodoxy.* Princeton Theological Monograph Series 175. Eugene, OR: Pickwick Publications, 2011.

Parca, Maryline. "Local Languages and Native Cultures." In *Epigraphic Evidence: Ancient History from Inscriptions,* edited by John P. Bodel, 57–72. London and New York: Routledge, 2001.

Park, Chris C. *Sacred Worlds: An Introduction to Geography and Religion.* London: Routledge, 2002.

Parkin, Tim G. *Demography and Roman Society.* Baltimore and London: Johns Hopkins University Press, 1992.

Pasachoff, Naomi E., and Robert J. Littman. *A Concise History of the Jewish People.* Lanham, MD: Rowman & Littlefield, 2005.

Pastor, Jack. *Land and Economy in Ancient Palestine.* London: Routledge, 1997.

Pearson, Birger A. "Earliest Christianity in Egypt: Some Observations." In *The Roots of Egyptian Christianity,* edited by Birger A. Pearson and James E. Goehring, 132–159. Philadelphia: Fortress, 1986.

Petersen, William L. *Tatian's Diatessaron: Its Creation, Dissemination, Significance, and History in Scholarship.* Leiden: Brill, 1994.

Phang, Sara Elise. *The Marriage of Roman Soldiers (13 B.C.–A.D. 235): Law and Family in the Imperial Army.* Columbia Studies in the Classical Tradition 24. Leiden: Brill, 2001.

Plummer, Robert L. *Paul's Understanding of the Church's Mission: Did the Apostle Paul Expect the Early Christian Communities to Evangelize?* Milton Keyes, UK: Paternoster, 2006.

Potter, David Stone. *The Roman Empire at Bay, AD 180–395.* London: Routledge, 2004.

Pounds, Norman J. G. "The Urbanization of the Classical World." *Annals of the Association of American Geographers* 59 (1969): 135–157.

Price, S. R. F. *Rituals and Power: The Roman Imperial Cult in Asia Minor.* Cambridge: Cambridge University Press, 1984.

Quasten, Johannes. *Patrology.* Utrecht: Spectrum, 1950. Reprint, Westminster, MD: Christian Classics, 1990.

Rainy, Robert D. D. *The Ancient Catholic Church: From the Accession of Trajan to the Fourth General Council (A.D. 98–451).* New York: Charles Scribner's Sons, 1902.

Rajak, Tessa. "The Jewish Community and its Boundaries." In *The Jews among Pagans and Christians in the Roman Empire,* edited by Judith Lieu, John North, and Tessa Rajak, 9–28. London and New York: Routledge, 1992.

Rathbone, D. W. "Villages, Land and Population in Graeco-Roman Egypt." *PCPS* 216, n.s. 36 (1990): 103–142.

Rebillard, Éric. "The West (2): North Africa." In *The Oxford Handbook of Early Christian Studies,* edited by Susan Ashbrook Harvey and David G. Hunter, 303–322. Oxford: Oxford University Press, 2008.

Reed, Jonathan L. "The Population of Capernaum." *Occasional Papers of the Institute of Antiquity and Christianity* 24 (1992): 1–19.

Reed, Jonathan L. *Archaeology and the Galilean Jesus.* Harrisburg, PA: Trinity Press International, 2000.

Reed, Jonathan L. "Instability in Jesus' Galilee: A Demographic Perspective." *SBL* 129 (2010): 343–365.

Remus, Harold. "The End of 'Paganism'?" *Studies in Religion* 33 (2004): 191–208.

Rhee, Helen. *Loving the Poor, Saving the Rich: Wealth, Poverty, and Early Christian Formation.* Grand Rapids, MI: Baker Academic, 2012.

Rich, John, and Andrew Wallace-Hadrill, eds. *City and Country in the Ancient World.* Leicester-Nottingham Studies in Ancient Society 2. London and New York: Routledge, 1991.

Richardson, Cyril C. "The Riddle of the 13th Canon of Ancyra." *CH* 16 (1947): 32–36.

Richardson, Peter. "An Architectural Case for Synagogues as Associations." In *The Ancient Synagogue from Its Origins until 200 C.E.,* edited by B. Olsson and M. Zetterholm, 90–117. Stockholm: Almquist & Wiksell, 2003.

Richardson, Peter. *Building Jewish in the Roman East.* Waco, TX: Baylor University Press, 2004.

Riggs, David. "Paganism between the Cities and Countryside of Late Roman Africa." In *Urban Centers and Rural Contexts in Late Antiquity,* edited by Thomas S. Burns and John W. Eadie, 285–300. East Lansing: Michigan State University Press, 2001.

Roberts, C. H. *Manuscripts, Society, and Belief in Early Christian Egypt.* The Schweich Lectures of the British Academy for 1977. London: Oxford University Press, 1979.

Robinson, Thomas A. *Ignatius of Antioch and the Parting of the Ways: Early Jewish-Christian Relations.* Peabody, MA: Hendrickson; Grand Rapids, MI: Baker Academic, 2009.

Rohrbaugh, Richard L. "The Pre-Industrial City in Luke-Acts: Urban Social Relations." In *The Social World of Luke-Acts: Models for Interpretation*, edited by Jerome H. Neyrey, 125–149. Peabody, MA: Hendrickson, 1991.

Rosenthal, Judah. "Bar Hebraeus and a Jewish Census under Claudius." *Jewish Social Studies* 16 (1954): 267–268.

Rosen-Zvi, Ishay, and Adi Ophir. "Paul and the Invention of the Gentiles." *JQR* 105 (2015): 1–41.

Roth, Norman. *Daily Life of the Jews in the Middle Ages*. Westport, CT: Greenwood Press, 2005.

Rousseau, Philip. *Basil of Caesarea*. Berkeley and Los Angeles: University of California Press, 1994.

Rubenson, Samuel. *The Letters of St. Antony: Monasticism and the Making of a Saint*. Minneapolis: Fortress, 1995.

Russell, J. C. *Late Ancient and Medieval Population*. Transactions of the American Philosophical Society, new series 48.3. Philadelphia: American Philosophical Society, 1958.

Rutger, Leonard Victor. *The Hidden Heritage of Diaspora Judaism*. 2nd ed. Leuven: Peeters, 1998.

Salmon, Pierre. *Population et dépopulation dans l'Empire romain*. Brussels: Latomus, 1974.

Salvemini, Gaetano. *Historian and Scientist: An Essay on the Nature of History and the Social Sciences*. Cambridge, MA: Harvard University Press, 1939.

Salway, Peter. "Roman Britain (*c.* 55 BC–*c.* AD 440)," in *The Oxford History of Britain*, 2nd ed., edited by Kenneth O. Morgan, 1–59. Oxford: Oxford University Press, 2010.

Sanders, Jack T. "Christians and Jews in the Roman Empire: A Conversation with Rodney Stark." *Sociological Analysis* 53.4 (1992): 433–445.

Sandgren, Leo Duprée. *Vines Intertwined: A History of Jews and Christians from the Babylonian Exile to the Advent of Islam*. Peabody, MA: Hendrickson, 2010.

Sandwell, Isabella. *Religious Identity in Late Antiquity: Greeks, Jews and Christians in Antioch*. Cambridge: Cambridge University Press, 2007.

Schaff, Philip. *History of the Christian Church*, vol. 1. New York: Charles Scribner's Sons, 1882.

Scheidel, Walter. "Progress and Problems in Roman Demography." In *Debating Roman Demography*, edited by Walter Scheidel, 1–82. Leiden: Brill, 2001.

Scheidel, Walter. "A Model of Demographic and Economic Change in Roman Egypt." *JRomArch* 15 (2002): 97–114.

Scheidel, Walter. "Demography." In *The Cambridge Economic History of the Greco-Roman World*, edited by Walter Scheidel, Ian Morris, and Richard P. Saller, 38–86. Cambridge: Cambridge University Press, 2007.

Scheidel, Walter. "Roman Population Size: The Logic of the Debate." Princeton/Stanford Working Papers in Classics (July 2007).

Scheidel, Walter, and Steven J. Friesen. "The Size of the Economy and the Distribution of Income in the Roman Empire." *JRS* 99 (2009): 61–91.

Schwartz, Joshua J. "The Material Realities of Jewish Life in the Land of Israel, 235–638." In *The Cambridge History of Judaism*, vol. 4, *The Late Roman-Rabbinic Period*, edited by Steven T. Katz, 431–456. Cambridge: Cambridge University Press, 2006.

Schwartz, Seth. "Political, Social, and Economic Life in the Land of Israel, 66–c. 235." In *The Cambridge History of Judaism*, vol. 4, *The Late Roman-Rabbinic Period*, edited by Steven T. Katz, 23–52. Cambridge: Cambridge University Press, 2006.

Schwartz, Seth. "How Many Judaisms Were There? A Critique of Neusner and Smith on Definition and Mason and Boyarin on Categorization." *JAJ* 2 (2011): 208–238.

Schwartz, Seth. *The Ancient Jews from Alexander to Muhammad.* Cambridge: Cambridge University Press, 2014.

Scroggs, Robin. "The Sociological Interpretation of the New Testament: The Present Stage of Research." *NTS* 26 (1980): 164–179.

Setzer, Claudia. "The Jews in Carthage and Western North Africa, 66–235 CE." In *The Cambridge History of Judaism*, vol. 4, *The Late Roman-Rabbinic Period*, edited by Steven T. Katz, 68–75. Cambridge: Cambridge University Press, 2006.

Shaw, Brent D. "Rural Markets in North Africa and the Political Economy of the Roman Empire." *Antiquités africaines* 17 (1981): 37–84.

Shaw, Brent D. "The Passion of Perpetua." *Past and Present* 139 (1993): 3–45.

Shaw, Brent D. *Sacred Violence: African Christians and Sectarian Hatred in the Age of Constantine.* Cambridge: Cambridge University Press, 2011.

Sider, Robert D. *Christian and Pagan in the Roman Empire: The Witness of Tertullian.* Washington, DC: The Catholic University Press of America, 2001.

Simonsohn, Shlomo. *The Jews of Italy: Antiquity.* Leiden: Brill, 2014.

Smallwood, E. Mary. *The Jews under Roman Rule: From Pompey to Diocletian.* Leiden: Brill, 1976.

Smallwood, E. Mary. "The Diaspora in the Roman Period before CE 70." In *The Cambridge History of Judaism*, vol. 3, edited by William Horbury, W. D. Davies, and John Sturdy, 168–191. Cambridge: Cambridge University Press, 1999.

Smith, Jonathan Z. "Religion, Religions, Religious." In *Critical Terms for Religious Studies*, edited by Mark Taylor, 269–284. Chicago: University of Chicago Press, 1998.

Snyder, Graydon F. *Ante Pacem: Archaeological Evidence of Church Life Before Constantine*, 2nd ed. Macon, GA: Mercer University Press, 2003.

Southern, Pat. *The Roman Empire from Severus to Constantine.* London and New York: Routledge, 2001.

Sowell, Thomas. *Migrations and Cultures: A World View.* New York: Basic Books, 1996.

Sowers, Brian. "Thecla Desexualized: The Saint Justina Legend and the Reception of the Christian Apocrypha in Late Antiquity." In *"Non-canonical" Religious Texts in Judaism and Early Christianity*, edited by Lee Martin McDonald and James H. Charlesworth, 232–233. London: T & T Clark, 2012.

Spigel, Chad S. *Ancient Synagogue Seating Capacities: Methodology, Analysis and Limits*, Texts and Studies in Ancient Judaism 149. Tübingen: Mohr Siebeck, 2012.

Stambaugh, John E. *The Ancient Roman City*. Baltimore, MD: John Hopkins University Press, 1988.

Stark, Rodney. "The Rise of a New World Faith." *RRelRes* 26 (1984): 18–27.

Stark, Rodney. "Antioch as the Social Situation for Matthew's Gospel." In *Social History of the Matthean Community*, edited by David L Balch, 189–210. Minneapolis: Fortress, 1991.

Stark, Rodney. *The Rise of Christianity: How the Obscure, Marginal Jesus Movement Became the Dominant Religious Force in the Western World in a Few Centuries*. Princeton: Princeton University Press, 1996.

Stark, Rodney. "Modernization and Mormon Growth: The Secularization Thesis Revisited." In *Contemporary Mormonism: Social Scientific Perspectives*, edited by Marie Cornwall, Tim B. Heaton, and Lawrence A. Young, 1–23. Champaign: University of Illinois Press, 2001.

Stark, Rodney. *Cities of God: The Real Story of How Christianity Became an Urban Movement and Conquered Rome*. New York: HarperCollins, 2006.

Stark, Rodney. *The Triumph of Christianity*. New York: HarperOne, 2011.

Starr, Chester G. *The Roman Empire: 27 B.C.–A.D. 476*. New York: Oxford University Press, 1982.

Stathakopoulos, Dionysios Ch. *Famine and Pestilence in the Late Roman and Early Byzantine Empire: A Systematic Survey of Subsistence Crises and Epidemics*. Birmingham Byzantine and Ottoman Monographs. Aldershot: Ashgate Publishing, 2004.

Stern, M. "The Jewish Diaspora." In *The Jewish People in the First Century*, edited by S. Safrai and M. Stern, I.117–183. Assen and Maastricht: Van Gorcum; Philadelphia: Fortress, 1987.

Stevenson, William. *Historical Sketch of the Progress of Discovery, Navigation and Commerce, from the Earliest Records to the Beginning of the Nineteenth Century*. Edinburgh: William Blackwood, 1824.

Still, Todd D., and David G. Horrell, eds. *After the First Urban Christians: The Socio-Scientific Study of Pauline Christianity Twenty-Five Years Later*. London: T & T Clark, 2009.

Streeter, B. H. *The Primitive Church*. London: Macmillan, 1929.

Tabbernee, William. *Montanist Inscriptions and Testimonia: Epigraphic Sources Illustrating the History of Montanism*. North American Patristic Society Patristic Monograph Series 16. Macon, GA: Mercer University Press, 1997.

Tabbernee, William, ed. *Early Christianity in Contexts: An Exploration across Cultures and Contexts.* Grand Rapids, MI: Baker Academic, 2014.

Tabbernee, William. "Asia Minor and Cyprus." In *Early Christianity in Contexts: An Exploration across Cultures and Continents,* edited by William Tabbernee, 261–320. Grand Rapids, MI: Baker Academic, 2014.

Tacoma, Laurens E. "Migrant Quarters in Rome?" In *Integration in Rome and in the Roman World: Proceedings of the Tenth Workshop of the International Network Impact of Empire.* Impact of Empire 17, edited by Gerda de Kleijn and Stéphane Benoist, 127–146. Leiden: Brill, 2014.

Tcherikover, Victor. *Hellenistic Civilization and the Jews,* translated by S. Applebaum. Philadelphia: Jewish Publication Society of America, 1959.

Testa, Rita Lizzi, ed. *The Strange Death of Pagan Rome.* Turnhout, BE: Brepols, 2013.

Testa, Rita Lizzi. "When the Romans Became Pagans." In *The Strange Death of Pagan Rome,* edited by Rita Lizzi Testa, 31–51. Turnhout, BE: Brepols, 2013.

Theissen, Gerd. *The Social Setting of Pauline Christianity: Essays on Corinth,* edited and translated by John H. Schütz. Philadelphia: Fortress, 1982.

Thompson, E. A. *Romans and Barbarians: The Decline of the Western Empire.* Madison: University of Wisconsin Press, 1982.

Thonemann, Peter. "Phrygia: An Anarchist History, 950 BC–AD 100." In *Roman Phrygia: Culture and Society,* edited by Peter Thonemann, 1–40. Cambridge: Cambridge University Press, 2013.

Townsend, John T. "Missionary Journeys in Acts and European Missionary Societies." In *SBL 1985 Seminar Papers,* edited by Kent Harold Richards, 433–438. *SBLSP* 24. Atlanta: Scholars Press, 1985.

Toynbee, J. M. C. *Death and Burial in the Roman World.* Baltimore: Johns Hopkins University Press, 1971.

Treadgold, Warren T. *A History of the Byzantine State and Society.* Stanford, CA: Stanford University Press, 1997.

Trebilco, Paul R. *The Early Christians in Ephesus from Paul to Ignatius.* Tübingen: Mohr Seibeck, 2004.

Trebilco, Paul R. "The Jews in Asia Minor, 66–c. 235 CE." In *The Cambridge History of Judaism,* vol. 4, *The Late Roman-Rabbinic Period,* edited by Steven T. Katz, 75–82. Cambridge: Cambridge University Press, 2006.

Trevett, Christine. *Montanism: Gender, Authority and the New Prophecy.* Cambridge: Cambridge University Press, 1996.

Trevett, Christine. "Montanism." In *The Early Christian World,* edited by Philip F. Esler, II.229–251. London and New York: Routledge, 2000.

Trombley, Frank. "Paganism in the Greek World at the End of Antiquity: The Case of Rural Anatolia and Greece." *HTR* 78 (1985): 327–352.

Trombley, Frank. *Hellenic Religion and Christianization c. 370–529.* 2 vols. Leiden: Brill, 1995.

Trombley, Frank. "Overview: The Geographical Spread of Christianity." In *The Cambridge History of Christianity*, vol. 1, *Origins to Constantine*, edited by Margaret Mary Mitchell and Frances Margaret Young, 302–313. Cambridge: Cambridge University Press, 2006.

Urman, Dan, and Paul V. M. Flesher, eds. *Ancient Synagogues: Historical Analysis and Archaeological Discovery*. Leiden: Brill, 1994.

Vaage, Leif E. "Ancient Religious Rivalries and the Struggle for Success Christians, Jews, and Others in the Early Roman Empire." In *Religious Rivalries in the Early Roman Empire and the Rise of Christianity*, edited by Leif E. Vaage, 3–19. Waterloo, ON: Wilfrid Laurier University Press, 2006.

Van De Sandt, Huub, and David Flusser, *The Didache: Its Jewish Sources and Its Place in Early Judaism and Christianity*. Minneapolis: Fortress, 2002.

Vryonis, Speros Jr. "Problems in the History of Byzantine Anatolia." *Ankara Univ. D.T.C. Fakültesi Tarih Arastirmalari Dergisi* 1.1 (1963): 113–132.

Walbank, F. W. "Nationality as a Factor in Roman History." *HSCP* 76 (1972): 145–168.

Wallace-Hadrill, Andrew. "Elites and Trade in the Roman Town." In *City and Country in the Ancient World*, edited by John Rich and Andrew Wallace-Hadrill, 241–272. London: Routledge, 1991.

Wallace-Hadrill, Andrew. "Introduction." In *City and Country in the Ancient World*, edited by John Rich and Andrew Wallace-Hadrill, ix–xviii. London: Routledge, 1991.

Ware, J. Patrick. *The Mission of the Church: In Paul's Letter to the Philippians in the Context of Ancient Judaism*. NovTSup 120. Leiden: Brill, 2005.

Ware, Timothy. *The Orthodox Church*, 2nd ed. London: Penguin Books, 1997.

Welborn, L. L. "The Polis and the Poor: Reconstructing Social Relations from Different Genres of Evidence." In *The First Urban Churches*, vol. 1, *Methodological Foundations*, edited by James R. Harrison and L. L. Welborn, 189–243. Atlanta: SBL Press, 2015.

Wenham, David, and Steve Walton. *Exploring the New Testament: A Guide to the Gospels & Acts*. Downer's Grove, IL: IVP Academic, 2005.

Wasserstein, Abraham. "The Number and Provenance of Jews in Graeco-Roman Antiquity: A Note on Population Statistics." In *Classical Studies in Honor of David Sohlberg*, edited by Ranon Katzoff, with Yaakov Petroff and David Schaps, 307–317. Ramat Gan, Israel: Bar Ilan University Press, 1996.

Watts, Edward J. *The Final Pagan Generation*. Oakland: University of California Press, 2015.

White, L. Michael. "Adolf Harnack and the 'Expansion' of Early Christianity: A Reappraisal of Social History." *SecCent* 2 (1985–1986): 97–127.

White, L. Michael. *The Social Origins of Christian Architecture*, vol. 1, *Building God's House in the Roman World: Architectural Adaptation among Pagans, Jews and Christians*. Valley Forge, PA: Trinity Press, 1990.

White, L. Michael. *The Social Origins of Christian Architecture*, vol. 2, *Texts and Monuments for the Christian Domus Ecclesiae in its Environment*. Valley Forge, PA: Trinity Press, 1997.

Wilhite, David E. *Tertullian the African: An Anthropological Reading of Tertullian's Context and Identities*. Millennium Studies 14. Berlin: Walter de Gruyter, 2007.

Wilken, Robert L., and Ramsay MacMullen. Review of *The Second Church*, by Ramsay MacMullen, with a response by MacMullen. *Conversations in Religion and Theology* 8.2 (2010): 120–125

Williams, Margaret H. *Jews in a Graeco-Roman Environment*. Tübingen: Mohr Siebeck, 2013.

Williams, Megan Hale. "Lessons from Jerome's Jewish Teachers: Exegesis and Cultural Interaction in Late Antique Palestine." In *Jewish Biblical Interpretation and Cultural Exchange: Comparative Exegesis*, edited by Natalie B. Dohrmann and David Stern, 66–86. Philadelphia: University of Pennsylvania Press, 2008.

Wilson, Andrew. "City Sizes and Urbanization in the Roman Empire." In *Settlement, Urbanization and Population*, edited by A. Bowman and A. Wilson, 161–195. Oxford Studies in the Roman Economy 2. Oxford: Oxford University Press, 2011.

Witcher, Robert. "Missing Persons? Models of Mediterranean Regional Survey and Ancient Populations." In *Settlement, Urbanization and Population*, edited by A. Bowman and A. Wilso, 36–75. Oxford Studies in the Roman Economy 2. Oxford: Oxford University Press, 2011.

Witherington, Ben, III. *Conflict and Community in Corinth: A Socio-rhetorical Commentary on 1 and 2 Corinthians*. Grand Rapids, MI: Eerdmans, 1995.

Woolf, Greg. "Beyond Romans and Natives." *World Archaeology* 28.3 (1997): 339–350.

Zetterholm, Magnus. *The Formation of Christianity in Antioch: A Social-Scientific Approach to the Separation between Judaism and Christianity*. London: Routledge, 2003.

Index

Printed in the USA/Agawam, MA
June 30, 2017